Comparative Literature in an Age of Globalization

The American Comparative Literature Association
Report on the State of the Discipline, 2004

Comparative Literature in an Age of Globalization

Edited by

HAUN SAUSSY

The Johns Hopkins University Press

Baltimore

© 2006 The Johns Hopkins University Press

All rights reserved. Published 2006
Printed in the United States of America on acid-free paper
2   4   6   8   9   7   5   3   1

The Johns Hopkins University Press
2715 North Charles Street
Baltimore, Maryland 21218-4363
www.press.jhu.edu

Library of Congress Cataloging-in-Publication Data
Comparative literature in an age of globalization / edited by Haun Saussy.
p. cm.
"The American Comparative Literature Association Report on the State of the
Discipline, 2004."
Includes bibliographical references.
ISBN 0-8018-8379-2 (hardcover : alk. paper) — ISBN 0-8018-8380-6 (pbk. : alk. paper)
1. Literature, Comparative.   2. Literature, Modern—History and criticism.
I. Saussy, Haun, 1960–   II. American Comparative Literature Association.
PN863.C585 2006
809—DC22   2005027706

A catalog record for this book is available from the British Library.

CONTENTS

In the spring of 2003, Margaret Higonnet and David Damrosch, president-to-be and president respectively of the American Comparative Literature Association, invited me to form a committee that would draft a report on the state of the discipline, something the association's bylaws require to be done once every ten years. My first thought was that I didn't want a committee report in the usual style—a consensus document studded with the magic phrases "We observe," "We advise," "We strongly recommend" and the like, of mysterious provenance and authority. I thought the need to form a consensus ought not serve as a filter for whatever diagnoses and recommendations might be made. The most provocative and readable parts of the previous ten-year report, *Comparative Literature in the Age of Multiculturalism,* had been the signed essays written in support or defiance of the committee's brief statement. I had nothing against manifestos, or even anathemas, but I was reluctant to pronounce them in the name of the Association. I hoped that we would find authors who would impress, alarm, delight, and stimulate our readership by disagreeing with me and with each other about the state of the field.

My second thought, which followed closely on the first, was that a book that consisted wholly of divergences from a set theme and expected the reader to synthesize the conclusions would do just as little to honor the ideal of dialogue as a book that corralled all divergences into a single policy statement. Readers already won to a particular point of view would read the chapter or two that confirmed their program for the future of comparative literature and ignore the rest. We needed other authors who would discover the shared patterns in the individual statements of Part One, sift their claims, and confront their disharmonies. The book, as I dreamt it before any words were actually on paper, would exemplify Heraclitus's "One differing in itself" and the "unity of difference and non-difference" proposed by the German Idealists, and would probably provide hints for the development of perpetual-motion and cold-fusion machines as well.

Margaret and David were receptive to the idea of a multivocal report, and with the help of the members of the advisory board of the ACLA, we sent out invitations to colleagues who had recently written on issues that seemed to us to loom large in the history and future of the discipline. I was happy to see that almost every person invited to contribute said yes, often within a few minutes of the sending of the e-mailed invitation. We then scheduled a series of meetings over the coming two years at which the pieces of the draft report, as they came in, would be discussed: by the contributors themselves; with respondents (often as a dress rehearsal for the essays in Part Two); and with members of the ACLA and our sister organization the Modern Language Association at the annual meetings of both groups. By now we had begun to think of it as a book, for which a title had to be found. The phrase "in an age of globalization" imposed itself, despite some resistance by all of us, as a marker of the times we endure and imagine, as an echo of the 1994 report, *Comparative Literature in the Age of Multiculturalism,* and as a reference to two of the models for the discipline currently prominent in comparatists' teaching and research, "world literature" and the politics of empire.

Somebody had to throw out the first ball. In October 2003 I began circulating a draft of my essay, an attempted general survey called "Exquisite Corpses from Fresh Nightmares." Partly because it appeared earliest, partly because it gave everyone at least something to disagree with, this essay came, by an unfortunate synecdoche, to be thought of by many as "the 2004 report." Several of the essays in what truly is the 2004 report refer to it and define positions in opposition to it. I claim only the virtue of convenience and am deeply flattered by the attention, but I hope the reader will understand that *everything* here, up to and including the responses, is the 2004 report on a field that we know to be so large, intricate, and various that no one person could reasonably be expected to report on it as a whole.

The variety emerges first in the kinds of texts we talk about. In "World Literature in a Postcanonical, Hypercanonical Age," David Damrosch elucidates the several senses in which "world literature" has become a different concern since the 1994 report. The canon of works under consideration, as represented by anthologies and teaching syllabi, has grown; more and more of us are involved in enlarging comparative literature; and the ways of thinking about it have ramified. And yet, as Damrosch notes, the field as encountered by students is, despite its internationalization and multiculturation, ever more strongly dominated by a few major writers. It is possible to imagine someone leaving college "having read *Things Fall Apart* three times and *Beloved* four times, but never having read Mahfouz or Ghalib." (Shakespeare is alive and well, thank you: despite the canard of their having been cast aside in favor of multiculturalism and small traditions, the new system has even increased the power of the Major Authors.) Damrosch suggests ways of resisting the star system while using the bankable Shakespeares, Joyces, and Tolstoys to introduce new writers and modes.

Emily Apter evokes several versions of a "comparatisme quand même" that seek to make connections despite the fatality of translation, above the walls separating linguistic families and literary genres, in spite of the riskiness of the category of the universal. Alain Badiou's attempts to produce a truth-bearing event through the encounter of disparate texts, the achievement of singularity that Peter Hallward attributes to certain postcolonial authors, and the planetarism of Gayatri Spivak's recent work are for her examples showing what is possible when the model of language as guarantor of community and identity disappears even as a thesis to be combated. These models disagree amongst themselves significantly: each offers its own account of the place of language, of literariness, and the role of interpreters in making connections.

Damrosch and Apter assume a form of literacy that, for the generation that came to maturity in the 1980s, underwrote most forms of comparison: literacy in the language of "theory." Richard Rorty's "Looking Back at 'Literary Theory'" gently questions the assumptions of reports on the state of a discipline, praising instead the "mutability and fashion-proneness" that makes the movement of ideas in a field unpredictable—as unpredictable as was, according to him, the sudden vogue of literary theory. For Rorty, it would be an error to see theory as having been the means of comparative literature's belated self-understanding; rather comparative literature, like any academic field, lacks a self to discover, be it through theory, expanded canons, or any other momentary conversation-starter.

For Djelal Kadir, practitioners of comparative literature in the United States now find themselves in an isolation "beyond dissensus," crystallized in the motto "Whatever," and incorporated willy-nilly into "universal global positioning systems" designed for the delivery of bombs, not the rescue of strayed mountaineers. Kadir notes the reversal of Marshall Plan America into its suspicious, hypersensitive Homeland Security avatar. The division of the world into those who are "with us" and those who are "against us" mirrors the unequal reception of works and scholars from different tiers of "abroad" into what is a recognizably American comparative literature; the more we talk, the less we know how to listen. In this light, the emergence of World Literature as a leading question suggests hegemony rather than hospitality, a "master construct" designed to produce the Same from the Different, and so the obsolescence of comparative literature.

"Indiscipline" names the question David Ferris asks about the survival of comparative literature within the contemporary university. Does the "discipline without a discipline" occupy a position of strategic flexibility (permitting it to develop free of the humanistic and national investments of other disciplines), or one of sheer nullity? The antinomy of "standards" and "comparison without bounds" serves as a reminder of the (in)ability of comparative literature to form itself as a discipline and indicates the Romantic themes of its intellectual origins: the nation as a project, the poetics of the fragment, the totalizing resistance to totality. World literature and the problem of "literature" both respond to the self-thematizing, self-diagnosed "impossibility" of the discipline.

As Sarah Lawall predicted in an essay cited by several contributors, the world-literature perspective is not one, but multiple. In "Cultivating Mere Gardens?" Françoise Lionnet narrates the ways "the global" emerges as a successor to the national in her own field of Francophone studies. Just as French feminism entered the United States on the wings of literary theory, so postcolonial theories exist in the French-speaking world largely as a subsection of Anglo-American studies, whereas writers from the former French and Belgian colonies are generally assimilated into the shared and single literary space of "la francophonie." A "transversal comparative approach," she argues, offers the best chances of overcoming the pressures to assimilation and ghettoization. Coline Serreau's film *Chaos* exemplifies for her the multiple unacknowledged points of contact between feminism and postcolonial francophone culture.

"What's happened to feminism?" Gail Finney imagines someone asking between the 1994 report and the present. What happened is, first, what was already at work in feminism: the adoption of interdisciplinarity as a matter of course, and the reframing of women's studies as gender studies. The consequent shift from the analysis and critique of binaries toward attention to pluralities has made feminism nearly unrecognizable, at least for those equipped only with a classic definition of the field. Judith Butler's work on performances of gender, the (at times edgy) coexistence of men and women within feminism, historical and social work on the body, the growth of queer studies, and even the paradoxical emergence of "postfeminism" have changed the context of feminism. As with comparative literature itself, the success of a style of thought leads both to its ubiquity and to its fading from view as a definite object.

"Writing in Tongues: Thoughts on the Work of Translation" is Steven Ungar's defense of a practice often grudgingly endorsed by comparatists, who after all distinguish themselves from colleagues in other disciplines by their reading of works from many different traditions "in the original," as we say. But what if the "original" is constituted through a relation to a "foreign language"? What if it emerges first as and in translation? Ungar questions a lingering logocentric bias through considerations of writers who speak of their use of French (a language Ungar cites "in the original") as shaped and plotted by intimacy with Arabic (a language he cites through the intermediary of French). The "perpetual translation" of bilingual or pluri-lingual writing, as exemplified by Abdelkebir Khatibi's *Love in Two Languages,* presents an allegory ("metaphora continua," as Quintilian put it—bilingually!) of comparative reading itself, and insists that the "original" is not a semantic or logical "prime." Translation as confrontation, not transparency: under these conditions, as Ungar recommends, "close reading"—of, not despite, translation—"will continue to be grounded in efforts to understand linguistic specificity as well as . . . broader factors of difference."

Medieval studies, an implicitly comparative field built around diglossic cultures in Europe and elsewhere, ought to have something to tell us about comparison, and Caroline Eckhardt's "Old Fields, New Corn, and Present Ways of Writing about the Past" contrasts the flourishing of medieval studies generally with its minor presence in comparative literature journals, associations, and conferences. Among the approaches in medieval research that bear implications for all fields and periods are a revived sense of manuscript reading and writing as a particular branch of media, the recovery of the internationalism of the Middle Ages, and attention to diverse contexts and functions of reading. Her recommendations seek to undo the temporal provincialism, as objectionable as the more often castigated vice of Eurocentrism, that too often concentrates comparative work in the last two centuries.

"Of Monuments and Documents: Comparative Literature and the Visual Arts in Early Modern Studies, or The Art of Historical Tact," by Christopher Braider, revives Erwin Panofsky's iconology in a new climate. The Renaissance, he reminds us, proposed a lingua franca of texts and ideas that bound together the vernaculars of Europe even as they diverged from Latin-based culture. Similarly, an "emulative rivalry" bound painting, sculpture, literature, and even historical action together. In our times, the iconology reserved to art historians has transformed into an "iconomachy" in which literary scholars, philosophers, historians of science, psychologists, media theorists, and others make images into an exceptionally serious kind of text, one that not just permits, but requires, interdisciplinarity.

In "Beyond Comparison Shopping: This Is Not Your Father's Comp. Lit.," Fedwa Malti-Douglas casts a backward glance on the changes in the field since her own initiation and describes her heeding of the "siren call" of "the world of the visual, the world of film, political cartoons, and comic strips" and the call of the "siren of law, medicine, and science." Arguing that these are all disciplines that do not stay within neatly defined realms but spread well beyond them in chains of consequence, Malti-Douglas calls on comparatists to take up their scrutiny and concludes with a *laudatio* of comparative literature as the realm of intellectual adventure.

Synthesizing partial perspectives and compensating for gaps in the essays comprising the report was the task originally planned for the "Responses" section. Inevitably, the responders were drawn to offer their original views on the direction of the field, though on the basis of the preexisting (or in-progress) report. Katie Trumpener offers a geopolitical reading of the chances of comparison, adopting Herder with his anthology *Voices of the Peoples in Songs* (1778) as predecessor figure. Reminding us of the headline stories of the last two generations—the construction and then the collapse of the Cold War system of nations—she charts the development of our field, through the migrations of its Central European sages, as a consequence of geographical and political shifts. Caryl Emerson, analogously "answering for Central and Eastern Europe," calls on us to acknowledge the contributions and distinctive points of view of scholars from the Slavic and Slavic-influenced world, the crucial difference, to her mind, being the place allotted to art in the scheme of human values. Roland Greene explains the place of cultural studies in the development of comparative literature, not as the definitive liberation from the tyranny of the text that it may have seemed to offer to some in 1994, but as a first move from an understanding of literature as a matter, not of "phenomena," but of "fields." Investigating "not works but networks," in the words of his title, comparative literature as Greene sees it will learn from colonial histories but not partition them off from their metropoles, investigate "non-Western" works but not on the basis of their "otherness" to Europe. We should "understand comparison as inherently problematic—a politics writ small," he urges.

In three commentaries on the report-in-progress presented at the 2004 Modern Language Association meeting, Linda Hutcheon, Zhang Longxi, and Jonathan Culler parse the discipline with local knowledge drawn from their exotic places of residence—Canada, Hong Kong, and the office of Cornell's Dean of Humanities, respectively. Their commentaries point up the fact, scarcely acknowledged elsewhere, that the organization sponsoring the present book is the *American* Comparative Literature Association, not the international association (which would have argued the issues of universalism and specificity as well, but differently), and above all, not a locationless, contentless Discipline of Everything filling a bureaucratic slot in the University of Excellence. But even that acknowledgment of local provenance leads into reflection on the universal pretensions ingrained, durably no doubt, in the intellectual forms of "Americanness" (a word that Hutcheon reminds us to take carefully).

Finally, Marshall Brown points out that geography is to some degree relative to the fineness of our perceptions: an attentive reader of the most classically European, standardly novelistic account of the bourgeois subject in its prime can nonetheless detect traces of languages and cultures not accounted for by the image of self-contained national cultures that comparatists have always striven against. In response to the sober tone of much of the report, the last word of his essay—and of the book—is "fun." So be it.

The present report has been discussed in various fora, posted on the Internet for the critiques of fellow comparatists, and even published in a partial (and premature) Chinese translation.[1] It now reaches print, thanks to the enthusiasm of Michael Lonegro, acquiring editor for the humanities at the Johns Hopkins University Press. I thank Elizabeth Yoder for her careful and sympathetic editing.

For its entire existence, comparative literature has benefited from intense self-scrutiny and proposals for renewal. The American Comparative Literature Association has helped to promote those meditations, and its ten-year reports imperfectly reflect them. Because our field has not yet found, or is disinclined to claim, a definitive place among the disciplines, and because its intrinsic restlessness makes it unsuited to adopting once and for all a common agenda, we practitioners need activist professional organizations like the ACLA and the Association of Departments and Programs of Comparative Literature to frame the never-ending discussion about what we do and why. This part of our work can happen only "seit ein Gespräch wir sind / und hören können voneinander," as the poet says with sublimity and bathos.[2] If this book had a dedication, it would be to those organizations, in gratitude for their steady willingness to renew the conditions of that conversation.

NOTES

1. "Guanyu bijiao wenxue de duixiang yu fangfa, shang" 關於比較文學的對象與方法, 上, (Objects and Methods in Comparative Literature, part 1). Translated by He Shaobin 何紹斌. *Zhongguo bijiao wenxue* 中國比較文學 56: 3 (2004): 11–30.

2. Friedrich Hölderlin, "Friedensfeier" (third untitled draft), in Hölderlin, *Werke* (Frankfurt am Main: Insel, 1983), 2:39. Rough translation: "since we have been a conversation / And are able to hear from each other."

PART I

THE STATE OF THE DISCIPLINE, 2004

CHAPTER ONE

Exquisite Cadavers Stitched from Fresh Nightmares

Of Memes, Hives, and Selfish Genes

HAUN SAUSSY

The Triumph of Comparative Literature

> Yes—I'm—the—
> Fellow that's hav-ing other peop-le's fan-tasies,
> Suffering what they ought to be themselves–
> —*Thomas Pynchon*, Gravity's Rainbow

Comparative literature has, in a sense, won its battles. It has never been better received in the American university. The premises and protocols characteristic of our discipline are now the daily currency of coursework, publishing, hiring, and coffee-shop discussion. Authors and critics who wrote in "foreign languages" are now taught (it may be said with mock astonishment) in departments of English! The "transnational" dimension of literature and culture is universally recognized even by the specialists who not long ago suspected comparatists of dilettantism. "Interdisciplinarity" is a wonder-working keyword in grant applications and college promotional leaflets. "Theory" is no longer a badge of special identity or a mark of infamy; everyone, more or less, is doing it, more or less. Comparative teaching and reading take institutional form in an ever-lengthening list of places, through departments and programs that may or may not wear the label of comparative literature (they may be configured as humanities programs, interdisciplinary programs, interdepartmental committees, or collaborative research groups). The controversy is over. Comparative literature is not only legitimate: now, as often as not, ours is the first violin that sets the tone for the rest of the orchestra. Our conclusions have become other people's assumptions.

But this victory brings little in the way of tangible rewards to the discipline. What comparatists elaborated, argued, and propagated in the laboratories of their small, self-selecting profession has gone out into the world and won over people who have no particular loyalty to institutional bodies of comparative literature. That is grounds both for satisfaction and for a restless kind of disappointment. We may all be comparatists now—and for good reason—but only with a low common denominator. Few think of themselves as primarily comparatists; the accidental or momentary comparatist is not about to give up her day job. The criteria for membership in our social network—in particular, the deep familiarity with three or more languages that most comparative literature programs still require—do not apply to the application of ideas pioneered in our discipline. Nor is it as if English or history departments had to pay a tax to the comparative literature department every time they cited Auerbach, de Man, Said, Derrida, or Spivak. The omnipresence of comparative literature ideas does not by any means betoken a large and powerful university department in that discipline; in fact, it might be used as an argument against the necessity of founding one. Comparative literature programs in most universities are thinly funded patch-works of committee representation, cross-listed courses, fractional job lines, and volunteer service. Our ways of thinking, writing, and teaching have spread like a gospel and have not been followed (despite what our friends in beleaguered language-and-literature departments may say) by an empire.

We might be forgiven for wanting to bring home the fruits of our collective intellectual influence. One nightmare scenario about genetically modified crops has poverty-stricken farmers obliged to pay heavily every year for special seed stock that is patented by the corporations that did the development; another has modified genes escaping, through pollen, out into nature and altering the makeup of wild and cultivated plants. In our case, it is certainly the second metaphor that applies. The successful propagation of traits from the comparative literature family has not been accompanied by mechanisms of identification and control (of "branding," to use a term shared by cowboys and marketing specialists). We are universal and anonymous donors—in ethical terms, a glorious role to play, but a perilous one in the scramble for resources, honor, and institutional legitimacy that we experience every day in the shrinking domain of the university humanities faculty. What is the reason for this anonymity? How might our discipline get the recognition it deserves?

—I'm sorry, I have to interrupt you. Isn't this discussion conducted in too small a compass, as if winning the support of deans and budget officers were the measure of success? Have you been a department chair for too long? A beehive can grow only to a certain size before its numbers begin to work against it; then a subset of its denizens leave, carrying a new queen bee, to form another hive. That comparative literature hives off into other departments and disciplines is proof of its vitality. Or have you mistaken the unit of analysis? In attempting to confute the Darwinian theory of natural selection, skeptics collected examples of traits and behaviors that did not advance the fitness of the individual; this then brought forth the clarification that the effects of selection are seen in the species, not the single animal. And others have proposed that the "invisible hand" behind natural selection is not the interest of the species but that of the gene, attempting (in some unconscious way) to provide for the greatest number of copies of itself in the succeeding generation. It may be that the present institutional form of comparative literature is only a transitional guise, preparing the way for an overhaul of the humanities generally. What needs propagating is the comparative reflex, the comparative way of thinking, not the departmental name; and if those are to be spread at the cost of identity and institutional reward, so much the worse for identity.

—It so happens that identity is the pivot of our triumph—and our wraithlikeness.

About Our Selflessness: An Origin-Story

人棄我取，人取我與。
What others cast off, I collect;
What others seek, I supply.
—*The merchant Bai Gui, recorded by Sima Qian*

If the discrepancy between the fortunes of comparative literature practices and comparative literature institutions is especially marked today, it can be seen retrospectively as operating at every moment of the history of the discipline—a history of counter-, supra-, and meta-institutional activities.

Comparative literature, as we all know, is a product of the nineteenth century. But in another sense, all literature has always been comparative, watered by many streams. The clay tablets of Mesopotamia yield evidence of rivalries and strategic mergings among the hero-narratives of neighboring cultures, as do the books of the Bible.[1] Seeking the true sublime in "examples that please all and always," the rhetor formerly known as Longinus examined passages from Greek, Roman, and Hebrew literatures.[2] Prolonged engagement with the Pali and Sanskrit idioms of Buddhist teaching first caused speakers and writers of Chinese to become aware of the characteristics of their own very differently structured language, such as tones and logographic characters.[3] Features of the morphology of written Latin that we take for granted—the distinctness of individual words marked by white space, for instance—were first elaborated by Celtic-speaking scribes who lacked the rhetorical and literary training of the typical Roman patrician and needed the extra help.[4] Not just influence, but consciousness of difference and relation, is at work in these collisions. "Languages in contact" spawn hybrid forms—translations, pidgins, creoles, bilingual villages—and stake out the points of view that allow languages and literatures to be known as (that is, *as if* they were) things in themselves.[5] The logic of comparative literature is as old as literature itself.

And yet this indeterminably ancient discipline of comparative literature has a particular origin in the era of nationalisms, which created the need for it.[6] For the purposes of manufacturing a mythology, three figures can be named as its patrons: Madame de Staël, Goethe, and Hugo Meltzl de Lomnitz.[7] Madame de Staël's *De l'Allemagne* described verbal art as the expression of a people, its culture, its spiritual life and institutions; and by describing those of Germany to her French fellow-citizens, she initiated what Michael Palencia-Roth has since denominated "contrastive literature," that is, reflection on national differences through the themes, attitudes, genres, devices, styles, and occasions of imaginative writing.[8] Her book showed French culture with all its unconscious universalism a corresponding image: another world of differently ordered thoughts and sentiments. (The argument that each nation had its own, irreducible, cultural personality and scheme of values had been made most vocally by Herder a generation previous, but Herder's writings did not meet with the instantaneous international welcome—and thus the comparative-literature effectiveness—of Staël's.[9])

Goethe, in the 1820s, foresaw (and by his translations and adaptations hastened) the coming of an age of "world literature," facilitated by travel and patterned on international commerce: "If such a world literature will soon come into being, as is inevitable given the ever increasing rapidity of human interaction, then we may not expect anything more or different from [this literature] than what it can and does achieve . . . whatever pleases the masses will expand without limit and, as we are already witnessing, find approval in all areas and regions."[10] That sounds like a distribution strategy, not an academic field; like a description, not a methodology. The field was to be initiated with the founding of the *Zeitschrift für vergleichende Literatur* (with renditions of its title in eleven other languages on the front cover) by Hugo Meltzl de Lomnitz in 1877. Meltzl's lead article, "The Present Tasks of Comparative Literature," announces the name and predicts the institution.[11]

So, as an institution, comparative literature can be traced back to 1877, the year of Nietzsche's *Human, All Too Human* and of Trollope's *Is He Popinjoy?*—twelve years after the conclusion of the American Civil War, seven years after Bismarck's Reich, five years after *Middlemarch* (with its unfortunate Casaubon and his "key to all mythologies"), three years after the International Postal Union. It is six years older than the Brooklyn Bridge and twelve years older than the Eiffel Tower. But a name, a birth date and a time line do not yet tell us what the discipline was designed to do. "Vergleichende Literatur" and its equivalents in various languages were the statement of a program, a call inviting a response. What were the terms of the call? Who responded, and how?

For the reader of 1877, "comparative" was a program (actually, multiple programs) in a single word. Since 1800, philological disciplines had emerged across Europe to enable the reading of texts in Old French, Old English, Middle High German, and the Scandinavian and Celtic languages; the literature of times that were previously considered barbaric was extracted from manuscripts and pored over with the attention formerly given only to Greek and Latin masterpieces. *Beowulf* (first edition 1815), the *Nibelungenlied,* the *Eddas,* the *Chanson de Roland,* and kindred epics were scrutinized for their bases in myth and history, and questioned for what they might have to say about the origins of the peoples whose cultural "property" they now had become. The *Deutsche Grammatik* (1819, 1840) and *Deutsche Mythologie* (1835) of the Brothers Grimm created Germanness as a cultural heritage before it could be achieved through political means.[12] National rivalries, particularly acute along the French/German axis, designated scholar-heroes who fashioned, through text editing and dialectology and in perpetual awareness of the identitarian needs of their state sponsors, versions of the "usable past." It was, in short, an age of "national philology."[13]

But the comparative method—the intellectual tool without which the grammars and mythologies would not have been achievable—if left to itself, had no respect for national frontiers. A consistent survey of the laws of phonetic drift and grammatical modification would lead to the conclusion that the Germanic, Romance, Celtic, Slavic, Persian, and Indic language-families, though riven with mutual unintelligibility, were at root forms of the same language. And the consequences of the comparative method were the same when applied to the content of utterances: Michel Bréal, for example, in the pivotal year 1877, proposed that "the *Râmâyana* and the *Iliad* may be based on the same premise, and it is certain that the *Odyssey,* the *Aeneid,* the *Nibelungenlied* and the *Shahnameh* contain episodes that retell, under different names, the selfsame fact."[14] Linguistic or literary chauvinism is beyond the point when all roads lead to the shores of the Indus, and no local hero is more than an avatar of one better known through the Vedas and Upanishads. Two models for literary study here collide, one drawn from manuscript editing, the other from linguistics. Whereas the historical method, as applied in New Testament or Homeric scholarship, sought to reconstruct the original form of a text by distinguishing it from the layers of subsequent accretion, the comparative method tended to dissolve identities, or at any rate their singular expressions, into a common source. One discipline seized on differences in order to pare them away; the other did so in order to neutralize them.

Meltzl de Lomnitz, in his program for comparative literature, announces "the principle of polyglottism" and prescribes ten languages as the basis for literary study: German, English, French, Icelandic, Italian, Dutch, Portuguese, Swedish, Spanish, and Hungarian. Such a list of prerequisites could perhaps only have been imagined by a nineteenth-century Central European nobleman; both admirably cosmopolitan and geographically restricted, it exhibits a certain Habsburg cut. (Romanian, the language of Meltzl's immediate surroundings, is excluded, presumably and unfairly as an idiom that had created nothing more than folklore; the omission of Russian is more serious and makes the list look more politically parochial.) Within its narrow geographic confines, however, polygottism does step outside the charmed circle of Indo-European cousinage. Philological study that incorporates both German and Hungarian cannot plot its course on cognates or common ancestors, for Hungarian belongs to a separate language family entirely; the science will have to suspend its allegiance to genealogical reasoning and take its bearings from reports of contact or similarity. The inclusion of Hungarian in an otherwise unremarkable list opens comparative literature to being something other than a science of origins. It can be seen as the first in a long series of gestures by which comparative literature questions the criteria for inclusion in the set of objects known as "literature," the ultimate ancestor of essays on orange juice jingles[15] or shopping malls,[16] and also the decisive swerve of an established academic discourse (the comparative philological method) toward a Goethean horizon in which world literature, coming from all directions, is whatever the world takes to be literature.

By not being a science of origins, comparative literature establishes an indefinite task for itself. Comparative philology could, in the end, use up its raison d'être: after a sufficient number of examples are adduced, laws can be formulated and historical accounts framed. In philology, the properly comparative moment came early in the discovery process, as parallel phonetic series were established for the different languages and the regularity of their differences showed them to be tributaries of a higher common source. Comparative philology found what it was looking for and then retreated from the foreground of scholarly attention once the floor plan of historical linguistics was complete. A similar fate lay in store for a related field, comparative anatomy, which by 1911 had become "a term employed to designate the study of the structure of man as compared with that of lower animals, and sometimes the study of lower animals in contradistinction to human anatomy; the term is now falling into desuetude. . . . The change of terminology is chiefly the result of modern conceptions of zoology. From the point of view of structure, man is one of the animals; all investigations into anatomical structure must be comparative."[17] By winning its case, comparative anatomy had made itself obsolete; it became simply a presupposition of general anatomy.

However, the inclusion, through Hungarian, of an irreducible philological exception, and all the exceptions to the definitions of literature and literary history that were to come, had the effect of impeding comparative literature's dissolution into one or another existing branch of the historical sciences.

As of 1877, no branch of learning was more involved with and indebted to national strivings than the study of modern languages and literatures. Chairs in rhetoric (a discipline indebted to the ancients and imbued with Renaissance universalism) had been turned over into chairs of philology and linguistics, whose new possessors fostered the study of English, French, German, Spanish, Italian—singly or in historically determined groups (*Germanistik,* Romance philology). Comparative literature with its ten concurrent tongues set itself against the model of national language and literature studies. In so doing, it certainly made finding a patron more difficult, for while particular ministries of education could and did always find it reasonable to appoint professors of the national heritage, a heritage that was at once everybody's and nobody's lacked the appeal of self-interest. Meltzl de Lomnitz, professor of Germanic philology at the University of Cluj in present-day Romania, published his grandly titled *Acta comparationis litterarum universarum* (Journal for the Comparison of the Totality of Literature) himself. It was in France, a country where culture had long spoken in the tones of confident universalism, and in the United States, a country of immigrants with an eclectic version of high culture, that comparative literature found its earliest institutional footing.

The interpretations of the term were correspondingly diverse: in France, it tended to be identified with "the study of the mutual relations of different literatures"[18] (which assumes that "a literature" is a well-defined object, usually one with national or linguistic frontiers); in the United States, it leaned toward systematic global perspectives, yielding common patterns of development. (Thus, for Charles Mills Gayley and Fred Newton Scott in 1899, comparative literature is "the general theory of literary evolution, the idea that literature passes through stages of inception, culmination and decline."[19]) There is room for a comparative study of comparative literature traditions.[20] What they have in common is a noncongruence with studies of the language and canon of particular nations (what we in the United States call a national-language-and-literature department) and, by consequence, a difficulty in determining their object of investigation. The history of comparative literature could provide a proof *a contrario* of the persistent power of the "nation," a relatively recent political unit, to define and shape culture. Circa 1777 in Europe, the disciplines that handled what we would today call literary texts were rhetoric, classical learning, philosophy, and theology—all of them based on ancient or late-antique models that were the common property of cultivated people. By 1877, it seemed self-evident that the proper disciplinary container for post-Renaissance literatures was the national language and culture. Comparative literature strove against this newer assumption.

Meltzl's comparative literature makes a nation of Europe. But this origin is a matter of anecdote, not necessity: indeed, for the East Asianist, the other end of the Eurasian continent is a far more promising place to host the international, interlinguistic, intercultural investigation. A far longer temporal series; a single dominant literary idiom shared by multiple dynasties, nations, religions, and languages; a common canon, parsed and combated in many ways; the emergence of vernaculars from and against the literary language; exchanges with peoples from different cultural backgrounds, and the consequent adaptations and revaluations—these and other factors combine to make East Asia a more "normal" ground for comparative literary history. South Asianists, Americanists, and others could no doubt say as much and do as well to cast doubt on the inevitability of Europe.

The "nation" of the discipline of comparative literature is perhaps most readily to be sought in the array of international organizations and scholarly societies that unfolded between 1850 and 1900: the International Expositions of 1851, 1867, 1889, 1900; the International Congresses of linguists, philosophers, psychologists, religious representatives; the International Committee of the Red Cross; the Socialist International; the Berlin Conference; the Universal Postal Union; the creation of time zones; the emergence of civil-society organizations for a universal language, against slavery, for female suffrage, for eugenics. (As this brief listing shows, such bodies, even when they aimed to overcome national egotism, were far from self-evidently beneficent.) An international organization gave quasi-political substance to professionally defined communities of practitioners (and presented opportunities for the political manipulation of each organization's "national section"). Comparative literature would not simply enter the newly created international space of such organizations but would, in the literary domain, express its logic.[21] Many comparatists have found this a congenial domain of extra-literary activity, and the proceedings of international congresses are replete with references to the encouragement comparatists of every country derive from being together.

If *literature,* as a word with implicit connotations of value, is an "essentially contested term" like *justice, truth,* or *beauty,* the purpose of making its study "comparative" can hardly be univocal.[22] Like "comparative philosophy" or "comparative religion," it suggests that what might have been, in isolation, simply Philosophy or Religion will take on a new look by being put next to other things of the same kind. (That there are "other things of the same kind" is what some adepts of Philosophy or Religion find impossible to admit.[23]) Comparative literature contests the definition of *literature* (as well as aesthetic norms, genre definitions, literary-historical patterns, and the rest) by throwing examples and counterexamples at it. Founded in the era of national and historical scholarship, comparative literature is neither.

That explains part of our disciplinary "selflessness": if (as the saying goes) a language is a dialect with an army and a navy, comparative literature is a committee with a list of good intentions. Another reason is our close dependency on the very national-language-and-literature disciplines that comparative literature was created to overcome. Without training in specific languages and canons, a comparatist will have nothing to work with. Ours is, in administrative terms, a metadiscipline or even a counterdiscipline, founded on the traditions of learning in national languages and literatures, inseparable from them but distinct from them in its purposes. It occupies a second floor and has no stairway of its own: the only way to get there is through a national language. The exception is courses in world literature in translation, which would probably benefit from being taught as, for example, English literature in a transnational mode, so as to preserve the very differences of language and historical moment that a wholesale "denationalization" of literatures into Literature would erode.[24]

In proposing to consider world literature as "an elliptical refraction of national literatures," "not a set canon of texts but a mode of reading," David Damrosch reminds us that there will be as many world literatures as there are national or local perspectives, that world literature is not a rival but an object, even a project, of comparative literature.[25] But comparative literature does not own world literature, as physics departments own cyclotrons and sociology departments own Erving Goffman. Comparative literature can assemble it—that committee structure again—from parts that various people, some in the university department structure and some out of it, own. Comparative literature supplies the instructions, the labor, and the glue. Our many "modes of reading" fix on texts from elsewhere, transform them, then send them out again. If part of our "selflessness" derives from not having a national "home," another part derives from our identification with the processes of interchange, our investment in methods rather than in subject matter.[26]

Of Objects and Methods

The dominant metaphor of conceptual relativism, that of differing points of view, seems to betray an underlying paradox. Different points of view make sense, but only if there is a common co-ordinate system on which to plot them; yet the existence of a common system belies the claim of dramatic incomparability. What we need . . . is

some idea of the considerations that set the limits to
conceptual contrast.

> —*Donald Davidson, "On the Very Idea of a*
> *Conceptual Scheme"*

To be a linguist these days, you do not have to know a lot of languages, despite the older meaning of the term *linguist:* in the last fifty or sixty years, linguistics has developed a set of autonomous research programs that do not involve engaging with language at that level of detail. Similarly, at moments in the last few decades, it has seemed possible to make a career in literary studies without making sustained reference to works of literature: one could study aesthetic theory, literary history, reception, pedagogy—even the history of theories of literature—as so many independent fields. But a field composed of examples (and of theories of what the examples are examples of) like comparative literature has little chance of declaring scholarly independence. What would we do all alone? This condition of imperfect autonomy keeps us awake at night and makes for a high degree of vulnerability to changes in the ecology of our institutions.[27] As Benedetto Croce said, "The comparative method, precisely because it is a mere method of research, cannot suffice to delimit a field of study"; "I cannot understand how a specialization can be constructed out of comparative literary history."[28] Little wonder that "no scholarly discipline has enjoyed as uninterrupted a tradition of doubts about its right to exist, expressed by its own adepts."[29] One way of addressing that doubt about whether comparative literature ought to exist is to think of it as a discipline defined by the search for its proper objects.

What is the object of comparative literature? What is it *about?* Some proposals have already been mentioned: literary foreign relations, the discovery of obligatory stages in the evolution of literary traditions. To consider in the same scholarly project works from two or three distinct traditions (which might as well, for the purposes of this argument, be couched in the same language: Petronius's *Satyricon* and Aquinas's *Summa theologica*), it is necessary to find some common point of reference, and naming such points has been the job of metatheory in comparative literature. The history of comparative literature as a university discipline is not one of steadily deepening understanding of a single object of study, but rather a history of attempts to locate that object of study. Receptive to changing definitions of "literature" to a degree unmatched by any other literary field, and also apt to reconsider its assumptions in response to newly prominent areas, periods, and languages of comparison, comparative literature has a discontinuous history in which it is not always the protagonist.

If comparative literature were more like comparative philology and comparative anatomy, the point of reference common to any two phenomena would be their latest shared ancestor: thus English *five* and Greek *pente,* distinct twigs on the tree of language, lead us back through branchings of sound and sense to an earlier Indo-European form, **penk^we,* as to a trunk. Comparison of the brain of man and the brain of the rat points out shared ancestral features as well as the history of development of each. In such comparison, as in a metaphor by Aristotle's account, the things to be compared lead the researcher to "solve for" their common factor, the *tertium comparationis* or ground. Where the third term is missing or simply too remote to be meaningful, the comparison fails. The assertion of historical sciences is that the third terms are not simply logical conveniences but reflect real states of affairs in the past. (In historical linguistics, hypothetical forms may be reconstructed from the evidence but must be marked as such, for the sake of maintaining a distinction between documents and conjecture.) To use an older language: the *tertium comparationis* was expected to be a *fundamentum in re.* Thus the comparative disciplines on the analogy of which comparative literature was first proposed thought of their subject matter as needing to be organized in the shape of a genealogical tree. Comparison enabled one to discover the distal events in the past that had produced branchings; it read difference as differentiation, a process unfolding in past time.

If comparative literature had espoused the pattern of historical linguistics and read literature as the growth of traditions from determinate beginnings, the phenomena of influence and translation would have had little interest for it; it would have been another national historical science, albeit one with a larger transnational scope (divided into provinces such as Indo-European, Semitic, Uralo-Altaic, etc.). It would have formed the literary corollary to historical studies in folklore and mythology, which do hew more closely to the patterns of linguistic diffusion and differentiation.[30] But by its interest in modern literary traffic across languages and borders, the "cosmopolitan character [of] production and consumption in every country" that creates the conditions for a "world literature,"[31] comparative literature could not but seek another basis, another kind of "third thing." Named for the tree-shaped disciplines yet not entirely like them, it had to find its own equivalent of a trunk.

What is the trunk—what does comparative literature discover? The most obvious, and usually untheorized, candidate for "trunk" status is simply the universality of human experience.[32] Situations, emotions, ideas, personalities seem to recur across any corpus of world literature, be it ever so diverse. If we will only take it for granted that the topics of literature refer to the same things, comparison becomes possible—indeed, all too possible—hence the need to keep calling into doubt the equivalence of similars. Although thematics, or subject matter, is the starting point of many an investigation, it is never enough simply to discover the same themes appearing in different places: an account of how the works make their subject matter manifest is the only thing that can save a comparison of nature poetry in Wordsworth and Xie Lingyun, for example, from platitude. An enabling hypothesis at best, the universality of selected themes cannot serve as a conclusion. Enumeration is a slender form of interpretation, and with a horizon of universality, one has never finished enumerating.

But for literature in translation, where nothing of the work may survive the process but the subject matter, there is no better place to start. Thematic reading is the constant pedagogical temptation in world literature.[33] But what works for world literature may not work for close comparative study, and vice versa. David Damrosch offers a hopeful case: "Kafka's haunting ironies play out in sentence structures that do not always translate well, yet 'the Kafkaesque' is fully visible in translation at the levels of the paragraph and the scene."[34] If so, good for Kafka, and good for Chekhov and many others; but not every author scales up so convincingly from sentence to paragraph or scene level. To perceive in Dante, Baudelaire, or Sei Shônagon only the incidents of plot and imagery would be to do them an injustice. Poets, for evident reasons, suffer from that treatment, and when reading goes far afield, the theme you identify may be your own.[35] What comes across in thematic reading (a tactic devised in response to conditions of our encounter with translated literature) is not necessarily what is most worth knowing about a work. A method of analysis that supposes content to have been acquired can only with difficulty ask if we know *how* to read.

World literature and translation are modes of understanding, and they are also filtering techniques: they unavoidably impart their selective bias to the literary field in the act of representing it. Not that representing the literatures of the world is all that world literature is good for: by putting traditions into contact and making a native language undergo "the test of foreignness,"[36] it has a productive and poetic role to play. But this role requires that language—the language of the original, but the language of the translation as well—be recognized as something more than a delivery system for content, that it be understood as having a weight and resistance of its own. No longer apologetic for teaching works they do not read in the original, some comparatists even present this necessity as a virtue, the consequence of a willingness to deal with remote traditions and to take collaborative risks. Unless specialist knowledge is maintained as the desired standard, such arguments are in danger of appearing merely self-serving. Comparative pedagogy must find a way to steer between the exclusivism of "I won't teach anything I don't already know" and the patronizing tone of "What matters is not my ability to learn from the text, but the fact that I am teaching it at all."

If the specific object of comparative literature is not found in the thematic content of works, perhaps it lies in a dimension of which works and their contents are only symptoms. Can something as impermanent as imagination and tale-telling give rise to true knowledge, as Socrates might have asked? Or do the fluctuating phenomena boil down in the end to something solid and necessary? Ideas of inescapable evolutionary rhythms shaped the comparative work of Alexander Veselovskij in the nineteenth century, and of his twentieth-century successor Viktor Zhirmunskij. Reading social history as a sequence of stages, and taking literature as the expression of social conditions, permitted comparative literature in this Russian style to find its proper object in the correlation of the stages in separate traditions. During much of the Soviet period, the subjection of literature to social science must have been a useful defensive strategy.[37]

One attempt to exploit the findings of folklore and oral tradition for comparative study was the symbolically titled *Growth of Literature* by H. Munro Chadwick and N. Kershaw Chadwick. The authors declared their aim to be "to formulate some general principles in regard to the history of literature" based on the results of the parallel treatment of a number of ancient European literatures—"we mean of course independent literatures."[38] This investigation harnesses together, in the style of comparative philology or mythology, the results of historical branching studies and typological classification. What were the original characteristics of the literatures, what genres and topoi obsessed them, and how did they change over time? The goal of comparative study as the Chadwicks formulate it precludes giving too much attention to lateral influences such as those borne by Greek and Latin written culture, as if borrowings would constitute meddlings with an experiment that should have been left to run its course. Their enterprise thus appears as the reversed image of the program devised for comparative literature by van Tieghem, the study of literary exports and imports. That comparative literary research could issue in two so well-stocked yet utterly contrary paradigms at the same time shows the capaciousness, or perhaps the incoherence, of the field circa 1930.

Another 1930s experiment with trunks and branches, R. D. Jameson's deployment of the theories of I. A. Richards and C. K. Ogden, founded comparative literature on semantic behavior:

> A national language is an infinitely complicated set of gestures. By means of symbols nations manipulate a universe, and at the same time relieve and stimulate emotions. . . . The establishment in a community of a range of sense, feeling, tone and intention for the words of its language serves to bring into view some aspects of its behavior and to hide others.
>
> If this rough account of meaning is acceptable, the comparison of literatures will become the comparison of the several kinds of meaning which the Germans, French, English and American peoples seek to elicit by the use of words.[39]

Here an anthropological category—human sign-using capacities—has taken the place of the common ground and serves as a metric for evaluating how far apart the nations of Europe have grown, or how much similarity remains to them, after hundreds of years of schooling in the vernacular languages of each.

A doctoral thesis that contained chapters about *Tristram Shandy,* Sherlock Holmes, *Don Quixote,* Dickens, Tolstoy, Bely, and Rozanov, with side excursions into all the major Russian authors, would certainly qualify in an American department of comparative literature. Viktor Shklovskij unwittingly pioneered the genre in 1925 with his *Theory of Prose.*[40] The common trunk to which all the exhibits in this wily, argumentative, intense book refer is the contention that writing is directed by technique, not subject matter, the thesis of "Art as Device." Here the intellectual leanings of the Formalist critics and the object-hunger of comparative literature are in alignment, or would have been had Shklovskij's work not been lost in the fog of Russian modern history for forty years. Literariness, *literaturnost',* to use a term made famous by Tynjanov, is the true object of literary studies, the common factor in all literary traditions, and it makes perfect sense for a cosmopolitan discipline like comparative literature to search out and describe it in all its contexts.

What Shklovskij did for prose, Roman Jakobson did for poetry, but with a significant difference: where Shklovskij's arguments could be made on the basis of translations and not suffer from that circumstance, Jakobson found that the available poetic devices were strongly constrained by the material offered by particular languages. Although a very abstract kind of description could uncover parallelism, symmetry, equivalence, iconicity, and the like as cross-linguistic features of poetry, the work that poets did was shaped, for example, by the opportunities furnished by differentiation between labialized and plain consonants (as in Russian), by classes of tone and rhyme (as in classical Chinese), and so forth.[41] A Formalist reading of poetry opened the details of the most advanced linguistic knowledge and the subtlest indications of stylistics, genre, and influence to comparison as a local case of the laws of literary art in general.

New analytic disciplines in the Formalist tradition—narratology, descriptive poetics, semiotics—as well as some originating outside it—for example, Foucauldian "genealogy," the "materialities of communication"[42]—have generated, like linguistics, specialized nomenclatures that seem to put the object of literary study at a remove from particular traditions. Collaborative work on dictionaries of literary terms helps to give plausibility to the idea that point of view, say, or anacoluthon, is a category that can be retrieved from the reading of works in Zuñi or Gikuyu as well as from works in French or Italian. But nothing should be taken for granted. When the effort is made to integrate contemporary vocabularies with the traditional lexicon of literary effects used in China, for example, the forced matches and awkward remainders of connotation on both sides reveal as much incompatibility as harmony.[43] If proposing equivalences is one job comparatists do well, their rejection by specialists is a further and instructive moment in literary-theoretical interaction. Comparative literature needs to run up against these limits as a reminder that the national boundaries it agrees to disregard are not *merely* arbitrary lines drawn on a continuous landscape.

The "linguistics of literariness" provides a rich conceptual framework and promises extension to an indefinite number of potential contexts of discovery: no human culture is without verbal art, and there are as many "devices" as there are ways of breaking with the expectations of ordinary, literal (as we figuratively call it) communication. Indeed, as Paul de Man held, literariness, redefined as "the rhetorical or tropological dimension of language . . . can be revealed in any verbal event when it is read textually"—even the Socratic dialogues of Archie and Edith Bunker.[44] Formalist reading is a great dissolver of canons. If all works of literature share a set of characteristics which it is the business of literary theory to explore, then any work, read with enough attention, is as good as any other.

The cases of critics as different, in almost every other respect, as Shklovskij, Jakobson, and de Man show the power and attractiveness for comparative literature of a concept of "literariness," however variously it may be put to work. It is not a concept for which national and linguistic frontiers or historical epochs matter much, so it promises to wave aside many of the standard objections to comparative research. While an attempt to define a priori what Literature is would certainly end in a chaos of disagreement, "literariness," as a differential concept correlated with ordinary language, creates an object of research for comparative literature through a modal argument: not that all literariness is alike, but that instances of literariness differ from instances of banal language in the same ways, is its message. The modal character of literariness makes it robust and context-independent, exactly what an expanding research project ought to be. That must account for its continuing vigor in periods when other ways of conceiving of the discipline's object have enjoyed favor.[45] But the term is not perfectly suited to be comparative literature's institutional totem. It does not adequately mark the fact that literariness *emerges from* contexts and methods of reading, rather than being a property of literature, and it suggests a category-slippage between a disciplinary product and a restricted class of objects.

Some paradoxes follow from the elevation of literariness (or repurposed language) to the status of characteristic object of study for comparative literature. Many activities normally carried out in the field do not find themselves reflected in it. Histories of literature have long been written—even comparative and international ones[46]—but a history of literariness is difficult to imagine. The kind of reading that discovers literariness, the kind of seeing appropriate to nonrepresentational painting, the kind of listening appropriate to atonal music—each announces and confirms the autonomy of the artistic medium under consideration. To discover language, paint, sound, not just as vehicles for the conveyance of general ideas, but as dense, specific habitats, makes it far harder to move from one medium to another. Even in the period of its strongest claim to disciplinary autonomy, comparative literature could not quite account for its actual range with a single coherent research program. The centrality of literariness to the discipline must therefore have always been a virtual model, an ideal condition to which literary history, inter-arts comparison, or other similarly heteronomous activities might aspire. Oddly, the moment in the history of comparative literature that saw it dwelling most insistently on the characteristics of its chosen object was also the moment at which it radiated outward, under the loose name of "theory," its strongest interdisciplinary energies.

In another paradoxical twist, the summoning of literariness from attention to the most specific properties of literary language so far transcended the concerns of national-language disciplines that it made their traditional concerns seem unimportant, passé. An Invisible College of Theory (sometimes but not always located in comparative literature departments) roamed the floor plans of previously distinct curricula. Everyone who made or applied Theory became a comparatist, if only by default, because of the undeniably specific and multiple historical origins of the theoretical vocabulary. Some twenty years after the moment of Theory's greatest influence, and for quite unrelated reasons, this neutralization of national literature projects has become an institutional reality. Across the country, programs in languages and literatures are being eliminated, consolidated into big, diverse departments of foreign languages and literatures, or subcontracted to units outside the humanities (international and overseas programs, for example). The academic environment that gave rise to comparative literature—one in which the national languages and literatures were the substantial, permanent disciplines and ours was the optional, occasional one—has been turned upside down and inside out, as foreign language departments take an interest in postcolonial literatures related to their metropoles or envision the national tradition in a larger context. Comparative literature can no longer play its previous part after this redistribution of the roles. These institutional changes deserve separate treatment in a later section of this report.

The 1993 ACLA report on the state of the discipline, later published with annexes as *Comparative Literature in the Age of Multiculturalism*, describes "comparative literature in the new millennium" as a field of fields, drawn to boundaries as opportunities for boundary crossing:

> The space of comparison today involves comparisons between artistic productions usually studied by different disciplines; between various cultural constructions of those

disciplines; between Western cultural traditions, both high and popular, and those of non-Western cultures; between the pre- and postcontact cultural productions of colonized peoples; between gender constructions defined as feminine and those defined as masculine, or between sexual orientations defined as straight and those defined as gay; between racial and ethnic modes of signifying; between hermeneutic articulations of meaning and materialist analyses of its modes of production and circulation; and much more. These ways of contextualizing literature in the expanded fields of discourse, culture, ideology, race, and gender are so different from the old models of literary study according to authors, nations, periods, and genres that the term "literature" may no longer adequately describe our object of study.[47]

The 1993 committee members were not so much declaring a new direction for the discipline as taking note of tendencies already at work. If the standard demarcations observed and transgressed by degree programs and books in comparative literature—language, genre, period—derive from the frameworks of national literary histories, the new orientations suggested here come from media studies, postcolonial studies, cultural studies, and the "politics of recognition" enacted by late-twentieth-century social movements.[48] Given the bearings of, say, Wellek and Warren's 1949 *Theory of Literature*, the suggested new approaches focus on the "extrinsic determinants" of literary production.[49] But the point is, precisely, to question the inwardness of the category of literature and whether such determinants are "extrinsic" at all: "worrying about the historical contingency of this category" is the cultural-studies task to which the Bernheimer committee summons us.[50]

No less than any other statement in the field, the 1993 report expresses a theory of what comparative literature does and what its object is. "Literary texts" are to be seen as "one discursive practice among many others in a complex, shifting, and often contradictory field of cultural production" (42). "Comparative literature should analyze the material possibilities of cultural expression, both phenomenal and discursive, in their different epistemological, economic, and political contexts" (45). The contention fits in well with our age-old disciplinary skepticism, indeed our traditions of "creative destruction."[51] "Culture (including literature)" joins the parade of intentional objects that have purported to define the profession. Just as an earlier comparative literature had replaced the national literary histories, which dwelt on identity and tried to minimize interchange, with its own universalisms and accounts of literary traffic, so in 1993 the "literature" without borders that had formed the disciplinary focus of comparative literature in the 1950s and 60s was to be redescribed as an illusory effect of momentary consensus. But what is "culture" in the "age of multiculturalism"?

In disciplinary terms, the "space of comparison" is mapped out as a result of negotiations that happen in the practices that form the objects of sociology (class, race, gender, sexual preference), historical geography (the West, the non-West; conditions before and after European colonization), the history of technology (forms of communication, the media of the different arts), and the disciplines that take "cultural construction" as their concern (anthropology, history, sociology, political science). These practices and their corresponding disciplines situate literature; it does not seem that literature is able to situate them. This is hard medicine for a discipline that, for all its ambitions, has no preestablished object of its own: if the theory of its field is couched in terms from outside its purview, comparative literature risks giving up what autonomy it has and becoming an area of application for the disciplines that define it. The fact that the standard-setting disciplines in this scenario are the relatively distant social sciences makes the threat of heteronomy even greater since few scholars of literature are in a position to respond in kind to social-science assertions or to do their anthropological groundwork in-house. (The impression that the 1993 report hands down conclusions arrived at elsewhere is strengthened by occasional value judgments offered as obiter dicta, without further justification.[52])

Hard medicine, but this map of knowledge is not inconceivable: better to serve in a practically existing arrangement of disciplines than to reign in an illusory one. What does comparative literature have to offer under the new dispensation? Since "progressive tendencies in literary studies, toward a multicultural, global, and interdisciplinary curriculum, are comparative in nature" already, those identified with the institution of comparative literature are in a good position to join with those tendencies (47). Cultural studies, which "has tended to be monolingual and focused on issues in specific contemporary popular cultures," shows by its shortcomings the need for comparatists to supply "knowledge of foreign languages, training in cultural translations, expertise in dialogue across disciplines, and theoretical sophistication" (45, 47). Comparative literature can guide debates about the literary canon by proposing new works and models of canonicity (44). Comparative literature seems tapped to become an art of the in-between, a diplomacy of disciplines, a clearinghouse for cultural specificities.

Being in-between also means owning up to multiple commitments. "History, culture, politics, location, gender, sexual orientation, class, race—a reading in the new mode [of 1993] has to try to take as many of these factors as possible into account. The trick is to do so without . . . suggesting that a literary work can be explained as an unmediated reflection of these factors . . . [to perform] contextualizing without reifying."[53] But the big money is in reifying, as it always is: studies of, for example, "mixed-race literature" attract attention because of their claim that literature by or about persons who describe themselves as belonging to multiple "races" is a special kind of literature.[54] It would be unusual for a study of, say, poetic rhythm in Japanese, Greek, and Norse to deny that there is any such thing as "poetic rhythm" independent of the comparative context. Nevertheless, it is possible that the referent of comparison is not some common substrate of the things being compared, but the act of comparing itself—a conclusion whose institutional consequences might be serious.[55]

Most disciplines are founded on successful reifications. Not to reify is to settle for a weak hypothesis about the identity of the thing one is describing, and that does not come naturally to describers. Certainly the canonical departments of literature—French departments, for example—came into existence because of a claim that the language and literature of a subset of the people living in France formed a meaningful unit with a narratable history; those pioneers reified Frenchness by trying to understand it. (When, one day, such claims fail to persuade, the "things" they referred to appear as reifications.) Comparative literature in the contextualizing mode finds itself once more an adverb among earthshaking nouns.

The reception of the 1993 report, as evidenced in the responses from a diverse and energetic group of scholars, provides a set of mental maps of the discipline as surveyed from various vantage points. The surprising thing is how much overlap there is, how much agreement about the shape of the territory, among people who disagree about much else. The downgrading of "literature" from the exclusive focus of the discipline to the status of one mode of cultural discourse among others is read by all as a gesture directed against both the high-cultural canon of European literatures and the legacy of "grand theory," whether the respondent thinks this downgrading is a good thing or a bad one. The adoption of categories from social science is perceived as a sacrifice of disciplinary autonomy, whether "borderline suicidal" or just a recognition that "in fact, there is no central activity of the field."[56] By their choice of examples, and sometimes by express argument, respondents indicate how styles of thought gravitate toward their elective objects. Tell me what your objects are, and I will predict your methodology. The "porosity" of disciplines registered in the 1993 report augurs a rise in status for narrative and documentary genres of writing, which are easily assimilated to biography and history and which, moreover, lend themselves to translation and thematic reading; and a neglect of poetry, which is tightly bound to language and has affinities with philosophy and logic.[57] Some see the future of comparative literature in a break with the very idea of nations and languages, so that the most comprehensive version of the discipline would be "comparative media."[58] Those less sanguine about the report's view of the field insist on the specificity of literature, its resistance to "full contextualization in other discourses,"[59] and the need for a self-aware theory of reading.

The battle between "literature" and "cultural studies," repeatedly correlated with a battle between "Eurocentric" and "non-Western" canons of text and theory, is often announced but has trouble taking place. Once we get into the details, the big picture suffers. The front line dissolves, and the opposing forces melt into one another. One of comparative literature's totems—the close reading of literary works in their original languages—is treated as expendable by the authors of the report in a gesture that announces openness but might be read as suggesting that not all languages and literatures are equally worth the trouble of learning: "The old hostilities toward translation should be mitigated . . . we would even condone certain courses in minority literatures in which the majority of the works were read in translation."[60] (The misprinting of exotic names in several essays—"Buchi Emchetta," "Vauri Viswanathan," for example—gives a further indication that close reading and multiculturalism are not yet one.)

Rey Chow observes that the integration of non-Western texts into the comparative literature canon may just mean confronting a new class of "Eurocentric" specialists in remote cultures; there is no guarantee that exposure to the alien canon will teach anyone to see it as the locals see it. Chow fires a preliminary shot across the bow of the heirs of "the great Orientalists, Sinologists, Indologists, and so forth,"[61] thus raising the question of what kinds of expertise will be considered valuable in the new comparative literature: will departments of world cultural studies have to cultivate their own specialists, uninfected by the Eurocentric virus? On all sides, the question is not *whether* to contextualize literature and admit new traditions and canons, but *how*; and asking how, quite rightly, leads us away from the delusional questions of identity and toward the pragmatic ones, away from statements such as "The proper object of comparative literature is . . ." and toward ones such as "What we do in comparative literature is. . . ."

For to frame the contest between "literature" and "cultural studies" as a difference in the objects of study would make sense only if comparative literature had an essential, as opposed to an occasional, investment in a particular set of objects. An Italian department that abruptly changed its focus to the languages and literatures of Sweden would soon undergo an identity crisis far profounder than would an economics department that stopped studying Russia and turned its attention to Latin America. The historical pattern of comparative literature's declared objects of study (always migrating, always retreating) gives no reason to think that the typical objects of cultural studies lie beyond its powers. We certainly can (and should) "do" cultural research, provided only that its topics are not handed to us as ready-mades in black boxes but can be subjected to the kinds of analysis, critique, and contextualization that the discipline has taught comparatists to perform. Such reanalysis is what happened, for example, with the theory of speech acts, an immigrant from the realms of law and ordinary-language philosophy: the idea was permanently modified by its passage through literary studies, and within our field it has been one of the crucial links between the conceptions of comparative literature as "comparison of literatures" to "comparisons with literature."[62]

There is no necessary conflict between "literature" and "cultural studies"; at most, speaking from the literary side, there is an antinomy between two properties of the object we know as "literature."[63] (The corresponding antinomy in social science would probably be formulated as that between structure and agency.) To quote once more from an alleged arch-Formalist, "The linguistics of literariness is a powerful and indispensable tool in the unmasking of ideological aberrations, as well as a determining factor in accounting for their occurrence."[64] Putting aside the connotations of de Man's favorite term "aberrant" (that would mean erring away from what precisely?), this formulation gives plenty of work to both cultural and historical studies (as the analysis of what "occurs" in and through the power of sign systems) and literary study (as the "unmasking" of that power by a "linguistics," or grammatical model, that accounts for the regularities in its performance).

To return to the politics of the adverb: Comparative literature is best known, not as the reading *of literature,* but as reading *literarily* (with intensive textual scrutiny, defiance, and metatheoretical awareness) whatever there may be to read. Contextualization is always a legitimate epistemological move, but let us not grant any context the final authority of the real. That would be to make comparative literature a portal for other, more meaningful, more conclusive disciplines, and so to cheat the world of the nonreductive model of critical relation that our work at its best can provide, whether in the modes of close reading, of world literature, of comparative literary history, or of interdisciplinarity. What is needed is a term similar to "literariness" but that will not suggest an exclusive focus on written texts, on imaginative "literature" (a subdivision of the written that has been current for only a couple of centuries) or, more misleadingly still, a particular canon of texts. "Culture" will not do it; culture is all about subsumption into historical identities and systems of value. What most needs to be preserved, what is at stake when we debate whether comparative literature still has a role to play or can be allowed to vanish, its work on earth accomplished, is *metadisciplinarity:* not because it sounds prestigious or guarantees our uniqueness, but because it is the condition of our openness to new objects and forms of inquiry.

The result of this short history of comparative literature's search for its appropriate *object* is to put us back in front of comparative *projects.* From a nominalist point of view, the point of reference of the discipline is the point of encounter of its various objects, which may have little else in common. It needs, as its manual of procedure, not a theory (a philosophy or an ideology) but a poetics (an elucidation of the art of making, as applied to its own practices). This does not mean that comparative literature does not know what it is doing. The individual comparatist, engaged on a project, knows or comes to learn quite well what she is doing. But the results of many projects do not add up to a cumulative body of settled law, do not prove for all future comers the "comparability" of item X and item Y, and thus, by some accounts, do not constitute a discipline. Comparative literature is engaged with specificity and relation: the specificity of the object whereby it exceeds established models of discourse, and the relations that a new reading creates among its objects. Every comparative project is in some measure an experiment, and the most imaginative ones best answer the peremptory challenge: Why should we be interested in this encounter? What can you show us that we could not have learned for ourselves by taking each object in the traditional perspective of its discipline? These are in fact the questions asked of the discipline as a whole, and on them hinge its independence within institutions.

The Age of What?

The fragility of comparative literature as an institution and its success as a set of ideas come down, then, to the same things: its lack of a permanent defining object, a position between and (methodologically speaking) above disciplines with determinate fields and canons, and an openness to lateral linkages and nomothetic generalizations. A discipline so conceived must watch for changes in its environment, in the boundary conditions that make it possible; and surveying these conditions is part of the task of a periodic "report on the state of the discipline" like this one. What we face, as much as who we are or what we do, marks out the paths that our discipline may follow in the coming years. Predictions are always unreliable, but recent mutations in the political and institutional structures within which we practice leave little unaffected. Some notes on these conditions follow—not, however, assembled under one title that might unify understanding of the present as the "age of" this or that.

An Age of Unipolarity

Ever since the world ended
There's no more black and white.
Ever since we all got blended
There's no more reason to fuss and fight.
—Mose Allison, *"Ever Since the World Ended"*

As a product of the nineteenth-century European nation system, comparative literature assumes the existence of a number of states, each with its divergent character and aims. An interlocutor, like the international organizations whose form it echoes, of all the recognized states, it cannot be identified with any of them (though of course in practice, particular forms of comparative literature have been very much identified with the projects of this or that state or region; the fact that this is admitted as a critique gives one hope).[65] World literature too exists in this international space, its anthologies and syllabi always open to challenge by newcomers; the new entrants alter, not only the allotments of pages per country, language, or continent, but the very structure and aims of the activity. Multiculturalism, an originally North American solution to the problem of overlapping identities in a heterogeneous state, creates a similar set of opportunities for groups to sue for recognition. Indeed, since much of the diversity in North American societies is the result of immigration, multiculturalism plays out as a domestic version of international politics with its quasi-representative institutions, spokespersons, campaigns, and crises. It would thus be easy for comparative literature to see itself playing a central role in mediating among different "nationalities," as it had done in the academy since its founding. In 1993 it seemed uncontroversial that "the age of multiculturalism" had arrived.

In her response to the Bernheimer report, Mary Louise Pratt traced multiculturalism to the conjoined effect of three transformations at work in recent years: "globalization, democratization, decolonization."[66] Ten years later, globalization has taken a different turn, so that in many ways it seems to be the practical opposite of multiculturalism.[67] The "increased integration of the planet, the increasingly rapid flows of people, information, money, commodities, and cultural productions" of which Pratt speaks continue apace, but the surface on which these flows occur is one sharply tilted by the interests of the one remaining superpower. Globalization is Americanization, not in the superficial sense of spreading a uniform consumer culture (for every McDonald's, an equal and opposite Pokémon can be adduced), but in the shaping of economic and political decisions on a world scale by the perceived needs of the United States. The "Washington consensus" about the shape of market reforms required before countries can obtain International Monetary Fund assistance (opening of financial markets, removal of subsidies to local industries, privatization of public services) favors American economic penetration at direct cost to citizens of foreign countries.[68] The United States unilaterally repudiates international agreements on trade, armaments, or the environment when these do not serve domestic purposes, a privilege it does not extend to other nations, and it seeks (explicitly, since 2001) to block the emergence of regional or global rivals. At this end of a century-long arc of the rise and decline of supra-governmental organisms, "irrelevant" is the current administration's favored term to describe the United Nations, whenever the General Assembly or Security Council attempts to set limits to the exercise of American power. (As literary scholars, we know a little about relevance and the work it does within institutions.) Unilateralism seems even to have conquered the domain of the interchange between fact and verification, as if repeating a claim often enough sufficed to make it true.[69] Merely to imagine the end of American dominance provokes outcry.[70]

The point of bringing up these familiar observations is not to clamor against American hypocrisy and short-sightedness but to point out the differences with the bipolar, potentially multipolar international situation under which comparative literature first established itself in this country. In 1947 (the year of the founding of the comparative literature department at Yale, with Wellek its first chair), Americans knew that they would have to engage with the rest of the world in mixed tones of threat and persuasion, that their desires were not going to be an adequate plan for action. As the rivals fade from view, American self-absorption grows. The terrorist attacks of September 2001 have not yet spurred great numbers of Americans to take up international studies of language, literature, religion, culture, or policy (despite a near-doubling of enrollments in Arabic).[71] Policy for the guidance and funding of language and area studies since 2001 has been highly instrumental in nature (training personnel who can read intelligence intercepts, rather than forming bicultural people) and may endorse specific outcomes for research, a departure from the pattern of previous government-university partnerships.[72]

Foreign language and literature teaching in general have much to lose: we may find ourselves one day teaching literature-in-translation and cultural studies because the infrastructure for our traditional concerns has collapsed. Comparative literature should take the side of foreign-language programs in the institutional competition for resources. However hard classical Chinese or Arabic may be, however crabbed and complex the traditions of annotation and interpretation, what comes across in even the best English translations of Laozi or the Quran is certainly not a patch on those works in the original. Books from far away or long ago are precisely the works that more people in the North American mainstream need to know intimately. A translation always brings across most successfully the aspects of a work for which its audience is already prepared; but what is most worth knowing may be what requires the most strenuous and imaginative adaptation from its readers. As members of national language departments (which most of us are, at least part of the time), we need to develop those readers; and as comparatists, we need to link readers and reading strategies together to fashion ever wider and deeper collaborations of reading.

Unipolarity forces us to consider our discipline from yet another standpoint: not only to remember its tacit complicity with one or another of the Great Powers, which can always be denounced by a rival Power, but to be mindful of the temptation of thinking its "space of comparison" to be a realm of pure contemplation above the grubby, interested dealings of the nations. Not just multiple "subject positions" are at issue, but multiple ways of coming to and through those positions. A Chinese-American student who chooses to reawaken a (possibly suppressed) "home language" in college, and advance it to literary competency, is in a different situation from his or her grandparents, who might have left Chinese behind as they received an English or French colonial education in Hong Kong or Shanghai. Though the two experiences have points in common, in either case the role of language, literature, canonical works, great authors; the ease or difficulty of translation and interpretation; and the greater or lesser demand to adhere to received models in one's own writing shape the readers and their experience of reading. Immigrants and colonized people (who might be said to have been immigrated upon) are already comparatists in much of their daily behavior, since their words and actions exist under two idioms, two scales of value, two legitimating vocabularies. The "double consciousness" articulated by W. E. B. DuBois admits of many variations. Thus, the meaning of comparative literature changes as the frame of reference shifts; although people share a disciplinary space, that space is organized differently for each. We are fortunate to inhabit a multipolar profession; the times make it a contrarian model.

An Age of Inequality

> If all the seas were one sea,
> What a *great* sea that would be!
>
> —*Mother Goose*

Claude Lévi-Strauss was haunted by the idea that the real name of his discipline was not anthropology but "entropology": "Every verbal exchange, every line printed, establishes communication between people, thus creating an evenness of level, where before there was an information gap and consequently a greater degree of organization."[73] Communication works in the same way as power transmission, equalizing the charge on all points of its system, seeking a point of rest. (Not coincidentally, Lévi-Strauss's journey to the Amazonian hinterlands followed the path cut through the brush for a telegraph line, a material connection, though often broken, between capital and outposts.) The ethnographer brings back information from remote peoples, dissolving the boundaries that separate them from others by translation as much as by overcoming the hardships and dangers of travel, and also leaves something of himself with the people investigated. In the long run, communication must reign unopposed and differences be reconciled in a universal "disintegration," the end of the world for ethnographic purposes.

Lévi-Strauss could have saved himself the worry. The (always unevenly distributed) realm of globalized interchange maintains difference as an essential part of its universalizing program. Lévi-Strauss's model was too simple: it failed to take into account the asymmetry and nontransparency of markets. Globalization puts us in a position to reflect on inequality all the time.[74] Indeed, that is part of the motive for globalizing an industry or a political system: to harness differentials in domains such as worker compensation, technological advancement, or popular sovereignty so as to maximize gains in economic efficiency or political control. Inequality is not on the way out; indeed, the elimination of some forms of privilege (such as protectionist policies restricting trade among countries) reinforces others (such as the difference between individuals who benefit from external trade and those who do not).[75] The two-way flow of commerce incorporates one-way flows in specialized products (sales of intellectual property rights in one direction, sales of raw materials or low-cost labor in another). The many states—which once could have been imagined as nearly self-sufficient entities, each with its own borders, language, main products, laws, customs officers—fold, in a certain sense, into the one global economy; but the single economy divides up what it unites.

How does the increasing inequality among states and between the rich and poor segments of states affect our work?

Comparative literature has always thought about difference, but inequality remains foreign to its usual vocabulary, transverse to its standing organization of differences. Our research nonetheless bridges domains on both sides of divides that we cannot ignore or assume to have been taken care of by the discipline's own inclusiveness. The more cosmopolitan our reach, the more evident the problem. Knowledge obtained across steep gradients of inequality is unreliable—one of the many arguments against torture as an intelligence-gathering tool. Much postcolonial scholarship (erroneously categorized as mere special pleading) has attempted to think about this condition. The reaction to postcolonial theory in the form of idealization of Western Civilization and its texts should perhaps be seen as a strategic attempt to create a protectionist bulwark or a nontransparent market in certain cultural goods.[76] Multiculturalism is often an attempt to establish a footing of equality among positions otherwise sharply up- or downhill from each other. The lore of "hybridity," too, teaches that "there's no more black or white." Comparative literature has long investigated so-called hybrids

(Imagist chinoiserie, the thousand forms of Cinderella). But hybridity as such often becomes a one-size-fits-all term good for blotting out specific interactions.[77] All these protocols need to be rethought, not simply as ideas in themselves, but as feedback mechanisms influencing the process of knowing.

Comparative literature does not leave untouched the objects of its arguments. A translator always perturbs the settled economy of two linguistic systems; operations among languages and cultures are not carried out by Maxwell's energy-conserving Demon. A task for comparative literature (and, all the more, for world literature) to take on would be evaluating the systematic, inescapable distortion effects of its critical terms. A border never looks the same from both sides, nor should we expect one worldwide realm of comparison in which local agendas reconcile (to raise Lawall's point about the multiplicity of "world literature" perspectives again). An example is the history of the Chinese disciplinary field *bijiao wenxue* 比較文學 (which translates as "comparative literature"), nonexistent before 1917 and created in order to answer the question, "What does modern China need to take from the cultures of the already modernized countries?" The resulting discipline is strongly marked by the need to define what is properly, uniquely Chinese, through contrast with the "others": its disturbance effects in modern Chinese culture have not been small.[78]

An Age of Institutional Transformation

The weakening of nations and the rise of an integrated global economy have consequences closer to home. The original purpose of founding a nation was, after all, protectionist: people needed walls and moats to "promote the general welfare." As multilateral trade agreements bind countries to remove their import-substitution regulations, and as international financial institutions require "structural adjustments" from client states, health care and education are no longer seen as universal benefits that governments are expected to provide. Privatization of institutions and a reorientation of public institutions for private ends are the rule; even professions such as medicine are becoming human resource pools for profit-seeking organizations. Under stress, the erstwhile containers of the public good buckle and leak.

The result is reinforced inequality, not just in terms of income or capital but of ways of life. Certain producers of high-quality goods are protected from market rationalization by the nature of the demand they serve. The producers of virgin olive oil from the hills outside Siena may not be running the most efficient industry possible, but they can absorb their costs by raising prices. An *ébeniste* can find enough commissions in Manhattan or Beverly Hills, whilst furniture workers in North Carolina have lost their jobs to lower-priced labor abroad. The highly skilled, proposing objects of rarity to a small public of patrons, prosper, but the market offers consumers lower down the scale only products put together by workers less comfortable than themselves. Jobs are exported or "de-skilled," and the only response of states with something to lose is protectionist legislation, ever less likely to succeed, that runs against the rules of world trade. Efficiency predetermines ends. Most of the good things in life are inefficiencies. When you are locked in the same space with a competitor that wins profits by size and economies of scale, and is necessarily always seeking to expand market share, watch out.

We see the same forces at work in academia, where budget pressures and the demand that research pay for itself deepen the differences between elite institutions and those with a more pragmatically defined service mission. The efforts of Allan Bloom, Samuel Huntington, and Sayyid Qutb to the contrary, hardly anyone believes anymore that wars are fought "for two gross of broken statues, / for a few thousand battered books." Once the core of the university, the departments that teach language, literature, and culture are now seen as clogs on the budget since they demand a high investment in personnel and yield little (whether products or people) that is immediately marketable. Subcontracting, a remedy often adopted for the clerical and technical labor pool, occurs where the university sees little point in long-term investment: hence the outsourced department, staffed by part-timers and non-tenure-track lecturers.[79] So the gulf widens between the institutions that can afford haute couture and those that have to buy from sweatshops; the middle zone of craft disappears.

Our reaction is typically to try to protect what we can from the ruthlessness of the market: to stand up for Medieval Russian or the Siglo de Oro. But such efforts may only delay or displace sacrifices. Long accustomed to thinking of fields in terms of "coverage," we have had to learn how the cultural market operates and how its rationality conceals (as do all markets) considerable irrationality—bubbles and shelters around which we can strategize.

Comparative literature has traditionally been seen as—been accused of being—an elite discipline. But it would be good to assess what happens to our graduates, relative to the national language graduates, in the context of overall transformations in the universities. Departments of comparative literature have often experienced a short-term benefit as other departments shrink. If comparatists are being hired regularly as Jacks and Jills of all trades, the economic rationality of such a move is transparent (getting two or more "fields" in one candidate). It may be the best decision a hard-pressed dean can make. But the history of the appointment and its larger context give it its main significance. Is the job on a tenure line? Does it replace a job (or more than one job) in national literatures? Is the teaching oriented toward electives, degree requirements, or courses for majors? What are the opportunities for research? The continued existence of comparative literature in hard times is reason for celebration, but ever more moderate celebration if it turns out that we are gaining at the expense of the sister disciplines that make our metadiscipline possible.

An Age of Information

> Cyberpunk, if it exists . . . I read as a species of literature about the
> unpredictable uses to which human beings always put technology,
> and the even stranger thoughts they breed out of those uses; about
> the way the world is always changing; . . . about the way politics and
> technology and economics and information flow and that element
> of expressive style in one's approach to them . . . are inseparable
> tangles rather than numerable discrete issues whose interfaces and
> interactions and implications can be analytically identified and
> plotted; . . . about the way information is slanted and stained and
> marked by its sources, and how it is not stacked monadic shoeboxes of
> fact but a thing that crossbreeds, multiplies, encysts, mutates, dies out,
> and competes ferociously for its own chunk of elbow room; about the
> new world that belongs to people who can walk with a light step and
> sharp discriminations through a howling murky noöspheric storm of
> competing thoughts.
>
> —*Teresa Nielsen Hayden,* Making Book

We live in an era of plentiful information, information so readily available as to be almost worthless. Wireless data appliances can serve as a metaphor for the condition: rather than being hooked up successively to different isolated communicating units, a wi-fi computer or telephone bathes in the ether of information around the clock. (So the current "space of comparison," rather than requiring that different works or traditions be deliberately wired up to communicate, sees them as always already connected; the question is just how.) What would Marcel have made of the inaccessibility of Albertine's mind if he had always before him her GPS location, heart rate, probable serotonin level, last 500 Google searches, past year's credit card transactions, status on Friendster, speed-dial list, and 25 most-played songs? The problem would become not one of having clues but of sorting them out. Marcel's desire for Total Information Awareness would need to be assuaged by ever more profound connections among ever larger groups of data. This is contextual interpretation with a vengeance. The question of what a person might mean to do becomes saturated with determinants. Neurobiology clutters the folk concepts of intention, blame, and feeling with its autonomous accounts of chemical and electrical transmission. Soon Radio Frequency

Identification Tags may come to enrich our lives, embedded in objects of daily use, each tag broadcasting its one of 18 thousand trillion potential values.[80]

In such a perspective, most of literature looks like a relic of an earlier, data-poor, low-bandwidth era of communications. The reader of literature is a paleontologist, scraping and fitting together a few poor bones to imagine a ten-story beast. A plain-text version of *War and Peace,* downloadable gratis, thanks to the Gutenberg Project, contains only 1.15 megabytes of data in ZIP format.[81] What carries an ordinary reader through weeks of immersion and intimidates nonreaders by its bulk on the library shelf takes up the same amount of informational space as:

— a freeware program that organizes your résumé,

— any of 19 songs in MP3 format posted by Eric and the Thin Line,

— a one-minute sample from "The Sounds of Moo: The Young Polish Real Electronic Music,"

— a PDF catalogue of bathroom window shades,

— or almost any one of the vacation pictures on my hard drive.

The close readings and paradoxes of traditional literary criticism must have been symptoms of the information-poor communications networks of the past, when details mattered. It mattered when the 1631 reprinting of the Authorized Version of the Bible gave the seventh commandment as "Thou shalt commit adultery," but the massive array of data points in a digital photograph could drop much more than three pixels without anyone's noticing. And indeed, the literariness of literature has a lot to do with focusing, giving disproportionate attention to small things. Reading precontemporary literature is a journey into a different epistemological world.

Our students, when asked to do research, go to Google and conduct word scans: "pierre natasha psychology love." It is hard—awkward, counterintuitive—to persuade them to go to the library, pull out a few books, read them, and take notes: why would anyone do that? The world according to Google is vast (and getting vaster all the time, now that whole libraries are being scanned into its database) and instantly searchable all the way to its farthest recesses. But the intellectual landscape it looks out on is flat: far flatter, indeed, than the flattened hierarchies that knowledge industry corporations were supposed to build for themselves through spontaneous organization.[82] A keyword occurs (or does not); it occurs on a page that is more or less frequently consulted, more or less often the goal of links on other pages, in greater or lesser proximity to other keywords, more or less highly ranked in a reputational algorithm that depends on following the behavior of other users of Google. Advertising may shuffle the results. For a reader whose experience of literature has been a matter of following arguments and assessing which statements are subordinated to which other statements; what moves are deliberative, concessive, epexegetic, or digressive; what turns and passageways are necessary to get from one point to another of the memory-palace that is a recollected book, a page of Google results on a familiar topic is apt to have a Cubist, crushed planarity, evoking by omission (and sometimes all the more vividly) the hollows, shadows, and implications it does not represent. But a generation used to having Google for its first-line encyclopedist and lexicographer may not see any Cubism there at all.

Google levels the world of text to a degree cultural studies might envy: for once, no "privileging" or aestheticizing, just "results"! The idea that a wider context will take care of hermeneutic problems, which is the assumption at the base of Google-mancy, takes for granted that text and context are co-present, "really," in some precritical fashion, a move that allows for a positivistic style of reading. But can one ask the right questions in such a positivistic setting? Is one condemned to wander a Google of endless quantitative correlations or a Yahoo! of preestablished categories narrowing down into preestablished subcategories?

With its poor bit-stream and its requirement that we slow down to its speed, quibble over every word, literature frustrates the economy of information in which more data and faster access is always better. A sociological study that has an n three times greater than the next study will be more reliable, within limits; a historical dictionary stands or falls by the copiousness of its database; but an anthology of three hundred Czech poems is not necessarily three times better, or more representative, as literature than an anthology containing one hundred. Literature in foreign languages opposes yet another layer of obstacles to the translation of text into data. The job of comparatists will be, increasingly, to show why this is worth the trouble.[83]

Someone once said—and was roundly derided for saying—that "il n'y a pas de hors-texte."[84] The translation into English as "There is nothing outside the text" did not help; the claim was rather that "there is no extratextual, tipped-in illustration [*planche hors-texte*] that I can send you to, no stone I can tell you to kick, that would not obey a textual logic or testify to the textual condition," a claim as modest as the usual translation is exorbitant.[85] A generation's pedagogy went to learning what "text" was. Likewise, there is no point to trying to escape the world of information—there is no outside to it, unless you want to depart from biology and physics as well. But literature is a kind of resistance to information's charm. An internal resistance, to be sure.

Informational orders are made, not natural (as if that case still needed rehearsing).[86] Yet we may find ourselves more and more acting as archaeologists of the information order of print, the people who remember the tacit knowledge that necessarily precedes any reading.

Envoi: The Age of Comparative Literature?

> "I can never bring you to realize the importance of sleeves, the
> suggestiveness of thumbnails, or the great issues that may hang from a
> boot-lace."
>
> —*Sir Arthur Conan Doyle, "A Case of Identity"*

One of our successful strategies has been interdisciplinarity. Comparative literature teaches us to adjust to multiple frames of reference and to attend to relations rather than givens. We are good at interdisciplinarity, which is so easy to do badly:

> For example, the historian proposed that the way to understand ethical problems is to look historically at how they evolved and how they developed; the international lawyer suggested that the way to do it is to see how in fact people actually act in different situations and make their arrangements; the Jesuit priest was always referring to "the fragmentation of knowledge"; and I, as a scientist, proposed that we should isolate the problem in a way analogous to Galileo's techniques for experiments, and so on.[87]

Comparative literature departments have been quick to take up what other departments have rejected—housing Continental philosophers or Marxist political theorists on some campuses, on others providing a place for noncanonical languages and literatures to be taught, and now and then giving a second chance to graduate students whose original advisors thought they "lacked focus." We sometimes have a hard time explaining ourselves in other than negative terms (we're not the English department, not the French department, not philosophy, not linguistics, not film . . .), and we may be viewed by deans as a sideshow—or as a Punch-and-Judy show: a comparative literature department without confrontations is a collection of inert elements.

The hospitality of comparative literature departments to the miscellaneous, disfavored, outmoded, or too-good-to-be-true approaches; to the leftovers and virtuosi of the better-organized disciplines; to margins and angles and all comers, may impede our forming a smooth corporate identity, but it gives us the opportunity to present ourselves as the test bed for reconceiving the ordering of knowledge both inside and outside the humanities. Why not graft Egyptian philology onto Japanese poetry, or phenomenology onto neurobiology? Don't multiplayer virtual reality games tell us something about Plato's dialogues that we might not have noticed before? As everyone knows, the old justifications for the existence of disciplines, or for keeping them separate, come more and more into question for intellectual as well as budgetary reasons, and comparative literature can move into the gaps between disciplines without (for once) a sense of sacrifice. The history of "theory," that still-controversial subject, in its migration across continents and contexts, from a base in philosophy to a nearly borderless field of new situations (not to say the banality of infinite repetition that comes with success), can stand as a precedent.

In a much-cited paper, Mark Granovetter reported that people secure important social connections—for example, get jobs—more often through chance acquaintances or friends of friends than through members of their established social networks.[88] The reason is that strongly defined groups tend to consist of individuals who already know one another and possess the same "social capital," so if anything new is to come into a person's world, it is likely to be through a less predictable avenue. The logic of "weak ties" could be a description of interdisciplinarity, or indeed of comparative literature. It is how we learn: not so much through coverage as through contact (or *synapse,* to mumble Greek). Most of the innovations in the sixty-year history of our profession in this country can be seen as capitalizations on weak ties (among disciplines, among methods, among canons), ties that eventually become strong, even unto tautology, and thus lose their power to bring in new intellectual or social resources. An eye for the unobvious connection distinguishes makers of metaphor, according to Aristotle (*Poetics* 1459 a 6), and perhaps comparative literature's institution builders as well.

Many departments have instituted interdisciplinarity by setting up, alongside the traditional three-literatures standard for degree programs, the option of preparing literatures in two languages plus a "field"—usually, in practice, a related humanities discipline such as history, film studies, philosophy, or art history, but occasionally something further off the beat: architecture, economics, law, computer science, studio art, biology. ("The humanities" appear less and less a self-contained province of discourse as "humanity" undergoes modifications.[89]) Students with such interests should be encouraged. The "two languages and a field" option is by no means a relaxing of requirements: for worthwhile interdisciplinary work to happen, the researcher must try to become a plausible "native speaker" of the idiom of a field, acquiring its legacy of results and controversy, and doing what others in the field do (running experiments, programming code, taking surveys, titrating blood samples). And, to satisfy the synthetic interests of comparative literature, the researcher must bring the lessons home, articulate conceptual and effective connections among the fields involved.

What adventurous students do shows us what the discipline can and should do. Always under threat of being classified as the rubric for the unclassifiable, comparative literature departments should attempt to work their emphases into a rationale, an explanation of what their internal conversation (lacking which, they may not deserve to be maintained) is about. It is always the season for rendering accounts in this most successful and most phantom-like of humanities disciplines; time we went knocking on doors and announced ourselves to all the disciplines that have borrowed our patterns of thinking. Ours too we owe to others.

NOTES

1. David Damrosch, *What Is World Literature?* (Princeton, N.J.: Princeton University Press, 2003), 39–77.

2. Pseudo-Longinus, *On the Sublime* 6.4.

3. Victor H. Mair and Tsu-Lin Mei, "The Sanskrit Origins of Recent-Style Prosody," *Harvard Journal of Asiatic Studies* 51 (1991): 375–470.

4. Paul Saenger, "Silent Reading: Its Impact on Late Medieval Script and Society," *Viator: Medieval and Renaissance Studies* 13 (1982): 367–414, p. 377.

5. Uriel Weinreich, *Languages in Contact: Findings and Problems,* 2nd ed. (The Hague: Mouton, 1953).

6. For a detailed examination of instances of the phrase from 1816 forward, see René Wellek, "Comparative Literature," in *Dictionnaire international des termes littéraires,* available at www.ditl.info. Most of Wellek's earliest examples could be paraphrased as "discussions of our native literature alongside some examples of foreign literature"; they do not indicate a method or an elaborate theoretical justification.

7. Why not Herder (see infra, Katie Trumpener, "World Music, World Literature: A Geopolitical View")? In a word: culture rather than nature, the need to fashion networks of communication rather than the desire to proclaim the unity of the species.

8. Michael Palencia-Roth, "Contrastive Literature," *ACLA Bulletin* 24 (1993): 47–59.

9. Goethe saw *De l'Allemagne* as having broken through "the Chinese Wall of antiquated prejudices that separated us from France"; cited by Horst Nitschack, "Die Rezeption Madame de Staëls in Spanien und Hispanoamerika," in *Madame de Staël und die Internationalität der europäischen Romantik,* ed. Udo Schöning and Frank Seemann (Göttingen: Wallstein, 2003), 139.

10. Cited and translated in Hendrik Birus, "The Goethean Concept of Comparative Literature and World Literature," *Comparative Literature and Culture: A WWWeb Journal* 2.4 (2000), available at http://clcwebjournal.lib.purdue.edu/clcweb00–4/birus00.html. The passage appears in Goethe's *Werke* (Weimar: Böhlau, 1887–1919), 42.2, pp. 502–3.

11. Hugo Meltzl de Lomnitz, "The Present Tasks of Comparative Literature," in *Comparative Literature: The Early Years,* ed. Hans-Joachim Schulz and Phillip H. Rhein (Chapel Hill: University of North Carolina Press, 1973), 56–62. Original: "Vorläufige Aufgaben der vergleichenden Literatur," *Zeitschrift für vergleichende Literatur* 1 (1877): 179–82.

12. On this period, see R. H. Robins, *A Short History of Linguistics* (Bloomington: Indiana University Press, 1967), 169–88.

13. See Hans Ulrich Gumbrecht, *Vom Leben und Sterben der großen Romanisten* (Munich: Hanser, 2002); R. Howard Bloch, "The First Document and the Birth of Medieval Studies," in *A New History of French Literature,* ed. Denis Hollier (Cambridge, Mass.: Harvard University

Press, 1989), 7–13. On Indo-European "nationalism," see Haun Saussy, "Always Multiple Translation: Or, How the Chinese Language Lost its Grammar," 107–23 in *Tokens of Exchange,* ed. Lydia
Liu (Durham, N.C.: Duke University Press, 1999).

14. Michel Bréal, *Mélanges de mythologie et de linguistique* (Paris: Hachette, 1877), 161.

15. Leo Spitzer, "American Advertising Explained as Popular Art" (1949), reprinted in
Spitzer, *Essays on English and American Literature,* ed. Anna Hatcher (Princeton, N.J.: Princeton
University Press, 1962), 248–77.

16. Rachel Bowlby, *Shopping with Freud* (New York: Routledge, 1993).

17. *Encyclopaedia Britannica* (11th ed.), s.v. "Comparative Anatomy."

18. Paul van Tieghem (*La littérature comparée,* 1931), cited by René Wellek, "Comparative
Literature."

19. Cited by René Wellek, "Comparative Literature."

20. For discussions of the distinct institutions of comparative literature—particularly the
ACLA and ICLA—see Gerald Gillespie, *By Way of Comparison: Reflections on the Theory and
Practice of Comparative Literature* (Paris: Honoré Champion, 2004), 163, 211–13.

21. See, for example, Albert J. Guérard's reminiscences of the activities of his father, Albert
L. Guérard, on behalf of Esperanto and world government: "Comparative Literature, Modern
Thought and Literature," in *Building a Profession: Autobiographical Perspectives on the Beginnings of Comparative Literature in the United States,* ed. Lionel Gossman and Mihai I. Spariosu (Albany: State University of New York Press, 1994), 89–97. George Woodberry's inaugural
editorial in the short-lived Columbia *Journal of Comparative Literature* strikes the pure note:
"The modern scholar . . . lives in a larger world—is, in fact, born no longer to the freedom of a
city merely, however noble, but to that new citizenship in the rising state which—the obscurer
or brighter dream of all great scholars from Plato to Goethe—is without frontiers or race or
force, but where reason is supreme. . . . [The *Journal* represents] a guild of scholars impanelled
from all nations, co-operating in the spirit of that great intellectual state" ("Editorial," *Journal
of Comparative Literature* 1 [1903]: 3–8).

22. An "essentially contested concept" is "any term . . . whose users, by adhering to compet-
ing traditions, contest the right to possession of the honorific appellation" (Max Black, *Caveats
and Critiques* [Ithaca, N.Y.: Cornell University Press, 1975], 255). Black credits W. B. Gallie with
the phrase.

23. For a case in point, see Ivan Strenski, "Durkheim, Disciplinarity, and the *Sciences Reli-
gieuses,*" 153–73 in *Disciplinarity at the Fin de Siècle,* ed. Amanda Anderson and Joseph Valente
(Princeton, N.J.: Princeton University Press, 2002).

24. In exactly this sense, Sarah Lawall proposes that "the world literature project should
be available inside any national literature department, in accord with its traditional mission to
relate a national heritage to the rest of the world. English, French, Spanish, Russian, Chinese,
Near Eastern Studies: all are potential centers for a nationally-based world literature course to
which extranational literatures are openly ancillary" ("Shifting Paradigms in World Literature,"
ACLA Bulletin 24 [1993]: 11–28).

25. David Damrosch, *What Is World Literature?* 281. See also Franco Moretti, "Conjectures
on World Literature," *New Left Review* 1 (2000): 54–68.

26. On the lack of "home" as biographical and disciplinary fact, see Emily Apter, "Global *Translatio:* The 'Invention' of Comparative Literature, Istanbul, 1933," *Critical Inquiry* 29 (2003): 253–81.

27. The collection of Gossman and Spariosu, *Building a Profession,* contains remarkably many narratives of bitterness in response to administrative decisions affecting the careers of comparatists.

28. Cited in Ulrich Weisstein, "Assessing the Assessors: An Anatomy of Comparative Literature Handbooks," in *Sensus Communis: Contemporary Trends in Comparative Literature, Festschrift für Henry Remak,* ed. Janos Riesz, Peter Boerner and Bernhard Scholz (Tübingen: Gunter Narr Verlag, 1986), 104.

29. Henry H. H. Remak, "Comparative Literature at the Crossroads: Diagnosis, Therapy, and Prognosis," *Yearbook of Comparative and General Literature* 9 (1960): 3. The observation is by now a ritual of surveys of the field: see René Wellek, "The Crisis of Comparative Literature" (1958): 282–95 in Wellek, *Concepts of Criticism,* ed. Stephen G. Nichols (New Haven: Yale University Press, 1963), and Charles Bernheimer, "Introduction: The Anxieties of Comparison," in *Comparative Literature in the Age of Multiculturalism* (Baltimore: Johns Hopkins University Press, 1995), 2.

30. On precisely this pattern, Ernst Robert Curtius's *European Literature and the Latin Middle Ages,* trans. Willard R. Trask (Princeton, N.J.: Princeton University Press, 1948) reconstructs the unity of Catholic culture before the emergence of the vernaculars. For a methodological confrontation with Erich Auerbach's *Mimesis: The Representation of Reality in European Literature,* trans Willard R. Trask (Princeton, N.J.: Princeton University Press, 1953), see María Rosa Menocal, *Shards of Love: Exile and the Origins of the Lyric* (Durham, N.C.: Duke University Press, 1994).

31. Karl Marx and Friedrich Engels, "Manifesto of the Communist Party," *Selected Works in One Volume* (New York: International, 1968), 38–39.

32. "Untheorized" in the main; but an articulation of literature as the province of "universal man" served René Wellek as his means to reject the narrow historicism of influence and reception studies in the "French" tradition. See Wellek, "The Crisis of Comparative Literature." Woodberry proposed that "if literature be regarded as the expression of the human spirit, the student of Comparative Literature . . . cannot be content with unsystematized knowledge with regard to the international diffusion of literature . . . the unaccomplished task . . . lies in the direction of the psychologies of the races that have produced literature, and in a strict sense of their metaphysics" ("Editorial," 6–7).

33. For a critical and historical survey, see Lawall, "Shifting Paradigms in World Literature."

34. David Damrosch, "Comparative Literature?" *PMLA* 118 (2002): 329.

35. See Paul Goldin, "Those Who Don't Know Speak: Translations of the *Daode jing* by People Who Do Not Know Chinese," *Asian Philosophy* 12:3 (2002): 183–95.

36. Antoine Berman, *L'épreuve de l'étranger* (Paris: Gallimard, 1984).

37. See René Wellek, "The Concept of Evolution in Literary History," in *For Roman Jakobson,* ed. Morris Halle et al. (The Hague: Mouton, 1956), 653–61; Victor Ehrlich, *Russian Formalism: History-Doctrine* (The Hague: Mouton, 1955), 10–15.

38. H. Munro Chadwick and N. Kershaw Chadwick, *The Growth of Literature,* 3 vols. (Cambridge: Cambridge University Press, 1932–40), 1:5, 1.

39. R. D. Jameson, *A Comparison of Literatures* (London: Kegan Paul, Trench, Trubner, 1935), 33–35, 29–30; the model is clearly I. A. Richards, *Mencius on the Mind: Experiments in Multiple Definition* (London: Kegan Paul, 1932; reprinted with an introduction by John Constable, London: Routledge, 2001).

40. Viktor Shklovsky, *Theory of Prose*, trans. Benjamin Sher (Elmwood Park, Ill.: Dalkey Archive, 1991).

41. Roman Jakobson, *Verbal Art, Verbal Sign, Verbal Time*, ed. Krystyna Pomorska and Stephen Rudy (Oxford: Blackwell, 1985).

42. Friedrich A. Kittler, *Discourse Networks 1800/1900*, trans. Michael Metteer and Chris Cullens (Stanford, Calif.: Stanford University Press, 1990); Hans Ulrich Gumbrecht and K. Ludwig Pfeiffer, eds., *Materialities of Communication* (Stanford, Calif.: Stanford University Press, 1994).

43. On literary terminologies, see, e.g., Earl Miner, *Comparative Poetics: An Intercultural Essay on Theories of Literature* (Princeton, N.J.: Princeton University Press, 1990), and Zong-qi Cai, ed., *A Chinese Literary Mind: Culture, Creativity and Rhetoric in 'Wenxin dialong'* (Stanford, Calif.: Stanford University Press, 2001). For a case in point, see Lydia Liu's discussion of the *style indirect libre* as used in translating premodern Chinese fiction. She argues that the technique was inconceivable to the authors of the originals and should not be imposed on them by translation (*Translingual Practice* [Stanford, Calif.: Stanford University Press, 1995], 104–6).

44. Paul de Man, *The Resistance to Theory* (Minneapolis: University of Minnesota Press, 1986), 17. The surprise is that for de Man, "this autonomous potential of language," when read "textually," "involves the voiding, not the affirmation, of aesthetic categories" (10). The device is to be defused, not just revealed. For the Bunker example, see de Man, *Allegories of Reading* (New Haven, Conn.: Yale University Press, 1979), 9–10.

45. As late as 1988, Adrian Marino was proposing to refashion the French university's understanding of comparative literature on the basis of universal poetics, as the study of "littérarité": *Comparatisme et théorie de la littérature* (Paris: PUF, 1988), 304–5.

46. See Mario J. Valdès and Linda Hutcheon, "Rethinking Literary History—Comparatively," *ACLA Bulletin* 25 (1995–96): 11–22.

47. "The Bernheimer Report, 1993: Comparative Literature at the Turn of the Century," in *Comparative Literature in the Age of Multiculturalism*, 41–42. Hereafter, parentheses in the text refer to this book.

48. See Charles Taylor, "The Politics of Recognition" (1992): 25–73, in Charles Taylor et al., *Multiculturalism: Examining the Politics of Recognition*, 2nd ed., ed. Amy Gutmann (Princeton, N.J.: Princeton University Press, 1994).

49. René Wellek and Austin Warren, *Theory of Literature* (New York: Harcourt, Brace, 1949), 65–135.

50. Charles Bernheimer, "Introduction," *Comparative Literature in the Age of Multiculturalism*, 10.

51. For this phrase, see Joseph Schumpeter, *Capitalism, Socialism and Democracy* (New York: Harper, 1942), 83. An oft-cited but highly technical update is Philippe Aghion and Peter Howitt, "A Model of Growth through Creative Destruction," *Econometrica* 60 (1992): 323–51.

52. For example, whereas the model of the discipline reflected in the 1965 and 1975 "Reports on Standards" is described as "defensive and beleaguered," the 1993 report endorses "progressive tendencies" (41, 47). While critical of earlier comparatists' complicity with nationalism (40), the authors of the 1993 report urge attention to "the role of a native tongue in . . . imagining communal structures, in forming notions of nationhood, and in articulating resistance and accommodation to political and cultural hegemony" (43), which sounds rather like Nationalism We Like as opposed to Nationalism We Dislike.

53. Charles Bernheimer, "Introduction," *Comparative Literature in the Age of Multiculturalism*, 8.

54. See Werner Sollors, *Neither Black nor White Yet Both: Thematic Explorations of Interracial Literature* (New York: Oxford University Press, 1997); Jonathan Brennan, ed., *Mixed Race Literature* (Stanford, Calif.: Stanford University Press, 2002).

55. Haun Saussy, "Comparative Literature?" *PMLA* 118 (2003): 336–41.

56. Peter Brooks, "Must We Apologize?" in *Comparative Literature in the Age of Multiculturalism*, 100; Roland Greene, "Their Generation," in ibid., 150.

57. See, among others, Marjorie Perloff, "'Literature' in the Expanded Field," in *Comparative Literature in the Age of Multiculturalism*, 175–86. Jonathan Culler analyzes the disciplinary shift away from poetry and toward prose narrative in "Comparing Poetry: 2001 ACLA Presidential Address," *Comparative Literature* 53 (2001): vii–xviii.

58. Rey Chow, "In the Name of Comparative Literature," in *Comparative Literature in the Age of Multiculturalism*, 116.

59. Peter Brooks, "Must We Apologize?" 105–6.

60. The Bernheimer Report, 1993: "Comparative Literature at the Turn of the Century," in *Comparative Literature in the Age of Multiculturalism*, 44.

61. Rey Chow, "In the Name of Comparative Literature," 111.

62. See Mary Louise Pratt, *Toward a Speech Act Theory of Literary Discourse* (Bloomington: Indiana University Press, 1977); Shoshana Felman, *Le scandale du corps parlant: Don Juan avec Austin, ou la séduction en deux langues* (Paris: Seuil, 1980), trans. by Catherine Porter as *The Literary Speech Act: Don Juan with J. L. Austin, or Seduction in Two Languages* (Ithaca, N.Y.: Cornell University Press, 1983); Judith Butler, *Gender Trouble: Feminism and the Subversion of Identity* (New York: Routledge, 1990).

63. See Kerstin Behnke, "Fragments, Not Wholes: Antinomian Thoughts in 'Literary Studies,'" in *The Future of Literary Studies / L'avenir des études littéraires*, ed. Hans Ulrich Gumbrecht and Walter Moser (Edmonton, AB: Canadian Review of Comparative Literature, 2000), 50–55. On the historical split between social and literary studies, see Tilottama Rajan, "In the Wake of Cultural Studies: Globalization, Theory, and the University," *diacritics* 31 (2001): 67–88.

64. Paul de Man, *The Resistance to Theory*, 11.

65. See Gayatri Chakravorty Spivak, *Death of a Discipline* (New York: Columbia University Press, 2003).

66. Mary Louise Pratt, "Comparative Literature and Global Citizenship," in *Comparative Literature in the Age of Multiculturalism*, 59.

67. For a perspective, see Frederick Buell, *National Culture and the New Global System* (Baltimore: Johns Hopkins University Press, 1994).

68. For a critique by an erstwhile IMF and World Bank advisor, see Joseph Stiglitz, *Globalization and its Discontents* (New York: Norton, 2003).

69. Thomas Powers, "The Vanishing Case for War," *New York Review of Books*, 4 December 2003, 12–17.

70. Dan Balz, "Clinton Sits Out Democratic Feud," *Washington Post*, 1 May 2003.

71. The figures for Arabic language enrollments are: 5,505 (1998); 10,596 (2002). Compare the figures for Latin, respectively 26,145 and 29,835. See Elizabeth B. Welles, "Foreign-Language Enrollments in United States Institutions of Higher Education, Fall 2002," *ADFL Bulletin* 35 (2004): 7–26.

72. See Spivak, *Death of a Discipline*, 103–5; Mary Louise Pratt, "Building a New Public

Idea About Language," *Profession* (2003): 110–19. At this writing, the Senate was considering an International Studies in Higher Education Act that would empower the Director of Homeland Security to name the members of a review committee charged with examining the "performance" of Title VI (Foreign Language and Area Studies) grants: see the draft legislation at http://edworkforce.house.gov/markups/108th/sed/hr3077/917main.htm.

73. Claude Lévi-Strauss, *Tristes tropiques* (1955; rpt., Paris: Plon, 1985), 478; here, trans. John and Doreen Weightman, *Tristes Tropiques* (New York: Penguin, 1992), 413–14.

74. James Kenneth Galbraith, "A Perfect Crime: Inequality in the Age of Globalization," *Daedalus* 131 (2002): 11–25.

75. On related questions, see Paul Farmer, *Pathologies of Power: Health, Human Rights, and the New War on the Poor* (Berkeley: University of California Press, 2003). Farmer shows how the concept of cultural difference, as a bone of contention in human rights discourse, obscures the perception of effects of inequality (213–46).

76. See Marcel Detienne, *Comparer l'incomparable* (Paris: Seuil, 2000). For an anecdote, see Edward W. Said, *Out of Place: A Memoir* (New York: Knopf, 1999), 229–30.

77. See, e.g., Homi Bhabha's remarks on the 1992 Los Angeles uprisings in Anna Deavere Smith, *Twilight: Los Angeles 1992* (New York: Anchor, 1994), 232–34.

78. See Chen Song 陳崧, ed., *Wu si qianhou dongxi wenhua wenti lunzhan wenxuan* 五四前後東西文化問題論戰文選 (The controversy around the problem of Chinese and Western cultures, circa 1919: an anthology, Beijing: Zhongguo shehui kexue chubanshe, 1985); Chen Guoqiu 陳國球, *Wenxueshi de shuxie xingtai yu wenhua zhengzhi* 文學史的書寫形態與文化政治 (Literary history: its modes of writing and cultural politics, Beijing: Beijing daxue chubanshe, 2004); and a forthcoming essay by Liu Dong 劉東, to whom I owe these thoughts about the nonequivalence of *bijiao wenxue* and "comparative literature."

79. See Martin Finkelstein, "The Morphing of the American Academic Profession," *Liberal Education* 89 (2003): 6–15.

80. Declan McCullough, "RFID Tags: Big Brother in Small Packages," CNET News.com., 13 January 2003 (http://news.com.com/2010-1069-980325.html). On the difficulties of archiving an information explosion, see Alexander Stille, *The Future of the Past* (New York: Farrar, Straus & Giroux, 2002). On the shift from scarcity to abundance of information, see Jeffrey Schnapp, "No Future," in *The Future of Literary Studies,* ed. Gumbrecht and Moser, 90–96.

81. See www.ibiblio.org/gutenberg/.

82. On "flatness," see Fredric Jameson, *Postmodernism or the Cultural Logic of Late Capitalism* (Durham, N.C.: Duke University Press, 1991), 6, 16. The title of the present essay was concocted to frustrate keyword searches, a possibly blameworthy piece of informational dandyism.

83. But see Franco Moretti's plea for "distant reading," "reading at second hand," in "Conjectures on World Literature," 56–57.

84. Jacques Derrida, *De la grammatologie* (Paris: Minuit, 1967), 227. One of Derrida's objects of attention, Claude Lévi-Strauss's *Tristes Tropiques,* boasts on its title page of "62 illustrations hors-texte de l'auteur."

85. The misunderstanding owes as much to reception and circulation as it does to translation: if a (U.S.) public had not been ready and willing to see in deconstruction a text-based solipsism, these few words would never have embarked on their career of endless reiteration. Translators slip, readers err. What happens next is beyond their control.

86. See Geoffrey Nunberg, "The Places of Books in the Age of Electronic Reproduction," *Representations* 24 (1993): 13–37; Lawrence Lessig, *Code and Other Laws of Cyberspace* (New York: Basic Books, 2000).

87. Richard P. Feynman, *Surely You're Joking, Mr. Feynman! Adventures of a Curious Character* (New York: Bantam, 1986), 258.

88. Mark Granovetter, "The Strength of Weak Ties," *American Journal of Sociology* 78 (1973): 1360–80.

89. See N. Katherine Hayles, *How We Became Posthuman: Virtual Bodies in Cybernetics, Literature, and Informatics* (Chicago: University of Chicago Press, 1999); Tim Lenoir, "Makeover: Writing the Body into the Posthuman Technoscape," *Configurations* 10 (2003): 203–20.

CHAPTER TWO

World Literature in a Postcanonical, Hypercanonical Age

DAVID DAMROSCH

World literature has exploded in scope during the past decade. No shift in modern comparative study has been greater than the accelerating attention to literatures beyond masterworks by the great men of the European great powers. The tellingly titled *Norton Anthology of World Masterpieces* was content in its first edition of 1956 to survey the world through a total of only seventy-three authors, not one of whom was a woman, and all of whom were writers in "the Western Tradition" stretching from ancient Athens and Jerusalem to modern Europe and North America. The numbers of included authors gradually expanded, and in the third edition of 1976, the editors finally found room for two pages of writing by a woman, Sappho. But the European and North American focus persisted into the early 1990s in the Norton as in most other "world" literature anthologies and the courses they served.

This situation was just beginning to change at the time of the Bernheimer report, and Rey Chow was rightly concerned at the time that the early efforts to broaden the spectrum of world literature weren't so much dismantling the great-power canon as extending its sway by admitting a few new great powers into the alliance. As she said in her response to the Bernheimer report:

> The problem does not go away if we simply substitute India, China, and Japan for England, France, and Germany.... In such instances, the concept of literature is strictly subordinated to a social Darwinian understanding of the nation: "masterpieces" correspond to "master" nations and "master" cultures. With India, China, and Japan being held as representative of Asia, cultures of lesser prominence in Western reception such as Korea, Taiwan, Vietnam, Tibet, and others simply fall by the wayside—as marginalized "others" to the "other" that is the "great" Asian civilizations.[1]

To a very real extent, the expansion of our understanding of world literature has improved this situation during the past dozen years. The major anthologies (such as those now published by Longman, Bedford, and Norton itself) today present as many as five hundred authors in their pages, often with dozens of countries included. It is even possible to consider that the old Eurocentric canon has fallen away altogether. As Christopher Braider puts it in his essay in this collection, contemporary postcolonial scholars "have not only completed the critical dismantling of the inherited literary canon but have displaced the European metropolis from the traditional center of comparatist attention."

This dismantling, however, is only half of the story, and not only because it hasn't yet occurred in practice to the extent that it has been achieved in postcolonial theory. We do live in a postcanonical age, but our age is postcanonical in much the same way that it is postindustrial. The rising stars of the postindustrial economy, after all, often turn out to look a good deal like the older industries: Amazon needs warehouses of bricks and mortar; Compaq and Dell have built huge assembly-line factories, complete with toxic chemicals and pollution problems, as they crank out an ever-growing number of quickly obsolescing products to overburden our attics, basements, closets, and eventually the world's landfills. This recrudescence of old-style industrialization is compounded by a second factor: many of the established industries have proven to do quite well in our supposedly postindustrial age. Consider the automobile, icon and mainstay of the old industrial economy: far from going the way of the stage coach in the age of the Information Highway, the automobile is more ubiquitous than ever. Not only that: there are more *luxury* automobiles on the road than ever. The Lexus, the Mercedes, and their high-end friends have profited precisely by adding value in the form of dozens of microprocessors that do everything from improving fuel economy to remembering their drivers' preferred seating positions.

World literature presents a comparable situation, partly because, as has often been noted, literary theory stepped in to provide an alternate canon to fill the gap left by the literature it was busy deconstructing. If we no longer focus largely on a common canon of fictional, poetic, and dramatic masterworks that we can require our students to study and expect our readers to know, we need some alternate basis to work from. So, it's said, we rely on Butler, Foucault, Said, and Spivak to provide the common basis for conversations formerly underwritten by a common fund of knowledge of Shakespeare, Wordsworth, Proust, and Joyce.

But *have* these old-economy authors really dropped by the wayside? Quite the contrary: they are more discussed than ever, and they continue to be more strongly represented in survey anthologies than all but a very few of the new discoveries of recent decades. Like the Lexus, the high-end author consolidates his (much more rarely, her) market share by adding value from the postcanonical trends: the James Joyce who used to be a central figure in the study of European modernism now inspires ambitious collections of articles with titles like *Semicolonial Joyce* and *Transnational Joyce.* Undeniably, comparatists today are giving more and more attention to "various contestatory, subaltern, or marginal perspectives," as the Bernheimer committee hoped we would,[2] yet these perspectives are applied as readily to the major works of the "old" canon as to emergent works of the postcanon.

How can this be? Something surely has to give. The number of hours in the day and the number of weeks in the semester haven't expanded along with the canon of world literature, yet we are definitely reading all sorts of works that are beyond the pale of the old "Western Masterpieces." We must be reading them in place of *something:* hence the frequent assumption, especially by the attackers of the recent expansion, that we're abandoning Shakespeare for Toni Morrison. But this is not so. Instead, just as in the postindustrial economy, what has happened is that the rich have gotten richer, while most others just scrape by or see outright declines in their fortunes. It's too simple to say that the old canon has vanished. Rather, the canon of world literature has morphed from a two-tiered system into a three-tiered one. Formerly, world literature could be divided into "major authors" and "minor authors." Even in the heyday of the "masterpiece" approach, a range of minor Western authors could still be found accompanying the major authors in anthologies, on syllabi, and in scholarly discussion: Apuleius and Petronius formed the frame from which Virgil and Ovid cast their radiance abroad to the world; the 1956 *Norton Anthology* included Aleksandr Blok along with its far more extensive selections from Tolstoy and Dostoevsky.

In place of this older, two-tiered model, our new system has three levels: a *hypercanon,* a *countercanon,* and a *shadow canon.* The hypercanon is populated by the older "major" authors who have held their own or even gained ground over the past twenty years. The countercanon is composed of the subaltern and "contestatory" voices of writers in languages less commonly taught and in minor literatures within great-power languages. Many, even most, of the old major authors coexist quite comfortably with these new arrivals to the neighborhood, very few of whom have yet accumulated anything like their fund of cultural capital. Far from being threatened by these unfamiliar neighbors, the old major authors gain new vitality from association with them, and only rarely do they need to admit one of them directly into their club. By "they," of course, I really mean "us": it is we teachers and scholars who determine which writers will have an effective life in today's canon of world literature.

As we sustain the system today, it is the old "minor" authors who fade increasingly into the background, becoming a sort of shadow canon that the older scholarly generation still knows (or, increasingly, remembers fondly from long-ago reading), but whom the younger generations of students and scholars encounter less and less. This process can be seen even within the national literatures, where pressures of time and range are much less pronounced than in the larger scale of world literature. Shakespeare and Joyce aren't going anywhere, and have actually added spacious new wings onto their mansions, but Hazlitt and Galsworthy are looking a little threadbare on the rare occasions when they're seen out and about. It may not be long until their cultural capital runs out and their ruined cottages are bought for a tear-down.

The shape of the new canon can be illustrated in various ways, both within national literatures and across them. A concise example is the situation of the "Big Six" British Romantic poets, as illustrated by the number of articles and books about them listed in the *MLA Bibliography*. Obviously, this is an imprecise measure, yet over time trends can be seen, particularly if we look at ten-year totals to smooth out the variations that can be caused by a centenary or a chance bunching of essay collections or special issues of journals. The figures for these major authors can be further contextualized by comparison with the numbers of entries for traditionally "minor" Romantic poets like Southey and Landor and for newly prominent countercanonical figures like Felicia Hemans and Anna Letitia Barbauld. The "Big Six" are particularly interesting as a test case, since their works were so central to the older New Criticism and then to Yale-style deconstruction before the advent of the current countercanonical criticism. It would be reasonable to expect that the Big Six would have suffered a significant decline during the past decade or two. Yet a survey of the *MLA Bibliography* reveals a startling continuity in the critical attention given to all of the Big Six. Even going back forty years, there has been remarkably little movement among the six, still less between them as a group relative to the field as a whole (fig. 1).

The Big Six dominated the field in 1964–1973, with upwards of 400 books and articles devoted to each of them (in whole or in part) during those ten years, whereas every other Romantic-era poet that I looked at had fewer than 100 entries for the same decade. This imbalance remains true today, and indeed, every one of the Big Six has had more entries for the most recent decade than they did for the first decade of this survey. Even more remarkably, there has been relatively little movement within the group. Byron began at the bottom of the hypercanonical group and remains there still. Shelley and Coleridge have each moved up a notch or two, and Blake and Keats have declined a notch or two, but no more. Blake did have a brief boom during the second of these four decades, but he then settled back to his prior level of attention. Wordsworth began at the top and remains there still, actually increasing his lead over the pack in the hypercanon: as in today's economy, the richest of the rich get richer still.

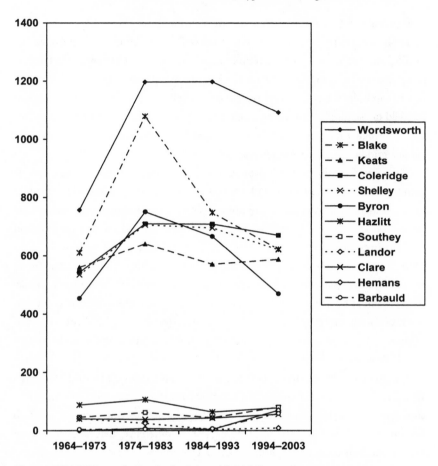

Figure 1. MLA Bibliography Entries for Selected British Romantics, 1964–2003

The formerly minor figures on this chart remain about where they were: John Clare went from 40 entries to 56; William Hazlitt has slipped from 88 to 78; Robert Southey has gone up and down, from 46 at the start to 62, then down to 44, and now up to 81, but he has never come close to breaking the 100 mark. Walter Savage Landor, on the other hand, has dropped sharply, from 41 at the start to 25, then down to 4 and now to 9. The countercanonical poets I looked at, Felicia Hemans and Anna Letitia Barbauld, have risen from next to nowhere during the past twenty years, but they' haven't risen all that far. They are now about where Southey and Hazlitt began, oc-cupying places that would formerly have indicated "minor" canonical status: Hemans went from no entries at all to 70; Barbauld from 4 entries to 59.

The emergence of the countercanon does mark a significant shift in the field, and if we extended the chart to include prose, we'd see the rise of Mary Wollstonecraft and Mary Shelley into the hypercanonical ranks as well as Jane Austen's ascent from a low "major" rank of 311 to a place high up in the empyrean (with 942 entries in the past decade, second only to Wordsworth). The neighborhood is certainly looking different today than it did thirty and forty years ago—yet it's clear that the larger structure of the field doesn't look as different as one might have expected. A few new occupants enjoy the higher range, but most hover far below them, and there are few if any writers in a middle range between 100 and 400 entries per decade.

This canonical bifurcation is pronounced even within a single period in a single country. However, the disparities of attention are more dramatic still when it comes to world literature, given the severe pressures of time and numbers involved. If we define "world literature" for this purpose as works that are read and discussed beyond home-country and area-specialist audiences, we see the hypercanon extending far beyond older fields formerly closely held by the New Criticism and its offshoots. In world literature, as in some literary Miss Universe competition, an entire nation may be represented by a single author: Indonesia, the world's fifth-largest country and home of ancient and ongoing cultural traditions, is usually seen, if at all, in the person of Pramoedya Ananta Toer. Jorge Luis Borges and Julio Cortázar divide the honors for Mr. Argentina.

A high degree of selectivity may be understandable in view of world literature's new scope, yet it is remarkable to see how the hypercanon has come to create divisions even among the select group of non-Western authors who have become well known in North America. Figure 2 may suggest the differences that can emerge even between authors of major standing in critical esteem.

The field of postcolonial studies has shown rapid growth during the past twenty years, and yet it is clear that this growth has affected authors in very uneven ways, to a degree that seems quite disproportionate to any differences of artistic quality or literary influence. A few favorite writers have emerged into a new, postcolonial hypercanon: Salman Rushdie, shown here, is by far the leader in this group, which would also include Chinua Achebe (with 407 entries over the past twenty years), Derek Walcott (309 entries in 1984–2003), and a handful of other authors. If we allow for the relatively small overall size of the field of postcolonial studies, we might include in the hypercanon Nadine Gordimer and anyone with a hundred or more entries during the past decade. Yet I haven't found many newly prominent postcolonial writers with that level of attention. Instead, after a few mid-list figures like Naguib Mahfouz, we quickly reach a very modest level of around two or three entries per year, the rate for Amos Tutuola, for example, or for Lu Xun. These highly respected yet rarely discussed writers could be called the Hazlitts of postcolonial studies—an odd way to think of

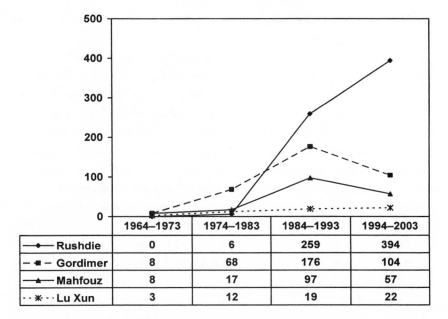

	1964–1973	1974–1983	1984–1993	1994–2003
◆ Rushdie	0	6	259	394
■ Gordimer	8	68	176	104
▲ Mahfouz	8	17	97	57
✳ Lu Xun	3	12	19	22

Figure 2. MLA Bibliography Articles on Rushdie, Gordimer, Mahfouz, and Lu Xun

them, surely, given their excellence as writers and their eminence in their home countries, but the numbers suggest that in world literature they have the secondary status
once accorded to "minor" Romantic poets and essayists.

Additionally, in postcolonial studies as in British Romanticism, there is a shadow
canon of figures everyone "knows" (most often just through one or two brief anthology pieces) but who are rarely discussed in print: Fadwa Tuqan and Premchand
have each been the subject of only a small handful of articles in the past twenty
years.[3] Some members of this shadow canon formerly loomed larger in discussions
of colonial and postcolonial literature but are now being rather directly eclipsed by
the ascendancy of other authors into the hypercanon: Alan Paton gives way to Nadine Gordimer, R. K. Narayan is upstaged by Salman Rushdie. The great ghazal poet
Ghalib was regularly discussed in the 1960s and 1970s but is almost never written
about today, perhaps not in favor of any specific other poet but as a consequence
of the general shift toward the twentieth century that Christopher Braider discusses
(chapter 11). All in all, even without the inherited underpinnings of author-specific
journals and special interest groups (*The Wordsworth Circle;* the Shakespeare Studies
Association), it appears that postcolonial studies is reproducing the hypercanonical
bias of the older Europe-based fields. What Rey Chow warned us about in the Bern-

heimer volume may have been averted at the level of the nation only to return at the level of the celebrity author.

How should comparatists respond to this situation during the years ahead? As readers, we should resist it; as scholars and as teachers, we should turn it to our advantage. We now have the resources available, in anthologies and in individual volumes, to read more widely ourselves and to present a wider range of materials to our students. Of course Rushdie, like Wordsworth, is a wonderful figure to discuss for many purposes, but we don't always and everywhere have to come back to the same few figures. In particular, we should take more care than we usually do to coordinate syllabi: far too often, a student will emerge from college having read *Things Fall Apart* three times and *Beloved* four times, but never having read Mahfouz or Ghalib.

We should resist the hegemony of the hypercanon, yet as long as it's a fact of life, we should also turn it to our advantage. Students may not enroll in a course on writers they've never heard of, so if we do want to broaden their horizons, it can be useful to include enough hypercanonical figures to catch their attention—not least because writers enter the hypercanon only when they really are exciting to read and talk about in a wide variety of contexts. Yet our offerings don't have to become all Rushdie all the time any more than they need to be all Shakespeare all the time. We can group hypercanonical and countercanonical works together, to the benefit of both.

Both in teaching and in scholarship there is a great deal of interesting work for comparatists to do via such conjunctions, and surprisingly little cross-cutting work has yet been done to link our countercanonical and hypercanonical writers beyond the boundaries of national or imperial spaces. This was brought home to me recently when the graduate students in my department made a special request for "a Joyce course" to be offered this year. As they recognized, Joyce's status is such that a course devoted to him offers valuable training for students interested in modernism, in postmodernism, in postcolonial studies, and in the history of the novel. I readily agreed to offer this course, but as a comparatist I wanted to expand the field, so I've surrounded Joyce's works with readings in precursors, contemporaries, and successors. Some of these readings show direct lines of influence (from Ibsen to Joyce; from Joyce to Lispector); others, such as *Swann's Way*, are intended to suggest something of the literary "field" within which Joyce was writing, or more generally, what was possible to write before him. For example, I wanted to start by giving some sense of the range of ways that realism was dealing with issues of gender in the 1890s as Joyce approached the period of writing *Dubliners*, so I assigned three works: Ibsen's *Doll's House*, which Joyce knew intimately, and then short stories by two writers he didn't know at all: Rabindranath Tagore and Higuchi Ichiyo.

Such conjunctions enable us to avoid an either/or choice between well-grounded but restricted influence study and an ungrounded, universalizing juxtaposition of radically unconnected works in the mode advocated by Alain Badiou (see Emily Apter's discussion elsewhere in this volume, and Djelal Kadir's response). Ichiyo's stories in particular proved to be extremely suggestive in relation to *Dubliners*, even though—and I will grieve Haun Saussy when I say this—we were reading her in translation rather than not read her at all. Yet we talked about much more than mere "themes." Formal issues of plot construction and the uses of dialogue came up constantly, as did issues of style and figurative language—only those features of style conveyed in Robert Lyons Danly's excellent translation, of course, but he conveys a great deal. Further aided by the introduction and notes in Danly's edition, *In the Shade of Spring Leaves*, we were also able to make comparisons in terms of intertextuality: whereas Joyce draws on Irish songs, Swift, and Dante, Ichiyo draws on Japanese street theater, Ihara Saikaku, and Murasaki Shikibu. The link to Joyce is indirect, but it goes beyond a coincidence of time, since Ichiyo and Joyce shared some important common precursors: one of Ichiyo's first reviewers, the novelist Mori Ogai, wrote that her characters "are not those beastlike creatures one so often encounters in Ibsen and Zola, whose techniques the so-called naturalists have tried imitating to the utmost. They are real, human individuals. . . . I do not hesitate to confer on Ichiyo the title of a true poet."[4] Like Joyce, Ichiyo was shaping her short stories in relation to Ibsen's and Zola's work, and like him she was seen as infusing poetic qualities into her prose.

This conjunction not only worked well in class: it points toward a much larger set of research opportunities, if we combine close analysis of individual texts with the study of "wave patterns" of the spread of genres like the short story, in the manner advocated by Franco Moretti.[5] Such comparisons are almost unknown once we move beyond a single national tradition or the trade routes of a colonial empire, and they can do much to illuminate hypercanonical and countercanonical authors alike. Such conjunctions can also ease the problems of audience faced by anyone who wants to work on either sort of author. If most nonspecialist readers have never heard of Ichiyo, much less read her, how are we to interest them in looking at her work, especially if we don't want to reduce it to yet another illustration of some European theorist's master-narrative? Conversely, with no fewer than 7,691 books and articles on Joyce published during the past forty years, who is going to want to read number 7,692, even supposing we feel like writing it? Every Irish ballad has already been tracked down, every chapter—almost every sentence—of *Ulysses* lovingly dissected, debated, re-interpreted: what can possibly be left to say? In this circumstance, crosscultural comparisons prove to be marvelously illuminating and refreshing. Making them, moreover, can help lessen the radical imbalance seen in figure 3.

As might be expected, comparisons have regularly been made within the hyper-

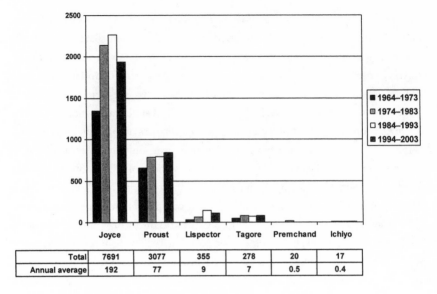

	Joyce	Proust	Lispector	Tagore	Premchand	Ichiyo
Total	7691	3077	355	278	20	17
Annual average	192	77	9	7	0.5	0.4

Figure 3. Books and Articles on Joyce et al., 1964–2003

canonical ranks: 55 of the above entries are on Joyce and Proust. Yet what of Joyce and Clarice Lispector? She is one of the most important writers of the second half of the twentieth century, a person who titled her first novel with a phrase from Joyce's *Portrait of the Artist* and whose collection of linked short stories *Laços de família* (*Family Ties*) is widely recognized as one of *Dubliners'* most creative successors. She has a substantial total number of entries in the *MLA Bibliography*, yet only three of these 355 items compare her and Joyce, and they barely begin to develop the comparison. And what of Joyce's contemporary, Tagore? He is a major short-story writer who shares Joyce's deep concerns with colonialism, interlinguistic tensions, and the impact of modernity on resistant traditional societies, yet there is only a single article on Tagore and Joyce. Less surprisingly, given the small number of articles, but no less regrettably, there isn't a single article on Premchand and Joyce, nor is there one on Ichiyo and Joyce.

We've come a fair distance in the decade since the Bernheimer report was published, but we have succumbed too readily to the pressures of time and the attractions of hypercanonical celebrity both within Western literature and beyond. Perhaps we've been too quick to take the advice of Joyce's elusive character Sylvia Silence, "the girl detective": "Though a day be as dense as a decade," she warns us, "you must, how, in undivided reawity draw the line somewhawre" (*Finnegans Wake,* 292). Not one line, but many: lines of connection across the conflicted boundaries of nations and of cultures, and new lines of comparison across the persisting divisions between the hypercanon and the countercanon of world literature.

NOTES

1. Rey Chow, "In the Name of Comparative Literature," in *Comparative Literature in the Age of Multiculturalism,* ed. Charles Bernheimer (Baltimore: Johns Hopkins University Press, 1995), 109.

2. *Comparative Literature in the Age of Multiculturalism,* 44.

3. That is, they have only been the subject of a few articles indexed in the *MLA Bibliography,* which most likely doesn't include many of the South Asian and Middle Eastern publications (newspapers as well as journals) where the work of these writers would often be showcased. The MLA's listings, though, do provide the best index of what is available to a general North American scholarly audience, suggesting an author's standing in the ambient of world literature as understood by North American comparatists.

4. Quoted in the introduction to Ichiyo in David Damrosch et al., eds., *The Longman Anthology of World Literature,* Volume E, 911.

5. See Franco Moretti, "Conjectures on World Literature," *New Left Review* 1 (2000): 55–67.

CHAPTER THREE

"Je ne crois pas beaucoup à la littérature comparée"

Universal Poetics and Postcolonial Comparatism

EMILY APTER

In a chapter of *Petit Manuel d'inesthétique,* his book of essays devoted to a comparison between the poets Labîd ben Rabi'a and Mallarmé, the philosopher Alain Badiou stridently emphasizes the chasms and gulfs of untranslatability that make the enterprise of comparative literature so tenuous. The chapter's opening line—"Je ne crois pas beaucoup à la littérature comparée"—prepares his case for disbelief in matters of literary comparatism, placing the onus of skepticism on the overdetermined failure of translations to transmit the genius of a source text.[1] In Badiou's view, translation itself is tantamount to a writing of disaster; and yet, for all the obstacles posed by translation, "great poems" surmount the difficulty of being worlds apart and manage to achieve universal significance. This textual singularity against all odds challenges the laws of linguistic territorialization that quarantine language groups in communities "of their own kind" (as in "Romance" or "East Asian" languages) or enforce a condition in which monolingualisms coexist without relation.

Badiou's literary universalism, built on affinities of the Idea ("une proximité dans la pensée") rather than on philological connections or shared sociohistorical trajectories, defines a kind of *comparatisme quand même* that complements the militant credo of his political philosophy (indebted to Beckett's formula for existence—"I can't go on, I will go on"). It argues for the ability of art to release the revolutionary possibility of an Event by making manifest Truth—a truth that surges forth unexpectedly from art's most "inaesthetic" philosophical expressionism. A comparison between two wildly divergent authors—one a nomad writing in classical Arabic in the pre-Islamic period, the other a bourgeois *salonnier* of Second Empire France—has just as much credence for Badiou as a comparison between authors hailing from a shared tradition. Indeed, it would seem that the greater the arc of radical dissimilitude and incomparability, the truer the proof of poetic universalism.

Badiou's *astuce*, which implies that comparativity with the least relation guarantees the maximum of poetic universalism, challenges shibboleths of translation theory and comparative literature alike. Translation and "Comp Lit" have traditionally supported each other in arguing for enhanced conduits of linguistic and cultural exchange. The principle of *adequatio*, based on values of equivalence, commonality, and aesthetic measure, has led to the professional triage of literary fields, with comparisons favored among language groups with a shared philological heritage. Even newer forms of postcolonial comparativism have inadvertently perpetuated neocolonial geopolitics in carrying over the imperial carve-up of linguistic fields. So, for example, in the case of the Caribbean: Haiti, Martinique, and Guadeloupe are placed under the rubric of Francophone studies; Cuba falls under the purview of Spanish and Latin American studies; and Jamaica remains sequestered in Anglophone fields. While there are obvious historical and pedagogical reasons for maintaining geopolitical relations between dominants and their former colonies, protectorates and client states (one wouldn't want, for example, to encourage European literatures to erase the past of their colonial encounters or to relinquish commitments to postcolonial literatures), there are equally compelling arguments for abandoning postcolonial geography. *Francophonie* might, then, no longer simply designate the transnational relations between metropolitan France and its former colonies, but linguistic contact zones all over the world in which French, or some kind of French, is one of many languages in play.

The idea of a postcolonial comparatism that doubles as a new form of global comparatism is anticipated by Charles Forsdick and David Murphy in their forward-thinking volume, *Francophone Postcolonialism*. In discussing the rationale for the book's four major organizing rubrics—Historical Perspectives: From Slavery to Decolonization; Language and Identity in the Francophone World; Postcolonial Axes: Nation and Globalization in Contemporary Francophone Cultures; and Postcolonial Thought and Culture in the Francophone World—the authors allude to a hypothetical fifth section that would focus on postcolonial comparatism. Postcolonial studies, they conclude,

> must be truly comparative if it is to develop, opening itself up to, among others, French, Dutch, Spanish, Belgian, Portuguese, Japanese, Turkish experiences. We must look beyond certain triumphalist discourses of a globalized, Anglophone uniformity in order to understand better the complexity and diversity—linguistic, cultural, political—of the world in which we live. As the rhetoric of empire seems increasingly to occupy a

prominent place in public discourse, the urgency of such a project becomes ever more apparent.[2]

Forsdick and Murphy are responsive to Anglophone dominance in postcolonial studies, particularly to the way in which the structure of the "Anglophone empire" that Amitav Ghosh associated with the "coalition of the willing" (U.S., Great Britain, and Australia) is reproduced. In establishing a disciplinary domain called "Francophone Postcolonial Studies," Forsdick and Murphy nudge postcolonialism closer to global, to translation studies, and to models of what Benedict Anderson has termed "long-distance nationalism." Anderson's *The Spectre of Comparisons* (1998), Louis-Jean Calvet's *La Guerre des langues et les politiques linguistiques* (1987), or Brent Hayes Edwards's *The Practice of Diaspora: Literature, Translation and the Rise of Black Internationalism* (2003) exemplify the charting of postcolonial cartography according to linguistic configurations. Demonstrating a willingness to cut large swaths of cultural space, these works complement others that compare by oceans—the Black Atlantic, the Pacific Rim, Archipelagian discourses, the literary Chunnel—or by North-South patterns of global hegemony.

Bringing postcolonial comparatism into alignment with language politics implies a recognition of the revolutionary potential available within oral and literary expressionism. A country such as France thus emerges as a *paysage* of regional and minority language groups set inside a wider linguistic world that includes but also traverses Europe. An essay such as Bernard Cerquiglini's report on "The Languages of France" (1999), which in the past might not have been considered germane to postcolonial criticism, acquires new heuristic relevance within the larger project of resectoring global language politics.[3] So too, though in a very different vein, does Patrick Chamoiseau's treatise *Ecrire en pays dominé* (1997), which introduces the idea of *omniphonie*, a condition of "all-language-ness" modeled after the vernacular experimentalism of Rabelais, Dante, Joyce, Faulkner, Mallarmé, Céline, Frankétienne, and Glissant. Postcolonial comparatism within these expanded parameters accords greater attention to the linguistic predicaments of minorities and micro-minorities, to what Lawrence Venuti has referred to as "the ethics of location" in translation studies, and to what Colin MacCabe characterizes as "the eloquence of the vulgar," or to the difficulties of defining the threshold of a discrete language when dialect, vernacular, creole, slang, and accent shear off from standard language.[4] These concerns are of especial significance in places with a history of colonial or neocolonial rule in which standard languages have been imposed and native tongues are over-managed, banned, or reduced to the status of endangered species.

Alain Badiou's comparatism could not be further from this location-conscious "translational transnationalism," a term I have used frequently in my own ongoing work on the politics of translation. If there is a global dimension in his reading practice, then it is produced collaterally, that is to say, as an unintended side effect of tracking the Idea wherever it might lead him. Whereas postcolonial comparatists have imagined a "trans" to "trans" space-time of literary analysis, reciprocally arraigning minority languages while bypassing metropolitan vehicular tongues (as in the translation of Scots dialect into Joual, Tagalog into Ogoni, Hinglish into Spanglish), Badiou pays little heed to linguistic class struggle. Comparative literature—even when it relies on the imperfect vehicle of translation ("toujours presque désastreuse")—rises to the political occasion precisely because it contributes to the unpredictable release of a revolutionary Truth-Event; this is what makes it an important "inaesthetic" praxis (with "inaesthetic" referring to the "strictly intraphilosophical effects produced by the independent existence of works of art"). Thus, Badiou's reading of Labîd ben Rabi'a and Mallarmé promotes a comparative literature that seeks out rather than shies away from parallels between languages of great discrepancy. Though he himself is not interested per se in making an argument about comparative literature as a discipline, his provocative opening salvo "Je ne crois pas beaucoup à la littérature comparée" hitched to a tempering "Et pourtant" stakes its claim on a Comp Lit willing to embrace linguistic nonidentity. Like Walter Benjamin, in "The Task of the Translator," he accepts translation failure as an a priori condition (Benjamin argues that to translate mere content is simply to repeat, badly, the most inessential nature of the original), and like Benjamin, he turns this failure to advantage, transforming it into an enabling mechanism of poetic truth.[5]

I must confess to having been initially very disconcerted by Badiou's blanket rejection of the ethics of location. But on further reflection, his paradigm of *comparatisme quand même* seemed bracing: a way of confronting the bare truth of translational dysfunction, while soldiering on. There was also theoretical significance accruing to the specific comparison between the Arabic ode (the *mu'allaqa*) of Labîd ben Rabi'a and Mallarmé's symbolist masterwork (*Un Coup de dés*). "We remain," Badiou insists, "between Mallarmé and the *mu'allaqa*" (p. 85). The choice to compare these particular Arabic and French texts is gradually revealed as arbitrary. Questions of democracy and subjectivation, terrorism, despotism, the nature of mastery, the seduction of sacred language, the influence of clans (the "call" of the *tribu*), the intoxicating desire for collective destiny and a *vita communis*, the sacrifice of civilization to science and technology, the spiritual "desert" or empty set of subjectivity, decampment, exile, and the defection of place—these ideas of paramount mutual concern to Labîd ben Rabi'a and Mallarmé constitute an Event in Badiou's sense of that term, even as they announce a universalist poetics that allows for linguistic relations of radical dissimilitude.

Badiou's argument, that "we remain between Mallarmé and the *mu'allaqa*," pointed me to a *mu'allaqa* by the contemporary Palestinian writer Mahmoud Darwish, "A Rhyme for the Odes (*Mu'allaqat*)," published in 1995. Darwish allows us to triangulate Badiou's anomalous pairing of Labîd ben Rabi'a and Mallarmé; it too contains a meditation on the autonomous, exilic status of the word:

> No one guided me to myself. I am the guide.
>
> Between desert and sea, I am my own guide to myself. . . . .
>
> Who am I? This is a question that others ask, but has no answer.
>
> I am my language, I am an ode, two odes, ten. This is my language.
>
> I am my language. I am words' writ: Be! Be my body!
>
> And I become an embodiment of their timbre. I am what I have spoken to the words:
>
>> Be the place where
>
> my body joins the eternity of the desert. Be, so that I may become my words.[6]

Darwish chisels a subjective space from the desert sand, itself an expanse defined by temporal portage and forced emigration: "They emigrated./They carried the place and emigrated, they carried time and emigrated." With a concluding line, "So let there be prose," Darwish would seem to echo Mallarmé's famous phrase in "Crise de vers": "Je dis: une fleur!" ("I say: a flower") or the categorical infinitive "Ecrire—" of "Quant au Livre." In the face of disaster—defined by Mallarmé as the crisis brought on by Victor Hugo's overdetermination of modern verse—these simple declarative utterances induce a revolution in poetic language, licensing prose to become a purveyor of the universal poetic idea ("la notion pure"). The last line of Darwish's *mu'allaqa:* "There must be a divine prose for the Prophet to triumph," also parallels Mallarmé's finale in "Quant au Livre": "L'air ou chant sous le texte, conduisant la divination d'ici là, y applique son motif en fleuron et cul-de-lampe invisibles."[7] Both poets accord the language of the everyday a prophetic, incantatory sway.

While the anomalous prospect of an "absolutely postcolonial" Mallarmé, of a Labîd ben Rabi'a jet-propelled into colloquy with the moderns, or of a Mallarméan Darwish disturbs conventional paradigms of literary comparatism, postcolonial or otherwise, it also re-activates the aesthetic. "The realm of the aesthetic," according to Peter Hallward, "invariably solicits the exercise of a thought-ful freedom."[8] To my knowledge, Hallward's book *Absolutely Postcolonial: Writing between the Singular and the Specific* is the sole experiment to date of a Badiou-inspired postcolonial comparatism. In recentering the aesthetic within postcolonial theory (displacing the field's preoccupation with what he castigates as a "deadened nativism"), Hallward harks back to an earlier era—the 1980s and early 1990s—before theory fatigue set in and before cultural critics stigmatized colonial ontology as an elitist threat to materialist *Verstehen*.

In practicing theory without apology, Hallward revisits the time when Anglophone and Francophone critics alike—among them Edward Said, Gayatri Chakravorty Spivak, Homi Bhabha, Ngugi wa Thiong'o, Paul Gilroy, and Robert Young on the Anglophone side; and Frantz Fanon, Albert Memmi, Edward Glissant, Abdelkebir Khatibi, Abdelwahab Meddeb, Achille Mbembe, Françoise Vergès, and Réda Bensmaïa on the Francophone side—availed themselves unabashedly of Continental theory, developing critical paradigms that engaged deeply with the work of Freud, Adorno, Lacan, Bakhtin, Benjamin, Althusser, Foucault, Derrida, Levinas, Deleuze, Irigaray, Cixous.

Hallward subscribes to Badiou's notion of singularity as a corrective to the postmodern relativism besetting postcolonial studies: its uncritical embrace of plural registers, its fetishization of the politics of difference, and its naive celebration of "the local." "The singular creates the medium of its own substantial existence or expression," he writes, in an affirmation drafted from Deleuze's pronouncement that "the One expresses in a single meaning all of the multiple."[9] Edouard Glissant, Charles Johnson, Mohammed Dib, and Severo Sarduy are elected for analysis by virtue of their invention of a singular postcolonial subjectivity. Representative of Francophone, Anglophone, Hispanophone, Caribbean, Maghrebian, and Latin American trajectories, these writers, considered together, offer a model postcolonial comparatism. But rather than focus on grounds of comparison common to all, Hallward explores how each writer, in a freestanding way, engages with the philosophical idea of the "univocity of being."

Absolutely Postcolonial, despite its vaguely comical echo of the TV-show title *Absolutely Fabulous,* produces a chilly comparatism tilted toward logic, ontology, and ethics. In this picture, the old Comp Lit utopia of global *translatio* and humanist dialogue gives way to an ascetic model of individuation in which the transcendence of specificity and relationality yields poetic singularity and solitude. "To write," Hallward maintains, in a paraphrase of Blanchot,

> is to undergo a radical detachment, to become absolutely alone, impersonal, isolated within an im-mediate atemporality ("the time of the absence of time"). Like the Deleuze he inspires, Blanchot tends to absorb all "actual writers as so many echoes of a singular "murmure anonyme."
>
> The "essential solitude" of the writer, then, is not that of an anguished isolation among others, but of a submersion within the aspecific or indifferent pure and simple, a space generally rendered in Blanchot's fiction as void, desert, snow, night or sea-spaces rediscovered, as we shall see, by the later novels of Mohammed Dib. Writing begins when the writer forgoes the "power to say I."[10]

Hallward's idea of postcolonial worldliness is truly other-worldly, suturing itself to Islamic constructs of *Islam* (surrender to God) and *Shadâdah* ("the assertion that 'there is no God but God'"), and to Buddhist notions of *sunyata* (void) and *nirvana* (self-extinction, transcendence of desire). These principles, allowed to shine through in their linguistic foreignness, inadvertently reveal the catastrophic state of untranslatability that has allowed the word *Islamic* to become a predicate of terrorism in Western parlance.

The challenge of Comp Lit is to balance the "singularity" of untranslatable alterity against the need to translate *quand même*. For if translation failure is readily acceded to, it becomes an all-purpose expedient for staying narrowly within one's own monolingual universe. A new parochialism results, sanctioned by false pieties about not wanting to "mistranslate" the other. This new parochialism is the flip side of a new globalism that theorizes place without ever traveling anywhere. Gayatri Spivak has taken direct aim at the way in which globalization theory treats real places like computer spaces "in which nobody actually lives." In proposing "the planet to overwrite the globe," Spivak embraces a humbling view of the alterity of humans, cast as temporary occupants of a planet on loan.[11]

Spivak remains firmly on the ground, so to speak, in her commitment to a radical alterity defined by the politics of translation. By contrast, Hallward, like Badiou, casts literary theory as cosmology, jumping parallel universes that share no philological common culture. Hallward's efforts to articulate the singularity of being might be seen as analogous to efforts in quantum cosmology to explain the origins of the universe as a "zero-moment of infinite density—a so-called singularity." In a chapter of *Absolutely Postcolonial* devoted to "the Buddhist path" in Sarduy, Hallward evokes *satori*, which he characterizes, quoting Daisetz Teitarô Suzuki's *Essays in Zen Buddhism* (published between 1949 and 1953), as "the Zen version of enlightenment. . . . a kind of instantaneous flash or explosion, 'a sort of mental catastrophe.'" This catastrophism brings in its train a new order of comparatism. The Idea of mental catastrophe in Buddhist enlightenment, set against the backdrop of the Hiroshima bombings, which loomed so large in the world's consciousness at the time of Suzuki's essay, evokes Heidegger's "zero-line [that] is suddenly emerging before us in the form of a planetary catastrophe." (This 1955 text addressed to Ernest Jünger, published as "Concerning 'The Line,'" responds to Jünger's reference to the "zero meridian" or "zero point" as "the world-historical moment of the planetary completion of nihilism.")

Walter Benjamin's observations on "The Railway Disaster at the Firth of Tay" also warrant mention as a signal text of planetary comparatism. Delivered as a 1932 radio lecture, this prescient "short history" of technology leads us from the baseline of small disasters (accidents) to an end-point of mass destruction:

Today we know what technology is . . . a new airplane, a space rocket, new machines receive the attention of the whole world. In the past, the most striking alterations to the globe in the course of the previous century were all in some way or another connected with the railway. I am going to tell you today about a railway disaster. Not so much to recount a horrifying story, but rather to put the event in the context of the history of technology and more particularly of railway construction. A bridge plays a role in this story. The bridge collapsed. This was without doubt a catastrophe for the two hundred people who lost their lives, for their relatives, and for many others. Nevertheless, I wish to portray this disaster as no more than a minor episode in a great struggle from which human beings have emerged victorious and shall remain victorious unless they themselves destroy the work of their own hands once more.[12]

Drawing Suzuki, Heidegger and Benjamin into orbit, catastrophism begets a planetary comparatism that subsumes postcolonial comparatism—or perhaps follows logically from it—if one acknowledges where two of postcolonialism's premier critics, Gayatri Spivak and Edward Said, seem to have moved theoretically. Spivak invokes "planetarity" as a rubric in her book on the fate of comparative literature titled *Death of a Discipline*. And in the late Edward Said's work on humanism, an anti-imperialist reinvention of Goethean *Weltliteratur* comes into focus as part of an expanded worldliness. Though Spivak and Said hardly share Badiou's poetic unilateralism and nondialectical notion of Truth, they too seem to be, so to speak, communists of the Idea, following "le grand écart" of cultural comparison in the name of militant principles of worldly dialectics and the transformative power of cognition in the historical process.

NOTES

1. Alain Badiou, *Petit manuel d'inesthétique* (Paris: Seuil, 1998), 85. Further references to this work will be included in the text.

2. Charles Forsdick and David Murphy, eds., *Francophone Postcolonialism: A Critical Introduction* (London: Arnold, 2003), 14.

3. Bernard Cerquiglini, "Les Langues de la France," available at www.culture.gouv.fr/culture/dgif. Accessed 16 September 2005.

4. Lawrence Venuti, *The Scandals of Translation: Towards an Ethics of Difference* (London: Routledge, 1998); Colin MacCabe, *The Eloquence of the Vulgar: Language of Cinema and the Politics of Culture* (London: British Film Institute, 1999).

5. Walter Benjamin, "The Task of the Translator," in *Illuminations,* ed. Hannah Arendt (New York: Schocken Books, 1969), 69–82.

6. Mahmoud Darwish, "A Rhyme for the Odes," in Darwish, *Unfortunately, It Was Paradise: Selected Poems,* trans. Munir Akash and Carolyn Forché with Sinan Antoon and Amira El-Zein (Berkeley: University of California Press, 2003), 90–91.

7. Stéphane Mallarmé, *Œuvres complètes,* ed. Henri Mondor (Paris: Bibliothèque de la Pléiade, 1945), 387.

8. Peter Hallward, *Absolutely Postcolonial: Writing between the Singular and the Specific* (Manchester: Manchester University Press, 2001).

9. Ibid., 2–3.

10. Ibid., 18.

11. Gayatri Chakravorty Spivak, *Death of a Discipline* (New York: Columbia University Press, 2003), 72.

12. Walter Benjamin, "The Railway Disaster at the Firth of Tay," in *Walter Benjamin: Selected Writings, Volume 2, 1927–1934,* ed. Michael W. Jennings (Cambridge, Mass.: Harvard University Press, 1999), 562.

CHAPTER FOUR

Looking Back at "Literary Theory"

RICHARD RORTY

In the 1970s, teachers in American literature departments began reading Derrida and Foucault. A new subdiscipline called "literary theory" took shape. The notion that a literary text could profitably be "theorized" helped make it easy for literature professors to teach their favorite philosophy books and for literature students to write their dissertations on philosophical topics. It also helped create jobs in literature departments for people who had been trained in philosophy rather than in literature.

I took advantage of this development to move from being Professor of Philosophy at Princeton to being University Professor of Humanities at the University of Virginia. Later I went to Stanford as Professor of Comparative Literature. These changes of title and of colleagues did not alter the content of my offerings, which were just straight philosophy courses—sometimes on analytic philosophers like Wittgenstein and Davidson, and sometimes on non-analytic philosophers like Heidegger and Derrida. Nor did they affect what I wrote. I would have written most of the books and articles that I wrote at Virginia and Stanford even if I had stayed on at Princeton.

As the years have gone by, however, I have come to realize that I was riding an ebbing tide rather than a rising wave. "Literary theory" (to which I have been bemused to find myself described as a contributor) has gradually become old hat. People in literature departments are beginning to suspect that all the juice has been milked out of the Nietzsche-Heidegger-Derrida intellectual tradition. Foucault has replaced Derrida as the one philosopher about whom every student of literature has to know something. "Cultural studies" has shoved "literary theory" aside. This means that there is less use for philosophy teachers in literature departments; although you cannot understand Derrida very well without knowing quite a lot about Plato, Kant, Nietzsche, and Heidegger, you can understand Foucault without much philosophical background.

I am glad that I was able to take advantage of the fact that philosophy was briefly in fashion in American literature departments, but it was never more than a fashion. There is no compelling reason why students of literature should read philosophy books. It is, to be sure, a good thing for students of literature to know something about philosophy. But it is also good for them to know about lots of other things—anthropology, psychoanalysis, and religion, for example. They should, ideally, read in several different literary genres. They should know several different languages well. They would certainly profit from a good understanding of sociopolitical history and of current political issues.

But they cannot do everything. Lots of first-rate literary criticism has been written by people who are monolingual, or who read lots of novels but almost no poems, or who have no political concerns, or who are philosophically illiterate, or who have little sense of what happened in history. Good criticism is a matter of bouncing some of the books you have read off the rest of the books you have read. The greater number of books you have read, and the more various they are, the likelier it is that the criticism you write will be of interest. But there is no natural order of priority, nor is there any set of methodological precepts, that should guide your decisions about which books to read first. All you can do is follow your nose. There is nothing special about philosophy books, or any other sort of book, such that reading them is likely to make you a better literary critic.

It was not a dialectical necessity, but rather a historical accident, that post-Nietzschean European philosophy entered the universities of the English-speaking world through literature departments rather than philosophy departments. The main reason those departments served as ports of entry for the books of Derrida and Foucault was that everybody in them had become, by 1970, bored stiff with New Criticism, with Marxist criticism, and with Freudian criticism. Graduate students who read Frederick Crews's *The Pooh Perplex* were determined never to write anything remotely reminiscent of the books that Crews had parodied. New gurus were desperately needed.

De la Grammatologie and *Les Mots et les Choses* were translated into English at exactly the right time. They hit the spot. Derrida and Foucault were not only brilliantly original thinkers, but they came out of an intellectual world that nobody in Anglophone literature departments (except for European émigrés like Paul de Man and George Steiner) knew much about. Reading their books gave people a sense that new horizons were opening. Graduate students of literature who had, as undergraduates, been bored or baffled by courses in analytic philosophy suddenly discovered that there was an intellectual world out there that their philosophy professors had never told them about. Exploring that world was great fun.

The excitement generated in literature departments by Derrida and Foucault (and by Nietzsche and Heidegger, who were discovered more or less simultaneously) was not due to these books having offered a new theory about the nature of literature. But the unhappy term "literary theory" deceived some hapless graduate students into thinking that they could write a worthwhile article or book just by "applying theory" to a text. This belief generated a great mass of barely readable, amazingly boring, articles and books. Fortunately, deconstructing texts is now as obsolete as spotting Christ-figures or vagina-symbols. Crews's *Postmodern Pooh* (2003) will, with any luck, mark the beginning of the end of this epoch, just as *The Pooh Perplex* (1965) did of an earlier one.

Derrida and Foucault are brilliantly original thinkers who can easily survive misuse, just as Marx and Freud have. Their books will become part of the philosophical canon. In coming decades, students of literature with a taste for philosophy will still be reading them. But the unfortunate idea that you could learn how to write well about a literary text by mastering a "theory" will gradually die out. Literary theory will be seen to be as optional for the practice of literary criticism as legal theory is for the practice of law.

Consider an analogy: A certain branch of mathematics is typically taught, under the sobriquet of "symbolic logic," in philosophy departments rather than mathematics departments. This too is an accident of history, having a lot to do with the fact that Anglophone students of philosophy in the 1930s were bored silly with realism-vs.-idealism, pragmatism-vs.-rationalism and various other dreary controversies. Symbolic logic, Russell and Carnap announced, was going to make philosophy lively and interesting again. So it did, for a while. But by the time Wittgenstein's *Philosophical Investigations* was published, in the mid-1950s, it had become *vieux jeu.*

Even now, however, you have to know something about Gödel's results before you can get a Ph.D. in most American philosophy departments (even though you plan to write your dissertation on, for example, the relation between Kierkegaard and Levinas). This is simply a matter of curricular inertia. Similar inertia may ensure that there will still be a "theory" section on the Ph.D. qualifying exams in comparative literature departments in 2050. Many students in that future time will be very glad they had to take a theory course, just as many philosophy students now get a lot out of the required course in symbolic logic. The rest will do their best to clamber over one more inexplicable curricular hurdle—a hurdle that was erected at a certain point in the twentieth century and may be dismantled at a certain point in the twenty-first.

As I see it, both comparative literature and philosophy departments should be places in which students receive plenty of suggestions about what sorts of books they might like to read, and are then left free to follow their noses. Members of these departments should not worry about the nature of their discipline or about what makes it distinctive. They should not fret about whether proving a theorem in set theory, or adjudicating the disagreements between Heidegger and Levinas, counts as "really doing philosophy." Nor should they speculate about whether to be a "true comparativist" one needs to know the literature of at least one non-European language as well as a few European ones. They should not fuss about what "a sound preparation" in their field consists in. They should just worry about finding intellectually curious students to admit to graduate study and about how to help such students satisfy their curiosity.

This laissez-faire attitude makes me dubious about Haun Saussy's suggestion that literariness is central to the discipline of comparative literature. I have the same doubts about this claim as about the idea that the search for conceptual clarity is central to the discipline of philosophy—a claim often made by "analytic" philosophers who believe that the study of logic conduces to such clarity. You can, I suspect, produce very illuminating comparisons between literary texts written in several different languages even if you have no use whatever for the term "literariness." You can write very good philosophy—even very good "analytic" philosophy—after you have come to think of "conceptual clarity" as a meaningless mantra.

I doubt that anything can ever be identified as central to an academic discipline any more than anything can be identified as the "core" of a human self. A self, Daniel Dennett has said, is best thought of as a center of narrative gravity. Like selves, academic disciplines have histories, but no essences. They constantly update their self-image by rewriting their own histories. So-called "crises" move the apparently peripheral to the center and the apparently central to outer darkness. The centers of gravity of biology, anthropology, and psychiatry are not where they were fifty years ago. The center of gravity of contemporary Scottish philosophy is a long way from that of philosophy in Brazil. As Spivak and Bhabha replaced Auerbach and Girard as exemplars, the center of gravity of comparative literature departments moved quite a distance. Where that center will be in 2050 is anybody's guess.

We should rejoice in the mutability and fashion-proneness of academic disciplines, for the only alternative is decadent scholasticism. Whereas crises in the natural sciences are sometimes provoked by encounters with brute facts, in the humanities there *are* no such facts. So paradigm shifts in disciplines such as classics, philosophy, or comparative literature are, typically, reactions to brilliant iconoclastic books: *The Birth of Tragedy; Language, Truth and Logic; Philosophical Investigations; The Anxiety of Influence; Of Grammatology; Metahistory.* There will be changes in fashion as long as such books are written—as I trust they always will be.

These paradigm-shifting books are sometimes written by people who are members of a different discipline than the one their books help transform. Then it is tempting for enthusiastic readers to conclude that what discipline A needs is more interdisciplinary cooperation with discipline B. But in the humanities at least, the whole idea of "disciplines" is pretty dubious, and so is that of "interdisciplinarity."

The difference between studying analytic and studying non-analytic philosophy, for example, is at least as great as the difference between studying either and studying comparative literature. The difference between Auerbach and Spivak is as great as the difference between Heidegger and Carnap. If you can profit from reading both members of either pair, you are already about as interdisciplinary as anybody could reasonably ask you to be.

Fifty years down the road, accounts of the nature of the discipline of comparative literature written with Spivak in mind will sound as quaint as those written with Wellek in mind do now. If they do not, then something will have gone wrong—not because there is anything wrong with Spivak, but because no healthy humanistic discipline ever looks the same for more than a generation or two.

CHAPTER FIVE

Comparative Literature in an Age of Terrorism

DJELAL KADIR

The reigning principle under whose aegis the current edition of the "decades" of comparative literature is being written is somewhat peculiar. That paradigm may be best expressed by the noncommittal ejaculation "Whatever . . . ," or, as one of the latest diagnoses of the discipline's fate would have it, the "same difference." This is Gayatri Spivak's pithy definition for what "will work only too well" (Spivak 2003, 4). These decennials are mandated by the constitution of the American Comparative Literature Association, and if the last report in the last decade of the twentieth century was composed during a time that sought consensus in plurality, as signaled by the title of its publication, *Comparative Literature in the Age of Multiculturalism,* the first ten-year report of the twenty-first century finds us beyond the need to domesticate dissensus. The actual possibility of dissensus itself may be an illusion in a world governed by transcoded terror defined as "full spectrum dominance" in the National Defense Strategy of the United States of America of September 2002. The pervasiveness of that encoding and its repercussions may well extend to the cognitive map and itinerary of comparative literature also.

Comparative literature, as the last report predicted, would indeed appear to have arrived at the individuated extreme of academic professional practices, as one form of discursive practice among many, now with each practitioner of this form of discourse being an isolate among many others, in turn. And were it possible for us to discern with any certainty, we might well discover ourselves so far along in that pluralist multiplicity as to be well beyond the perils of dissensus and at even greater risk than the absence of *sensus communis.* Irreconcilable dissensus haunted the 1993 report. Its immediate antecedent in the decade of the 1980s had been consigned to silence and oblivion precisely because differences among the comparatist redactors could not be breached. The chair of that report committee, we are told, "was so dissatisfied with the document that he exercised a pocket veto and never submitted it" (Bernheimer 1995, ix). This is an interesting event in itself, one that merits due historicization in the annals of the discipline. My own attempts to ferret out that impasse reached as far as the moment the tracks submerged beyond institutional memory and into history.

The crucial question for us, then, becomes, what follows the sought-after consensus of the 1990s that follows the irreconcilable dissensus of the 1980s? What, in other words, does a post-consensus and post-dissent discourse and cultural formation consist in? "Whatever" would not appear to be a serious desideratum, nor would the "same difference." Neither would seem to hold a resolute purchase on anyone's cultural or disciplinary franchise. And yet, reigning principles have no obligation to be either serious or desirable. The farcical and the adverse can reign with just as much determinacy—and, historically speaking, they often have—in the affairs of the intellect and of disciplines as in the affairs of state (as is the case presently, and with deadly consequences, even as these lines are being written in January 2004).

Coexistence with difference in an age of "whatever" tacks an intricate and portentous itinerary symptomatic of the hyper-differentials that link our hyper-connectivities as navigable web that can be negotiated from the privacy of one's individual cyberspace with no undue peril of commitment or risk of compromise, or so we would like to think. In the year 2004 and the age of the cybernetic flat screen, the contours of complexity are smoothed out, the global arc flattened, the overlaps paratactically arrayed, and forthrightness elliptically skewed. And lest there be the need to negotiate network imbrications or collective synergy, discursive geometry easily reverts to Euclidean linearity, thereby foreclosing on all possibilities for multilinear convergence or perspectival cross-hatching, except as "optional" exercise on the part of those who may "choose" to bring elective trajectories into counterpoint from the safety of their respective Internet modules and navigational command posts. I put quotes around "optional" and "choose" because, under invisible regimes of control and panoptic lurking, one's optic may well be duly safeguarded in its trajectory, the *taglio* of one's field of vision protected from any possible obstruction, one's positionality unmitigated by any contestation, and personal space may well be secured against undue proximity and unwarranted questions. The subject agency of such security, however, remains as inscrutable as the free agency of the individuated comparatist may be virtual. We read, we are under the illusion that we read, from and within the distance of our margin of safety; we conjecture and conjugate at our convenience and on individual expediency. "Whatever," then, would appear to be the screen saver of our cultural moment, of our epoch of comparative literature, and of our praxes as comparatists in the global metropolis under the security cover of ubiquitous surveillance.

If this self-reflexive assessment of our constitutionally decreed exercise is an accurate diagnosis of this 2004 report's mode of production, it would also have to be the contradiction of such a diagnosis. It would be so because this reflection itself crisscrosses (one can only hope, not at cross-purposes) with all the other discretely arrayed parts of the whole. Such self-consciously wrought convergence may not amount to a conjunction or a *sensus communis*. And furthermore, an embedded self-critique as self-effacement inevitably raises yet another question: To what extent is self-checking a move of efficacy and yet another screen saver, or its illusion, for one's exposure? To what degree, in other words, is reflexivity yet another reflection screen, a shield of deflection that safeguards one's self-representations and occludes potential embarrassment in the event of slippage from self-searching to yet another level of self-seeking, if not for anything else, for a modicum of cover from the panopticon and its regimes of control and the security state?

Overheard conversation in the year 2004:
    —Why raise such impertinent questions?
    —What is this, a report, or a confession, or an inquest?
    —Yes?
    —And why are we answering a question with another question?
    —But, yet again, did the founding scriptors of the ACLA constitution mean this mandated decachronic exercise to be a decalogue, a chronicle, a self-palpation, a periodic rite of atonement, a disciplinary sanction, a redemptive self-reconfirmation, a penitential act of catharsis, or what?
    —Or, whatever . . .
    —Whatever is a pretty powerful template. What's the default; is it an imputable setting?
    —Hey, you talkin' to me, or is your name Hamlet?
    —Yes . . . ?
    —Oh . . . ! Anyone at the other end of the line?
    —Line . . . ? Dude, where've you been?
    —Whatever . . .

Conversation overheard in the year 2014:
    —Was comparative literature already that wireless, and the ACLA comparatisti that wired in 2004?
    —No doubt. They lived under the illusion of distant reading, distant relations, distant learning, and virtual hyperconnectivity.
    —And distended surpluses and tumescent deficits.

—And they were already being lined up for our imminent manned mission to the new Mars theme park of interplanetarity at Disney World.

—And for other martial missions. . . .

—Their comparatistic decade culminated in the mother of all credos of mass construction.

—You don't mean world literature?

—I mean world literature.

—Ever wonder what their distance was from credo to credulity?

—We'll have to calibrate the distance between their Templar and their template. Their comparative literature in 2004, it turns out, negotiated that distance at the speed of light.

—Indeed, their move from the historical density of the literatures of the world to the abstracted construct of world literature is the best example of their efficiency, second only to their enthusiasm for achieving their country.

—So, what happened?

—They proved too efficient. We've spent the decade since 2004 trying to revive the discipline from the dead.

Meanwhile, back in 2004, American comparative literature, having cycled through all three of its terms to immolate the final noun on the pyre of multiculture ten years earlier, now declaims the postmodern postmortem of its own discipline ("Today, comparative literature is in one sense dead," Bassnett 1993, 47; see also Spivak, *Death of a Discipline*). And the triune American comparative literature now reverts back to its first term to be, foremost and perforce, like the rest of the planet in 2004, American. *Pace* Spivak's recuperation of it as alternative to globalization—"I propose the planet to overwrite the globe" (72). Planetarity is the shrink-wrapped version of the longitudinally and latitudinally bounded gridwork of globalization. The planet is no less a political space than the globe. And while Spivak idealizes planetarity as a space beyond reclamation, a "species of alterity belonging to another system; and yet we inhabit it, on loan" (72), she does not see it as immune to "the auspices of a Comparative Literature supplemented by Area Studies," noting with a flush of confidence, "The planet is easily claimed" (72).

Indeed. But what Spivak overlooks is the belatedness of staking comparative literature's claim to a planet whose every inch is already platted on universal global positioning systems, whose interplanetary space is thoroughly weaponized, and whose planetarity, rather than "undivided 'natural' space" (72), is already naturalized into martial containment. Any elliptical tangents that would be drawn by comparative literature, with or without the cooperation of area studies, could no longer have any chance of being tangential, but would inexorably prove to be segments of ubiquitous circumscriptions with opportunistically shifting centers and expedient circumferences. Any emancipatory agency we might exercise as comparatists, then, may be no more than symptomatic illusion of a potently determined cultural indeterminacy or discursive undecidability. Ours may be little more than the calculated freedom accorded to radical fractiles and delusionary isolates in free-floating orbits that justly suspect their own putative autonomy but cannot muster the capability to move beyond isolation, silence, or the "cool" of whatever.

The result is a default complicity with regimes of truth whose truth derives from the leveraging of terror. Just how complicit American comparative literature may be in such regimes in 2004 may remain for the comparatists of 2014 to determine. One mathematical tabulation through which they might well do so will be by calculating the correlation between the transnational flows of comparatistic focus/activity and the directionality and scope of biometric control of bodies and their worldly movements, a control regime of bodies on a scale that exceeds the bodies and measures thus managed in Auschwitz and the rest of the hellholes such regimes created in twentieth-century Europe. What, in other words, is the ratio of comparatistic activity between the United States of America and the twenty-seven countries on the planet whose citizens are exempted from the biometric regime of fingerprinting and racial and ethnic profiling, on the one hand, and the level of comparatist focus and activity between the United States and the rest of the planet's countries whose citizens are subject to such management, on the other hand?

Such calculations are likely to be actionable sedition and professionally less than decorous in 2004. The question now might be, how far in extremis can the illusion of individuated detachment and free agency move before slipping into a status of vestigial excrescency? And if our historical present shares with all other presents the common status of being the past's vestige, what is our era vested in when it comes to the futures of comparative literature if the very space we occupy is already under full-spectrum occupation? The question is more problematic than topical, more rhetotropic—in the political argot of 2004, "spinnable"—than negotiable. Futures do, after all, constitute a putative investment, a wager that would find us and our place somewhere intended as destination, a future anteriority as terminus ad quem.

The trouble is that in 2004 we find ourselves as practicing comparatists under the aegis of something no longer innocently nameable as the American Comparative Literature Association, and no longer credibly or humanely definable as destination. Rather, in the context of 2004's planetary realpolitik, which is incontestably circumscribed as the domain of the Project for the New American Century, we form, whether we would wish to or not, an inextricable part of a terminus a quo, a radial point of emanation. Perforce, we function as *envoyants* rather than as *destinataires*, emitting envois of unpredictable consequence and indeterminate effect in a decidedly asymmetrical flow and permeability that finds our envois and formative constructs unimpeded in their penetration and diffusion, while we remain properly isolated and screened from what may be trying to flow our way. Cognitive constructs such as world literature and comparativity that originate in our metropolitan centers, for their part, need no visas or biometric clearances to arrive at what we deem to be our periphery. And these asymmetries continue to be progressively inflected by the officially usurped and transcoded agendas of global terrorism.

Those versatile codes of terror become transmuted into official instruments of panoptic surveillance, legislative regimes of control such as the Patriot Act, administrative regimes of interdiction such as the Department of Homeland Security, and regimes of preemption at the heart of the National Defense Strategy of the United States of America of September 2002, security apparatuses all in the service of the security state whose existence and self-perpetuation depend on the perpetual state of insecurity. Political expediency and economic profitability have finally perfected the efficacy of "worlding" the world and "achieving our country" (Rorty 1998, passim). Comparative literature and the inexorable complicity of its practitioners could be more efficaciously integrated into these transcodations than comparatists may realize or might wish to realize.

As an integral part of what was the Marshall Plan in post–World War II Europe, American comparative literature spent the second half of the twentieth century defining itself as the terminus of comparatism, a haven for comparatists in flight, a refuge from exilic displacement. Now, in the year 2004, the era of the Martial Plan as decreed in the National Defense Strategy of the United States of America of September 2002, otherwise known as the Bush Doctrine for a planetary realpolitik that neatly maps the planet on the grid of an unbreachable divide between the axis of evil and the nexus of good, that twentieth-century definition of comparative literature in America is made moot by a profound reversal, a reversal that may well have been in process since the last two decades of the last century and that now stands in stark light. The terminus ad quem has mutated into the terminus a quo.

Beginning with the first self-reflexive diagnosis in the critical writings of René Wellek at mid-twentieth century, "crisis" was the perennially defining condition of American comparative literature. And crisis would prove to be its métier, the dynamic that drove the engine of criticism, as Paul de Man would note a few years later. The last ACLA report of the century exacerbated that crisis, not by its intended "splicing of Comp. Lit. and Cultural Studies/multiculturalism" (Spivak 2003, 4), but by its unintended splintering of the critical fragments into supernumerary multiples of cultural identity claims clamoring for consensus on irreconcilable difference and nonnegotiable grounds, which Gerald Gillespie (2004, 157) characterized by invoking John Donne, "Tis all in peeces, all cohaerence gone."

We, in the year 2004, find ourselves in post-entropy's emergent state and in systematically reiterated states of emergency. Our condition is not critical but acute, the engine of our crisis generates not criticism solely but the urgency to seek after what lies as, in, and beyond the humbug of "whatever" and the unstoppable celerity of its spin. We are fated to construe disciplinary poesis beyond prosodic syllogism and in the catastrophic, since where epode would predictably ensue from strophe and antistrophe in dialectical three-step, we confront catastrophe instead. More than criticism, our perennial crisis, now in extremis, generates not just criticism but terror. "Comparative Literature in the Age of Terrorism," then, may be an appropriate reprise to last decade's report.

Reactively eschewing the regimes of identity and the cultural politics of difference that were so overdeterminative in the decade covered by the last ACLA report, comparative literature in an age of terrorism is obliged to negotiate some form of habitation in the space between an animadversion to difference and the bugbear of incomparability. In fact, the two are symbiotic. Incomparability is the dynamic, not of criticism or of comparatistic counterpoint, but a handmaiden of terror. Terror thrives on unbreachable difference, on exceptionalism, on the cultural and political monads that lie beyond the plausibility of dissensus and outside the possibility of the negotiable consensus. That is to say, terror thrives on the eradication of difference through the hyperbole of self-differentiation into Self-Same and of identity as self-equivalence, or as Spivak refers to it, the "same difference" (2003, 4). It might be more forthright to view this as the indifference that could well infect with deadly banality the execrable default that is the nonchalance of "whatever." And this is why I think we ought to read ethicists of post-difference such as Alain Badiou with due caution, lest we fall into a recidivist ethic of Heideggerian quiescence in anticipation of the apocalyptic "Nondum," the "not yet" (see Kadir 2000, 75) to which Badiou takes us perilously close in his "indifferent differences" of recognition that hang agency and ethical impulse into abeyance in anticipation of "the Same," which Badiou glosses as "the coming-to-be of that which is not yet" (2002, 25).

"Same," much like the unbreachable different, the indifferent, and the exceptional, is as inimical to comparative literature as it is nurturing and abetting of terrorism. Exception has historically functioned as the path to, and as the cover for, genocide. It now functions as instrumentality of self-exemption that transcodes the legitimate need for immunity from terror into impunity for its practice, first as preemptive strike, then as vengeful reaction. "Same" under these conditions spells indifference to difference. This is not merely a logical contradiction but an ethical predicament where comparative literature is concerned. In the absence of difference, replaced by modular individuality and exceptionalism that become the private redoubt of each comparatist, comparative literature in America is not only a self-contradiction. Occupying as it does the hegemonic locus of a terminus a quo, it easily and inadvertently slips into complicity with regimes of terror.

In 2004, the greatest danger for this slippage resides in the overheard conversation, above, from the year 2014, when the next ACLA report on the state of the profession is being drafted, namely, the construct we call world literature. The facility with which we seem to move from the literatures of the world to World Literature (Moretti, Damrosch, inter alios), Global Literature (Dimock, Shih), and Planetary Literature (Spivak) is indeed awesome. And coming as these master constructs do at a historical moment when historical density is elided into the comfort zone of post-difference and the contextual specificity of culture is taken up into the local academic debate of culturalism (by which I mean a re-anthropologization of the different as "untouchable," either due to felt perils of essentialism or to the risks of dissipation in universalism), world literature discourse, and analogous narrative structures, run the greater risk of instrumentalizing the literatures of the world as objects of neocolonial usurpation and imperial subsumption in a process telegraphed by Shu-mei Shih, after Badiou, as "technologies of recognition" (Shih 2004, 16 et passim). At that juncture, any promise for bridging difference into negotiable transculturations becomes moot, co-opted by the hegemonic appropriation that colonizes comparativity and instrumentalizes the comparatist as an isolate device for purposes of streamlining the processes and honing the efficacy of such technologies. I have noted elsewhere the peculiar coincidence throughout history between the rise of imperial hegemony and the surge in the discourse of "world literature" or "world civilization" (Kadir 2004). The level of our cooptation as comparatists in this regard may not be as fully evident to us now as it may become to the future anteriority that will be the time of the chroniclers of the next decade of comparative literature in 2014.

The foregrounding of regional and area studies in projects as diverse as those of the ICLA Executive Bureau, which carved up the globe into field regions whose literatures are documented principally by native comparatists of each respective region, and Gayatri Spivak's *Death of a Discipline* may be not as odd a coincidence as it might seem, despite Spivak's searing recollection of her experience with the ICLA Executive Bureau (see Spivak 2003, 5). In this re-privileging of auto-ethnography and the native informant by both projects, the ICLA's is little more than a reversion to a balkanization of world literary cultures that harks back to the Cold War era of reduction and containment. Spivak, for her part, in pursuit of what she terms the "specificity of the autochthone" (14) and "exemplary singularity" (22), betrays a peculiar form of nostalgia and, hence, the necessity of a return to the linguistic and cultural particularity that underwrote area studies, with whose revival and collaboration she envisions a "new Comparative Literature" (21) with which she would have us supercede the "monolingual, presentist, narcissistic" (20) aegis of cultural studies. The multiculturalist 1993 ACLA report continues to resonate in Spivak, and as reaction formation, the cultural studies that so inflected that report continue to be determinative through Spivak's felt need to surmount them.

One would be hard-pressed to find a comparatist who would argue against the supersession of monolingualism, presentism, and narcissism. The difficulty in the historical moment of 2004 is to differentiate between multilingualism and forked tongues, historical scope and self-serving historicism, non-narcissist self-effacement and self-critique as cloak of invisibility. In the age of terror every gesture becomes transcoded in the guise of security and as disguise for the survival of security's preemptions. Being in the world, comparative literature may not always be able to discern when and to what degree it is of the world, and other-worldly constructs such as world literature could well be deflective mechanisms for disciplinary equanimity and for keeping the world at a safe distance, albeit never out of reach. Between far- and near-sightedness, our cultural scale leaves little choice in the order of value. And distance rather than nearness, individuation rather than collectivity, solipsism rather than communion, unbridgeable contestation rather than conversation are of optimal usefulness to regimes of terror. The first term in each adversative binomial would appear to be the paradigm that subtends comparative literature in 2004. The degree to which this might be so symptomatically or otherwise may not be as clear to us as we diagnose the historical moment that defines us. That may become clearer to the authors of the next decennium.

WORKS CITED

Badiou, Alain. *An Essay on the Understanding of Evil.* Trans. Peter Hallward. London: Verso, 2002.
Bassnett, Susan. *Comparative Literature: A Critical Introduction.* Oxford: Blackwell, 1993.
Bernheimer, Charles, ed. *Comparative Literature in the Age of Multiculturalism.* Baltimore: Johns Hopkins University Press, 1995.
Damrosch, David. *What Is World Literature?* Princeton, N.J.: Princeton University Press, 2003.
De Man, Paul. *Blindness and Insight: Essays in the Rhetoric of Contemporary Criticism.* Minneapolis: University of Minnesota Press, 1983.

Dimock, Wai Chee. "Literature for the Planet." *PMLA* 116 (2001): 173–88.

Gillespie, Gerald. *By Way of Comparison: Reflections on the Theory and Practice of Comparative Literature.* Paris: Honoré Champion, 2004.

Kadir, Djelal. "Heidegger, Hölderlin, and the 'Essence of Philosophy': An Adversative Conversation." *Neohelicon* 27:1 (Winter 2000): 69–78.

———. "To World, To Globalize: Comparative Literature's Crossroads." *Comparative Literature Studies* 41:1 (2004): 1–9 .

Moretti, Franco. "Conjectures on World Literature." *New Left Review* 1 (2000): 54–68.

Rorty, Richard. *Achieving Our Country.* Cambridge, Mass.: Harvard University Press, 1998.

Shih, Shu-mei. "Global Literature and the Technologies of Recognition." *PMLA* 119.1 (January 2004): 16–30.

Spivak, Gayatri Chakravorty. *Death of a Discipline.* New York: Columbia University Press, 2003.

Wellek, René. "The Crisis of Comparative Literature." In *Concepts of Criticism,* ed. Stephen G. Nichols Jr., 282–95. New Haven, Conn.: Yale University Press, 1963.

CHAPTER SIX

Indiscipline

DAVID FERRIS

Andromaque, je pense à vous . . .

One can imagine the response if a latter-day Hegel, writing not on art but on the university, were to proclaim that the humanities are a thing of the past. Fingers will no doubt point with ironic confidence at the continuing presence of the humanities as if this proclamation were nothing more than a denial of the mere existence of our departments of history, philosophy, English, French, Italian, German, East Asian, classics—even comparative literature. The empirical evidence that the humanities survive is just too plainly to be seen—and there can be no question about the evidence of the empirical, can there? Yet even the continuing survival of these departments fails to counter the sense that their claim on the intellectual life of the university has diminished significantly over the last forty or so years. Is this because the humanities are no longer in tune with fundamental changes in what now constitutes knowledge, changes that have already taken place but whose consequences have not yet wrought their full effect on how the university has historically organized its knowledge? Or is this because the humanities really *are* a thing of the past? Are the humanities already living on beyond their means, awaiting a significance promised by their mere surviving?

Given that the nature of the university changed greatly in the latter half of the twentieth century, whether the humanities can articulate a significance for themselves within the contemporary transformation of the university is now a pressing question. More pointedly, can they do so without resorting to incantations of the value of being human, of the value of the history of the humanities, of the value of the illimitable transportability of those skills of close reading (who does that anymore?) to more professional vocations? Can they do this in an age that appears to be experiencing a transvaluation of all values even if it has not has not registered the consequences of such a transvaluation? To ignore this transvaluation is human, or, as Nietzsche would say, all too human. Only by ignoring such a transvaluation can the shell of the past persist in the form of a shelter for the humanities. But to accept this transvaluation is to accept its repercussions for the methods of study that have long claimed the value of being human as their crowning value. And to accept these repercussions is to pose a question about the humanities and their current configuration within the university. Do the humanities have a place within this transvaluation beyond the mere survival of what they have been, and beyond strategic reconfigurations of their traditional division?

Within this situation the case of comparative literature appears to merit special consideration. A relative newcomer institutionally, it did not come into existence until after the traditional divisions of literary study had been established—after all, it needed something to compare. Does this meta-humanities position then mark comparative literature as different from the traditional divisions of the humanities? Does this mean that comparative literature should be claimed as the one area of study that can escape the difficulties the traditional disciplines of the humanities now face within the transvalued university? Such a claim easily fuels the sense of exception that comparative literature has fostered for itself. It also fuels one of the common refrains of our times, at least where comparative literature is concerned. On the basis of such a claim, could we not say that comparative literature is the discipline that is not a discipline? As such, is it *the* discipline of our allegedly postmodern and transvalued times, the discipline that eschews definition of itself as a discipline? And is not this resistance to definition the sign of having rejected not just certain values but the value of defining values, the value of a historically suspect past?

To situate comparative literature as this avatar of our times does, however, require caution, and not only because of the ease with which a resistance to definition quickly becomes a value in its own right. Can we really say that the difficulties comparative literature has experienced in defining itself as a discipline are the reflection of a particular era or time? The temptation to see such a connection between our age and the disciplinary elusiveness of this field of study is strong but hardly accurate. Difficulties in self-definition defined the history of comparative literature even from its institutional beginnings in the very un-postmodern milieu of the 1870s. In an essay that Haun Saussy's contribution has recalled from the 1870s, none other than Hugo Meltzl de Lomnitz already writes that "*Comparative Literature* . . . is . . . by no means a fully defined and established discipline. As a matter of fact it is still far from that goal" (1973, 56). To return to this observation almost 130 years later is to return with a conflicted response. For Meltzl, definition and establishment go hand in hand, and their separation is a source of weakness. For us, however, establishment and definition are easily separated from one another. Consequently, we have little difficulty seeing comparative literature in the same light as other established disciplines while at the same time renouncing any need to define precisely what has been established in its name. Here it is tempting to assert the self-contradictory and evasive rhetoric of our age and define comparative literature as the discipline that is not a discipline. Let us have our cake and eat it too. What Meltzl saw as a weakness is now our strength.

But why has the enduring theme of comparative literature and its history, an anxiety about defining what it is, an anxiety that now produces reports in the form of reports about reports, why has this theme finally emerged and found its reflection in the general historical condition of our age? Was comparative literature then always, and *avant la lettre*, postmodern? Or is there something else at work in the history of its development, a logic that drives comparative literature to question continually what constitutes it as a discipline? Is this a logic that also ensures, in its calculation, that the answer to what comparative literature is should always fail in order to preserve the question? This inability to define itself, this failure to become a discipline, in effect, this *indiscipline*—why does it not disappear in the distraction of our presumed postmodernity? But what does it mean that we should still be brought to this question now, at this moment in the history of the humanities, in our presumed postmodernity?

Confronted with such questions, the example of Meltzl is again instructive. Faced with a field of study but no defined discipline, Meltzl founded a journal in 1877, a journal known from 1879 on as *Acta comparationis litterarum universarum*. This footnote in the history of comparative literature is worth recounting for only one reason: the claim that a field lacks definition is met with the attempt to substantiate this same field in a series of examples or "acts." This tendency has been widespread and is nowhere more present than in volumes devoted to the subject of comparative literature. It has been easier to offer a demonstration, to *do* something called a "comparative reading" than it has been to conceptualize the project of comparativism. Why this is so is a question comparative literature needs to ask, but only in the knowledge that it is a question addressed *to* comparative literature. It may not, in fact, be a question that can be asked from within comparative literature or even in its name, lest the response end up being one more comparative act, one more comparative performance. But if it has to be asked from somewhere else, this necessity also has to be recognized as part of the current situation of comparative literature. The question is: where is this elsewhere from which the situation of comparative literature can be discerned?

To know the current situation of comparative literature is of course the reason the ACLA engages in its ten-year exercise on the state of the discipline. This, the fourth report, comes at a time when the field reflects the increased presence of literatures other than those of its classical European past. This inclusion now points comparative literature toward the question of the institutional position it will be called upon to play as the university registers distinct shifts in what constitutes the meaning of foreignness as well as how it provides an educational experience. Accompanying this shift, there arises a changing sense in the value of certain foreign languages, languages that once formed the core of comparative literature's classical past, the period of its "Eur-iquity." An initial effect of this shift is that comparative literature now finds itself situated within the humanities between the expansiveness of English programs that look increasingly comparative (even if the medium of every text is English) and the continuing growth of departments of Hispanic literatures and languages. Comparative literature, along with the non-Hispanic foreign literatures, is increasingly positioned between these two poles. Given this situation, it is not beyond possibility that the evolution of the study of literature within humanities will, in the short term, yield a tripartite division in which the disciplinary structure of the past will preserve itself, albeit in greatly reduced form. There will be English, Hispanic literatures, and Comparative Studies—the latter acting as a "home" for languages and literatures no longer able to sustain departmental status (a balkanization based on institutional rather than intellectual needs). It is at this point that the tendency toward global studies and world literature within comparative literature can easily become a rationale for the administrative exigency that would form an umbrella department under the title of Comparative Studies. What happens to comparative literature at such a juncture is worth contemplating now if this field is to retain a signature for itself rather than be shaped by such an exigency.

To pose this question now is to pose it at a time when the traditional departmental support structure for comparative literature is entering a critical phase. The most recent statistics show that the foreign literatures historically most closely associated with comparative literature have achieved, at least temporarily, smaller declines in their enrollments. However, a downward trend continues, and it is a trend that indicates increasing difficulties ahead for comparative literature as it has been traditionally conceived.[1] This is so not only because these departments are producing fewer students but because, as these departments grow smaller, their ability to sustain doctoral study and therefore provide courses for comparative literature students diminishes. In this respect, the fate as well as the purpose of this model of comparative literature is tied directly to the condition of language and literature study in the modern university. Here the anxiety about standards voiced in the Levin (1963) and Greene (1975) reports becomes a luxury we can no longer indulge. It is no longer simply a question of locating where or how high the standard should be. The question now, if Levin and Greene were to ask it, would be whether there will be something for their comparative literature to standardize. Or has this field of study evolved beyond the kind of restriction within which such standards are conceivable? A world already translated?

Bernheimer's report (1995) clearly reflects a commitment to such an evolution. In doing so, comparative literature takes on the task that the modern university has also taken up: to institute as its own the same global forces whose allure informed the Bernheimer report. This move beyond limited cultural pluralism, this move to a horizon seemingly without limit, does not, however, completely escape the question posed symptomatically in the previous reports by Levin and Greene. Their insistence on standards may have been defined in the form of European literatures, but to dismiss why they insisted on standards merely because such standards have been articulated in European terms evades the opportunity to address the ongoing consequences of two defining and contrary forces within comparative literature: comparison without bounds, and the possibility of a discipline. The latter force marks the reflection on comparative literature until Bernheimer—and it is present both in an insistence on standards and in the repeated anxiety, from Meltzl to Wellek, about how to define comparative literature, to bring it to discipline. To escape into a world, or more precisely, to take up *the* world as the subject of comparative literature gives a radical, all-encompassing emphasis to the former force—as if to say that the failure of the latter can be mitigated by pursuit of the former. But even here, and *pace* Bernheimer, comparative literature is once again faced with confronting the question of standards for its own expanded horizons and for access to those horizons.

In the past (increasingly mythical), such standards were easier to articulate: a knowledge of three literatures in their original language and a level of theoretical sophistication appropriate to the conceptual nature of a field no longer confined to national restrictions. Such a model works, according to the traditions of comparative literature, as long as the three original languages do not wander far from the language menu prevailing in the modern university. Thus, an argument runs, comparative literature should not expand beyond the foreign literary and linguistic infrastructure of its institutional situation—in effect, it should replicate and sustain this situation. But, if comparative literature is to do more than shore up graduate study in certain foreign literatures, it must decide whether the linguistic requirements of its past are still in force although no longer European in character. If such requirements are held to, then the specter of standards returns here. As a result, the Bernheimer report is forced to face what might be its own worst nightmare: the ghostly appearance of a multicultural Levin, perhaps still dressed as a plumber, but armed with the knowledge of every conceivable literature and its language, chanting "This is the standard, this is the standard."[2] If comparative literature is to distinguish itself from English at this point, the question of such standards threatens to return. As comparative literature radicalizes its inmost comparatist gesture in an unashamedly expansionist model, it poses ever more insistently the question of the intellectual identity of such a model within the university of late capitalism, the question of its discipline, the question of its distinction and identity.

The ghostly return of a multicultural Levin is the return of the perennial question of comparative literature: is there a limit to its expansive trajectory? Because Levin, and later Greene, sought an answer to that question in a standard accentuating the acquisition of the original languages of a literature (read, available languages), comparative literature became an easy target for just about anyone from late capitalism possessed with a minimal awareness of ideology. Standards equal Eurocentrism. The boldness of this claim would sweep away in a single gesture another issue, an issue more central to comparative literature than its historical Eurocentrism (which can be read as a symptomatic response to this issue). It is an issue present from the very inception of comparative literature as a field: the translatability of a subject speaking from within a national identity, which establishes the possibility of comparing literature. In the heady atmosphere of an incipient multiculturalism, Bernheimer's report could not see that the narrowness observed in Levin, for instance, was a restricted form of what, the later report argued, should take place in the study of literature. The stake is not Europe but access to the model Europe had held, quite literally, in exile for itself: the right to compare without restriction, the right to exemplify comparison. Without such a right there could never have been a Eurocentric comparative literature. At the same time, without such a right there could never be a comparative literature beyond such a Eurocentrism. What Bernheimer reiterates is this right, a right whose existence goes to the very center of comparison as we have come to understand it, while validating the value of that center as crucial to the critical enterprises that define our times.

Yet rather than reflecting on the theoretical issue that haunts comparative literature wherever this right is exercised—its claim to exercise such a right and to place it at the center of the humanities, in short, a claim to found a discipline in comparison—Bernheimer advocates an imperative (hence, as Peter Brooks has pointed out, its many "shoulds") that exports the most essential historical right of traditional comparative literature in order to welcome its return in the form of its own displaced subject. In this odyssey, the relation of such a subject to literature remains unchanged: its unchanged status is the effect of a comparative project whose first expansionist steps emphasized Europe; whose development stalled in front of the seductive prospect of a discipline, the prospect of standards, the prospect of a method for comparative literature; and whose most recent turn picks up once more the thematic rationale of its history. First Europe, then the world.

The logic that informs this tendency can already be discerned in Meltzl. With the second volume of the journal he founded in 1877, a new motto is adopted. It comes from Schiller and reads as follows: "It would be a pitiful, petty ideal to write for *one* nation only: for a philosophical spirit this limitation is absolutely unbearable. This spirit could not confine itself to such a changeable, accidental, and arbitrary form of humanity, a fragment (and what else is the greatest nation?)" (Schiller, 25:304). In taking up this remark (from a letter written by Schiller in October 1789), Meltzl's incipient comparativism reveals its dependence on an idea central to the romantic critical project: the fragment. The concept of a nation, according to which the study of literature was to organize itself within the university, no longer retains its integral role. Now it is more appropriate to speak of literatures within these units as they register the failure of a nation to sustain its previous significance. This development not only reflects a tendency present in comparativism from its beginning, but it is also witness to the sense of fragmentation that Schiller expresses and that the first journal of comparative literature takes up as its guiding motto.

If the greatest nation is still a fragment—and what else could have been at stake in comparative literature's Eurocentrism than such a nation?—this Euro project is already fated to disintegrate, to become one nation among other nations, to join, as it were, an organization of fragments, each assuring the failure of the other's hegemony. Here the status quo threatens to become a paralysis as the task of comparativism is defined more and more as the task of limiting nationhood, of producing the nation in its failure, as the fragment it already was. The movement toward a reinvention of the idea of world literature is a logical consequence of this task—a world that no part can lay claim to as its world except by laying claim to the world as an essentially fragmentary experience.

But, as always, where the fragment arises, a desire for totality is never far behind. The literary theory of Iena Romanticism already understood this aspect of the fragment and developed it in such a way as to totalize the world in its fragmentation: the fragmentary experience of totality becomes totalizing in itself. Has comparative literature become the institutional form of this theory? The discipline of fragmentation, the medium in which other disciplines are made to reflect an essential fragmentary tendency? To borrow a coinage by Walter Benjamin, has comparative literature become the *Reflexionsmedium* of the humanities? The discipline that undoes the concept of discipline through its reflexive mediation of all other disciplines? Or is this undoing, this desire to be undone, no more than the endgame of a history of aesthetic experience that Hegel also sought to end, an experience only able to reproduce its own unending end as the condition of its survival? Because it was Hegel who sought to end such an experience, it would be tempting to see his rejection of Iena Romanticism as the rejection of something anti-Hegelian, of something that undermines the resolutely totalizing character of his thought—never mind his judgment on the future of art. To do so is not only to refuse to recognize that there is a totalizing tendency at work in both, but it is also to evade the question of what is at stake now as we align comparative literature with an essentially Romantic project.

Meltzl's turn to Schiller is symptomatic of the forces now traversing comparative literature as it seeks a new postmodern institutional identity. To argue that this identity favors incompletion over totality is not to argue a merely formal concern. It is also to take up the question of a nation, a question that has always been in play within comparative literature. Schiller is instructive in this respect. Limiting the nation to the status of a fragment is, in Schiller's words, to affirm the nation as "a changeable, accidental, arbitrary form of humanity." That Schiller is capable of this awareness should give us pause for thought. Aren't we accustomed to attribute to Schiller the ideological basis of politics in Western nations? But aren't the terms in which Schiller describes the concept of a nation close to the terms that the world, after postcolonialism, is accustomed to using to criticize the historic emphasis of comparative literature on core European languages and literatures? Europe, now recognizable as a changeable, accidental, arbitrary form of humanity. And is it not in the name of a future for humanity, as well as the humanities, that this criticism is made? What kind of history can sustain such a contradiction? But the question that really needs to be posed here is whether this future is not still essentially European in effect, a Europe that would no longer be Europe but a Europe effaced into other names: nation, earth, world, planet . . . in these words our progression and our enlightenment, indeed, our comparison, now puts itself at stake, as recent publications insist.

Nowhere has this stake been more pronounced than in the tentative steps comparative literature has made in articulating a future for itself in the form of a world. But as David Damrosch's recent work in this area witnesses, comparative literature, even as it expands beyond a European base and becomes the foster home of world literature, is still faced with the anxiety René Wellek experienced within that base. In his 1958 essay "The Crisis of Comparative Literature," Wellek writes that "the most serious sign of the precarious state of our study is the fact that we have not been able to establish a distinct subject matter and a specific methodology" (Wellek 1963, 283).[3] The very fact that Damrosch's book has been or can be written reflects the difficulty in establishing, in Wellek's words, a distinct subject matter and a specific methodology for the literature we know in terms of the world.[4] It is also a sign that the persistent question of comparative literature is still at work, if only in a displacement.

It is no longer the question of one discipline. Rather, that discipline's questioning of the nationalization of literary study now poses the question of what literature must now belong to when, to reframe the beginning of this essay, the value of nation has been transvalued. What is posed by the advent of world literature is not only the question of what defines literary study, but more importantly, it is the question of where and how, in the modern university, is the world to be located? The question is pressing if comparative literature is to avoid becoming no more than the gatekeeper to the new cultural, and increasingly virtual, Grand Tour—to PowerPoint and beyond? Damrosch offers an answer to this question (which he calls, not unadvisedly, "the comparatist's lurking panic") when he writes, "World literature is not an immense body of material that must somehow, impossibly, be mastered; it is a mode of reading that can be experienced *intensively* with a few works just as effectively as it can be explored *extensively* with a large number" (Damrosch 2003, 299). Here, Damrosch's approach would displace the will to master that has driven and plagued the history of comparative literature when faced by the impossible extensiveness of its field. By displacing the emphasis from a body of literature to a mode of reading, Damrosch is able to overcome the challenge posed by this extensiveness: world literature is not a body of literature but a way of reading literature, in effect, an experience of the world.

But even in this displacement there remains the tendency that has haunted comparative literature throughout its history. The purpose of this intensive reading is to experience what could otherwise be experienced if it were not so impossible a task: the experience of the world through its extensive multiplicity. Damrosch asserts that the *in*tensive reading experience achieves, "just as effectively," what the *ex*tensive experience of the world also promises. What is to be known, in effect, mastered, is what a world is—whether this is achieved through a restricted or extensive reading experience. Here comparative literature, faced with the impossible—and not for the first time in its history but always at those points where it poses the question of its theoretical and methodological foundation—justifies its retreat into the confines of the possible: the possibility of what would otherwise be an impossible experience of literature, literature in its totality as a world. The goal has not changed; rather, the experience of that goal has been relocated. It is here, displaced into a mode of reading, that the imperative to master the field, the world, lives on and does so despite, but perhaps also because of, the evidence of its impossibility. The same imperative that surfaces with such regularity in the history of comparative literature (and signaled by the suspicion that such mastery will always be impossible, that comparative literature is impossible as a discipline) is now channeled through a mode rather than an object.

One is tempted to conclude that it is between this imperative and its impossibility that what is at stake in the world of world literature takes place: a constant struggle between the project of comparison and what continues to evade that project, namely, the world (despite the fact that it is only conceived from within that project). To mediate this difficulty (which means, Hegel-like, to give the project of comparison a future in the face of its most difficult task, comprehending what a world is, bringing it within the sphere of comparison), Damrosch promotes an intensive reading experience in strict analogy to an extensive experience (the latter being the kind that gives graduate students, as well as ourselves, dreams of plumbers who compare the literature). The analogy is clearly weighted in favor of the intensive as a means of sustaining the comparative project as it contemplates its fate in the impossible experience of the world. Thanks to this intensiveness, the world can be read as if it had been read in its extensiveness.[5] Harry Levin's ghost need not return to haunt our waking days. The plumber, it appears, has been laid to rest.

But, does the plumbing work? Does it lay to rest the need to take up once again the question of comparative literature, or does it run the risk of divorcing comparative literature from its only vital question, the question always lurking in its history even when it takes custody of the world, namely, why is it so *indisciplined?*

It is increasingly clear that the humanities, as we know them today, have developed greatly from the impulse comparative literature gave to them in the last fifty years. As Haun Saussy points out in his chapter, this has occurred to such an extent that comparative literature is now suffused throughout the humanities. The consequence of this extension is that the question comparative literature has historically posed about itself and its place within the humanities is no longer its proper question; it is no longer a question it can simply pose to itself, no longer a question it can pose about itself. The question of comparative literature has become everyone's question, a fact reinforced by its pursuit of the world. To refuse this pursuit is to dream that one could fall asleep and reawaken as René Wellek circa 1958. The question of comparative literature is now the question of the humanities at a time when the past is no longer enough to ensure their future.

Where then does this future lie? In a world? In the world? But, to ensure this future under the rubric of a world or even the world—is this one more attempt to rescue comparative literature from the failure Wellek had already sensed in his own time, or is it a definitive break with the conditions governing that past and its failure? Did one comparative literature die to give rise to another? Or has the logic of comparison against which Wellek, and later Levin and Greene, struggled survived to claim the world in an impossibly other voice, the voice of the world, a totality of fragmented nations only able to speak in the exile of their nationality, that is, in comparative literature? If the latter, then another question awaits us: Is comparative literature a distinct activity, or is it merely the particular form of a more general comparative project, the comparative project of the humanities?

If the latter, the guiding logic at stake here has taken a long time to find its voice within the humanities. This logic, and its effects, as Jean-Luc Nancy points out at the beginning of his *La création du monde ou la mondialisation* has a decidedly Hegelian provenance. Nancy cites the following passage from Hegel, which, despite being stated in terms of commerce, reads like an account of the recent history of comparative literature and the humanities: "The extension, according to natural necessity, of commerce with foreign nations, as for example the commerce between Europe and a new continent, has had a skeptical effect on the dogmatism of their sense of community such as it existed before and on the irrefutable certitude of a host of concepts concerning law and truth" (Hegel, "The Relation between Skepticism and Philosophy"; cited by Nancy 2002, 15). Invested in this extension, then as now, is a sense of advancement, a sense of overcoming a dogmatic past whose strictures made it clear precisely what constituted "the literature." Although the passage cited by Nancy gives a strong sense of the logical consequences of the project of globalization, it is not, as Nancy goes on to remark, an accurate account of our current situation. This situation, Nancy observes, is one in which the West "is no longer even able to encounter the relativity of its norms and its doubt about its own assurance" (15).

The time of relativity and doubt already occurs in Hegel. The difference between Hegel and today is that the "skepticism in which Hegel saw the richness of the shaking up of dogmatisms no longer has today, as it had for him, the resource of a future in which the dialectic would carry reason further, more in advance, more to the forefront of a truth and a sense of the world" (Nancy 2002, 15). To insist that we are in this stage of relativity is to harbor the hope that what we call the world conceals a truth and a sense accessible through the relativity of our fragmentary certitudes. It is also to reveal the Hegelian character of our own attempts to make Hegel a thing of the past. But more than this, Nancy warns that it is in this very same movement through which skepticism aims at a greater "truth and sense of the world" that "the assurance of historical progress is suspended, that the convergence of knowledge, of ethics, and of living well together is taken apart, and that the domination of an empire united in technical power and pure economic reason is affirmed" (15).

If the recent history of comparative literature finds its rationale in a skepticism about the assumed certainties of a European past, has it unwittingly subscribed to the will of a university that now bows to technical power while transforming reason into economic reason? Has it in fact affirmed the very forces it claims to resist? In this context, has the very idea of literature, understood in terms of the world, become the means by which the comparative project has sought to suspend its historical progress one more time?

The fear of such a suspension plays a strong role in the imperative to master that Damrosch gives voice to at the end of *What Is World Literature?* There it takes the form of an impossibility that has haunted both the dreams and the waking hours of those who have sought to know comparative literature. This persistent statement of anxiety about comparative literature's impossibility indicates that the history of comparative literature has only ever been thought from the perspective of a discipline. In this respect, the character of this history has invariably been dialectical, always seeking to incorporate what remains other to it and always suspending itself before this other. In the periodic suspension of its own sense and reason has comparative literature assured its future. This is why Wellek's anxieties about comparative literature are not simply his own, nor do they mark a privileged point of consciousness in the history of comparative literature; rather, they are one of the many points of suspension present in this history. To have a history marked by such suspensions is to have a history founded on an impasse that must be periodically reproduced but always in a different form so at least the illusion of progress is maintained. The logic that governs this reproduction is the logic of comparison. It is present in the passage Nancy cites from Hegel: through commerce and the exchanges it establishes between Europe and new continents comparisons are made, comparisons that provide an awareness of the means by which Europe has projected itself as Europe (a means it cannot see without the awareness initiated by comparison). Europe can no longer simply refer to itself as Europe but must recognize the fragmentary limitation of an existence without comparison. Here the double bind of comparison makes itself felt most forcefully: Europe is brought to the recognition that it cannot affirm itself as Europe without comparison. But with comparison, it cannot sustain itself as the entity it wants to affirm through comparison. Confined to such a situation, comparison produces no other results; it is, to use a formula easily adopted by our times, nothing more than the possibility of its own impossibility. In short, what is at stake here is not Europe but a logic whose purpose is to assure its own impasse and reproduce itself as this impasse. Such a logic can take us to many different places, to many futures, even different worlds, but each journey returns to the same as if, like some amnesic Odysseus, we are fated to set off for home one more time because we have forgotten we are already where we have set out to go.

In her Wellek Lectures on Comparative Literature, Gayatri Spivak states a version of this problem when she says, "Globalization is the imposition of the same system of exchange everywhere" (2003, 72). This recognition provides the awareness that comparative literature, as indicated by the title under which these lectures were subsequently published, *Death of a Discipline,* has experienced its death. This never means that it no longer exists. After all, for something to *experience* its death means that it is not dead, at least not yet. Spivak's lectures are positioned between such an experience and an anticipated death. This is why Spivak, in her preface, expresses the hope that her book "will be read as the last gasp of a dying discipline" (xii). And after that last gasp? The silence of apocalyptic wisdom? Spivak's hope that her book will be read as the last gasp of a dying discipline seems far from the original title of these lectures when they were given at Irvine in 2000: "The New Comparative Literature." Seems far, but isn't really. The desire for the new, the modern, and the desire for an end (that modernity should be the end) have always been closely related. They have also always involved a curious rhetoric whose temporality gives all the force of occurrence to something that has not yet occurred—what Spivak invokes as "a definitive future anteriority, a 'to come'-ness, a 'will have happened' quality" (6). Thanks to this future anteriority, what is written here as the last gasp of comparative literature can only be read as such from a point at which no more comparison and no other gasp is possible. For Spivak to see her lectures in this light is to reveal comparative literature as the carefully rehearsed performance of a desire, the desire for its impossibility, the impossibility of itself in the form of its radical *indiscipline*. To articulate such a state is no mean feat, but to articulate it only in the hope that "there may be some in the academy who do not believe that the critical edge of the humanities should be appropriated and determined by the market" (xii) may be to miss the point of why this state can be and has been articulated now.

To pronounce the death of a discipline, particularly the "old" discipline of comparative literature, is to claim that its internal ordering, its disciplining of literature, is no longer vital. The order at stake here is nothing other than discipline itself, the concept of discipline through which so much of the history of comparative literature has registered its self-uncertainty. What Spivak envisages as the "new" comparative literature arises from the attempt to cross over from the impasse that resonates throughout this history even in its globalization phase. Spivak rightly sees that such globalization, despite its name, remains a restricted economy. Her call for a crossing over to a "new" comparative literature indicates her awareness of the need to break with this system of exchange and its Hegelian character. Yet the rhetoric of crossing that sustains this break, along with a reiterated call for a "new" comparative literature, invites suspicion that what is being played out in this death is the history comparative literature has repeatedly bequeathed to itself in moments of self-inflicted crisis—not to mention, once more, that what is also at stake in these moments is the renewal of comparative literature as a kind of reason.

To voice this renewal in terms of old and new comparative literatures is to invoke comparison as the purpose of difference, as the purpose of all those crossings that academic work now seems so intent on rehearsing over and over again.[6] But more is at stake here than just another crossing. Rather, what is at stake is crossing as the modern form of the comparative project of humanities: crossing as the gateway to a "new" comparative literature in which crossing becomes an end in itself. This is tantamount to saying that comparative literature can only take its method, comparison, as its subject if it is to survive its own history. Here comparison not only understands crossing as its most necessary step but, as crossing, it is understood as the opening to "a species of alterity" that Spivak names as the planet. This step, necessarily strategic, is essentially comparative, since it derives its force in comparison to what it supplants: the "old" comparative literature—comparative literature as conflict of Eurocentrism and cultural studies, globalization, world. Even in this most strategized of forms, the logic that drives the history of comparative literature persists—the logic that seeks and fails to find standards, the logic that confines comparative literature to the productive paradox of a discipline without disciplinarity, the logic of its *indiscipline*. But no new comparative literature is foundable on these terms since what is founded as the new is predicated on what comparative literature has repeatedly experienced as its history, namely, its impossibility. Comparative literature is, in this respect, an essentially Kantian undertaking—a critique that seeks to sustain the limits within which it operates; in effect, it is a theoretical account of the humanities in general.

Despite the strong sense of the "pastness" of a certain comparative literature, Spivak's strategic turn to "planet" and "planetary" is symptomatic of a situation that is not simply the situation of comparative literature but the situation of the humanities as they evolved in the modern university. For Spivak, the planetary arises as a result of "cross[ing] borders under the auspices of a Comparative Literature supplemented by Area Studies" (72). Earlier in her lectures, she had explained this "new" comparative literature as one "that would work to make the traditional linguistic sophistication of Comparative Literature supplement Area Studies (and history, anthropology, political theory, and sociology) by approaching the language of the other not only as a 'field' language" (9). How this would occur relies, Spivak claims, on "a reader with imagination ready for the effort of othering, however imperfectly, as an end in itself" (13). Alterity is not only central to this project of a "new" comparative literature, but it is also, by implication, central to the possibility that the humanities can survive their own history. The effort of "othering" referred to here is also the effort that produces crossing. By making this effort an end in itself, the comparatist can now offer an answer to the most embarrassing question comparatists are confronted with: What do you compare? No longer need we shyly reply that we really don't compare anything, that our field of study is misnamed. The answer is now, "We compare what cannot be compared." The logic that used to drive comparative literature toward an end, toward a sense of discipline, while depriving it of just such an end, now becomes its possibility, the possibility of its impossibility.

Such is the force of the planet envisaged by Spivak, this "species of alterity" that, in the almost final words of her lectures performs the following role: "The 'planet' is here, as perhaps always, a catachresis... Its alterity, determining experience, is mysterious and discontinuous—an experience of the impossible" (102). Beyond the protective "perhaps" and the "however imperfectly"—strategies that protect the impossible from actually being experienced, strategies that therefore protect comparative literature from a decisive death—the question of comparative literature's history remains in force: why must comparative literature always be transfixed before the seduction of the impossible?

As already argued, it is not simply comparative literature that is at stake here but the possibility of the humanities in late modernity—specifically, the possibility of the disciplinary formation out of which comparative literature emerged and to which it responds. To say that this disciplinary formation is at stake is, however, also to say that what is in play now is the concept of Enlightenment modernity out of which the humanities and its disciplines developed. What the history of comparative literature registers is an essential *indiscipline* at the very core of this concept, but not an *indiscipline* that can be simply accorded the value of alterity with respect to the Enlightenment and modernity—as if the "rationality" of the Enlightenment and the modernity it inaugurates could be confined to an exclusion of alterity. But to bring this force of *indiscipline,* this impossibility we would know as alterity, out of its confinement by modernity—is this not already the still most essential gesture of modernity? Let us not forget that modernity is itself founded on impossibility, as Winckelmann put it, the impossibility of imitating an inimitable antiquity.

In this impossibility, modernity founds its future as what is other to antiquity, founds itself as the possibility of what would be, in effect, an other antiquity, our future antiquity, our future anterior. Such a modernity is an unfailingly comparative project: it originates in an unflattering comparison of itself to antiquity, and it aims at achieving the comparability of itself to antiquity to the extent that it would supplant antiquity. The apparent unraveling of this project, so easily assignable to what we call postmodernity, does not, however, mean that we have crossed over and therefore crossed out of the comparative logic so essential to the founding and continuation of this project. Rather, it means that the incomparability assigned to antiquity is the impossibility on which modernity is founded. Modernity did not compare itself to what was incomparable but only to what was *conceived* as incomparable, and it did so by means of comparison. Because such incomparability is complicit with comparison, the impossibility it represents is already claimed by comparison. This is the comparative logic that drives our modernity—even beyond itself. To cross over or out of this logic by invoking the impossible is to subscribe to this logic one more time. Our modernity is, in effect, founded on the invocation of its impossibility. No postmodernity escapes this logic; it is also its foundation, or, as an indifferent postmodern would have it, its foundation without foundation, its impossible foundation.

Wherever impossibility is invoked, the comparative project of modernity is never far away. Within the humanities, the history of comparative literature has expressed this project more purely than other "disciplines." Whether this takes the form of the impossibility of defining this field of study (which can then become a definition of itself as a discipline), the impossibility of knowing a world for world literature (which then sustains an intensive analogy), or alterity as impossibility (which then claims a planet in a strategic displacement of the world), each authorizes the comparative project in terms of an impossibility that becomes ever more radical (radical also meaning ever more extensive here). This is not just any impossibility but an impossibility that institutes literature and the reading of literature as the medium in which the possibility of the humanities is to be defined and redefined and re-redefined again precisely because, at its core, it preserves its impossibility like a talisman ensuring its future, ensuring that it can always be compared.

Such impossibility is the guardian of comparison. Between old and new, Europe and the world, again and again. It is thus through the articulation of its own impossibility that comparative literature survives until a periodic crisis, as arbitrary as Schiller's nations, announces that it is time to find something new to compare itself to, one more time. And where do we find this comparison nowadays if not in the impossible other—an other commensurate with, but not other to, impossibility? But what is *this* impossibility if not a discipline in its *indiscipline?* What is comparative literature if not a discipline transfixed with, and distracted by, the totality of its impossibility as well as the infinite task of translating and transforming this impossibility, a discipline only able to survive in the failure of its own inmost tendency, and nowhere more spectacularly, as Hegel already knew and was fond of pointing out, than after the owl of Minerva has taken flight?

Transfixed and distracted by its own history, comparative literature is forced to radicalize its own acts of comparison. Yet comparative literature is not alone in this radicalization. In honor of postmodernity's hyper-reflexiveness, it is now a tendency within the humanities to transform its own impasses into the reason for their existence. Thus, the humanities prepare themselves for the role of alterity within the university of late capitalism, but an alterity appropriated and determined into impossibility—in effect, a determined impossibility, an impossibility that now affords their last gasp possibility.

It is in this last gesture, both radical and extreme, that a world whose future is staked on comparison can be read as the gesture toward an impossibility in which the promise of alterity is always made. But can Europe, the world, or even the planet ever lay claim to such a promise without subjecting alterity, making it a subject of analogy, giving it the voice of impossibility, essentializing impossibility to authorize comparison? Alterity, finally comparable, contained? Can there be any comparison for alterity? If this promise can never be made without such a subjection, then comparative literature could, of course, be rightly described as a discipline of exile. It can be nothing other than the discipline that produces itself by exiling itself from a place whose impossibility will always affirm its exile. Such a comparative literature can have no other task than to produce something from which it is permanently exiled while thematically repeating that exile in the form of one nation or another, one continent or another.[7] And what could fulfill that permanent exile more spectacularly than exile itself? To be exiled, not from a nation or a continent, but from exile itself? And what could be more reassuring than this hyper-reflexive situation in which our modernity preserves itself as its failure, as its postmodernity? What can be more comforting (or a better example of undisciplined thought) than to claim that, in our relation to exile, we also find ourselves in the state we say we are exiled from? And yet, as we rely upon this dialectical extrication, can we really claim that Hegel is a thing of the past?

In its history, this "exile" of comparative literature has taken various forms: the "standard" of Levin; the absence of definition in both Meltzl and Wellek; more recently, the extensive knowledge of a world; and finally, impossibility. To have come to this point is to have named the concept that appears with greater and greater insistence in each of these manifestations. Whether coming to this point marks the death of a discipline or whether it marks one more instance of a project whose (predictably impossible) object is its only promise of survival remains to be seen (remains, since this is the logic of comparative literature, its *indiscipline*)—and will be seen when it arrives yet again ten years from now when "the status of the discipline" is interrogated once more. We should expect as much; after all, art did not end with Hegel—and, unfortunately, neither did Hegel.

The question is whether comparative literature can take up the question that the project of comparison has historically been unable to confront, the question of an incomparable impossibility, an impossibility without condition, an impossibility no longer understood from the perspective of the possibility of a discipline or field of study, an impossibility that is no more than a lack of discipline.[8] To take up this question is to take up the issue of where and from what position literature, the other word in this "discipline," can still be thought within late modernity—assuming, of course, that literature no longer needs to be exiled in the politics of representation or in the politics of comparison through which modernity exacted its revenge on antiquity, an assumption that will be as difficult to resist as it is to pursue. In pursuing this question, it is worth remembering that, strictly speaking, alterity can have no analogy, not even an impossible one. To bring such alterity within the sphere of comparison is to refuse such a question in order to confine the humanities to the possibility of an impossible future and an equally impossible past: an alterity whose impossibility is only too possible.

That comparative literature should have pursued this impossibility as the most essential characteristic of its history as well as its future affords us an opportunity to reflect on the project to which the humanities belong as well as the seduction of its unending impossibilities. But to fall prey to this seduction over and over again indicates that our values have not yet suffered their fullest transvaluation but remain caught within the comparative logic that sustains our modernity even as we proclaim its demise. To fall prey to this seduction is also to confirm the extent to which we still, despite our modernity, define literature and its interpretation in terms of its possibility—precisely the definition that allowed Aristotle to overcome the impossibility Plato laid at the door of the poetic. For Aristotle, what Plato dismisses as the impossibility of the poetic (its inability to distinguish between representations of what exists and what does not, what is real and what is only possible) becomes the source of its value: in Aristotle's hands the poetic is not confined to dealing with what is or what already exists, but with what could exist, what is possible.[9]

Whether the study of literature can give up the comparative logic that sustains this history and find its critical significance within the transformation of the university remains to be seen.[10] It is still there, more than anywhere else—more than Europe, the world, or the planet—that the most decisive intervention awaits us. Otherwise, our significance will be *as* a thing of the past, surviving our own end through the promise of its repetition while embracing, as Baudelaire put it when he describes in "Le Cygne" that distant moment of modernity figured in Andromaque's exile, "ce Simoïs menteur"—an old world made new, again, the essential gesture of our modernity, this comparative project and its self-inflicted *indiscipline*.

To begin to interpret this project and its hold on the disciplines of the humanities is to promise a future that is neither a thing nor the past, and it is to make this promise while refusing to displace the question of literature into what literature is said to represent, reflect, or imitate, that is, into the past of all the things it has been compared to. To understand the difference between this displacement and its interpretation is to understand why there has been such a thing as comparative literature as well as why this field suspends itself before the prospect of the humanities and their discipline. And, to understand this difference, is it not also to understand the question posed by a criticism without condition, an interpretation without condition, in short, literature, that is, a literature no longer confined to the *indiscipline* of being compared to the impossible?

1. The most recent report by the MLA on enrollment trends in foreign languages and literatures has registered a slower rate of decrease if not an equilibrium. These indications are hard to
interpret in any prognostic way, however, since the last few years have also registered significant
increases in the overall enrollment at many universities and colleges. If the overall enrollment
increases by, say, 10 percent, but enrollment figures in some departments remain the same or
show growth less than 10 percent, then even an increase in the overall number of students
studying a particular language cannot conceal a decreased overall demand for that language
amongst current students. The most recent report by Elizabeth B. Welles, "Foreign Language
Enrollments in the United States Institutions of Higher Education Fall 2002," does not reflect
this issue, nor is it yet able to interpret fully the consequences of expanding the definition of
foreign language to include American Sign Language (which has had a statistically significant
effect on undergraduate enrollment in foreign languages since it accounted for 21,613 students
in 2003, up from 852 in 1995).

As always in such reports, the statistics need to be interpreted with care, particularly when
read from the perspective of a discipline such as comparative literature that intensively emphasizes graduate study. In this respect, Table 2a (Welles 2004) provides a salutary picture of
languages that have either sustained increases or have remained at roughly the same level of
enrollment for undergraduates in four-year colleges but have experienced a significant drop
in graduate enrollment. At the graduate level, between 1995 and 1998 there were significant
enrollment declines in French (29%) and German (30%); however, both experienced lesser
declines between 1998 and 2002 (French, 5%, German 4.5%). A different picture occurs at the
undergraduate level though: German increased slightly between 1998 and 2002, while French
continued to decrease but at a lesser rate. Graduate enrollment in Italian increased by 13% between 1998 and 2002 after dipping between 1995 and 1998; it also showed a significant increase
at the undergraduate level between 1995, 1998, and 2002 (up by 43%). Asian languages (Chinese,
Korean, and Japanese) all showed significant increases in undergraduate enrollment between
1995, 1998, and 2002; but at the graduate level, all registered declines between 1998 and 2002
(Chinese declined 23.5%, Korean declined 36%, and Japanese declined 30%). Overall, graduate
enrollment in foreign language departments between 1998 and 2002 increased by 11.9%, but
this was still not enough to make up for a decline of 15.2% between 1995 and 1998. This 11.9%
increase results from enrollment growth in Ancient Greek (35%), Arabic (20%), Hebrew (56%),
Italian (13%; in 2002 Italian returned to its 1995 level), Latin (17%; in 2002 Latin also returned to
its 1995 level), Spanish (10%), and other languages (50%). Of these languages, Hebrew, Ancient
Greek, and Spanish account for an increase of 4,457 students at the graduate level between
1998 and 2002. Although the languages experiencing the next largest increases were significant
percentage-wise (Arabic, Italian, and Latin), they only yielded a net increase of 359 graduate
students. The group "other languages" showed an increase of 601 students for the same period
after falling between 1995 and 1998. While these gains amount to a total of 5,417 additional students at the graduate level, they are offset by losses or zero growth in the other languages, so that
the net gain for all languages is 3,912 students. This means that, in languages other than Hebrew,

Ancient Greek, Spanish, Arabic, Italian, Latin, and the group "other languages," a decline in the order of some 1,505 students was experienced.

If we concede that the university has now become an enrollment-driven entity, the advice these figures could be said to offer to comparative literature would follow (with some expansion, although for different reasons) what Alexandre Kojève is reported to have given a group of radical students in 1968: learn Greek. On the strength of the percentages just cited, we would now say: learn Hebrew too. Despite high percentage increases in Latin, Italian, and Arabic, the numerical increase for these three languages is very small (Italian gained 122 graduate students; Latin, 151; and Arabic, 86) when compared to Hebrew and Greek (gains of 1,991 and 1,562 graduate students respectively). But statistics and institutional pressures aside, the question remains: is the fate (and therefore the definition) of comparative literature only tied to the fate of foreign language teaching in the United States?

2. On this anecdote concerning the appearance in a graduate student's dream of Harry Levin dressed as a plumber, see Peter Brooks's response to the Bernheimer report, "Must We Apologize?" Brooks recounts the story as follows: "A persistent piece of graduate student lore at Harvard in the early 1960s concerned the dream of a student in comparative literature on the eve of his oral exams. The doorbell rang, the student stumbled from bed, opened the door, and found himself faced with Harry Levin and Renato Poggioli (the two professors in the department) dressed as plumbers, carrying pipe wrenches and acetylene torches, who announced: 'We've come to compare the literature'" (Brooks 1995, 97).

3. Marjorie Perloff, in an essay included in the Bernheimer volume, also returns to this sentence and comments: "This is the malaise that has haunted comparative literature from its inception and that continues to bedevil it in the 'age of multiculturalism'" (Perloff 1995, 178).

4. To this may be added a recent anthology of essays on the subject of world literature: *Debating World Literature,* ed. Christopher Prendergast (London: Verso, 2004).

5. It is not only in the world that this extensiveness is given expression. The difference that distinguishes comparative literature from national literature study is marked by extensiveness—and to such an extent that comparative literature must pursue this extensiveness as the sign of its distinction while lamenting the difficulty this poses for its self-definition.

6. That "crossing" is the rhetorical banner of our age can be implied from the number of books published within the last ten years that contain either "crossing borders" or "crossing boundaries" or some variation of these words as part of their titles—not to mention the numerous conferences that take "crossing" in one form or another as their thematic focus.

7. If, as Emily Apter recalls in her contribution to the volume of essays sparked by the Bernheimer report, it is only through a Europe experienced in exile, experienced in a foreign context, that comparative literature is established in the United States, then what is at stake in the world of our comparative exile is the fragmentary experience that Schiller perceives in nationhood. To speak of the nation in this fragmentary way is to recognize that a nation, in order to be recognized as a nation, is already in a relation of exile to itself. Isn't this why exile, whether internal or external, has had such a long history as a punishment for dissidence? Through the ability to exile, the state acclaims its existence as a state.

8. It is in this sense that Derrida has broached the question of the future of the humanities in his text "The Future of the Profession or the University without Condition" (2001). The

sense of the impossible developed by Derrida in this text is not something calculated to resist the progress of the humanities and thereby define them in terms of what is always possible (an impossibility understood only from the perspective of a "masterable possible" [53]). Rather, Derrida poses the question of what happens, of what future the humanities will face, once the possibility they have pursued loses its condition, becomes impossible. Here the impossible is no longer thought of as a resisting force against which the possibility of a field or discipline within the humanities articulates itself. For Derrida, the impossible marks the limit where what arrives without condition, without calculation, therefore without comparison, can take place with all the singularity of an event. For Derrida, it is at such a point that the humanities and the university that fosters them are "in the world" they are "attempting to think" (55). Since the singularity of this event requires a future that is no longer simply possible or impossible, it opens a project for the humanities in terms of a future that is not just confined to the impossible and is therefore not just enclosed within the humanities and their history. The task of the humanities, then, is to think about the nature as well as the consequences of a limit that not only makes the humanities *possible* but that also opens the humanities to a future no longer subject to what they have been—not to mention the comparative project according to which they have been organized.

9. In the *Poetics,* Aristotle refers to the production of what could exist (*tà dunatà:* possible, potential things [see 1451a36–38]) as the essential role of the poet. On the fundamental importance of a concept of possibility to Aristotle's founding of our critical history, see David Ferris, "The Possibility of Literary History," in *Theory and the Evasion of History* (Baltimore: Johns Hopkins University Press, 1993), 1–36.

10. That comparison inaugurates the value of literature and art after Plato becomes apparent in Aristotle's explanation of the causes of mimesis: "The reason why we enjoy seeing likenesses is that, as we look, we learn and infer what each is, for instance, this because of that [*hóti hoûtos hekeînos*]," *Poetics* 48b17.

WORKS CITED

Bernheimer, Charles, ed. 1995. *Comparative Literature in the Age of Multiculturalism.* Baltimore: Johns Hopkins University Press.

Brooks, Peter. 1995. "Must We Apologize?" In *Comparative Literature in the Age of Multiculturalism,* ed. Charles Bernheimer, 86–106. Baltimore: Johns Hopkins University Press.

Damrosch, David. 2003. *What Is World Literature?* New York: Columbia University Press.

Derrida, Jacques. 2001. "The Future of the Profession or the University without Condition." In *Jacques Derrida and the Humanities,* ed. Tom Cohen, 24–57. Cambridge, UK: Cambridge University Press, 2001.

Greene, Roland. 1995. "The Greene Report, 1975." In *Comparative Literature in the Age of Multiculturalism,* ed. Charles Bernheimer, 28–38. Baltimore: Johns Hopkins University Press.

Levin, Harry. 1995. "The Levin Report, 1965." In *Comparative Literature in the Age of Multiculturalism,* ed. Charles Bernheimer. Baltimore: Johns Hopkins University Press.

Meltzl de Lomnitz, Hugo. 1973. "Present Tasks of Comparative Literature." In *Comparative Literature: The Early Years,* ed. Hans-Joachim Schulz and Phillip H. Rhein, 53–62. Chapel Hill: University of North Carolina Press.

Nancy, Jean-Luc. 2002. *La création du monde ou la mondialisation.* Paris: Galilée.

Perloff, Marjorie. 1995. "'Literature' in the Expanded Field." In *Comparative Literature in the Age of Multiculturalism,* ed. Charles Bernheimer, 175–86. Baltimore: Johns Hopkins University Press.

Schiller, Friedrich. 1943–2003. *Schillers Werke.* Edited by Julius Petersen and Gerhard Fricke. 42 vols. Weimar: Böhlaus.

Spivak, Gayatri. 2003. *Death of a Discipline.* New York: Columbia University Press.

Wellek, René. 1963. "The Crisis in Comparative Literature." In *Concepts of Criticism,* ed. Stephen J. Nichols Jr., 282–95. New Haven, Conn.: Yale University Press.

Welles, Elizabeth B. 2004. "Foreign Language Enrollments in the United States Institutions of Higher Education Fall 2002." *ADFL Bulletin* 35.2 (Winter 2004): 1–20.

CHAPTER SEVEN

Cultivating Mere Gardens?

Comparative *Francophonies*, Postcolonial Studies, and Transnational Feminisms

FRANÇOISE LIONNET

"We are going, first, to bring Greece to its knees," Pyrrhus said.

"And then?" asked Cinéas.

"Then we'll annex Africa."

"After Africa?"

"We will move on to Asia to conquer Asia Minor and Arabia."

"And then?"

"We'll go all the way to the Indies."

"And after the Indies?"

"Ah!" said Pyrrhus, "then I am going to rest."

"Then why," asked Cinéas, "don't you just rest right now?"

—*Simone de Beauvoir,* Pyrrhus et Cinéas

Soleil levé, soleil couché, the days slip past. . . . But I shall die here, where I am, standing in my little garden. What joy!

—*Simone Schwarz-Bart,* The Bridge of Beyond

I must confess to feeling a bit like Cinéas with respect to comparative literature's conquering Pyrrhus. Our discipline's protean reach makes it a bit harder now to take a "position" with regard to its best practices and the new "projects" that we might formulate. Over the past two decades, we have redefined comparative literature and its neighbor disciplines in such broad-ranging ways as to be left wondering whether there are any more territories to explore, any fresh landscapes to invest, any new spaces of comparison to lay siege to. Haun Saussy points out in his contribution to this report that our field has "won its battles . . . our conclusions have become other people's assumptions. . . . But this victory brings little in the way of tangible rewards to the discipline. . . . Our way of thinking, writing, and teaching have spread like a gospel and not been followed . . . by an empire."

We seem to be the victims of our own success: but successful all the same. If we are to use military metaphors, then let's boast that ours has been a peaceful conquest in which *we* have been transformed just as much as we have influenced those disciplines across whose critical terrains we have traveled. Comparatists now do, inter alia, what francophonists, anthropologists, sociologists, musicologists, women, or ethnic studies folks have been doing for quite some time. But comparatists also lead the way and provide examples of good practice for burgeoning global studies programs that are scrambling to move international relations out of obsolete "area studies" models and into sophisticated transnational approaches that are not reductive, market-driven, or propelled by rational choice theories.

So perhaps it is time to "just rest," as Cinéas suggests to Pyrrhus? To rest, if not exactly on our imperial laurels, still with the not insignificant comfort of knowing that we have accomplished a global mission, and that the time may have come to let our own smaller gardens bloom?

Comparative literature *is* what its various practitioners do—it is the sum of its many parts. And now I am not entirely sure that having a "report" that takes the temperature of the discipline is such a wise idea. . . . Does one take the temperature of a healthy body? I think the field *is* healthy, but somehow, we feel insecure about the many directions in which specific programs or individual comparatists tend to go these days. So we look for standards, for examples of good practices—in other words, for "norms." Gayatri Spivak has called for a "new" comparative literature that would take over—and transform—some of the approaches of the old area studies while maintaining the value of "teleopoiesis," of slow literary reading, of an understanding of the multiple and ambiguous forms of meaning-making that are the domain of the "literary." While I agree completely with the need both to include a diversity of languages and to stress the importance of the "literary," or the slow "reading and teaching of the textual" (Spivak 2003, 101), I am uneasy about any kind of prescription that purports to be "planetary" and proposes that we imagine (only now?) a "drastic epistemic change" (87). Such epistemic changes have been on the horizon for quite some time, provided we take notice of what is actually going on in the field and take into account the alternative modernities that many scholars and writers have foregrounded in their own work.[1]

The theoretical tools that comparative literature scholars have borrowed and honed, and that everyone now utilizes and transforms, have countless good uses. But some tools may be best suited for more minimalist purposes. That's why comparative literature's uncanny success at bringing the whole world within its purview makes me just a bit chary. So let me turn to Simone de Beauvoir for existential reassurance. Borrowing from Plutarch's *Lives* in her *Pyrrhus et Cinéas* (1944), de Beauvoir struggles to understand the point of our actions, the justification for going on when goals become diffuse and our freedoms are infinite. "Why stop there? Why not go further? What's the point?" (10), she imagines Cinéas would ask. Why act if the end is only (eternal) rest (or lethal budget cuts? . . .). She finds the beginnings of an answer in Candide's famous injunction: "We must cultivate our own garden," which she relates to the Gospels' "Who is my neighbor?" arguing that it is by our actions and our choices that we create both gardens and communities, put ourselves in ethical relation with others, and can develop a vision of future possibilities that might simply be a cyclical, seasonal return to unfinished business, rather than the teleological progress toward new conquests and transcendent viewpoints (10, 12, 122).

I am not convinced that we need prescriptions—just encouragement to keep on doing what we collectively do in our respective gardens. My own garden of choice has always been comparative francophone postcolonial and feminist studies, although the coupling of "francophone" and "postcolonial" is a rather recent phenomenon. These still rather distinct fields have much in common but do not quite speak the same language. And I would argue that there is much disciplinary "unfinished business" between these two domains on the one hand, and gender studies on the other.

In their introduction to *Postcolonial Theory and Francophone Literary Studies,* H. Adlai Murdoch and Anne Donadey make some illuminating comments on the points of intersection among these three areas. Focusing on questions of language and translation, they note that whereas the "*imperium* of English" (Spivak 1993, 277) has led to uneven development and unfortunate misreadings of the fundamental critical and cultural parameters of *francophonie,* the translation of influential postcolonial theorists into French also lags behind, thus resulting in their neglect both in France and in the broader francophone world. "The point of entry of postcolonial theory into francophone studies," they suggest, "has been primarily through postcolonial feminist theory," even if few francophone studies scholars took up "the term *postcolonial*" in the 1990s, or if they did, it was often "simply as a temporal marker" without the theoretical apparatus it implies (Donadey and Murdoch 2001, 8). This insightful remark goes a long way toward explaining some of the difficulties that have delayed the *rapprochement* of the two fields.

Indeed, if feminism has been the ground of their mediation in the U.S. academy, such a foundation is not available in literary and critical practice in France and the broader francophone world, where feminism has never played a central role. In the United States, postcolonial studies has been notoriously anglocentric, except when making use of the writings (in poor translations) of figures like Fanon or Memmi, who have been appropriated and often misunderstood, to the point where some students do not even realize that they actually wrote in French! But as Charles Forsdick and David Murphy have stressed, postcolonial studies must now become "truly comparative if it is to develop itself up to, among others, French, Dutch, Spanish, Belgian, Portuguese, Japanese, Turkish experiences." To which they add this cautionary note: "As the rhetoric of empire seems increasingly to occupy a prominent place in public discourse, the urgency of such a project becomes ever more apparent" (2003, 14). Linguistic parochialism is beginning to crumble, so let's rejoice in the fact that the campus victories of comparative literature are of a more honorific than imperial nature—ours is an influential *succès d'estime.*

Due to the theoretical fortunes of "French feminism" in the 1970s and 1980s, comparatists in the United States and Britain were attuned to French feminist research even as it evolved and interacted with Anglo-American and other "ethnic" feminisms. An ideal terrain for the rise of interdisciplinarity in the U.S. academy was thus created. That was decades before comparative literature and cultural studies began to claim interdisciplinarity as their own. If the three main "French" feminist critics, Cixous (born in Algeria), Irigaray (born in Belgium), and Kristeva (born in Bulgaria) continue to be studied by U.S. scholars, their own work has since moved in new and sometimes unexpected directions, whereas vocal critics of their poststructuralist and dialectical methods have pointed to the limitations of these approaches in a multicultural or multiracial context. Their focus on language and psychoanalysis, in particular, led to charges that these theories ignored history as well as social realities and could not account for agency in the individual subject.[2]

During the 1980s and 90s, intellectual and political engagements between different "schools" of feminist theory and the fields of "postcolonial, indigenous, and emergent" feminisms played themselves out in the pages of such journals as *Yale French Studies, Signs, Genders, Critical Inquiry, differences, L'Esprit créateur, Studies in Twentieth-Century Literature,* and *Callaloo,* to name but a few.[3] Today, "feminism" continues to expand as an academic discipline in the United States. In many institutions, women's studies and gender studies have large undergraduate majors and important M.A. programs. Furthermore, doctoral programs have been instituted at a growing number of research universities, from the University of Minnesota to UCLA.

In France, by contrast, many intellectuals today take a very negative view of "feminisms," as evidenced by Elisabeth Badinter's *Fausse route* (2003), in which the former women's rights activist now accuses feminists of seeing "victims" everywhere, arguing that this tendency is in part the result of twenty-five years of (damaging) radical American feminist influence (*à la* Andrea Dworkin and Catharine MacKinnon).[4]

Badinter thus seems unaware of the vastly more complex debates that have since flourished in gender studies, from the focus on performance and performativity to the widely negative reviews of universalizing tendencies implied by some Western versions of feminism, not to mention Judith Butler's 1994 critique of MacKinnon's "structurally static account of gender, its pro-censorship position, and its falsifying cultural generalizations about the eternally victimized position of women" (15).[5] Indeed, Butler's *Gender Trouble* has recently been translated into French.[6]

There is only one program of "études féminines" in France: Hélène Cixous's at Paris VIII-Vincennes, and its future is perpetually in question. All too often, due to the time lag (and disinterest) in translating the most current theoretical works of U.S. feminists and postcolonial theorists, French intellectuals are "en retard d'une guerre" (one war behind), as we say, when it comes to understanding the issues and engaging with the existing debates and internal critiques within these disciplines, whether the topic is the "war of the sexes" or the "culture wars." Like feminism, "ethnic studies" is viewed in France as a political field, based in narrow communitarian ideologies, too earnest and too "PC" to be worth the intellectual effort required to understand what it has contributed to the transformation of our contemporary *mentalités*.[7]

When postcolonial and ethnic studies have made inroads in the French academy, it has been in departments of English and American studies, and more recently in some comparative studies programs such as those of Paris IV and Lille. There the intellectual, literary, and cultural history of the English-speaking world is part of the curriculum, and scholars are better informed about U.S. multiculturalism and British, Indian, or Australian postcolonial contexts. It is thus worth noting that several scholars of *francophonie* working today in the United States were first trained in departments of English and American studies in France and then arrived in the U.S. already familiar with American ethnic literatures and the political theories and critical methodologies that differ markedly from those used most often by scholars trained in departments of French or comparative literature in France or elsewhere. The paradox and difficulty, therefore, for comparative francophone studies arises from its natural "affinity" with a broad range of debates about nationalism, colonialism, immigration, diaspora, identity, orientalism, "subalternity," and transnationalism—debates that have so far had little or no purchase in literary studies in France, where formalism is still pretty much de rigueur. The tendency there seems to be more toward "integrating" the complex ethnic, cultural, and discursive patterns of both the French and the francophone corpus under the broader umbrella of *francophonie*, as one influential anthology has done.[8] Francophone writers who get anointed by Parisian publishing houses and receive critical acclaim followed by major literary awards are the ones who make it into the canon of contemporary literature, and their works generally are subsumed under established national, aesthetic, or formal categories. That is, they become legible in terms of such categories instead of providing an opportunity for a radical rethinking of the existing parameters of formal, let alone cultural, analysis.

But as Edward Said has taught us, it has become imperative, in a multipolar world, "to think through and interpret together experiences that are discrepant" (1993, 32). As he explains in *Culture and Imperialism,* a "comparative, or . . . contrapuntal perspective" can illuminate connections between seemingly disparate entities. He advocates a move "beyond insularity and provincialism . . . to see several cultures and literatures together . . . [as] an antidote to reductive nationalism and uncritical dogma" (43). I would like to suggest that *comparative* francophone, ethnic, and "minority" studies can be such an "antidote" to cultural nationalism and to the theoretical generalizations that lead to an unnecessary opposition between knowledge and culture or theory and literature. This opposition has had the unfortunate result of "feminizing" the expressive cultures of the periphery in relation to the more "masculine" intellectual capital that broad conceptual categories and universalizing theories tend to acquire within the field of comparative literature (be it in the United States or elsewhere). A transversal comparative approach that allows us to link the cultures of decolonization, immigration, and globalization within a conceptual framework that seeks common denominators—while remaining suspicious of simplistic generalizations—can help us go a long way toward a rethinking of the place and nature of theoretical investigation within our discipline. In my collaborative work with University of California colleagues, this is what we have been trying to do in a working group on Transnational and Transcolonial Studies (see Lionnet and Shih 2005).

> An ethics of ambiguity will be one that will refuse to deny *a priori* that
> all separate beings can, at the same time, be bound to one other, that
> their individual freedoms can forge laws valid for all.
>
> *Simone de Beauvoir,* Pour une morale de l'ambiguïté

It is telling that the volume edited by Donadey and Murdoch offers no sustained engagement with feminist discourses as such and no major attempt to investigate the new avenues opened up by transnational feminist ethics, a rubric under which much innovative "First World" and "Third World" feminist theorizing is now being done.[9] Are there no new French or francophone "feminist" writers and theorists to inspire the critics and bridge the gap between Western theories of the subject and new approaches to feminist ethics in our globalized academies? Or have these two modes of inquiry become too "discrepant" in view of the widespread academic indifference to gender studies in France and parts of the francophone world?

Taking my cue from Said's call for a "contrapuntal" reading of "discrepant" spheres of experience, I would like to dwell on the current "disconnect" between feminism and comparative francophone studies, since each indeed has its own "particular agenda and pace of development, its own internal formations, its internal coherence and system of external relationships, all of them co-existing and interacting with others" (Said 1993, 32). By describing the "discrepant experiences" of empire in the preceding terms, Said points to the logic internal to each experience and to the networks that can either connect them or enforce their separation. If gender studies and francophone studies now pursue "parallel tracks," the phrase Donadey and Murdoch (2005, 1) use to describe the trajectories of comparative postcolonial and francophone studies, it may be interesting to ask why and to think about ways of foregrounding their respective blind spots. Is it because we have entered the era of "theory fatigue" (Apter, ch. 3) or because we have reached "the stage of metafeminism" (Finney, ch. 8), as two contributors to this report explain? What can the relationship be between transnational feminist theory and comparative literature? Let me make a first stab at bringing together some elements for further research. An example from contemporary French cinema can explain what I have in mind.

What I find especially compelling in Said's description of "discrepant" spheres is the strong echo that it creates for me with the interpersonal "ethics of ambiguity" formulated by Simone de Beauvoir some fifty years earlier (in 1947). Taken together, Said's and de Beauvoir's perspectives may help to demarcate a fertile terrain for rethinking feminist questions within a transnational or globalized francophone frame. As de Beauvoir states in the epigraph above, "an ethics of ambiguity will be one which will refuse to deny *a priori* that separate beings [*existants*] can, at the same time, be bound to each other, that their individual freedoms can forge laws valid for all" (1947, 26). Her emphasis on "separate beings" resonates with Said's description of "discrepant" experiences, although she is more concerned, as a philosopher, with the individual and the personal, whereas his focus is on culture, intellectual history, and the disciplines. Nonetheless, de Beauvoir's contention that separate or distinct entities can also be "bound to each other" in a way that may subject them to the same "laws valid for all" is an important one for thinking through an existential ethics of coalition and solidarity in a global context. Transnational feminism attaches much value to questions of solidarity, for such an ethics implies that we remain respectful of differences while arguing for universal human rights in a multipolar world. I was thus especially gratified to discover that the latest Coline Serreau movie, *Chaos* (2001), is a witty "case study" of a French bourgeois woman who cannot go on with her "normal" life once she has witnessed the appalling indifference to suffering that characterizes her class.

Serreau's film provides a "transnational" feminist perspective by dealing humorously with serious questions of women's rights. She vigorously denounces the dehumanizing global forces that now contaminate all aspects of our private and public lives. She crafts a tale of friendship and selflessness that foregrounds an ethics of relationality across multiple sites of encounter in which differences are not blurred but become the ground on which solidarity can begin to be conceived. As a deft manipulator of emotions, images, and situations, Serreau gingerly elicits a recontextualization of some important ethical questions faced by postcolonial and feminist theorists today. Using her film as my guide, I propose that we take seriously her portrayal of feminine solidarity and appropriate it for comparative francophone studies in a transnational frame.

In the final scene of the movie, we see four women sitting together in silence on a bench in the oceanfront garden of a beautiful old house, set on what appears to be the coast of Normandy. They are facing the sea, and their faces express different emotions. Two of them are French, and two of them are Algerian-born French citizens. The two immigrant sisters are sitting between the French women. The youngest, Zohra, is frowning, and appears puzzled; while her sister, Malika, has a serious, determined, and thoughtful look. The middle-aged French woman, Hélène, has a vacant stare; while Mamie, her mother-in-law, appears, by contrast, to be quietly blissful. The camera lingers on each face in turn and finally comes to rest on a close-up shot of the beaming white-haired and blue-eyed grandmother, played with understated style by the veteran actress Line Renaud.

The country house in the background might appear to connote the ultimate Franco-French traditional "home" of nationalist literary and cultural history (Balzac's, Flaubert's or Proust's), as it attempts to "integrate" into its midst the immigrant women framed here by Hélène and Mamie. But this venerable mansion is not what it seems. True to Serreau's style of reversing stereotypes and playing with our *idées reçues* (commonly held beliefs), the final shots succinctly make fun of nationalist rhetoric, bourgeois domesticity, and fundamentalist familial arrangements.[10] For the house does not belong to the French women. Rather, it was just purchased by Malika. She has brought all the women here, and they seem to be facing together an uncertain, hazy, but wide-open horizon of possibilities in the soft light of the setting sun. Granted, the French women "frame" the immigrants, but they are also in the debt of the latter, especially of Malika, who has provided companionship and shared stories during her convalescence.

Chaos is a biting social satire that indiscriminately stereotypes men, Frenchmen as well as Eastern European and Maghrebian immigrants, as being, without exception, uncaring monsters.[11] But Serreau's female characters are not their "victims":

they take charge, fight back, leave "home" in order to create this new and temporary community in a world depersonalized by greed and callousness, globalization and the Internet. Malika is the one who is now in control. She has fulfilled her dream of owning a house by the sea. Serreau's final images seem to suggest that theirs is now a "postcolonial" and "feminist" future. But what that future may be made of is left to our (amused) imagination at the conclusion of this charming, fast-paced, and gyno-centric movie that mixes slapstick comedy with humane dramatic vignettes.

The frantic opening scene of *Chaos* features the upper-class bourgeois couple, Paul and Hélène, as intimate strangers going through their high-velocity morning routine on a background of jazzy techno music by the group St. Germain. By contrast, the peaceful and quiet final shot of transgenerational and transnational "sisterhood" is underscored by the music of J. S. Bach. The Aria from the *Goldberg Variations* plays on. The movie hints hesitantly and amusingly at the dream of a common feminist future in which tradition is not what it seems and where women might achieve a pro-visional form of solidarity that transcends age, race, class, culture, and history. Their very different facial expressions and affects reveal, however, that Serreau's vision is by no means a utopian construction of postcolonial and postpatriarchal harmony. As de Beauvoir might indicate, the women here are presented as "separate beings," "bound to each other" but each with her own particularities and reactions to this unusual state of newfound freedom from alienating familial, sexual, social, or professional relations. As the camera moves from one face to the next, we take in the irreducible subjectivity of each woman, captured in each one's singular look: emptiness (Hélène), puzzlement (Zohra), weariness (Malika), or contentment (Mamie).

The uncertainty and weariness expressed by Malika is contrasted by the peaceful-ness conveyed by Bach's music as the final still shot of Mamie concludes the film and the credits roll. Even though Serreau chose to use only the Aria, one cannot help but think of Bach's fugues, of what Edward Said, in *Musical Elaborations* (1991), called music's utopian vision and its ability to dissolve difference and to underscore a secu-lar form of humanism.[12] According to my Funk & Wagnall's dictionary (which dupli-cates the *Petit Robert* exactly, since the meaning of "fugue" is identical in French and English), the "fugue" is both (1) a musical "form in strict polyphonic style in which a theme is introduced by one part, harmonized by contrapuntal rule, and reintroduced throughout," and (2) an episode or "an interval of flight from reality." This "contra-puntal" quality of the music evokes Edward Said's own use of the term, his call for "contrapuntal criticism" in postcolonial studies in order to achieve a better form of mediation between the West and its Others, the First World and the Third. I would argue that French filmmakers such as Serreau contribute a broad view of postcolonial and gender issues and that they struggle with an *ethical* understanding of their own positionality in relation to the cultures they traverse. Here the subaltern can indeed speak, so long as the transnational encounters occurring on uneven thresholds of power and knowledge (Hélène is a lawyer; Malika, "just" a prostitute with business savvy) do not repress differences, if only for the moment of a "fugue."

It is significant that Malika's physical injuries initially leave her paralyzed and speechless—a situation treated with much (respectful) good humor by the film-maker. After Malika recovers the full use of her faculties, Serreau makes her tell her *own* story, bearing witness and sharing her tale in one of the many moments of physical proximity that become a metaphor for the "coming home of solidarity." Hélène's privileged difference (note the homonymy with Cixous's own first name) does not preclude the possibility of being "bound to" another whose individuality, freedom, and agency are separate and radically *other*. Serreau's film, like Cixous's *Les Rêveries de la femme sauvage* (to a certain extent) or de Beauvoir's *Pour une morale de l'ambiguïté*, does not advocate the loss of boundaries between distinct subjects. Rather, it calls for new ways of imagining solidarity and coalition. This might well be a model for our own disciplinary practices as scholars working at the intersection of comparative postcolonial, francophone, feminist, ethnic, and transnational studies, and as scholars who care deeply about the shape of knowledge in a broad context of rights. As Serreau says in an interview, "Most people just don't care. If you take five people on this planet, one is on a diet and four are starving. Yet that doesn't seem to prevent us from going on. What I'm showing in this movie is one person *who can't go on in the old way* [my emphasis]. She's stopped in her tracks" (Abeel 2003). In the end, Hélène has cultivated a personal ethics of the neighbor that creates the conditions of possibility for justifying peaceful, "restful" proximity with others.

Serreau's creative insights add a funny twist to de Beauvoir's existentialist ethics, to recent scholarship in the fields of gender and transnationalism, and to the comparative perspectives of scholars who worry about the moral dimensions of personal and professional encounters. Might Serreau's image of women in an Eden-like garden serve as *one* possible "test bed for reconceiving the ordering of knowledge inside and outside the humanities" (Saussy, ch. 1)? Might it be possible to cultivate mere gardens and find, close to home, an order of things that echoes and opens up global epistemological and ontological concerns?

"Soleil levé, soleil couché . . . ," the owl of Minerva, as we know, needs twilight and *demi-teintes*, stillness and neighborliness. Let's give it a chance to take flight.

NOTES

Translations are mine unless otherwise indicated. Parts of this paper were previously published as "Afterword: *Francophonie,* Postcolonial Studies, and Transnational Feminisms," in *Postcolonial Theory and Francophone Literary Studies,* ed. Anne Donadey and H. Adlai Murdoch (Gainesville: University Press of Florida, 2005).

1. For Francophone writers (such as Assia Djebar or Simone Schwarz-Bart), language has an inherent internal multiplicity, and their borrowings across linguistic and colonial lines cut across the kinds of linguistic "silos" that are the basis for the "world literature" comparative model *and* for area studies. I must admit that Spivak's critique of the limited form of national "destabilization" introduced by "Francophony, Teutophony . . . Hispanophony" (2003, 9) along what she calls "the lines of the old imperialisms" baffles me, for it reveals a limited understanding of the "irreducible hybridity of all languages" that she purports to value and that the postcolonial Francophone, Hispanophone or Sinophone corpus exemplifies time and time again.

2. The first influential anthology of French feminism in the United States was Marks and de Courtivron's *New French Feminism* (1980). See also Moi, *Sexual/Textual Politics* (1985); Fraser and Bartky, *Revaluing French Feminism* (1992); Grosz, *Sexual Subversions* (1989); and Scott, "Universalism" (1995).

3. For example, Spivak, "French Feminism in an International Frame"; a special issue of *Signs* on "Postcolonial, Indigenous, and Emergent Feminisms"; a special issue of *Yale French Studies* on "Post/Colonial Conditions: Exiles, Migrations, and Nomadisms"; a special issue of *L'Esprit créateur* on "Postcolonial Women's Writing"; Woodhull, "Unveiling Algeria"; a special issue of *Studies in Twentieth-Century Literature* on "Contemporary Feminist Writing in French"; and special issues of *Callaloo* on "The Literature of Guadeloupe and Martinique" and on Maryse Condé.

4. Badinter also critiques contemporary French feminist sociology influenced by Bourdieu's concept of male domination. For a scathing review of *Fausse route,* see de Champs 2003. For a more nuanced report, see Remy 2003a, and her interview with Badinter (Remy 2003b).

5. See also other contributors to this special issue of *differences* edited by Butler. An important volume on *Pleasure and Danger* (Vance 1984), published more than twenty years ago, testifies (contrary to Badinter's views) to American feminism's lasting engagement with questions of sex, passion, and pleasure.

6. Judith Butler, *Trouble dans le genre: Pour un féminisme de la subversion,* trans. Cynthia Kraus (Paris: La Découverte, 2005).

7. See Lionnet 1998. For a controversial and critical engagement with postcolonialism in the arts, see Amselle 2003.

8. Jean-Louis Joubert (and a team of collaborators) use this approach in the major anthology *Littérature francophone* (1992). This volume includes works from the sixteenth to the twentieth century, and covers all areas of the francophone world.

9. See the articles by Donchin, Nussbaum, and Nnaemeka in *Signs;* Lionnet and Shih, *Minor Transnationalism;* a special issue of *Signs* on "Globalization and Gender"; Mohanty, Russo, and Torres, *Third World Women and The Politics of Feminism;* Fuss, *Essentially Speaking* and *Inside/Out;* Cheng, *The Melancholy of Race;* Khanna, *Dark Continents;* Stoler, *Race and the Edu-*

cation of Desire; Alexander and Mohanty, *Feminist Genealogies;* Springfield, *Daughters of Caliban;* Smith, *Global Feminisms since 1945;* DeKoven, *Feminist Locations;* Kaplan, Alarcón, and Moallem, *Between Woman and Nation.*

 10. For another look at Coline Serreau's use of stereotypes, see Rosello 1998.

 11. Several women characters are also typecast, for example, the busy, chatty, and distracted nurses or the female university students. One could argue that the main female characters, too, correspond to particular "types"; but my point here is that Serreau never sees any one of them as simply "victims," even as she denounces the sexual exploitation of immigrant women. Her "feminist" vision is thus at odds with Badinter's simplistic view of feminist ideology.

 12. I thank Susan McClary for drawing my attention to this point.

WORKS CITED

Abeel, Erica. "Fast-Paced Feminism; Coline Serreau Talks About *Chaos.*" www.indiewire.com/people/people_030130serreau.html (accessed May 2003).

Alexander, M. Jacqui, and Chandra Talpade Mohanty, eds. 1997. *Feminist Genealogies, Colonial Legacies, Democratic Futures.* New York: Routledge.

Amselle, Jean-Loup. 2003. "Primitivism and Postcolonialism in the Arts." Trans. Noal Mellott and Julie Van Dam. *MLN* 118.4 (September): 974–88.

Badinter, Elisabeth. 2003. *Fausse route: Réflexions sur trente années de féminisme.* Paris: Odile Jacob.

Beauvoir, Simone de. 1947. *Pour une morale de l'ambiguïté.* Paris: Gallimard.

———. 1944. *Pyrrhus et Cinéas.* Paris: Gallimard.

Butler, Judith. 1994. "Against Proper Objects." *differences: A Journal of Feminist Cultural Studies* 6.2–3 (Summer-Fall): 1–26.

Callaloo. 1992. Special issue on "The Literature of Guadeloupe and Martinique." Edited by Maryse Condé. 15.1.

Champs, Emmanuelle de. 2003. "Femmes: fausse route ou marche arrière?" *Le Monde,* May 17, 2003, available on the Web site of the organization Mix-Cité: www.mix-cite.org/communique/index.php3 (accessed May 2003).

———. 1995. Special issue on Maryse Condé. Edited by Delphine Perret and Marie-Denise Shelton. 18.3.

Cheng, Anne. 2001. *The Melancholy of Race: Psychoanalysis, Assimilation and Hidden Grief.* Oxford and New York: Oxford University Press.

Cixous, Hélène. *Les Rêveries de la femme sauvage: Scènes primitives.* Paris: Galilée, 2000.

DeKoven, Marianne, ed. 2001. *Feminist Locations: Global and Local, Theory and Practice.* New Brunswick, N.J.: Rutgers University Press.

differences: A Journal of Feminist Cultural Studies. 1994. Special issue on "More Gender Trouble: Feminism Meets Queer Theory." Edited by Judith Butler. 6.2–3 (Summer-Fall).

Donadey, Anne, and H. Adlai Murdoch, eds. 2001. *Postcolonial Theory and Francophone Literary Studies.* Gainesville: University Press of Florida, 2005.

Donchin, Anne. 2004. "Converging Concerns: Feminist Bioethics, Development Theory, and Human Rights." *Signs: Journal of Women in Culture and Society* 29.2 (Winter): 299–324.

L'Esprit créateur. 1993. Special issue on "Postcolonial Women's Writing." Edited by Elizabeth Mudimbe-Boyi. 33:2.

Forsdick, Charles, and David Murphy, eds. 2003. *Francophone Postcolonial Studies: A Critical Introduction.* London: Arnold.

Fraser, Nancy, and Sandra Bartky, eds. 1992. *Revaluing French Feminism: Critical Essays on Difference, Agency, and Culture.* Bloomington: Indiana University Press.

Fuss, Diana. 1989. *Essentially Speaking: Feminism, Nature, Difference.* New York: Routledge.

———, ed. 1991. *Inside/Out: Lesbian Theories, Gay Theories.* New York: Routledge.

Grosz, Elizabeth. 1989. *Sexual Subversions: Three French Feminists.* Sydney, Australia: Allen and Unwin.

Joubert, Jean-Louis, et al., eds. 1992. *Littérature francophone.* Paris: Nathan.

Kaplan, Caren, Norma Alarcón, and Minoo Moallem, eds. 1999. *Between Woman and Nation: Nationalisms, Transnational Feminisms, and the State.* Durham, N.C.: Duke University Press.

Khanna, Ranjanna. 2003. *Dark Continents: Psychoanalysis and Colonialism.* Durham, N.C.: Duke University Press.

Lionnet, Françoise. 1998. "Performative Universalism and Cultural Diversity." In *Terror and Consensus: The Cultural Singularity of French Thought,* ed. Jean-Joseph Goux and Philip Wood, 119–32. Stanford, Calif.: Stanford University Press.

Lionnet, Françoise, and Shu-mei Shih, eds. 2005. *Minor Transnationalism.* Durham, N.C.: Duke University Press.

Marks, Elaine, and Isabelle de Courtivron. 1980. *New French Feminism.* Amherst: University of Massachusetts Press.

Mohanty, Chandra Talpade, Ann Russo, and Lourdes Torres, eds. 1991. *Third World Women and the Politics of Feminism.* Bloomington: Indiana University Press.

Moi, Toril. 1985. *Sexual/Textual Politics: Feminist Literary Theory.* London: Taylor and Francis Books.

Nnaemeka, Obioma. 2004. "Nego-Feminism: Theorizing, Practicing, and Pruning Africa's Way." *Signs: Journal of Women in Culture and Society* 29.2 (Winter): 357–85.

Nussbaum, Martha. 2004. "Women's Education: A Global Challenge." *Signs: Journal of Women in Culture and Society* 29.2 (Winter): 325–35.

Remy, Jacqueline. 2003a. "Le *J'accuse* d'Elisabeth Badinter." *L'Express,* 24 April 2003. www.lexpress.fr/Express/Info/Societe (accessed May 2003).

———. "L'Homme n'est pas un ennemi à abattre." 2003b. Interview with Elisabeth Badinter. *L'Express* 24 April 2003: www.lexpress.fr/Express/Info/Societe (accessed May 2003).

Rosello, Mireille. 1998. *Declining the Stereotype: Ethnicity and Representation in French Cultures.* Hanover, N.H.: University Press of New England.

Said, Edward. 1993. *Culture and Imperialism.* New York: Knopf.

———. *Musical Elaborations.* 1991. New York: Columbia University Press.

Scott, Joan Wallach. 1995. "Universalism and the History of Feminism." *differences: a Journal of Feminist Cultural Studies* 7.1 (Spring): 1–14.

Signs: Journal of Women in Culture and Society. 2004. Special issue on "Development Cultures: New Environments, New Realities, New Strategies." Edited by Françoise Lionnet, Obioma Nnaemeka, Susan Perry, and Celeste Schenck. 29.2 (Winter).

———. Special issue on "Globalization and Gender." 2001. Edited by Amrita Basu, Inderpal Grewal, Caren Kaplan, and Liisa Malkki. 26.4 (Summer).

———. 1995. Special issue on "Postcolonial, Indigenous, and Emergent Feminisms." Edited by Iris Berger, Elsa Chaney, Vèvè Clark, Joanna O'Connell, Françoise Lionnet, Angelita Reyes, and Mrinalini Sinha. 21:1 (Autumn).

Smith, Bonnie G., ed. 2000. *Global Feminisms since 1945.* New York: Routledge.

Spivak, Gayatri Chakravorty. 1994. "Can the Subaltern Speak?" In *Colonial Discourse and Post-Colonial Theory: A Reader,* ed. Patrick Williams and Laura Chrisman, 66–111. New York: Columbia University Press.

———. 2003. *Death of a Discipline.* New York: Columbia University Press.

———. "French Feminism in an International Frame." 1981. *Yale French Studies* 62: 154–84.

———. 1993. "Scattered Speculations on the Question of Culture Studies." In *Outside in the Teaching Machine,* 255–84. New York: Routledge, 1993.

Springfield, Consuelo López, ed. 1997. *Daughters of Caliban: Caribbean Women in the Twentieth Century.* Bloomington: Indiana University Press.

Stoler, Ann Laura. 1995. *Race and the Education of Desire: Foucault's History of Sexuality and the Colonial Order of Things.* Durham, N.C.: Duke University Press.

Studies in Twentieth-Century Literature. 1993. Special issue on "Contemporary Feminist Writing in French: A Multicultural Perspective." Edited by Laurie Edson. 17 (Winter).

Vance, Carole, ed. 1984. *Pleasure and Danger: Exploring Female Sexuality.* Boston: Routledge & Kegan Paul.

Woodhull, Winifred. 1991. "Unveiling Algeria." *Genders* 10.1: 112–31.

Yale French Studies. 1993. Special issue on "Post/Colonial Conditions: Exiles, Migrations, and Nomadisms." Edited by Françoise Lionnet and Ronnie Scharfman. 82–83.

CHAPTER EIGHT

What's Happened to Feminism?

GAIL FINNEY

If we don't encounter the word *feminism* as much as we used to, I would suggest that this is not because the ideology has vanished but rather because it has proliferated and been assimilated by other theoretical approaches. Feminism is much less literature-specific than most of the other topics explored in this volume, several of which take comparative literature as their point of departure. The heterogeneity of feminist theory may be traced to two developments that began in the 1970s: its transformation into gender studies, and its assimilation of a wide variety of disciplines. Margaret Higonnet acknowledges these developments in her treatment of comparative literature and feminism in this volume's predecessor, *Comparative Literature in the Age of Multiculturalism*, published in 1995:

> A wide spectrum of comparatists, as the Bernheimer report points out, now use methods borrowed from cultural studies, new historicism, feminism, or subaltern studies as they gravitate to localized and historicized models of cultural production. In recent years many feminist critics have likewise sought to move beyond theoretical and historical claims whose universalism masked particularist assumptions, whether national, class bound, or tacitly racial. [...] These critiques have pushed feminists, first, from women's studies toward cross-cultural gender studies, and second, from a generalizing but basically national literary study toward historically anchored comparative analyses.[1]

Similarly, Haun Saussy, in the first chapter of this book, intimates the transliterary purview of feminism in his introduction to the volume at hand: "In disciplinary terms, the 'space of comparison' [quoted from the 1995 Bernheimer report] is mapped out as a result of negotiations that happen in the practices that form the objects of sociology (race, gender, sexual preference), historical geography (the West, the non-West; conditions before and after European colonization), the history of technology (forms of communication, the media of the different arts), and the disciplines that take 'cultural construction' as their concern (anthropology, history, sociology, political science)." Feminism has steadily moved in the direction of openness. To anticipate the argument of this chapter, feminism has progressed, or has continued to progress, from an orientation around binaries to an orientation around pluralities. This evolution may be illuminated by a brief rehearsal of the early stages of feminist literary criticism.

Even in its initial phases, feminist literary criticism was by no means a homogeneous phenomenon; methodological approaches abounded. But feminism can in general be categorized according to whether its point of departure is women as readers or women as writers. The resulting types of feminist literary criticism are aptly described by the terms formulated by Elaine Showalter in her now-classic article "Feminist Criticism in the Wilderness" (1981).[2] The first category, which focuses on images and stereotypes of women in literature, on omissions and misreadings of women in criticism, and on women as signs in semiotic systems, Showalter terms the "feminist critique," famously inaugurated in 1969 by Kate Millett's *Sexual Politics.* The second category (and second phase chronologically), which Showalter calls "gynocritics," is concerned with the history, styles, themes, genres, and structures of texts by women. Showalter goes on to postulate the existence of national tendencies or characteristics in feminist literary criticism: work by British critics is predominantly Marxist, emphasizing oppression; French feminist literary criticism is largely psychoanalytic in orientation, highlighting repression; and American feminist criticism tends to be focused on the text, stressing expression. Although such large generalizations have their problems, this typology does point to differing, decisive intellectual influences in the three traditions—Marx, Lacan, and empirical, anti-metaphysical philosophy in England, France, and the United States, respectively. Comparative literature gets short shrift, but presumably, comparatists can extrapolate.

The genre of tragic drama offers a particularly graphic example of the sexual morphology of "gynocritics": conventional tragedy is associated with the male sexual experience, consisting of foreplay, arousal, and ejaculation (catharsis). Further elements of a tragedy, such as complication, crisis, and resolution, are also linked to phallic experience. By contrast, a feminine form of tragedy, reflecting female sexuality, might have multiple climaxes rather than the dramatic focus on ejaculation or on a single climax. In contrast to drama by men, feminine theater would be characterized by simultaneity rather than linearity, and by multiplicity and fragmentation rather than wholeness.[3]

The ahistoricism of such thinking is evident. Especially in France, "gynocritics" was often taken to extremes, and charges of essentialism frequently undermined this line of theorizing. Although the biological dualism underlying essentialism is an especially striking manifestation of binarism, the "feminist critique," or the critical analysis of images of women in literature, is also based on the male-female duality, even as it is motivated by a desire for sexual equality. A category of work that can be seen to have profited from both of these modes of feminist criticism is what has come to be known as "body theory." Susan Suleiman's rich and diverse anthology, *The Female Body in Western Culture: Contemporary Perspectives* (1986), can, in retrospect, be regarded as a launching pad. Divided into thematic sections on eros, death, mothers, illness, images, and difference, the essays explore the roles the female body has played during the past two millennia, both as an actual entity and as a symbolic construct.

Despite the expectations that might be raised by the term "body theory," work in this field explores, not the inevitable differences between the sexes, but rather the ways in which the body is socially constructed. In *Thinking Through the Body* (1988), for example, Jane Gallop writes against the age-old polarity that associates woman with maternity, the family, sexuality, the domestic sphere—the body—and man with power, knowledge, the public sphere—the mind—and instead concentrates on the ruptures in this dichotomy. Rather than stressing sexual difference, she is interested in the ways in which new acculturation based on knowledge can break through old layers of conditioning based on biology. She warns, for instance, against taking Luce Irigaray's *Ce Sexe qui n'en est pas un* (1977) (*This Sex Which Is Not One*) too literally, purely as a rendering of female sexuality, and advocates instead a symbolic reading in terms of the plurality of modern textuality.[4] Similarly, in *Volatile Bodies: Toward a Corporeal Feminism* (1994) Elizabeth Grosz emphasizes that "the body must be regarded as a site of social, political, cultural, and geographical inscriptions, production, or constitution. The body is not opposed to culture, a resistant throwback to a natural past; it is itself a cultural, *the* cultural, product."[5]

The body's embeddedness in culture is compellingly demonstrated by a rich three-volume collection of essays on the history of the human body edited by Michel Feher.[6] The essays illuminate an eclectic range of perspectives on the body in cultures around the world, drawing on insights from history, anthropology, and philosophy and informed by gender studies. The first volume deals with the relationship between divinity and the human body, including the links between humanity and animality; the second treats psychosomatic relations—the ways in which external bodily features reflect internal states, and the effects of emotions and the erotic on the body; the third volume studies the figurative use of the body, for example, the ways in which bodily organs and substances are used as metaphors for the functioning of society, or the relation between bodies and the status of the individuals they incarnate.

The focus on the sociocultural rather than the physical basis of bodily difference lies at the heart of the gradual supplanting of the term "sex" by "gender" and, concomitantly, of "feminist studies" by "gender studies." One of the most important contributions to the discourse on gender was Teresa de Lauretis's *Technologies of Gender: Essays on Theory, Film, and Fiction* (1987). The title previews de Lauretis's elaboration of gender as a representation constructed by culture—by the schools, the media, the courts, the family, the institutions with which we interact. In this definition she is indebted to the first volume of Foucault's *History of Sexuality*, which illuminates the ways institutions of power have encouraged a discourse of sexuality, albeit one whose taboos and prohibitions produce sexual oppression. Yet in de Lauretis's view, Foucault's theories deny gender insofar as his conception of sexuality is one-sidedly male. Her book supplies a corrective: "*The construction of gender is the product and the process of both representation and self-representation.*"[7] We are represented, and we represent ourselves, as male or female.

The notion of gender as constructed reflects the legacy of poststructuralist thought, a dominant tenet of which is the rejection of essentialism. This line of thinking owes much to the work of Friedrich Nietzsche, in particular to his emphasis on the arbitrary nature of linguistic signs and his equation of truth with perception, which is necessarily relative—ideas argued most pithily in his essay "On Truth and Lying in an Extra-Moral Sense." Elsewhere he associates woman, too, with relativity and the lack of an essence, and he takes the next logical step of equating truth with woman. According to Jacques Derrida, for Nietzsche woman was a "non-identity, a non-figure, a simulacrum."[8] Although such thinking has invited a good deal of critique on the part of feminist scholars, it should be noted that, like many topics, woman is a subject about which one can find varied and even opposing views in Nietzsche's writings.[9]

The anti-essentialism of Nietzsche and Derrida links deconstruction and other modes of poststructuralist thought to comparative literature, in which the tendency has long been to question traditional boundaries, to open up literary genres and traditions, to test conventional definitions. It is possibly for this reason that many comparatists have been more receptive to poststructuralist thought than have scholars of individual national literatures. Similarly, as a transdisciplinary field, feminism has increasingly embraced poststructuralism as it has moved away from essentialism.

From the poststructuralist notion of gender as representation and self-representation, we are only one step away from one of the most influential feminist studies on gender, Judith Butler's *Gender Trouble: Feminism and the Subversion of Identity* (1990). Pursuing the feminist distinction between sex and gender, she writes:

> If gender is the cultural meanings that the sexed body assumes, then a gender cannot be said to follow from a sex in any one way. Taken to its logical limit, the sex/gender distinction suggests a radical discontinuity between sexed bodies and culturally constructed genders. . . . When the constructed status of gender is theorized as radically independent

of sex, gender itself becomes a free-floating artifice, with the consequence that *man* and *masculine* might just as easily signify a female body as a male one, and *woman* and *feminine* a male body as easily as a female one.[10]

Extending this reasoning, Butler claims that "the substantive effect of gender is performatively produced and compelled by the regulatory practices of gender coherence. ... Gender is the repeated stylization of the body, a set of repeated acts within a highly rigid regulatory frame that congeal over time to produce the appearance of substance, of a natural sort of being."[11]

Butler's landmark conception of gender as not only liberated from biological sex but performed, which has been assimilated by theoreticians from a wide range of disciplines, epitomizes the pluralistic direction that feminist studies have increasingly taken. One of the most striking manifestations of this pluralism has been the entrance of men into feminism. This development takes a twofold form that to some extent parallels the shape of early feminist literary criticism: men first as readers and then as subjects of feminist work. The first impulse is represented by male feminist criticism, the second by masculinity studies. The groundwork for the first of these is laid in a by now well-known section of Jonathan Culler's *On Deconstruction* (1982) entitled "Reading as a Woman," which he defines as "to avoid reading as a man, to identify the specific defenses and distortions of male readings and provide correctives."[12] The following two decades witness a rich body of feminist-inspired work by men that, on the one hand, could be seen to ask what it is to be a woman, and on the other, to explore what it is to be a man.

An especially noteworthy example of the first category is *Men in Feminism* (1987), edited by Alice Jardine and Paul Smith. The collection includes Elaine Showalter's often-cited article "Critical Cross-Dressing: Male Feminists and the Woman of the Year" (1983), in which Showalter describes the feminist work of several prominent male colleagues. In addition to Culler's remarks, cited above, she mentions Wayne Booth's self-declared "conversion" to feminist criticism, Robert Scholes's chapter in *Semiotics and Interpretation* on the literary suppression of the clitoris, and Terry Eagleton's Marxist-feminist reading of *Clarissa*. The ambivalence of Showalter's attitude toward male feminist critics—to what extent is this just another power play?—is reflected by association with her reading of the film *Tootsie,* also included in the chapter: "*Tootsie*'s cross-dressing is a way of promoting the notion of masculine power while masking it. ... [*Tootsie*] says that feminist ideas are much less threatening when they come from a man."[13]

Hence, it would seem that during this stage of feminist thinking, men can't win: they are criticized for their obliviousness to women's problems, yet they are received with skepticism when they attempt to see things from women's perspective. Thaïs Morgan organized a special session at the 1988 MLA convention on precisely these issues. Entitled "The Future of Men with Feminism, the Future of Feminism with Men," the session formulated some guidelines in this area. Jardine exhorted the audience to prevent the connection between men and feminism from becoming just another subject of discussion in the academy; Culler warned men practicing feminist criticism against taking themselves as universal subjects, thereby perpetuating exactly the problem feminist approaches attempt to thwart; Leslie Rabine encouraged male feminists to resist the dualistic hierarchies that link men with theory, spirit, and mind, and women with practice, matter, and body; and Scholes wore an apron to emphasize his conviction that "we are all in this together until the job is done."

Paul Smith's ironic claim—as one of a minority of men contributing to *Men in Feminism*—that "men, some men, now . . . are entering feminism, actively penetrating it,"[14] was not welcomed by all feminists. Tania Modleski calls him a "would be 'breaker and enterer'" and criticizes anthologies like this one (bringing together male and female contributors on feminist issues) for "bringing men back to center stage and diverting feminists from tasks more pressing than deciding about the appropriateness of the label 'feminist' for men," for having a "heterosexual presumption," and for promoting a "liberal notion of the formal equality of men and women."[15] Subsequent anthologies on the subject have shown an increasingly sensitive and sophisticated awareness of the issues involved. Joseph Boone and Michael Cadden intimate this development in introducing their collection *Engendering Men: The Question of Male Feminist Criticism* (1990):

> Bringing together a community of male critics whose insights into issues of sexuality and gender have been enabled and empowered by feminist insights, we hope to make more visible the efforts of all those individual men throughout the academy who have already begun the task, perhaps too often in isolation, of reconceptualizing themselves as men and hence as critics of the literary and cultural texts that we have inherited and are in the process of recreating. In engendering ourselves, in making visible our textual/sexual bodies, we thus acknowledge our part in a movement whose time, we hope, has come.[16]

Divided into the categories of "Men, Feminism, and Critical Institutions," "Power, Panic, and Pathos in Male Culture," "Cleaning Out the Closet(s)," and "Revolutionary Alliances: Call and Response Across Gender," the essays in this volume focus on masculine subjectivity, the ramifications of patriarchy, and issues of sexuality. As with most of the work cited in this chapter, the primary texts treated belong primarily to American and English literature; it is the literary theory that reflects a comparative dimension.

Another collection worth singling out for mention is *Men Doing Feminism* (1998), edited by Tom Digby. A mixture of academic and personal, even autobiographical essays, the volume has an eclectic theoretical orientation, containing pieces by male and female feminist philosophers, political theorists, sociologists, scholars of Afro-American studies, and specialists in women's studies. The editor candidly reveals that when he tells people he is a feminist, most respond with acute embarrassment, but with a difference: "With women it's as if I had just announced that I like to wear fuzzy animal slippers, while with men, it's as if I had just said that I am a turnip."[17] If such an avowal smacks excessively of the anecdotal mode, the analogy with racism made by Sandra Bartky in the book's foreword is worth taking to heart in connection with the project of male feminism: just as many whites are repelled by racism and devote considerable energy to combating it, numerous men come to recognize the injustice of sexism and to resist participating in the subordination of half the human race.[18]

Whether one views the activity of male feminist criticism or men doing feminism as their pursuit of the limelight or as a gesture toward solidarity, another reaction to feminism can be recognized at least in part as defensive, the new field of masculinity studies. The line between male feminist work and masculinity studies is often a fine one, and sometimes the same critics engage in both. To cite one early example, Paul Smith's analysis of the ways in which feminist theory can be used to talk about male sexuality points toward masculinity studies.[19] Some interesting historical work has been done in the field of masculinity studies, such as Angus McLaren's *The Trials of Masculinity: Policing Sexual Boundaries, 1870–1930* (1997) or Gerald Izenberg's *Modernism and Masculinity: Mann, Wedekind, Kandinsky through World War I* (2000). Izenberg, for example, argues that Thomas Mann, Frank Wedekind, and Wassily Kandinsky all experience a crisis of masculine identity that directly affects their creativity. He shows that in all three cases the crisis of masculinity is closely related to the artists' conceptions of femininity and that this relationship bears significantly on the "modernism" of their art. Izenberg's study is typical of the way much work in masculinity studies represents a departure from the work of the feminist critique. Many feminist treatments of the turn of the century concentrate on femininity—often types, such as the femme fatale, the femme fragile, the New Woman, and so forth. By contrast, Izenberg's approach, investigating not only femininity but masculinity as well, is pluralistic. Furthermore, whereas (as he points out) earlier discussions of the turn-of-the-century crisis of masculinity are more limited in scope, focusing on either anti-Semitism or fin-de-siècle aestheticism, or relying on very general theoretical frameworks, Izenberg's study is not only multipronged—dealing with both masculinity and modernism—but also interdisciplinary—treating a dramatist, a prose writer, and a visual artist. Hence, this book is of interest to specialists in modernism (in theater, narrative fiction, and painting), in the turn of the century, in gender studies, and in each of the three artists.

While masculinity is only one of the parameters Izenberg studies, a large and growing body of literature takes the concept of masculinity as its point of departure. The recent proliferation of readers such as *The Masculinities Reader* (2001), *Men and Masculinity: A Text-Reader* (2001), and *The Masculinity Studies Reader* (2002) signals the burgeoning of interest in masculinity and its ramifications. The fact that the field of masculinity studies is often referred to as "men's studies" intimates both its separation from and its debt to feminist theory and women's studies—a link explicitly explored by the volume *Masculinity Studies and Feminist Theory* (2002), edited by Judith Kegan Gardiner. With essays studying such issues as the relationships of men, masculinity, and male bodies to feminism and feminist theory; the teaching of masculinity studies; masculinity and feminist mothering theory; masculinity and violence; racial differences in masculinity; and feminist theories of sexual violence and masculine strategies of Black protest, Gardiner's collection constitutes a locus of both conjunction and differentiation for feminist theory and masculinity studies. The solidification of men's studies or masculinity studies as a field is reflected in the existence of journals like *The Journal of Men's Studies,* published by Men's Studies Press; *Men and Masculinities; Men's Studies Review;* and (formerly) *Masculinities.* Research groups and conferences on the subject abound: at my own institution, UC Davis, a faculty research cluster on "Masculinities" thrived for some time during the late 1990s, and several programs cosponsored a colloquium on "Sub-Cultural Fashion and Masculinities" in early 2004.

Insofar as feminism represents a reaction against the inegalitarianism of patriarchy, and insofar as the foundation of patriarchy is heteronormative sexuality, feminism has from its beginnings been linked, both in some of its doctrine and in the popular imagination, with lesbianism. Although it is of course grossly inaccurate to equate feminism with lesbianism, in the early phase of "women's liberation" some viewed lesbianism, in its eschewal of sex with men, as the consummate form of feminism. Hence, there exist attitudinal and often actual links between feminism and queer theory, which poses an even more radical challenge to the heteronormative status quo. While queer theory is not a direct outgrowth of feminism, the theoretical apparatus of LGBTG (Lesbian, Gay, Bisexual, Trans-Gendered) queer theory stems indirectly from the same liberationist-activist moment as feminism—the 1960s and 1970s. And for both feminism and queer theory, the object of scrutiny and revaluation is gender and sexuality. For these reasons I find it appropriate to include a consideration of queer theory, which has become an increasingly more visible and influential presence in literary and cultural studies since the early to mid-1990s, in this chapter on the later development of feminism.

The slang usage of "queer" as a pejorative term for homosexual reflects the word's etymological development from the Low German for "oblique or off-center" into the contemporary German *quer*—"diagonally, sideways, or against the grain"—and the English *queer*—"strange, odd, deviant." A decisive step in the revaluation of "queer" was the formation of Queer Nation in April 1990, which originated in New York City as an offshoot of the AIDS activist group ACT UP in order to thwart the hate crimes against gays that were on the rise in the East Village. The militantly gay, lesbian, bisexual, and transgender members of Queer Nation sought to reinvest "queer" with a positive valence and to energetically publicize this new, productive identity. Although Queer Nation lasted for only two years, it played a crucial role in the dissemination and redefinition of queerness.

A brief look at the recoded term will indicate the ways its meanings have shifted and broadened. In the words of Joseph Bristow and Angela Wilson, *queer* is used as an "enabling point of definition against the extremely narrow identities produced by the hetero-homo binary."[20] Even this short definition, however, reflects the extent to which poststructuralist theory and postmodernist culture, with their skepticism toward binary oppositions, participate in the context of queer.[21] Eve Sedgwick illuminates the broadened significance of the queer project in noting that "intellectuals and artists of color whose sexual definition includes 'queer' . . . are using the leverage of 'queer' to do a new kind of justice to the fractal intricacies of language, skin, migration, state."[22] One of the most far-reaching goals of queer theory is to undermine or denaturalize essentialism of all kinds—as Holger Pausch writes, "to destabilize heterocentrism and its power position as norm-giver, to communicate the fact of its historical construction, to clarify its moral and ethical relativity and incidental structure in the social order, and . . . to break down the barriers of racism, sexism, and homophobia."[23] Michael Warner offers a comparable insight into the multidimensional and far-reaching implications of queer endeavors: "Because the logic of the sexual order is so deeply embedded by now in . . . social institutions . . . queer struggles aim not just at toleration or equal status but at challenging those institutions and accounts."[24] The anti-essentialist, pluralistic, ultimately revolutionary thrust of queer theory, transcending the male-female, masculine-feminine, women's studies–men's studies binaries, is paradigmatically encapsulated in Judith Halberstam's 1998 study, *Female Masculinity*.

If queer theory has been inflected by feminism and gender studies, it has influenced these fields in turn. The case of German studies is representative, as documented by Evelyn Annuss and Robert Schmidt in "The Butler Boom: Queer Theory's Impact on German Women's/Gender Studies."[25] Similarly, the discourse of camp, long associated with gay culture, has profited from elucidation by queer theorists.[26] In a nonscholarly context, undergraduates at UC Davis are working toward the establishment of a minor in Queer Studies, which they hope will have a significant impact on the LGBTG community at the university. And even popular culture has embraced the notion of queer: the success of the television show *Queer Eye for the Straight Guy* is reflected in the fact that it has already been spoofed—in a show called *Straight Plan for the Gay Man*.

Mention of popular culture brings us finally to the phenomenon known as postfeminism. Although the word was coined in the media of the early 1980s and is sometimes traced specifically to a *New York Times Magazine* article of October 1982 entitled "Voices From the Post-Feminist Generation," there is little agreement about what the term actually means. Some postfeminist discourse emphasizes the "post," suggesting that women are no longer oppressed and that feminism has therefore been rendered superfluous. A fairly innocuous definition focuses on the idea that women, especially younger women, can and should be as involved with the Internet as men. But most often the term refers to a conservative reaction against feminism, which is lambasted for its portrayal of women as victims. This anti-feminist impulse has been viewed as a campaign on the part of corporate media, vigorously stimulating women's desire for the endless stream of products that are supposedly necessary to achieve and sustain feminine beauty, and as a backlash against feminism perpetrated on women by popular culture, the government, the medical profession, self-help books, and evangelism.[27]

Perhaps the most compelling conception of postfeminism is one that could be understood as dialectical, combining the accoutrements of traditional femininity with masculine privilege. On an anecdotal level, this is the mode I most often recognize in my female students: they embrace conventional ideals of feminine beauty yet expect that they as women will have equal access to the same institutions, rights, and privileges that their male fellow students do. They reject the label "feminist," but they have internalized—perhaps unconsciously—the goals of the ideology. For educated, largely middle-class women like these, who do not perceive themselves to be victims of sexual inequality, feminism has perhaps indeed been rendered superfluous—in a positive sense.

Globally, practices previously regarded as barbaric toward women are being reassessed. In discussing *sati*, the ritual Hindu practice in which a widow immolates herself on her husband's funeral pyre, Gayatri Spivak takes as her point of departure the case of the Rani of Sirmur, an actual woman in colonial India who was prevented against her wishes from committing *sati*. Employing what might be called deconstructionist detective work, Spivak traces the Rani's history, or lack thereof, to illuminate the ways in which the practice of *sati* is complicated by the imperialist project and the ways in which the narrative of the instrumental woman is elided.[28] Similarly, historian Dorothy Ko has published one volume of a projected two-volume study reexamining the practice of foot-binding in China, in which she neither attacks nor defends the practice but rather seeks to explain it. Her nuanced treatment, presenting the origins and development of foot-binding in terms of women's culture, contends that foot-binding made sense for women living according to a Confucian system of values.[29]

It is possible that feminism has moved to the stage of metafeminism, to judge at least from a very recent study by Lynne Pearce, *The Rhetorics of Feminism: Readings in Contemporary Cultural Theory and the Popular Press* (2004), a stylistic and rhetorical analysis of contemporary feminist theory and journalism. In demographic terms, there is no doubt that in the academy the discipline of comparative literature, like those of English and the other national literary fields, has become feminized: the current president, vice-president, and secretary-treasurer of the ACLA are women, as are six of its ten advisory board members. In an article published in 1991, I expressed the hope that the increasing presence of women in academia could lead to a humanization of the profession.[30] In the interim, the University of California has adopted a policy whereby the tenure clock can be delayed for women because of childbirth, and the maternity leave policy has been expanded so that both partners may take a leave or modified leave of absence to care for a newborn or adopted child. This is a very practical example of the way the impulse of feminism, with its original aim of equality for women, has evolved to the point of breaking down binary distinctions in a way that improves the condition of people of both sexes and of all sexualities. As the academy steadily diversifies, one can hope for a continuation of this process.

NOTES

1. Margaret Higonnet, "Comparative Literature on the Feminist Edge," in *Comparative Literature in the Age of Multiculturalism*, ed. Charles Bernheimer (Baltimore: Johns Hopkins University Press, 1995), 156–57.

2. Elaine Showalter, "Feminist Criticism in the Wilderness" (1981), rpt. in Showalter, ed., *The New Feminist Criticism: Essays on Women, Literature, and Theory* (New York: Pantheon, 1985), 243–70.

3. Cf. Sue-Ellen Case, *Feminism and Theatre* (New York: Methuen, 1988), 129–30.

4. Jane Gallop, *Thinking Through the Body* (New York: Columbia University Press, 1988), 92–99.

5. Elizabeth Grosz, *Volatile Bodies: Toward a Corporeal Feminism* (Bloomington: Indiana University Press, 1994), 23.

6. Michel Feher, ed. with Ramona Naddaff and Nadia Tazi, *Fragments for a History of the Human Body,* 3 vols. (New York: Zone, 1989).

7. Teresa de Lauretis, *Technologies of Gender: Essays on Theory, Film, and Fiction* (Bloomington: Indiana University Press, 1987), 9; emphasis in the original.

8. Jacques Derrida, *Spurs: Nietzsche's Styles / Éperons: Les Styles de Nietzsche* (Chicago: University of Chicago Press, 1979), 49.

9. See, for example, Kelly Oliver, *Womanizing Nietzsche: Philosophy's Relation to the 'Feminine'* (New York: Routledge, 1995); and Peter J. Burgard, ed., *Nietzsche and the Feminine* (Charlottesville: University Press of Virginia, 1994).

10. Judith Butler, *Gender Trouble: Feminism and the Subversion of Identity* (New York: Routledge, 1990), 6.

11. Ibid., 24, 33.

12. Jonathan Culler, *On Deconstruction: Theory and Criticism After Structuralism* (Ithaca, N.Y.: Cornell University Press, 1982), 54.

13. Elaine Showalter, "Critical Cross-Dressing: Male Feminists and the Woman of the Year," in *Men in Feminism,* ed. Jardine and Smith (New York: Methuen, 1987), 123.

14. Paul Smith, "Men in Feminism: Men and Feminist Theory," in *Men in Feminism,* 33.

15. Tania Modleski, *Feminism Without Women: Culture and Criticism in a 'Postfeminist' Age* (Routledge: New York, 1991), 69, 6.

16. Joseph A. Boone and Michael Cadden, eds., *Engendering Men: The Question of Male Feminist Criticism* (New York: Routledge, 1990), 7.

17. Tom Digby, ed., *Men Doing Feminism* (New York: Routledge, 1998), 1.

18. Ibid., xiii.

19. Paul Smith, "Vas," *Camera Obscura* 17 (1988): 89–111.

20. Joseph Bristow and Angela Wilson, eds., *Activating Theory: Lesbian, Gay, Bisexual Politics* (London: Lawrence & Wishart, 1993), 9.

21. See for example, Steven Seidman, "Identity and Politics in a 'Postmodern' Gay Culture: Some Historical and Conceptual Notes," in *Fear of a Queer Planet: Queer Politics and Social Theory,* ed. Michael Warner (Minneapolis: University of Minnesota Press, 1993), 105–42.

22. Eve Sedgwick, *Tendencies* (Durham, N.C.: Duke University Press, 1993), 9.

23. Holger Pausch, "Queer Theory: History, Status, Trends, and Problems," in *Queering the Canon: Defying Sights in German Literature and Culture,* ed. Christoph Lorey and John L. Plews (Columbia, S.C.: Camden House, 1998), 3. For a provocative collection of interdisciplinary essays exploring key issues engaging queer theory at the turn of the millennium, see Joseph A. Boone et al., eds., *Queer Frontiers: Millennial Geographies, Genders, and Generations* (Madison: University of Wisconsin Press, 2000).

24. Warner, *Fear of a Queer Planet,* xiii.

25. Article translated by Silke R. Falkner, Elizabeth Penland, and Cathrin Winkelmann, in *Queering the Canon,* ed. Lorey and Plews, 73–86.

26. See, for example, Fabio Cleto, ed., *Camp: Queer Aesthetics and the Performing Subject: A Reader* (Ann Arbor: University of Michigan Press, 1999); and David Bergman, ed., *Camp Grounds: Style and Homosexuality* (Amherst: University of Massachusetts Press, 1993).

27. See, for instance, Susan Faludi, *Backlash: The Undeclared War Against American Women* (New York: Crown, 1991).

28. Gayatri Spivak, *A Critique of Postcolonial Reason: Toward a History of the Vanishing Present* (Cambridge, Mass.: Harvard University Press, 1999), 227–311.

29. Dorothy Ko, *Every Step a Lotus: Shoes for Bound Feet* (Berkeley: University of California Press, 2001), 15.

30. Gail Finney, "Iphigenie in *Germanistik,* or the Feminization/Humanization of the Profession," in *Rethinking Germanistik: Canon and Culture,* ed. Robert Bledsoe et al. (New York: Lang, 1991), 31–43.

CHAPTER NINE

Writing in Tongues

Thoughts on the Work of Translation

STEVEN UNGAR

Translation is the most intimate act of reading.
—*Gayatri Chakravorty Spivak*

All of this so-called Maghrebian literature of French
expression is an account of translation. I am not
saying that it is nothing but translation; it is a matter
of an account that *speaks in tongues.*
—*Abdelkebir Khatibi,* Maghreb pluriel

The Most Intimate Act of Reading

Consider this a position paper. Translation has remained central to comparative philology as well as to European and North American models of world literature since the early nineteenth century. Yet the centrality of translation within literary studies is at odds with the fact that it often remains under-analyzed and under-theorized. Rather than simply bemoan this condition, I want in what follows to consider how issues surrounding practices of an emergent field of translation studies over the past twenty-five years has contributed to the evolving discipline, discourse, and institutions of comparative literature. To put an edge on this consideration, I want to state from the start that what draws me to translation is less a matter of what it is, and how to do it, than what it *could* and *should* be doing. No poetics of translation, then, without its concomitant politics and ethics.

"No better place to start," writes Haun Saussy concerning literature in translation, where "nothing of the work may survive of the process but the subject matter." The assertion occurs about a third of the way into his introduction to the current ACLA report, during a brief overview of world literature. It precedes a reference to thematic reading as a constant pedagogical temptation and examples of Kafka and "the Kafkaesque" borrowed from David Damrosch in order to illustrate that what works for world literature may not work for close comparative study. Here is Saussy's sentence in full: "But for literature in translation, where nothing of the work may survive the process but the subject matter, there is no better place to start."

What strikes me first in this assertion is how vocabulary and grammar set the second of two dependent clauses apart from the independent clause that completes the sentence. That second clause jumps out at me, grabbing my attention on the order of what Barthes theorizes in *Camera Lucida* as the *punctum*.[1] I am likewise drawn to the terms "work," "process," "survival," and "subject matter," whose convergence discloses a judgment—implied, indirect, and rapid—concerning the process of translation. As used here, the terms "work" and "survive" allude to what translation adds to or detracts from a verbal entity whose designation as "work" connotes an assumption of aesthetic value that presumably warrants survival.

To state the point somewhat differently, I propose that what the clause refers to in terms of process and work is grounded on assumptions of value ascribed in a positive way to the literary work of art at the cost of the specific activity of translation. For I continue to see the literary work first of all as a textual entity (post-1960s Barthes again) whose minimal units of meaning can be analyzed at a level of detail for which aesthetic values such as literariness are secondary. The term "process" likewise also fails to account adequately for the work of the translation. It is *this* work—*travail* rather than *œuvre*, *Arbeit* (or even *Werk*) rather than *Kunstwerk*—for which I want to be an advocate and for which Saussy's remarks provide an apt point of departure. Finally, I admit to a degree of doubt concerning Saussy's contention that the process of translation fails to affect the subject matter that it purportedly conveys. To the contrary, elements of inscription that I take as essential to the work of translation inevitably bear on the nature of a communication as a process that is never direct or transparent.

For the record, I mean to "speak"—actually write—here less as a theorist of translation than as chair of the University of Iowa's Department of Cinema and Comparative Literature, in which former colleagues Stavros Deligiorgis, Gayatri Spivak, Fred Will, and Daniel Weissbort were among the first to teach literary translation in the United States nearly forty years ago. In fact, all of us who study and teach language and literature are comparatists—and even professional foreigners of sorts, in deed if not always by title.[2] George Steiner, for one, has long been an eloquent advocate for a model of comparative literature centered in the eventuality and defeats of translation under the sway of what he calls the multiplicity of languages after Babel:

Every facet of translation—its history, its lexical and grammatical means, the differences of approach that extend from the word-by-word interlinear to the freest imitation or metamorphic adaptation—is absolutely pivotal to the comparatist. . . . It is, furthermore, a close hearing of the failures or incompletions of even the finest of translations which, more than any other means of access, helps to throw light on the *genius loci* as it were, in any language. Labor as we may, *bread* will never wholly translate *pain*. What, in English, French or Italian is *Heimat?*[3]

Steiner's remarks point to the conundrums surrounding translation as an activity engaged with language as the material expression of cultural difference. The terms "failure" and "incompletion" imply the persistence of a model of translation whose virtues would entail precisely overcoming failure and incompletion. Accordingly, a successful and complete translation would presumably be one that succeeded in excluding any and all alternatives. Yet the criteria of such completion would, I believe, be of less interest to Steiner than what a "close hearing" of translation's failures and incompletions might disclose concerning the nature of cultural difference, whose interpretation Steiner identifies elsewhere as the never-ending task of the translator.[4]

Lost in Translation?

The work of translation is often dismissed within literary production as a second-order representation, with the translator accordingly invisible as an extension—faithful or unfaithful—of the original work attributed to the author.[5] Only when a translation reads clumsily in the target language do the figurative eye, ear, and hand of the translator lose their invisibility. Recasting the work of translation instead as rereading and rewriting engaged with the production of meaning counters received understanding in the form of a prejudice that stigmatizes translation as always already derivative.[6] The efforts of translators whose work I use and admire—Richard Howard, Barbara Wright, and Ralph Manheim are among the names that first come to mind—fully warrant parity with that accorded to authors because they succeed in conveying the linguistic specificity of the source text . . . in another language. What is distinctive about such translations is the extent to which they succeed in conveying a sense of a French text in English beyond conventions of prose meaning in the latter language. The fact that these translations in English read ("feel") close to the French results less from their transparency in the target language than in a quality of abusive fidelity located first in the agency of the translator and only secondarily in the attentive reader.[7]

While it may be tempting for the sake of argument to assert the primacy of language over the respective agencies attributed to the figures of author, translator, and reader, a focus on these figures posits the irreducible nature of translation as an act of communication among individuals and/or groups. Such communication obtains even in instances where etymological and historical links between transposition, transfer, and translation conveyed by the Spanish noun *traslado* prompt a convergence of unpaired domains seldom on a par with each other.[8] Recognition alone does not suffice to rectify this lack of parity. But it illustrates the extent to which the work of translation falls all too easily into aspects of contrast rather than comparison. As in the case of the translator's invisibility, interaction between the two domains is often unequal.

The work of translation is most evident in detail and thus in a sensitivity to language and style grounded in poesis and poetics; that is, in the making and critical understanding of how that making occurs. At the same time, translation enters fully into areas of force, influence, and power that set poetics by necessity alongside politics of varying kinds and degrees. To the extent that current usage of the term "globalization" can be understood as including an increase in the circulation of capital—symbolic and cultural as well as material—the import of translation cannot be determined simply by the accuracy, grace, or faithfulness of the product. Instead, it centers, as Gayatri Spivak argues, on choices made by the translator: "In the translation from *French* to *English* lies the disappeared history of distinctions in another space—made by the French and withdrawn by the English—full of the movement of languages and peoples still in historical sedimentation at the bottom, waiting for the real virtuality of our imagination."[9] Spivak's position is, in fact, among the strongest that I have seen in support of what she refers to several pages earlier in the same book as "the irreducible work of translation, not from language to language but from body to ethical semiosis, that incessant shuttle that is a 'life.'"[10]

Exactly what do we mean when we refer to the politics of translation? Jacques Derrida describes translation as a political-institutional problem of the university linked to the values of traditional teaching.[11] Lawrence Venuti characterizes it as a cultural political practice that opens onto ethical dimensions involving greater respect for linguistic and cultural difference.[12] For Sherry Simon, translation is a feminist practice and "a mode of *engagement* with literature necessarily involved in a politics of transmission, in perpetuating or contesting the values which sustain our literary culture."[13] Spivak, Derrida, Venuti, and Simon all seem to agree on the potential of translation to contest received practices and values related to language as communication. Where Derrida emphasizes teaching and the institution of the university, Venuti analyzes power relations at work in the commerce of literary translation whose academic variant he describes as "a deep unwillingness among foreign-language specialists to think about the differences introduced by moving between languages and cultures."[14] Venuti argues forcefully for moving beyond linguistic-based approaches that block the ethical and political agenda of a minoritizing practice of translation. Spivak and Simon follow Venuti while they focus on cultural aspects of identity related to the long history of subjugation (Spivak) and gender as a distinctive construction emerging enunciated at multiple sites (Simon).

What Simon describes as the cultural turn linking translation studies to a feminist practice promotes a change in critical perspective and the foundational questions: "Instead of asking the traditional question which has preoccupied translation theorists—'How should we translate, what is a correct translation?'—the emphasis is placed on a descriptive approach: 'what do translations do, how do they circulate in the world and elicit response?'"[15] Referring to the writings of Spivak, Salman Rushdie, and Homi Bhabha, Simon argues for an altered understanding of translation as an activity "which destabilizes cultural identities, and becomes the basis for new modes of cultural creation" (135). The model that she proposes is that of Third World literature, whose translation into English discloses imbalances inherent in a willful monolingualism and its corollary of a "flat international translatese" wholly inadequate to the transmission of literary and cultural specificity (142). (Spivak makes a similar point when she writes of what happens when "all the literature of the Third World gets translated into a sort of with-it translatese, so that the literature by a woman in Palestine begins to resemble, in the feel of its prose, something by a man in Taiwan."[16])

The questions that Simon raises for translation as a feminist practice and the case studies on which she draws illustrate not just what translations do, but also (and more to the point) what they fail to do. Simon also follows Spivak by extending the politics of translation toward a revised pedagogy affecting the recognition of difference within the postcolonial nation as well as the institutional site of this pedagogy in college and/or university curricula. The logic that links writing, translation, and pedagogy is one of transmission. Accordingly, the prospect of making translation integral to the new comparative literature is most evident in cases that illustrate the limits of current models and practices: that is, when they disclose what translation does as well as what it does *not* do. Simon invokes Christine Brooke-Rose's 1968 novel *Between* and Eva Hoffman's 1989 essay *Lost in Translation: A Life in a New Language* as recording an economy of difference and loss growing out of new forms of postwar internationalism. Without understating the pertinence of Simon's examples, I want to explore how a similar economy of difference and logic of transmission bear on translation faced by Moroccan, Algerian, and Tunisian writers following the formal end of colonization under France in 1962. I take my cue here especially from Abdelkebir Khatibi, Assia Djebar, Abdelwahab Meddeb, and others whose writings disclose a cultural layering that casts their authors as occupying an "in-between" space between Arabic, French, and other languages. To bring this layering back to the level of language, I want to explore how the specificity of enunciation and inscription bears on translation in the context of globalization and difference.

It is helpful to start by distinguishing between the phenomenon of the bilingual (which Khatibi often equates with the pluri-lingual) and conventional usage that posits the former term as fluency in more than one language. Differences between the two usages emerge exactly when the assumptions grounding translation as a finite process no longer obtain in a reading practice that recognizes a core of language that resists translation. Accordingly, the phenomenon of the bi- or pluri-lingual discloses an "infraliminal level of writing and thinking that renders the dualistic opposition that has dominated Maghrebi literary production obsolete."[17] It recasts translation less as a process leading to transparency in the target language than as a confrontation in which multiple languages and cultures square off against each other and "*meet without merging . . . without* a reconciling *osmosis* or *synthesis.*"[18] Curiously, a secondary meaning of the French verb *traduire,* designating the legal phenomenon of bringing someone before a court ("traduire en cours de justice") conveys the adversarial nature of this interaction. It heightens the strategic force that Khatibi grants to the *bi-langue* and *pluri-langue* as a means of disclosing the play of power that always bears on a diglossic condition whose inequality conventional translation all too often glosses over. Retaining the italicized term *bi-langue* in English likewise contends with the corporeal sense of "bi-tongue" or "forked tongue" apart, at a distinct remove, from standard usage of the English word *bilingual.*[19]

For more than thirty years, Khatibi has written decidedly between languages in order to destabilize hierarchies of the colonial period that fixed Arabic language and cultures as inferior to their French equivalents. In *La Mémoire tatouée,* he writes that "at school, with a secular education imposed on my religion, I became a triglot: I read French without being able to speak it, I played with some fragments of written Arabic, and I spoke the dialect as my everyday language. Where in the midst of this confusion is coherence and continuity?"[20]

A decade later Khatibi transforms this condition between languages and cultures into a critical wedge when he writes:

> As long as the theory of translation, the *bi-langue,* and the *pluri-langue* does not advance, certain North African texts will remain impregnable via formal and functional approaches. The mother tongue is at work in the foreign language. Between the one and the other occur a permanent translation and an interchange of infinite recession that is

extremely difficult to elucidate. . . . Where does the violence of the text take shape if not in this cross-over, this intersection that is truly irreconcilable?[21]

As described above, *pluri-langue* and *bi-langue* promote a literary production in which the marks and traces of multiple languages resist traditional translation grounded on binary distinctions between source and target languages. For Samia Mehrez, the *pluri-langue* asserts the untranslatable as a mark of resistance and subversion: "With this literature, we can no longer merely concern ourselves with conventional notions of linguistic equivalence, or ideas of loss and gain which have long been a consideration in translation theory. For these texts written by postcolonial bilingual subjects create a language 'in between' and therefore come to occupy a space 'in between.'"[22]

The evocation of *pluri-langue* and *bi-langue* entails interaction among calligraphies of French and Arabic whose incommensurability Khatibi transforms from deficiency to advantage—he refers to luck, energy, and his third ear—as a performance of writing equated with the force of enunciation. Of Abdelwahhab Meddeb's 1979 *Talismano*, he writes:

> Here the book is torn, sometimes bursting into pieces. Something that belongs to the madness of speaking in tongues in a unified writing, inhabits the imagination of those who suffer the inversion of the ordinary relations from one language to another: relations that specify to each language its distinct property, its separate territory, and its resistance to all translation. The extraordinary thing would be to write so to speak in multiple hands a text that is nothing but a perpetual translation.[23]

Both passages cited above convey the essential differences of language and culture bearing on North African texts whose impregnability also embodies an otherness that *Love in Two Languages* extends to sex and affect. Once again, translation remains a key element of Khatibi's deployment of *bi-langue:*

> What was translated by this love? Reply slowly, it's still going toward an encounter without actually reaching it, and recovering from it in reality. Neither expectation nor return: maintain the constraint of the undetermined. In thinking of you in other terms, I'll add that a dissymmetric rapture took place: I transcribed you in your native tongue as I abducted you from my own, which you didn't recognize.[24]

The indispensability of Khatibi's *bi-langue* for the interpretation of Maghrebi texts is heightened by the affective charge of sexual difference and an otherness that *Love in Two Languages* conveys in its full complexity. This otherness does not, however, lend itself to deployment on the part of the presumably male narrator, a deployment to which an anonymous female referred to throughout the text as "she" seemingly has no access.[25] Jacques Derrida provides an additional take on the phenomenon of *bi-langue* when he asserts, just before noting that he and Khatibi share a certain "state" as far as language and culture are concerned, that the double postulation

> —*We only ever speak one language* . . .
> *(yes, but)*
> —*We never only speak only one language* . . .

is not only the law of what is called translation but also the law itself as translation.[26] Derrida is referring to the linguistic hierarchy imposed on him in his youth by the educational system in colonial Algeria, and this in the context of a cultural complexity conveyed via the invented term "nostalgeria" that serves as a measure of both distance and persistent proximity.[27]

Challenging Translation

The sites of translation work that I have invoked above range from academic discipline and pedagogy to insurmountable difference and otherness cast in sexual and affective terms. Khatibi's staging of translation as an extended set of attempts at exchange and understanding recalls the format of Maurice Blanchot's *L'attente l'oubli* (1962), and this not least by the suspension of full and adequate understanding through an infinite series of failed attempts that result in misunderstanding. Khatibi's advocacy of *bi-langue* and *pluri-langue* derives from cultural and political conditions in North Africa that impose a linguistic space constructed out of two kinds of Arabic (dialectal and classical), Berber, French, and (in parts of Morocco) Spanish. This plurality also bears on the status of French as a language continually made, unmade, and remade by the internal and external languages that surround and inhabit it: "And in fact, all Maghrebian literature of so-called French expression is an account of translation. I don't mean that it is only translation, but more specifically that it is an account that *speaks in tongues*."[28]

The challenges that Khatibi's *bi-langue* and *pluri-langue* raise for translation recall those associated with a third space of hybrid culture in which translation likewise imitates and displaces the priority of what traditional translation posits as the source language.[29] As hybridity becomes less an exception than a fact of daily life, a translation pedagogy attuned to difference can contribute to recasting the model and practices of a new comparative literature in line with the realities of globalization in its multiple expressions. Part of that model and practice should extend the decolonization of knowledge by showing the extent to which knowledge remains entrenched in the irreducible difference of language. For Khatibi, this difference links the geohistorical location of the Maghreb between Orient, Occident, and Africa as a crossing of the global in itself to a condition in which the regional languages of classical Arabic, its local dialects, French, and Spanish contain the inscription of the other languages that surround and inhabit it.[30] How best to convey this difference and its essential dissymmetry is a prime challenge for what translation studies can contribute to understanding the range of local, regional, and global contexts with which the new comparative literature increasingly contends.[31]

As formulated through the set of problems that Khatibi raises in conjunction with the phenomena of the *bi-langue* and *pluri-langue,* translation enhances rather than resolves linguistic difference by pointing to the collapse of clear and stable distinctions between source and target languages:

> A foreign tongue is not added to the native tongue as a simple palimpsest, but transforms it. When I write in French, my entire effort consists of separating myself from my native language, of relegating it to my deepest self. I am thus divided from myself within myself, which is the condition for all writing inured to the destiny of languages. Dividing myself, reincarnating myself—in the other's language. Henceforth, little by little, my native tongue becomes foreign to me. Bilingualism is the space between two exteriorities. I enter into the telling of forgetting and of anamnesia. Henceforth, "I am an/other" in an idiom that I owe it to myself to invent—a limit experience inherent in this situation.[32]

For Khatibi, then, the turning point in contending with the phenomenon of the *bi-langue* in its Maghrebian specificity involves taking charge of—rather than merely resisting—the plurality among Arabic, French, and Berber even (and especially) when what it imposes is a radical experience of melancholia and loss. To assert difference, to speak and write this loss, is thus to contend with the war between languages in the formation of self as a more personal setting of the impact of this war in the formation of nations and states.

Among the strategies that might promote this understanding of difference, the condition that Khatibi asserts in terms of *bi-langue* and *pluri-langue* lends itself by extension to the context-dependent practice of a thick translation linked to a "genuinely informed respect for others."[33] The irreducible difference on which Khatibi grounds his practices of *bi-langue* and *pluri-langue* can be tempered with reference to the more moderate position that Benjamin adopts when he asserts that while languages are not strangers to one another, "all translation is only a somewhat provisional way of coming to terms with the foreignness of language."[34] Close reading will continue to be grounded in efforts to understand linguistic specificity as well as to recognize how broader factors of difference bear on the linguistic choices made by the writer.[35] As comparatists learn to contend with the full range of this difference and foreignness, translation becomes even more essential to literary study across languages and cultures such as the teaching of literature in translation that Saussy aptly designates as the best place to start.

NOTES

1. Roland Barthes, *Camera Lucida: Reflections on Photography*, trans. Richard Howard (New York: Hill and Wang, 1981).

2. The expression "professional foreigners" appears in Abdelkebir Khatibi, *Figures de l'étranger dans la littérature française* (Paris: Denoël, 1987), 211. Translation must continue to ally itself with literary studies and their institutional corollaries in academic departments of language and literature. Translation activities at Iowa have long been allied with creative writing, especially with the International Writing Program, a residency program founded in 1967 by Paul Engle and Hualing Nieh that brings writers to spend a semester in Iowa City. Because the writers often live in countries where freedom of expression and human rights are restricted, the opportunity to interact across languages with students and faculty responds to the challenge raised by Gayatri Spivak and others to make a new "Comp. Lit." with a human import.

3. George Steiner, "What is Comparative Literature?" in *No Passion Spent: Essays 1978–1995* (New Haven, Conn.: Yale University Press, 1996), 151–52.

4. Steiner elsewhere connects open-endedness of translation to reading and hermeneutics. See, for example, his "Understanding as Translation," in *After Babel: Aspects of Language and Translation* (New York: Oxford University Press, 1975), 48.

5. Lawrence Venuti, *The Translator's Invisibility: A History of Translation* (New York: Routledge, 1995), 6. Walter Benjamin makes a similar point in "The Task of the Translator" (1921) when he writes that "just as translation is a form of its own, so the task of the translator may be regarded as distinct and clearly differentiated from the task of the poet" (*Walter Benjamin, Selected Writings, Vol. 1: 1913–1926*, ed. Marcus Bullock and Michael W. Jennings [Cambridge, Mass.: Harvard University Press, 1996], 253). Much of what I advocate in this chapter draws on Venuti's work over the past fifteen years. I thank Venuti and Christopher Merrill for their comments on an initial draft.

6. Lawrence Venuti, *The Scandals of Translation: Towards an Ethics of Difference* (New York: Routledge, 1998), 1.

7. See Philip E. Lewis, "The Measure of Translation Effects," in *Difference in Translation*, ed. Joseph F. Graham (Ithaca, N.Y.: Cornell University Press, 1985), 31–62.

8. Octavio Armand, *Refractions*, trans. C. Maier (New York: SITES/Lumen Books, 231); cited in Carol Maier, "Translation, *Dépaysement*, and their Figuration," in *Translation and Power*, ed. Maria Tymoczko and Edwin Gentzler (Amherst: University of Massachusetts Press, 2002), 184–85.

9. Gayatri Chakravorty Spivak, *Death of a Discipline* (New York: Columbia University Press, 2003), 18.

10. Ibid., 13.

11. Jacques Derrida, "Living On/Border Lines," in *Deconstruction and Criticism* (New York: Continuum, 1979), 93–94.

12. Venuti, *Translator's Invisibility*, 19; *Scandals of Translation*, 6.

13. Sherry Simon, *Gender in Translation: Cultural Identity and the Politics of Transmission* (New York: Routledge, 1996), viii.

14. Venuti, *Scandals of Translation*, 33.

15. Simon, *Gender in Translation*, 7. Subsequent citations are in the text.

16. Gayatri Chakravorty Spivak, *Outside in the Teaching Machine* (New York: Routledge, 1993), 182. Along similar lines, I have heard derisive reference to a practice known as "MacTranslation."

17. Réda Bensmaïa, "Translating or Whiting Out Language: On Khatibi's *Amour bilingue*," in *Experimental Nations: Or the Invention of the Maghreb*, trans. Alyson Waters (Princeton, N.J.: Princeton University Press, 2003), 104.

18. Ibid.

19. Richard Howard's decision to retain the term *bi-langue* in his English translation of *Amour bilingue*—see *Love in Two Languages* (Minneapolis: University of Minnesota Press, 1990)—is fully in line with the model and practice of writing in the 1983 French text published under the title of *Amour bilingue*.

20. Abdelkebir Khatibi, *La Mémoire tatouée* (Paris: Denoël, 1971), 64; cited in Samia Mehrez, "Translation and the Postcolonial Experience: The Francophone North African Text," in *Rethinking Translation: Discourse, Subjectivity, Ideology*, ed. Lawrence Venuti (New York: Routledge, 1992), 120.

21. Abdelkebir Khatibi, "Bilinguisme et littérature," in *Maghreb pluriel* (Paris: Denoël, 1983), 179. I have italicized the two key terms for emphasis.

22. Mehrez, "Translation and the Postcolonial Experience," 121.

23. Khatibi, "Bilinguisme et littérature," 205.

24. Khatibi, *Love in Two Languages*, 101–2.

25. Winifred Woodhull asserts this indispensability but remains critical of the extent to which Khatibi's use of deconstruction and Freudian psychoanalysis reinforce patriarchal attitudes (*Transfigurations of the Maghreb: Feminism, Decolonization and Literatures* [Minneapolis: University of Minnesota Press, 1993], xiii). See also Lucy Stone McNeese, "Decolonizing the Sign: Language and Identity in Abdelkebir Khatibi's *La Mémoire tatouée*," *Yale French Studies* 83 (1993): 12–29; and Bensmaïa, *Experimental Nations*, 99–124.

26. Jacques Derrida, *Monolingualism of the Other*, trans. P. Mensah (Stanford, Calif.: Stanford University Press, 1998), 10.

27. Ibid., 52.

28. Khatibi, *Maghreb pluriel*, 186.

29. See Homi Bhabha, "The Third Space," in *Identity, Community, Culture, Difference*, ed. J. Rutherford (London: Lawrence & Wishart, 1990), 210.

30. On Khatibi and border thinking, see Walter D. Mignolo, *Local Histories/Local Designs: Coloniality, Subaltern Knowledges, and Border Thinking* (Durham, N.C.: Duke University Press, 2000), 64–71.

31. This dissymmetry is neither neutral nor negligible. In the Maghreb, it has led to the death of three languages linked, respectively, to colonization (Arabic) and to independence (French and Berber). It has prompted an apparent impasse in which "literary Arabic is misunderstood by the majority, while dialectical Arabic and Berber are limited to oral usage while French, often

poorly spoken, remains the language of colonial alienation" (Djamila Saadi-Mokrene, "The Algerian Linguicide," in *Algeria in Others' Languages,* ed. Anne-Emmanuelle Berger [Ithaca, N.Y.: Cornell University Press, 2002], 44–46).

32. Khatibi, "Diglossia," in Berger, 158.

33. Kwame Anthony Appiah, "Thick Translation," in *The Translation Studies Reader,* ed. Lawrence Venuti (New York: Routledge, 2000), 427. Appiah's title evokes the model of a culturally informed and context-dependent interpretation that Clifford Geertz sets forth in "Thick Description: Toward an Interpretive Theory of Culture," in *The Interpretation of Cultures* (New York: Basic Books, 1973).

34. Benjamin, "The Task of the Translator," 255, 257.

35. William H. Gass, *Reading Rilke: Reflections on the Problems of Translation* (New York: Basic Books, 1999), 55.

CHAPTER TEN

Old Fields, New Corn, and Present Ways of Writing about the Past

CAROLINE D. ECKHARDT

Some six hundred years ago, a Londoner whose day job might have come under the designation of Civil Servant (he collected taxes, inspected bridges, delivered confidential messages for powerful government figures, and in general made himself useful), and whose night job might have been designated Poet or Public Intellectual, was having an epistemological moment. In other words, he was pondering the nature and the production of knowledge, and in particular, the relations between earlier knowledge, as preserved in writing, and present knowledge, as derived from experience. His resolution, while not new either then or now, captures in metaphor several concepts useful for any attempt to assess the status of a field of knowledge or an academic discipline:

> For out of olde feldes, as men seyth,
> Cometh al this newe corn from yer to yere,
> And out of olde bokes, in good feyth,
> Cometh al this new science that men lere.[1]

The poet, as some readers may have recognized, is Chaucer, and the poem is his "Parlement of Foules," an allegorical narrative in which most of the speakers are birds, many of their utterances are what we would call bird-brained, and the doubly punning title suggests a parliament (a speaking or discourse) both of birds and of fools, as well as pointing toward the British Parliament in particular.[2] With those multiple referents, the poem goes on to incorporate a critique of language, of representative government, of human love and desire, and of literature itself.

The epistemological position offered in the brief lines just quoted, which Chaucer will later complicate, seems simple enough here: just as new grain comes from old fields, so new knowledge comes from the cultivation of old books. The metaphor offers comfort food for the mind, for it draws upon ingredients that are familiar and reassuring. Old fields were within almost everyone's ordinary experience in Chaucer's day, even for city dwellers like himself; and old books too, especially religious books, were often nearby, although relatively few people had their own copies. The production of new knowledge, according to this analogizing theoretical framework, would be contingent on industrious labor, patience, and successful collaboration with the material environment in recuperating and renewing the fruits of the past. But as long as there were no natural or human disasters, the harvest should be good. Though the process of producing and disseminating knowledge might undergo natural cycles of dormancy and regeneration, and though the work of individual laborers might fail, the field of knowledge production was always already incubating the next development: it was inherently a growth industry. It was also inherently a comparatist industry, at least in Chaucer's hands. The old books that nourished his "Parlement" included, for example, Cicero's *Somnium Scipionis* [the Dream of Scipio, part of the *Republic*], Boethius's *Consolatio philosophiae* [Consolation of Philosophy], the *Roman de la Rose* [Romance of the Rose], Alain de Lisle's *De planctu Naturae* [Complaint of Nature], Dante's *Commedia*, and Boccaccio's *Teseida*. These and other works constituted a most fertile Latin, French, and Italian grounding for Chaucer's English poem.

How different are things now?

Our terminology and metaphorical frameworks have shifted utterly from Chaucer's green and pleasant metaphor, which may now appear—well, corny. More important, our commitment to the old fields and the old books has undergone a fundamental transformation. Comparative literature in the first decade of the twenty-first century is frequently a presentist discipline, as others have noted. Having largely discarded the canonical thinking that once gave many of the old books an automatic centrality in syllabi and scholarship, we new comparatists are often preoccupied with objects of knowledge and kinds of discourse that entail direct engagement with the social and political issues of our own times. Nevertheless, even if sometimes only from the margin, the old books continue to assert their significance. I will attempt here, first, to document the place of medieval studies in particular—approximately a thousand years' worth of old books, ca. 500–1500 C.E.[3]—within our current professional praxis, and then to argue that these old books are still *dulce et utile*, pleasurable and useful, to borrow the literary criteria of an even older era, and that they can speak to us now as compellingly as ever before.

Professional Praxis: In Our Name

As others have pointed out, academic disciplines are not only institutional and theoretical constructs but also behavioral and performative phenomena, so comparative literature can be defined, at least in part, by what we *do*.[4] What is the place of medieval studies in practices that carry the name of our discipline? I will offer a brief empirical excursus to assess the presence of medieval contributions in several contexts: the work of new scholars, as evidenced in dissertations; the research presented under the aegis of our professional association, the American Comparative Literature Association, as seen in its recent conference programs and the prizes it has given; and the articles recently published in two central journals that bear the title of our discipline, *Comparative Literature* and *Comparative Literature Studies*.[5] Both in the choices of data to collect and in the interpretations offered, this assessment is admittedly only approximate and inevitably partly subjective.

To begin with dissertations, given that no single year is likely to be diagnostic, I have used data from the period 2000–2004—in other words, the most recent five years documented in *Dissertation Abstracts International* (at the time of this search the majority of the abstracts for 2005 were not yet available). For comparison, I have also used data from the corresponding five-year periods a decade ago: 1990–94; and a decade before that, 1980–84. A subject search on the term "Literature, Comparative" in the *DAI* database located a total of 671 dissertations for the earliest of these periods, 1980–84; 1,338 dissertations for 1990–94; and 1,482 for 2000–2004.[6] It should be noted that not all of these dissertations necessarily represent Ph.D.s granted by graduate programs in comparative literature, since the search engine relies on subject-terms assigned by *DAI*'s editors and does not separately reveal the name of the student's degree. In some cases, such as studies of one author, the *DAI* editorial decision to categorize a dissertation as "Literature, Comparative" might well be questioned. Nevertheless, it is easy to see the great variety and vigor of comparative literary research, labeled as such in this major database and thus permanently (one supposes) associated with the name of our discipline.

In order to permit patterns to appear, all these dissertations were arrayed into a taxonomy according to chronology, region, theme, and other categories, using their titles, and sometimes the abstracts, to decide the taxonomic categories (usually, multiple categories) in which each should be listed.[7] Only a small part of the somewhat unwieldy results from this venture will be relevant to our present discussion of medieval studies, though the data could be interrogated for other inquiries too. Out of the total of 3,491 dissertations in the data set, 327 of them, or just under one-tenth (9.4%), focused on or included medieval topics. There were 86 such dissertations (12.8% of the whole) in 1980–84; 131 (9.8%) in 1990–94; and 110 (7.4%) in 2000–2004.

As for the regional taxonomy, within the medieval group it is not surprising to find that a great majority of the dissertations dealt wholly with Western European literatures (including those of the British Isles). However, in all three sets of years studied, there are dissertations on topics outside Europe. For example, the 1980–84 cluster includes projects on Arabic and Hebrew texts of broader Mediterranean circulation; the Persian Renaissance of the Abbasid period; *tsa-chu* drama of the Yuan period in China; the works of the eleventh-century Tibetan poet-saint Milarepa in comparison to European hagiographic literature and art; a comparison of Japanese *kyōgen* drama and fifteenth-century English comic plays; a study of love in Tang Dynasty tales and twelfth-century European courtly literature; the influence of Chinese on Japanese poetry in the tenth century C.E., and so forth. The most recent cluster, 2000–2004, includes studies of an eleventh-century courtly Japanese poet with comparisons to a twelfth-century Provençal poet; Tang fiction compared to Ming drama; Greek and Latin traditions in the work of the first patriarch of Constantinople during the Ottoman period; scholarship on the Byzantine poem *Digenes Akrites* in comparison to scholarship on the *Chanson de Roland;* patricide, the classical Arabic ode, and Abbasid court poetry; African and medieval European mysticism; Abu Bakr al-Wasiti's Sufi glosses on the Qur'an as they survive in later texts; Islamic mysticism and the Spanish *Libro de Buen Amor;* and the *Tale of Genji* in comparison to Spenser's *Faerie Queene.*

This search among the archives of *DAI* shows that work on medieval literature has long constituted, and continues to constitute, a modest but significant (if somewhat decreasing) proportion of dissertations that are labeled "Literature, Comparative." Furthermore, for doctoral students in medieval literature to work not only on Western Europe but also on other regions, in particular the Mediterranean rim and East Asia, is not new. However, in what *DAI* regards as comparative research on literature for our thousand-year time span, it seems that scholarship on the medieval literary cultures of sub-Saharan Africa, or the lands we now call the Americas, is scarcely visible at all.

Let us turn now to the place of medieval studies in the research presented under the aegis of the ACLA. A scan of the titles of papers scheduled for the annual ACLA conferences in 2001–2005 (conveniently available via the ACLA Web site, www.acla. org) yielded a total of only 59 papers with evidently medieval topics out of the approximately 2,600 papers presented at these five conferences altogether: 14 papers in 2001 (9 of them from one panel, "Rethinking Time and Space in Dante's Worlds"); 3 papers in 2002; 15 papers in 2003 (8 of them from one panel, "Alterity Revisited: Pre-

and Early Modern Literatures," and 4 from another, "Premodern Texts and Hypertexts"); 7 papers in 2004 (4 of them from one panel, "Crossing the Pre-Modern and Post-Modern: Challenges to Global Ethnic Networks"); and 20 papers in 2005 (8 from one panel, "Medieval Canonicity: Transmission, Authority, and Authorship," and 5 from another, "Medieval and Early Modern Translation"). Evidently, if members of the association take the initiative to organize an explicitly medieval (or premodern) panel, it will attract participants, and a scattering of medieval papers may appear in other sessions; but overall, the representation is small indeed. Moreover, there is little continuity: among the authors of the 59 medieval papers on the programs for 2001–2005, only three appear more than once—or, to put it differently, only three of the scholars who presented medieval papers in 2001, 2002, 2003, or 2004 have appeared on the program in this capacity again.[8] This situation suggests that ACLA presentations by medievalists may be mostly adventitious, or dependent on the energies and professional networks of particular session-organizers, rather than representing the participation of scholars who feel integrated into the association as a whole. However, I do not know whether such discontinuity is peculiar to medievalists because I have not studied "return rates" for presenters in other fields.

Beyond its organizational sponsorship of the conference papers on its programs, the ACLA calls attention to individual achievements in research through the prizes it awards. Among the winners of ACLA book prizes, to judge from the titles provided on the association's Web site, there have been only two books substantially on medieval topics, published fifteen years apart: Mary E. Wack's *Lovesickness in the Middle Ages: The Viaticum and Its Commentaries,* published in 1990 and awarded the Harry Levin Prize in that year; and Seth Lerer's *Error and the Academic Self: The Scholarly Imagination, Medieval to Modern,* published in 2002 and awarded the Levin Prize in 2005. There have evidently been no winners on medieval topics among the association's other prizes for books or dissertations (the Wellek, Frenz, and Bernheimer prizes), though there have been two recent awards in Renaissance or early modern studies.[9] As for journal articles, though the association does not give an award for a best journal article published by a faculty member, there is an award for the best graduate student article (the Aldridge Prize); no winners are listed in medieval studies, though again there have been two recent winners in Renaissance or early modern studies.[10]

Turning very briefly to periodicals that use the name of our discipline, as a sample I have glanced at only two such journals, *Comparative Literature* (University of Oregon) and *Comparative Literature Studies* (Penn State); at only the past five complete years, the time span of 2000–2004; and at only articles per se, not also book reviews or other short items. Thus, this tally represents no more than a small step in the direction of studying the place of medieval literature in our journals. *Comparative Literature* published a total of 82 articles during these years, with 5 articles (6.0%) explicitly including medieval topics; *Comparative Literature Studies* published a total of 98 articles, again with 5 (5.1%) on medieval topics. The representation is smaller than the proportion of medieval dissertations, but it is considerably greater than the proportion of ACLA conference presentations.

Putting all three types of data together, and again acknowledging the insufficiencies of this survey, it appears that in these venues associated with the name of our field, research on medieval literature over the past twenty-five years has occupied a position that is always under 10 percent, ranging from occasional presence (some 2% of the papers at ACLA conferences, just under 4% of the ACLA prizes, around 5–6% of the *CL* and *CLS* journal articles), to a significant minority component (around 9% of dissertations). I do not mean to suggest, of course, that our discipline has been inhospitable to medievalists, for that would not be either fair or true, and there are specific initiatives to the contrary.[11] Nevertheless, for whatever reason, in recent years the representation of medieval studies has not been extensive.

Although the subject of this volume primarily concerns comparative literature as an academic discipline in the United States, a brief broader glance may also be pertinent. The International Comparative Literature Association (ICLA), founded in 1954 at Oxford University, has a global scope, since it serves as a partner or umbrella association for many "national" comparative literature associations around the world, including the ACLA. Though its Web site (www.byu.edu/~icla) does not include information on previous conference presentations or on prizes, the ICLA has an internal committee structure based partially on subject-areas and sponsors its own publications program, and in these respects we can consider the pragmatic definitions that are implied.

That implied research identity is firmly postmedieval: the association's structure includes a Research Committee on Modernity and Literature, for example, but no Research Committee on Premodernity and Literature. More important, the ICLA has been hosting an ambitious project to sponsor a series of collaborative volumes on comparative literary history, a project founded, quite rightly, on the principles that (as the Web site puts it) "the writing of literary histories confined to specific nations, peoples, or languages must be complemented by the writing of literary history that coordinates related or comparable phenomena from an international point of view," and that "it is almost impossible for individual scholars to write such comprehensive histories, which implies we must now rely on structured teamwork, drawing collaborators from different nations." This project has so far produced nineteen volumes under the guidance of an international coordinating committee. Although the avowed aim of the series is historical, to judge by their titles, the earliest period that has been included is early modern (two volumes deal with the *époque de la renaissance*). Since the series is unfinished, its final shape (if indeed it is to be completed) remains unknown, and of course we should not assess the research scope of the ICLA or its members by this one project; yet once more it seems that medieval literature as such is nearly invisible.[12]

This omission seems particularly ironic if we consider the ICLA's own history as an institution founded in the postwar European context: two profoundly important comparative studies, still indispensable for medievalists (and others), came out of the intellectual conditions of wartime and postwar Europe and, at the time, represented pioneering and courageous achievements in pushing back the borders of narrow literary nationalisms. These two monumental works are Erich Auerbach's *Mimesis* (1946) and Ernst Robert Curtius's *Europäische Literatur und Lateinisches Mittelalter* [European Literature and the Latin Middle Ages] (1948).

Praxis: In Other Names

The preceding pages should not be taken to suggest that there is a dearth of medieval comparative studies overall, for that is emphatically not the case. Much of it is simply taking place outside the named associations and journals of our discipline (as well as, occasionally, within them). Indeed, the study of medieval literature is a flourishing field, with the old books, to return to Chaucer's metaphor, serving as fertile ground for the constant (re)production of knowledge. Each year in May, nearly two thousand papers on medieval topics, many of them literary and comparative, are given at the annual International Medieval Congress (www.umich.edu/medieval/congress). The archive of book reviews at *The Medieval Review* (www.hti.umich.edu/t/tmr/) includes an average of about two hundred new medieval books per year over the last five years (156 in 2000, 160 in 2001, 191 in 2002, 243 in 2003, 244 in 2004); not all of these books are either literary or comparative, but given the broadening, in medieval as in later fields, of categories such as "literature" and "cultural text," many of them are surely relevant to comparative literature. In response to a search on the subject-term "Literature," the *International Medieval Bibliography* (www.leeds.ac.uk/imi/imb/imb.htm) lists between 1,084 and 2,089 publications, mostly journal articles, for each of the years between 2000 and 2003 (data for 2004 have not been completed at this time). Again, not all of the articles are necessarily comparative, but many of them are.

It would not be possible within the scope of this paper to represent the major trends and achievements of this energetic scholarship, but I would like to comment on a few significant characteristics or directions.[13] Research involving the production and dissemination of texts, the recovery of neglected texts, women's cultural production, expanded geographical ranges, colonial and postcolonial discourses, and a renewed attention to aesthetics accompanies the continuation of traditional literary history and textual scholarship, both of which supply the material that medieval studies cannot do without. The foundation for some of the new kinds of work on textual production and dissemination was partly laid in the mid-1990s, with works such as John Dagenais's *Ethics of Reading in Manuscript Culture* (1994), which concentrates on the *Libro de Buen Amor* but deals in wide-ranging ways with the nature of the act of reading ("it was above all an ethical activity," xvii); or the collection *The Whole Book: Cultural Perspectives on the Medieval Miscellany,* ed. Stephen G. Nichols and Siegfried Wenzel (1996), which associates the technologies and visual spaces of composite manuscripts with the characteristics of hypertext. A few of the more recent and noteworthy works of textual scholarship that display interdisciplinary methodologies include Jonathan M. Bloom, *Paper Before Print: The History and Impact of Paper in the Islamic World* (2001); Andrew Taylor, *Textual Situations: Three Medieval Manuscripts and Their Readers* (2002); Mary C. Erler, *Women, Reading, and Piety in Late Medieval England* (2002); Marilynn Desmond and Pamela Sheingorn, *Myth, Montage, and Visuality in Late Medieval Manuscript Culture: Christine de Pizan's* Epistre Othea (2003); Sophia Page, *Magic in Medieval Manuscripts* (2004); Alison I. Beach, *Women as Scribes: Book Production and Monastic Reform in Twelfth-Century Bavaria* (2004); and A. C. Spearing, *Textual Subjectivity* (2005).

Work that helps bring attention to texts that are inadequately known, as well as presenting geographical and linguistic dimensions beyond Western Europe, includes Karl Reichl's *Singing the Past: Turkic and Medieval Heroic Poetry* (2000), which ranges from England to Anatolia to Siberia, "collating . . . non-cognate traditions," as reviewer John F. Garcia puts it (*The Medieval Review* 04.02.03), and raising methodological questions about that praxis. Another "non-cognate" enterprise, the collection *Crossing the Bridge: Comparative Essays on Medieval European and Heian Japanese Women Writers,* ed. Barbara Stevenson and Cynthia Ho (2000), includes chapters that examine topics such as the rhetoric of entreaty, male and female epistolary dynamics, the communicative value of silence, and women situated in gardens, in texts not previously brought together in this way.

Several works insist on the breadth of cultures within Europe itself, contesting the silent equation, still all too common, of medieval Europe with Christendom. María Rosa Menocal's *The Ornament of the World* (2002), for example, reinvestigates tolerance at the conjunction of Islamic, Jewish, and Christian traditions in Spain. Canonical Western European texts and authors are also receiving new attention. For example, Michelle R. Warren's *History on the Edge: Excalibur and the Borders of Britain, 1100–1300* (2000) reads medieval chronicles through the lens of postcolonial theory and argues that several of these chronicles are border writing. Renewing an earlier field of comparison in a way that combines recent theory with fine textual analysis is Robert R. Edwards's *Chaucer and Boccaccio* (2001), which shows how through Chaucer's reading of Boccaccio both the classical past and medieval modernity are portrayed.

Several of the newer approaches are visible in articles in the recently founded periodical *New Medieval Literatures* (1997-), as the following titles suggest: "Dante in Somerset: Ghosts, Historiography, Periodization," by David Wallace (1999); "Panopticon Is Her Bedroom: Voyeurism and the Concept of Space in the Love Lyrics of Early Medieval China," by Anne Birrell (1999); " 'Now you see it, now you don't': Nation, Identity, and Otherness," by Wendy Scase (2001); " 'Reading Is Good Prayer': Recent Research on Female Reading Communities," by Jocelyn Wogan-Browne (2002); "Medieval Literature and the Cultures of Performance," by Bruce Holsinger (2004); and "Urban Utterances: Merchants, Artisans, and the Alphabet in Caxton's Dialogues in French and English," by Lisa H. Cooper (2005).

Topics such as these bear obvious similarities to investigations into more recent literatures, but I do not mean to suggest that scholarship on medieval literature has painlessly joined ranks with cultural studies and with modern and postmodern theory. The angry controversy over the "New Philology," a debate of (mostly) the 1990s that ostensibly focused on different methods of text-editing but that became the site of struggles to control both the past and the standards of scholarship, exemplifies the anxieties and internal ruptures that have occurred as some medievalists accept, and others reject, the work of previous generations.[14] The tenuous position of medieval studies (and hence the professional prospects of medievalists) in some departments of "national" literatures—and, allegedly, the low status of medieval literature in the hierarchy of value among practitioners of other fields—have led to concerns about the preservation of an appropriate space for these thousand years in our future mappings of literary topography. Moreover, there are complexities entailed by the inescapable fact that the writers to whom medievalists intensely devote their professional lives are all utterly beyond our reach, as Sarah Kay, in a Kristevan analysis of recent controversies, explains:

> The past is irrecoverable. At different times, in trying to grapple with this disconcertingly simple fact, scholars have stressed the modernity of the Middle Ages, or else they have underlined its alterity. . . . [W]hereas the ethical question of how to respond to the contemporary other is urgent and delicate, the Otherness of medieval writers is in a way

more radical since they are all dead. Indeed, it would be impossible to count the corpses that litter the centuries between us and the Middle Ages. Profoundly depressing, this vision can also be liberating; are we not free to say what we want about poets who lived 800 years ago? . . . Determinedly, we elaborate for ourselves an image of that which is absent, and defend it against impairment from the criticisms of others. Our attention to the past is the more elegiac as our love for the dead reminds us of our own deaths.[15]

One might reply that love for the dead can remind us of life too, as the medieval writers of elegies knew; and that love for the living, who are also incompletely recuperable, can remind us of death: all literary study is a mediation between the possible and the impossible, presence and absence, yearning and finding and loss.

Planting Seeds, or A Brief Agenda

I should like to propose that in plowing and seeding our academic fields and cultivating our gardens, we seek a fuller partnership between the production of medieval comparative scholarship and the institutional site of comparative literature. That is a general call, but there are particular things we can do.

First, it is time for the ACLA or the ICLA to sponsor a comparative history of medieval literatures, not in the earlier sense in which the geocultural referent of "medieval" was primarily Christian Western Europe, perhaps with occasional glances at its immediate adjacencies (the Mediterranean rim, Eastern Europe, Western Asia), but instead in the current sense in which we recognize the global simultaneity, though without claiming the cultural interconnectedness, of all parts of the globe in all times. The cultural world of the Aztec or the Inca was *there,* for example, in the year 1400, just as much as Chaucer was *there* completing his literary career on the "best of islands, set far in the Western Sea."[16] The residue of Aztec or Inca literary productions is far harder for us to capture at this point than is the residue of fourteenth-century English literary productions, but at least let us include it to the extent we can—along with, for example, from the period around or shortly after Chaucer's death, the Noh plays of Zeami in Japan and the narratives of the Mali Empire in West Africa, among others. It is not that these cultures or texts remain unstudied, but instead, that they are not often enough studied on the same grounds as medieval European literature is. Perhaps such a global venture would even lead to the choice of a new name to replace "medieval" and "Middle Ages," those apologetic labels whose insufficiency, even for the West, has long been evident: why do we denominate a thousand years of cultural production by the fact that they are located "in between" other ages? Does not every age, except perhaps for the last, constitute the middle element of a chronological sandwich?

Though the task of a globally comparative history of medieval literatures may have long seemed impossible (leaving aside the question of naming), in the past few years that situation has changed as the groundwork has recently been laid. The context in which this has occurred is pedagogical, for the new world literature anthologies already incorporate the collaborative work of teams of scholars, exemplifying a broadened scope not only for the nineteenth and twentieth centuries, in which globalization is now virtually taken for granted, but also for earlier times. With no intention to ignore other anthologies, I will use as an example *The Medieval Era,* the second volume of the six-volume *Longman Anthology of World Literature,* which is among the most recent of the collaborative world literature anthologies and the one most closely identified with comparative literature as a discipline.[17] Its breadth is evident at once. On its front cover this volume displays a detail from an early eighteenth-century portrait of Murasaki Shikibu (ca. 978–1014 C.E.), the woman who wrote the Japanese classic *Genji monogatari* [Tale of Genji]. The world map inside the anthology's front cover, dated ca. 1154 C.E., is attributed to the Arab geographer al-Idrisi, who was born in Morocco, educated in Spain, and made maps for the European ruler of Sicily. The timeline that forms part of the anthology's introduction for students includes columns for Year, The World, and Literature; and in these columns it is easy to see that the poets Judah ha-Levi (a Jewish poet of Muslim Spain) and Guillaume d'Aquitaine (a Christian poet of the south of France) were twelfth-century contemporaries, and that Gottfried von Strassburg's *Tristan* (Germany) and the first version of *Heike monogatari,* the *Tales of Heike* (Japan) date from approximately the same time (early thirteenth century).

I must note that even this volume has not fully achieved a global approach: South Asian texts from the twelfth through fifteenth centuries do not appear here, but are oddly separated from their contemporaries and chronologically displaced into the anthology's next volume, *The Early Modern Period,* as are Mesoamerican texts taken to be representative of cultural traditions prior to Columbus. Furthermore, all of Africa is, on the whole, less well represented than some rather small individual nations elsewhere in the world. Decisions such as these were probably influenced by market research, which dictates that no more than a modest amount of innovation can be incorporated into a textbook if it is to sell well. Despite these limitations, the collaborative teams of scholars brought together for this anthology (and similarly for others) have prepared so much of the ground for a truly global comparative history of medieval literatures that such a project would surely be feasible now.

I will briefly mention a few further components for a potential agenda, realizing that in some institutional settings these initiatives are already in place.

As a second item, perhaps more of the journals whose titles include the name of our discipline could try to attract papers on medieval topics, commissioning such papers if necessary, or could sponsor special issues, sometimes with a more than European (or European-plus-adjacent) scope. Similarly, if conference organizers do not see medieval session proposals or papers arriving in due time, they could invite a few major scholars to participate. Our journals and conferences are, of course, very open to medieval scholarship already, but it may be necessary to seed change (or change the seeds that are planted), because this further growth may not happen on its own. In time, seeing those participants, medievalists should become more likely to think of ACLA meetings and our disciplinary journals as obvious places to submit their work, and special attention should no longer be necessary.

Third, I will make the controversial suggestion that the requirements of all our comparative literature degree programs should include some acquaintance—*any* acquaintance—with literary cultures prior to the early modern era and also that non-European cultures should be included within this early purview, for we should not pretend that those cultures came into existence only when Westerners encountered and translated them. If a more nearly global range is now included in world literature anthologies designed for undergraduate general education courses, should we not have even higher expectations for our majors, particularly for the graduate students who will become the next generation's teachers and scholars?

There are many ways in which such a graduate-level curricular goal could be accomplished. In my own doctoral programs (both the one from which I took my Ph.D. and the one I am now part of), this modest aim of "some acquaintance" has been met through a few readings in the year-long course on the history of literary criticism and theory as well as (in my current program) through the proseminar that all new graduate students take and, in most cases, through their individual doctoral reading lists. In a recent debate about the contents of the theory courses in graduate programs in comparative literature, participants acknowledged that it is difficult to use such courses as a means of expanding our students' global awareness without resorting to tokenism or superficiality, but I believe it is preferable to accept those risks rather than not to make the attempt.[18]

The effect of an agenda such as that sketched here would be to reaffirm and expand our discipline's connectedness to approximately a thousand years of literary and cultural production—approximately one-fourth of the entire duration of written literature. One could easily argue that there is too much else to do now, or that much of this earlier cultural work addressed the problems of its own times and places but does not directly address ours, or that the strangeness of some of these texts constitutes too great a barrier to serious understanding and invites only the familiar kinds of unsatisfactory readings—either an orientalist othering in which we find these works to be "exotic," or else a coercive assimilation in which we find these works to resemble ourselves. The judgment of those who recognize these sibling dangers is often that medieval texts should be left to those few specialists who choose to become fully immersed in their particularities (such as their languages) and are thus less likely to err in either direction. Those arguments against what might be called an amateur reading certainly carry weight. The sum of that weight, however, if not counterbalanced, would be to rob us of this segment of our human past—and to rob that past, in turn, of its future, at least of whatever future it can have in our hands.

An amateur reader can also be a lover, as the word suggests: someone who desires the literary object and finds pleasure and value in it despite the imperfections of the relationship. Among the characteristics that can make the old books desirable companions, suitable for a constant relationship with some of us, or for occasional engagements with comparatists who are committed primarily to more contemporary projects, or for students in any field of study, is their usefulness in helping to defeat foolishness or ignorance about our own predicaments—as when I have heard, from those who are uninformed about the past, that racism is an invention of the United States, or that Jews and Muslims are always enemies, or that the voices of women were always suppressed until the twentieth century (those are real examples, each needing only a single literary reference as a cure). I do not think we can agree with Chaucer that "al this new science," all this new knowledge, comes from the old books, for there are other sources of knowledge, as he himself elsewhere describes, but at least some forms of old knowledge are readily obtainable from these texts. Moreover, the old books, especially if they come from less familiar domains and can take us out of our comfort zones, can offer the stimulation of discovery; counteract the risk of isolation or parochialism, which for individuals still exists despite all the phenomena of globalization; state ethical problems in alternative frameworks that clarify our own; and relieve us from loneliness by reminding us that the fundamental human joys and sorrows with which we necessarily deal are not unique or new.

And finally, as one of my students said, on a first reading of the Provençal comic romance *Jaufre*, "Whoever wrote this is a real cool dude—this is *fun*." The pleasure of the text is a valid reason for its perpetuation too.

1. Geoffrey Chaucer, "The Parliament of Fowls" [Parlement of Foules], ed. Vincent J. Dimarco and Larry D. Benson, in *The Riverside Chaucer*, 3rd ed., ed. Larry D. Benson (Boston: Houghton Mifflin, 1987), ll. 22–25, p. 385.

2. Regarding the double punning: (1) *parlement*, the French word for "discourse, commu-

nication, speaking," had come by Chaucer's time to refer also to the British Parliament, as it does now; (2) the words for "fowl" and "fool" have different etymologies (Old English *fugol* for "bird," Old French *fol* for "fool"), but in the range of Middle English forms, they shared the spelling "foul" and were presumably close in pronunciation. See *Middle English Dictionary*, ed. Robert E. Lewis et al., 118 fascicles (Ann Arbor: University of Michigan Press, 1952–2001); rev. ed. online at http://ets.umdl.umich.edu/m/med.

3. I am not unaware that at the margins, this chronological range might be defined somewhat differently by other scholars and that it has been applied variously within geographical or linguistic domains, particularly at the assumed borderline between "medieval" and "Renaissance" or "early modern." An evident example is that Petrarch and Boccaccio (long classified as "Renaissance" and now "early modern" writers) antedate Chaucer (long considered medieval) and serve as sources for him. One could defensibly regard Petrarch as medieval, Chaucer as early modern, or the distinction as dysfunctional—but that argument belongs to another day.

4. Claudio Guillén, for example, tends to define comparative literature in terms of desire ("let us consider our field as a yearning rather than as an object") and praxis, "an activity chosen over other activities" (*The Challenge of Comparative Literature*, trans. Cola Franzen [Cambridge, Mass.: Harvard University Press, 1993], 4); cf. the inclusion of praxis in several older works, such as in the statement "Whoever is concerned with the international rather than the nationalistic mode of the study of letters is practicing comparative literature" (François Jost, *Introduction to Comparative Literature* [Indianapolis: Bobbs-Merrill, 1974], vii); Robert J. Clements, *Comparative Literature as Academic Discipline: A Statement of Principles, Praxis, Standards* (New York: MLA, 1978); and *Vergleichende Literaturwissenschaft: Theorie und Praxis*, ed. Manfred Schmeling (Wiesbaden: Akademische Verlagsgesellschaft Athenaion, 1981).

5. I thank Annika Farber, doctoral student in comparative literature at Penn State, for compiling data on dissertations and other types of information, and for much additional assistance.

6. This discussion of dissertations is based on *Dissertation Abstracts International*, searched online during Spring 2004 and Summer 2005, using the subject term "Literature, Comparative" (*DAI*'s subject category 0295). A subject search was chosen rather than a keyword search because the latter brought up only abstracts that used the words "comparative" and "literature" in their text. Category designations are supplied by the *DAI* editors. I thank Dana Ouellette and Karen Kaltz of ProQuest for the following information about *DAI*'s methodology: "The subjects are assigned by a group of editors. . . . The classification has not changed substantially since 1979, except to add or modify subjects (although Comparative Literature as a subject has not changed in that time). The guidelines they use to make the determination are the name of the department and the subject of the actual manuscript. In a nutshell, the comparative literature subject is assigned to manuscripts that compare or contrast multiple authors, or compare/contrast literature from multiple countries, regions, or languages" (personal communication to Annika Farber, 25 March 2004).

7. The taxonomy included ten time periods, ancient through twenty-first century, along with "general"; eleven regional categories, plus "general"; and an optional category for emphasis or theme or approach, such as theory, translation, or globalization/diaspora. Each dissertation was listed in as many categories as applied. There was necessarily some subjectivity here, and in some cases Ms. Farber and I were reduced to sheer guesswork because not even careful perusal of the abstract yielded any clear sense of what a dissertation was about. (I would like to

put in a plea that we all urge our students, as a courtesy to readers and a guide to the perplexed, to write abstracts that include the names of authors or texts, dates, translations of key terms, and other such basic information.)

8. However, during these years some of these scholars have reappeared on the program in other capacities.

9. Levin Prizes have been awarded to the following books on Renaissance or early modern topics: Leonard Barkan's *Unearthing the Past: Archeology and Aesthetics in the Making of Renaissance Culture* (1999), prize awarded in 2001; and Julie Stone Peters's *Theatre of the Book, 1480–1880: Print, Text, and Performance in Europe* (2000), prize awarded in 2003. The scope of Peters's book, while primarily postmedieval, begins prior to 1500, and it is possible that some of the other award-winning books also touch on medieval literature.

10. The Aldridge Prize, sponsored jointly by the ACLA and the journal *Comparative Literature Studies (CLS)*, has been awarded to the following articles on Renaissance or early modern topics: Mary Frances Fahey's "Allegorical Dismemberment and Rescue in Book III of *The Faerie Queene*," Aldridge Prize for 1997, published in *CLS* 35.1 (1998): 49–71; and Thérèsè Migraine-George's "Specular Desires: Orpheus and Pygmalion as Aesthetic Paradigms in Petrarch's *Rime sparse*," Aldridge Prize for 1998, published in *CLS* 36.3 (1999): 226–46.

11. One such project is a forthcoming special issue of the *Yearbook of Comparative and General Literature* (vol. 51, 2003–4), guest ed. Heather Richardson Hayton, which will focus on premodern topics.

12. This information is based on the Web site www.byu.edu/~icla/ and the links to which that site leads; I will gladly welcome corrections and more recent information. The volumes in the comparative literary history series are: (1) *Expressionism as an International Literary Phenomenon*, ed. Ulrich Weisstein (1973); (2) *The Symbolist Movement in the Literature of European Languages*, ed. Anna Balakian (1982); (3) *Le tournant du siècle des lumières 1760–1820: Les Genres en vers des lumières au romantisme*, ed. György M. Vajda (1982); (4) *Les avant-gardes littéraires au XXe siècle: Histoire*, ed. Jean Weisgerber (1984); (5) *Les avant-gardes littéraires au XXe siècle: Théorie*, ed. Jean Weisgerber (1986); (6) *European-Language Writing in Sub-Saharan Africa*, ed. Albert Gerard (1986); (7) *L'époque de la renaissance (1400–1600). I. L'avènement de l'ésprit nouveau* (1400–1480), ed. Tibor Klaniczay, Eva Kushner, and Andre Stegmann (1987); (8) *Romantic Irony*, ed. Frederick Garber (1988); (9) *Romantic Drama*, ed. Gerald Gillespie (1994); (10) *A History of Literature in the Caribbean: Hispanic and Francophone Regions*, ed. A. James Arnold (1994); (11) *International Postmodernism: Theory and Literary Practice*, ed. Hans Bertens and Douwe Fokkema (1997); (12) *A History of Literature in the Caribbean: Cross Cultural Studies*, ed. A. James Arnold (2001); (13) *L'époque de la renaissance (1400–1600). IV. Crise et essors nouveaux* (1560–1610), ed. Paul Chavy, Eva Kushner, and Hans Runte (2001); (14) *Die Wende von der Aufklärung zur Romantik 1760–1820: Epoche im Überblick*, ed. Horst Albert Glaser and György M. Vajda (2001); (15) *A History of Literature in the Caribbean:* Volume 2: *English-and Dutch-speaking regions*, ed. A. James Arnold (2001); (16) *L'Aube de la Modernité 1680–1760*, ed. Peter-Eckhard Knabe, Roland Mortier, and François Moureau (2002); (17) *Romantic Poetry*, ed. Angela Esterhammer (2002); (18) *Nonfictional Romantic Prose: Expanding Borders*, ed. Steven P. Sondrup and Virgil Nemoianu (2004); and (19) *History of the Literary Cultures of East-Central Europe: Junctures and Disjunctures in the 19th and 20th Centuries*, ed. Marcel Cornis-Pope and John Neubauer (2004).

13. An overview is provided by Stephen G. Nichols, "Writing the New Middle Ages," *PMLA* 120 (2005): 422–41.

14. See Sarah Kay, "The New Philology," *New Medieval Literatures* 3, ed. David Lawston, Wendy Scase, and Rita Copeland (Oxford: Oxford University Press, 1999), 295–326.

15. Ibid., 313–14.

16. In medieval foundation-narratives about Britain, as in some medieval maps, the geographical perspective is often Mediterranean, from which vantage point the British Isles, praised as being the best of islands for their fertility, are depicted as being situated at the margin of the known world, in what was called the Western Sea: "Of all the ylys, Brutayne the best, / . . . / Closyd within the West Se it standys, / Betwyx France sole and Irlandes" (*Castleford's Chronicle, or The Boke of Brut*, ed. Caroline D. Eckhardt, I, EETS [Oxford: Oxford University Press, 1996), ll. 255, 257–58, p. 8).

17. *The Longman Anthology of World Literature*, gen. ed. David Damrosch, Vol. B, *The Medieval Era*, eds. David L. Pike, Sabry Hafez, Haruo Shirane, Pauline Yu, et al. (New York: Pearson Longman, 2004).

18. Katherine Arens and Elizabeth M. Richmond-Garza, "The Canon of Theory," with responses by Caryl Emerson, John Neubauer, Aparna and Vinay Dharwadker, Caroline D. Eckhardt, and Christine Froula, *Comparative Literature Studies* 34 (1997): 392–427.

CHAPTER ELEVEN

Of Monuments and Documents

Comparative Literature and the Visual Arts in Early Modern Studies, or The Art of Historical Tact

CHRISTOPHER BRAIDER

I have been invited to comment on the recent efflorescence of comparative scholarship devoted to the intersections of literature and the visual arts in early modern Europe. As former ACLA president David Damrosch has noted with depressing pertinacity, early modern studies—indeed, studies focused on anything prior to the nineteenth century—have been increasingly pushed to the margins of our collective consciousness. However interesting and important ongoing work in premodern eras may be, the vast majority of our colleagues almost exclusively focus on the period since 1800.[1] To the extent, moreover, that most of us remain aware of developments prior to the nineteenth century at all, it is as the wicked laboratory of the technologies of cultural fabrication and control embodied in Michel Foucault's favorite icons of the hegemonic modern state—the insane asylum, the panoptic prison, the public scaffold, and the school. Nevertheless, beyond representing a rewarding field of research in its own right, the interdisciplinary analysis of early modern literature and art may prove exemplary for comparatist scholarship generally.

For one thing, it serves as a prime instance of how the comparatist impulse has evolved over the past two or three decades in the direction of a broader, cultural-historical conception of what we used to think of as distinctively literary issues. But it also suggests how deeply the concomitant attempt to fuse the rival claims of formalism and historicism (of "text" and "context") is embedded in the underlying logic of comparative literature itself. In the process, it may further remind us of something that, in the "post-humanist" (and even "post-human") era of what the title for the 2004 meeting of the ACLA calls "global ethnic networks," we too readily forget. To borrow a phrase that the great art historian Erwin Panofsky used to define the art historical practices that he and his sometime collaborators at the Warburg Institute

were engaged in reinventing, comparative literature is a *humanistic* discipline.[2] By
that I mean, as in the article in question Panofsky did, that our fundamental task is
a work of at once learned (philological) and imaginative (sympathetic) understanding, grounded in a sense of the character and value of the acts of inventive (if also
mediated, often violent, and as often both alienating and alienated) self-creation of
which cultural artifacts are the instruments and deposits. The case of literature and
visual art in the early modern West may thus help renew what I can only call the *faith*
in human creativity (whatever the medium and whatever the aim) that sustains the
humanities, the beleaguered family of disciplines to which, happily or not, comparative literature belongs.

But before trying to make the case for the exemplary interest of interdisciplinary
comparatist work in the early modern era, let me briefly review certain more general
considerations bearing on the nature of what, for all its newfound interdisciplinarity,
remains comparative literature's fundamental object. A major contribution that early
modern literary scholars concerned with the visual arts have made is the extension
of methods formed for the analysis and interpretation of texts, to aesthetic artifacts
whose sensitivity to such methods is not (or was not, at least, until recently) immediately obvious. Conversely, if so many literary scholars have found themselves
drawn to the visual arts, it is because the analysis of works of art has enabled them
to *see* in the texts with which they normally deal things they otherwise could not, including otherwise hidden phenomena bearing not only on the nature, but, as Joseph
Margolis would say, on the *career,* the evolving uptake or receptive afterlife, of texts
themselves.[3] For both of these reasons, then, let me begin by trying my hand at the
question (and the alternative) that Paul Ricœur poses in a classic essay, "Qu'est-ce
qu'un texte? Expliquer et comprendre,"[4] one of whose many salient features is the way
it mirrors both the arguments and the ethics informing Panofsky's "The History of
Art as a Humanistic Discipline."

To talk about "the text" is always, in the first instance, to talk about what endures
in the dimensions of space and time. Indeed, talk of "the text" is talk of what is *meant*
to endure even if, in the forensic spirit of the "symptomatologies," "genealogies," "eti-
ologies," and topological "transvaluations" by which so much current criticism and
theory is dominated, it is also talk of what (like evidence left at a crime scene) remains
behind to trip up and condemn us. As lawyers like to remind us, now by insisting on,
and now by urging against it, in committing ourselves to writing, and more especially
to writing addressed beyond the immediate circle of associates and friends and the
practical contexts we share with them, we lay claim to at least a relative transcendence.
This is why texts may in general be classed with the group of cultural artifacts that,
in the article alluded to a moment ago, Panofsky has distinguished by the name of

monuments: objects that, unlike the humbler documents scholars use to establish the historical framework for monuments' purposes and meanings, demand that we engage them on something approaching their own terms, as ends rather than means, and as works rather than as interpretive fields or instruments.

Texts are, of course, of many kinds and do many things. This fact underscores a whole problem entangling much French theorizing on the subject in Blanchot or Barthes, in Derrida, Lacoue-Labarthe, or Quignard,[5] all of whom tend to measure what is meant by "text" against an implicitly literary (and more specifically, Romantic) model that, however central and interesting to the likes of us, nonetheless constitutes only one among many others. Think, for instance, of medieval *muniments*— charters, say, recording acts of donation or treaty. While a feature of such documents is the residual orality with which they performatively embody the acts they identify and register, serving indeed as metonymic pledges of the exchanges they minute, the ethical horizon they inscribe conspicuously fails to respond to the kind of symbolic pressure evinced by the undertone of pathos associated with the Blanchotesque Book, the literary Absolute, Derridean *différance,* or Quignardian specularity. But whatever texts do—instruct (with or without delight), exhort, argue, persuade, extenuate, entreat, narrate, mythologize, worship, divert, minute, move, provoke, invoke, evoke, enjoin, protest, interpret, *re*-interpret—they do it in the perspective of the far-reaching and ever-lasting.

This accounts for the positive face of Socrates' famous criticism in Plato's *Phaedrus:*

> The fact is, Phaedrus, that writing involves a similar disadvantage to painting. The productions of painting look like living beings, but if you ask them a question they maintain a solemn silence. The same holds true of written words; you might suppose that they understand what they are saying, but if you ask them what they mean by anything they simply return the same answer over and over again.[6]

Even in the manuscript culture to which both Socrates and Plato belong, where the text is notoriously exposed not only to the abuses and misinterpretations to which Socrates turns in the continuation of his attack, but to the vicissitudes of scribal errors, variant copies, and silent editorial excisions, additions, and reworkings, writing inherently gestures toward the fixity and permanence that, in enabling it to travel from place to place and era to era, enables as well as obliges it to say the same thing ever and again. In this sense, print—together with the codex in which print finds its ideal material embodiment—exhibits writing's *destiny,* proclaimed not only by what early modern theologians liked to call "universal consent" (with few exceptions, people abandon hand-written scrolls as soon as opportunity permits), but in the *verbatim* practices even the most agile and inventive hermeneut will affect. To cite an example that a reading of Gibbon's *Decline and Fall of the Roman Empire* recommends, the Arian crisis of the reign of the odious Constantine can be fairly represented as stemming from the interpretive pressure placed on the form of a single word as determined by that of a single syllable. Is the relation between the divine Father and his only "begotten" (or "created"?) Son best expressed by the term *homoousia,* indicating an identical substance, or by the slacker *homoiousia,* denoting a mere substantial likeness?[7] Or consider the turn exegesis takes in the era of Erasmus's *Novum instrumentum* and the Lutheran Reform it helped foment precisely by raising questions about the exact form of words (and about the exact historical sense of the words) laid down in the Greek New Testament. In both of these cases, what at once authorizes and provokes dispute is the fact that there is a *text* and that, *as* a text, it says only and always one thing and the same.

Still, as the ambiguous status of the medieval *muniment* reminds us, and as Panofsky further notes in the essay I have been citing, texts are also *documents*—instruments (Erasmus's very word) whose value, though depending on permanence and on the survival permanence makes possible, nevertheless lies in the contingent uses to which they are put rather than in the claims to quasi-transcendent autonomy they make and project. Here we move from the act and aim that occasions to the cultural *activity* of which the text (*any* text) provides the practical index: at once a constituent of what we have come to call the "historical record" and a tool we use to *establish* that record. In this light, the text is preeminently the target of what Gibbon styles "the bold and sagacious spirit of criticism."[8] If the monument, as an *arti*-fact, demands attention to the *telos* that presides over its making, the document is a *fact* that helps determine the artifact's conditions and point, often at the expense of the teleology it explains.

Put another way, if the monument is the object of a certain *idolatry* of which, again, as iconomachically "deconstructive" as it may conceive itself to be, French theory offers an uncomfortable example, the document is finally and unavoidably iconoclastic. Operating as it does in the historical mode of the "just what," it imposes the reductive logic of "nothing but." Whence, in our earlier locus in Gibbon, what an irreverently philological rather than dogmatically exegetical stance reveals about the triumphant Church in the era of Constantine: the ignoble collusion of interests uniting the all-too-worldly ambition of bishops and the monstrous imperial egotist on whom the bishops conferred a legitimacy belied by the usurpations, murders, and luxurious extravagance that characterize Constantine's rise to power and personal reign.[9] True, in sifting not only such imperial missives, orations, edicts, and clerical records as survive, but also the epistles, treatises, canons, and anathemata that churchmen produced, Gibbon erects a monument of his own: the *Decline and Fall* itself, a literally colossal work that begins and ends in the ruins of Rome on which it is founded (and feasts).[10] Yet (giving the term something of the force it has in Kant) a *peculiarity* of the work is the antinomic way in which it consciously presents itself as a monument of and to the at once scrupulous and ironical ethos of a skeptical (Gibbon, with an eye to his contemporary hero Hume, likes to call it "philosophical") documentarity. A measure of the greatness of the *Decline and Fall* is its at least fitful awareness of the material condition (one is tempted to say the historical fate) its basic method entails: its acknowledgement of its own inevitable conversion into the kind of historical document it deploys and (as a means to that end) "criticizes."

Gibbon's example illuminates a resource available to even the most hubristic monuments: the capacity to indict the imminence of the documentary ruin that *will* sooner or later overtake and consume them. This too is already at work in the *Phaedrus.* Thus the sophist Lysias is not there to answer for the discourse on love entrusted to the dialogue's beautiful eponym and cannot therefore defend it against the critical reduction it nonetheless licenses; and the theme of the reduction is the phallic scroll concealed in Phaedrus's garments and the gesture of simultaneous concealment and exposure with which a shame-faced Socrates prefaces his first, lying speech about love by pulling his robe over his head to unmask the silent organ whose salience prompts the seductive lies Lysias propounds.[11] The reduction to the status of a document is indeed what, in its very monumentality, the monument sets out to counter, exorcise, or preempt, deploying the arts of beautiful persuasion in order to anticipate and thereby (in the dual French sense of the word) *prevent* the iconoclastic reckoning to come.

Nothing is easier for us today than to recognize the lamentable anti-Semitism shaping of, say, Shakespeare's *The Merchant of Venice:* whatever the Bard thought he was doing, whatever complex moral perspective he intended to defend against the lethal letter of the emergent modern institution of the Law, there is no mistaking the putrid subsoil of unthinking racial prejudice, scholarly superstition, religious anxiety, and proto-national fantasy that transforms the hapless Shylock into "the Jew," embodiment of the law of which the action makes him the victim. Yet there is much to bring us up short in the contemporary testimony of Marlowe's *The Jew of Malta,* a play that documents Shakespeare's anti-Semitism the more powerfully precisely because it not only corroborates but *anatomizes* the Elizabethan construction of "the Jew." The scapegoating of Shakespeare's Shylock is the more visible (and unpardonable) just because Marlowe's Barabas *becomes* "a Jew" by consenting to play the role his Christian compatriots foist on him to justify their expropriation of his wealth. Marlowe's Jew is the beam in Shakespeare's eye, a monument to the documentary self-consciousness the same era could afford even if Shakespeare blinked.

So it is against this background, and in particular as illuminated by the monument/document dialectic Panofsky formulates, that I propose to turn to the subject at hand as a means of understanding not only the exemplary potential that the interdisciplinary turn of early modern comparative literature illustrates, but the light it sheds on the at once epistemological and ethical dilemma that the methods of critical historicism pose for the humanities at large.

Though Haun Saussy overlooks it in the otherwise exemplary pocket history of the field provided in the introductory chapter to the present volume, the sprawling composite once called "the Renaissance" and now more commonly referred to as "early modernity" emerged as a precocious terrain for comparatist exploration. It is true that, dating from the immediate postwar generation of the 1950s and 60s, the widespread interest in the novel, in literary modernism, and in existentialist philosophy tended to identify comparative literature with the Iron Triangle of nineteenth- and twentieth-century English, French, and German. The emphasis on English, French, and German modernity was seconded by the concomitant currency of Freudian psychoanalysis and the "phenomenological" methods that characterized the Francophone (as opposed to Anglo-American) New Criticism of Georges Poulet, Jean Starobinski, or the Roland Barthes of *Le Degré zéro de l'écriture* (1953) or *Sur Racine* (1963). Subsequent developments reinforced the narrow linguistic and historical scope of mainstream comparatism. The embrace of French structuralism in the late 1960s and early 70s; René Wellek's assertion of the need to provide literary criticism with a rigorous theoretical foundation informed by readings in German literary and philosophical speculation since Goethe; the growing preoccupation with Anglo-German Romanticism, French symbolism, and post-Enlightenment philosophy (especially Hegel, Nietzsche, and Heidegger) attending the triumph of Derridean and de Manian deconstruction in the 1970s and early 80s; and the complementary if also in many respects rival rediscovery (in Fredric Jameson, notably) of the Marxian cultural criticism of the Frankfurt School—all confirmed the dominant focus on the literature of nineteenth- and twentieth-century England, France, and Germany.

As chronicled in the Bernheimer report of 1994, the cultural turn inaugurated not only by Frankfurt School materialism, but also by the advent of Foucauldian "archaeologies" aimed at unearthing the hegemonic social "discourses" conditioning the both cultural and colonial order of the modern West, enriched and complicated the kinds of materials comparatists studied, the range of questions they asked about those materials, and the methods (and metaphors: in Foucault, for instance, the two are often indistinguishable) those questions in turn engendered. Thanks in part to the example of the structuralist Barthes of *Mythologies* (1957) or *Le Système de la mode* (1967), the study of literature began to make room for meditations on popular culture as exhibited in the electronic as well as print media, thereby inaugurating the wave of interest in advertising, comic books, and TV shows that is still very much with us. Similarly, Kaja Silverman, Laura Mulvey, or Teresa de Lauretis's critical feminist challenge to the Lacanian theory of the "subject" stimulated research on the problematically gendered character of vision enacted in photography and film. Crossed with Deleuze and Baudrillard's anti-Platonic revaluation of the "simulacrum," François Lyotard's demonstration of the eminently deconstructable ahistorical pretensions of high literary modernism and the "grand narratives" that buttressed them prompted increasing engagement with the self-consciously self-consuming ironies of the "postmodern condition." Foucault's monumental *Histoire de la sexualité* (1976–84) fueled the exploration of the constructed nature of sexual identities and desires deepened by Judith Butler's analyses of the performative nature of gender and power. More recently, the perspectives of "world literature" promoted by Edward Said's classic exposé of Western Orientalism and by Gayatri Spivak, Homi Bhabha, Ariel Dorfman, or Anthony Appiah's efforts to think in the genuinely global perspective of postcolonial experience have not only completed the critical dismantling of the inherited literary canon but have displaced the European metropolis from the traditional center of comparatist attention.

It is nonetheless worth remembering that, even before receiving its now-familiar proper name, comparative literature was forged in the study of early European modernity. Many of the discipline's basic models are to be found in the Romance studies of Erich Auerbach, Ernst Robert Curtius, Leo Spitzer, and Paul Oskar Kristeller, pioneers to whose example we owe, as it were, the apostolic succession of their North American descendants, Harry Levin, Thomas Greene, David Quint, William Kennedy, or Gordon Braden. Much of the original impetus behind what we now call comparative literature thus came from scholarship on the "long" European Renaissance reaching from the late Italian Middle Ages of Dante, Petrarch, and Boccaccio through the "high" Renaissance of Ariosto, Tasso, the Elizabethans, and the Pléiade down to the period of cultural crisis associated with the baroque and its neoclassical aftermath.

There are obvious and important reasons why this should have been so. One of the many historical byproducts of—or, to put the same idea in a more energetic light, one of the many historical tasks undertaken by—the early modern era was to frame, invent, or (to borrow Benedict Anderson's influential term) "imagine"[12] the nations and national traditions on which comparative literature depends in order precisely to "compare" them: long before Herder, Staël, and Goethe laid the proximate basis for Meltzl's historic inauguration of the *Zeitschrift für vergleichende Literatur* of 1877, Du Bellay's *Deffence et illustration de la langue françoyse* (1549) and Camden's *Brittania*

(1586) had asserted the autonomous national identities of France and England. Still, the major features of at any rate élite period culture were inherently international phenomena. As Anthony Grafton and Peter Miller have shown, humanism and the increasingly critical philological protocols that were at once its chief instrument and its characteristic expression enlisted the collaborative efforts of scholars throughout Europe. Behind this collaboration and the networks of correspondence, libraries, and exchanges of manuscripts that sustained it lay the active conviction of both continuity with the classical past and community in the intellectual present, whose locus was the transnational Republic of Letters of which all humanists saw themselves as citizens.[13] Similarly, the Reformation and the radical collective experience of alterity, provoked not only by the great schism itself but by the humanist discovery of history, the growing success of the demystificatory methods of modern science, and Europe's violent encounter with and colonial conquest of the Americas, united Europeans even as it divided them into ever more stridently irreconcilable camps.

What was true of the content of the new European experience of self and world was equally true of the media that propagated that experience: print and the (by period standards) vast and rapid circulation of information and opinion that print made possible; the cultivation and use of an increasingly refined form of Latin conceived precisely as an international medium of communication and expression; the shared "places" and models drawn from classical antiquity; the great Neoplatonic Idea by which, from Ficino and Pico della Mirandola on, European writers were consistently drawn and in relation to which they measured their productions; or the ever larger and (thanks to the editorial and commercial efforts of Italian or Dutch scholars and printers) ever more widely broadcast corpus of literary and historical *exempla* with which writers compared and defined the emergencies of present occasions—all of these formed a consciously shared legacy and a set of consciously shared principles that shaped not only what writers from diverse regions understood themselves to have in common, but even how they conceived their ever more pointed historical and national differences. To cite an example recently expounded by Harry Berger, the writings of the Roman Tacitus, and in particular his annals of the Cæsars, supplied a mode of historical and political discourse that served as a *lingua franca* of European social thought from Machiavelli and Bodin to Grotius and Hobbes. Yet in the same author's *Germania,* describing the barbaric but nonetheless noble freedom of Rome's uncouth Gothic enemies, European intellectuals found a paradoxically shared model of cultural and historical *difference* that would enable Luther, notably, to formulate the dialectic of uncompromising Northern veracity versus denaturing Southern sophistication that characterized what he saw to be fundamentally at stake in his rejection of Roman orthodoxy.[14]

It is significant, however, that, as much of the preceding already indicates, the early modern period was tailor-made for interdisciplinary as well as comparative literary scholarship. Before the notorious specialization of the term's meaning in the nineteenth century—that is, not at all coincidentally, in the era whose analysis is so closely linked to the advent of theory and the dominance of English, French, and German studies—"literature" was the slightly barbarous synonym for "letters," itself a synonym for "learning." As such, the literary crossed disciplinary boundaries its practitioners did not in any case systematically recognize or acknowledge. Historians and poets, dramatists and philosophers, philologists, antiquarians, and divines were in continuous intimate conversation because they pursued complementary (if often contradictory) perspectives on the same world and on the same canonical corpus of texts. Poets, for example, were expected to be "polyhistors," steeped in the rival "liberal" traditions among which poetry was numbered. If this was so, it was in part because humanists like Castelvetro, Casaubon, or the Scaligers were not merely students of the poetic forms whose textual histories they reconstructed, but their theorists. The tragedies and Stoic epistles of the ancient Seneca formed the common patrimony of philosophy and drama alike, an idiom Lipsius or Montaigne actively shared with the playwrights who succeeded them: Shakespeare, Corneille, Calderón, and Racine. And what was true of poets, philosophers, and philologists was equally true of the historians to whom dramatists in particular turned for the subjects (or "fables") on which their art depended. If Machiavelli was a playwright as well as the historian and theorist of the political disasters of late-fifteenth-century Italy, it is not just because he drew on the same classical sources in Tacitus, Livy, or Suetonius, but because the fundamental theme of history and political theory was a kind of poetics of historical events whose models were as self-consciously dramatic as they were critical and documentary.

We observe the same kind of synergy in the "scientific" disciplines and professions with which our later "literature" has come to be contrasted—a contrast reinforced by the largely anti-scientific claims to access to the "absolute" that Romantic poets were pleased to make. Like Ficino and Pico or Erasmus and More before them, the new "natural philosophers" of the later sixteenth and early seventeenth centuries remained *gens de lettres* even as they grew more skeptical of the idealisms to which poetry and traditional philosophy were alike committed. Campanella and Kepler, Bacon and Descartes were thus quite naturally the authors of masques, dialogues, utopias, and science fictions that form an integral (if today subaltern) part of the early modern literary corpus. Moreover, though historically fated, as Mary Campbell has recently demonstrated, to part ways with its fictional counterpart, the idiom of the new science was initially literary in its own right.[15] Bacon's aphorisms; Descartes'

adaptations of the mode of Loyolan spiritual exercises for the purpose of metaphysi-
cal rather than pious meditation; the Epicurean thought-experiments of Kepler, God-
win, or Cyrano de Bergerac, conducted in the form of imaginary voyages to distant
islands or to the moon—these are not merely evidence of the weight of historical
inertia, symptoms of the mental difficulty early moderns encountered in adopting
what Campbell calls the properly "anaesthetic" discourse of professional philosophy
and science. They are also tokens of the continuum in which this discourse stood and
from which it progressively labored (as indeed it *had* to labor) to differentiate itself.

What was true in the domain of letters was also true in that of the arts more
generally, and in particular the visual arts. A central theme of early modern aesthetics, as crucial for the intelligence of poetry as for that of period art, is the doctrine
ut pictura poesis—"as is (or as in) painting, so is (or so in) poetry." The doctrine
generated both an endless stream of pointed "parallels" and "comparisons" between
poetry and painting and the notorious *paragone,* the struggle to determine which of
the two was the "first" or "original" and thus the preeminent of the so-called "sister
arts." At the heart of early modern aesthetics, then, was an emulative rivalry in many
respects analogous to and even continuous with that between ancients and moderns—a point that emerges with particular clarity in Leonardo's contribution to the
genre, where painting's privileged connection with visual *sperientia,* the increasingly
scientific analysis of visual experience, is systematically opposed to the Neoplatonic
Idea blinding poetry to the true because empirical form of things. The rivalry was
nonetheless grounded in, and indeed only possible, on the underlying assumption
of a fundamental "sisterhood" and the active exchange of values that the notion of
sisterhood endorsed and decreed. It is to this extent a measure of the degree to which
painters inhabit the same literary realm and draw on the same literary inheritance as
the poets and *gens de lettres* with whom they disputed aesthetic priority. This is indeed why, like poets, painters present themselves as "polyhistors" laying claim as such
to the same bookish "liberality." And it is also why—as attested by Michelangelo's
sonnets; Leonardo's notebooks and the unfinished literary project they were intended
to prepare; the treatises of Alberti, Dürer, and Van Hoogstraten; Vasari's *Lives of the
Artists;* Bernini's work as a comic playwright; Poussin's correspondence with Chante-
lou; or the lectures of the French Academician Le Brun—so many painters turn out
to have been writers of considerable authority, ingenuity, and power.

Whence another, notably German and, in philosophical terms, late Romantic
strain of comparatist scholarship that dates from the first third of the twentieth century, a development the more telling for arising within the then only recently institutionalized field of art history. I am thinking here of the Warburg Institute and of
the precocious sense of art's place in the broader intellectual and cultural scheme of

things that inspires the work of the Warburg's first generation of scholars—Erwin Panofsky, Fritz Saxl, and Rudolf Wittkower—as well as their patron, Aby Warburg himself. The object of study the Warburgers propose for themselves is not yet the environing and in every sense disciplinary "discourse" explored by Foucault and his disciples in contemporary cultural historicism. They speak rather the at-once neo-Kantian and neo-Hegelian language of Alois Riegl's *WeltanscHaungsphilosophie,* and above all of Ernst Cassirer's three-volume *Philosophie der symbolischen Formen* (1923–29): a monumental work of philosophical synthesis that is also (and integrally) a history of the evolution of the philosophical ideas in which it trades and that, as such, furnished Panofsky in particular (whose first book, *Die Perspektive als 'symbolische Form'* [1927], cites Cassirer's key concept in its title) with a key model for his own research. It is true that the idealist modes of historical reflection that the Warburgers practiced now seem dated and even suspect, especially in their tendency to fetishize historical epochs by treating them as unique and somehow naturally occurring formations, organically self-sufficient, strangely eternal, and therefore ahistorical. Still, their scholarship remains exemplary for its commitment to a highly textured and inventive excavation (an "archaeology," indeed) of the common cultural language, the ambient ethos and sensibility, the habits of perception and thought, and even the general "mentality" of which visual art, conceived as an inescapably historical phenomenon, bears the imprint. Nor should it escape our notice that the Warburgers articulated a decisive model for Walter Benjamin's Arcades Project. For all Benjamin's consistently unhappy yet stubborn commitment to the materialist modes of analysis dictated by his correspondents in the Frankfurt School, what Adorno notoriously derided as his at-once naïve and idolatrously positivistic fascination with semi-digested bodies of cultural "facts" owed a great deal to the quite comparable accumulations set forth in Warburg *Vorträge.*

This leads, on one side, to a highly developed documentary conception of art in historical context. For example, to cite another of Panofsky's works, *Gothic Architecture and Scholasticism* (1951), to understand or, more pointedly, to know how to look at and thus take in the abbey churches and cathedrals of twelfth- and thirteenth-century France demands knowledge of the intellectual program they fulfill. And this in turn requires knowledge of the fourfold method of Thomist allegoresis, the triadic patterns of high Gothic Trinitarian thought, and the structures of scholastic disputation—the habit of expounding the *sic et non* or *pro et contra* of any theological or philosophical question in pursuit of the mediating *tertium quid* by which apparently insuperable opposition might be resolved. Conversely, precisely because art emerges as the plastic exhibition of the modes of sensibility and thought that make it possible, it becomes in turn a documentary ground for those forms of literary, philosophical, doctrinal, or historical representation that help contextualize and explain it. As a remarkable result, in order to perform his tasks as an art historian, Panofsky had not merely to rely on the philological work of others, but to make himself a philologist in his own right. Thus, in *Hercules am Scheidewege und andere antike Bildstoffe in der neueren Kunst* (1930), on the theme of the Judgment of Hercules in European art from Locher's *Stultifera navis* (1494) down to the eighteenth century, Panofsky was obliged not only to mine the relevant literary remains of classical antiquity (e.g., Prodicus's rehearsal of the Hercules story as reported in Xenophon's *Memorabilia*, Cicero's commentary on the Dream of Scipio in *De republica*, or the symbolic valence Pythagoreans attached to the form of the letter Y) for the intelligence they offer; he had at points to actively *reconstruct* the tradition as a means to that end. As he writes in a passage in the introduction that Peter Miller also quotes:

> It is in the nature of the thing that the investigation had to proceed, here and there, in the domain of purely literary-historical and even text-critical discussions. No single science can be ready with answers to all the questions that a sister-discipline, from its completely different intellectual context, can address to it. And when the historian of images sees himself led to specific textual problems, he cannot expect to find exactly these problems—which from the standpoint of the philologist or literary historian are often not visible at all—already completely solved, but he will have to help himself as best he can.[16]

The art historian, then, is also a classicist. Furthermore, in what is surely Panofsky's greatest and most famous contribution to humanistic as well as art historical method, his grasp of the fundamental dialogue in which art and letters stand led to the invention of *iconology*, a science of visual signs and of the means required to interpret them that was later to help shape, in Foucault and Marin notably, the semiotic turn at the heart of the contemporary enterprise of literary and cultural analysis.

Needless to say, a great deal has changed in the interval, and not least—thanks to Michael Ann Holly's *Panofsky and the Foundations of Art History* (1984), documenting the idealist underpinnings of the Panofskian model—our sense of Panofsky himself. The prestige of Warburg iconology and its erudite reconstructions of the intellectual as well as iconographic subsoil of the European artistic canon has given way to the still-rising authority of the kind of ideological suspicion that informs the work of the precisely contemporary Institute for Social Research: a collective whose leading lights, Theodor Adorno and Max Horkheimer, challenge the viewpoint represented by Panofsky's aestheticizing fusion of Kant and Hegel. More specifically, and despite the dialectical use Benjamin's *Ursprung des deutschen Trauerspiels* (1928) was able to make of Panofsky and Saxl's collaborative exploration of the early modern literary and iconographic portrayal of the theme of melancholy,[17] the Warburg's unquestioning allegiance to high culture evinced by Panofsky's late Romantic embrace of Kantian humanism (see, e.g., the opening pages of "The History of Art as a Humanistic Discipline") inevitably blinded its members to the materialist insights behind Benjamin's own later immersion in the low-cultural detritus zealously assembled in the Arcades Project. It is indeed in this critical light—with Foucault, Barthes, and the semiotic turn the Louis Marin of *Etudes sémiologiques* (1971), *Détruire la peinture* (1977), and *Des pouvoirs de l'image* (1993) gave art historical analysis as guides—that new historicists and their counterparts in the "new" art history have been led to read and above all to *revise* the Renaissance legacy.

One sign of the change is the energetic pertinacity with which students of literature have turned to early modern visual art. Perhaps the most spectacular example is Norman Bryson, a sometime director of English studies at Cambridge whose pathbreaking application of the methods of French semiotics to the business of interpreting the painterly language of French classical art in *Word and Image* (1981) and to the reassessment of the fundamentals of Renaissance naturalism in *Vision and Painting* (1983) established his credentials as the professional art historian he has since become. But literary styles of interpretation and thought have also produced startling new insights in a wide variety of contexts and modes. To cite only a few particularly memorable examples, Mieke Bal's *Reading Rembrandt* (1991) and *Quoting Caravaggio* (1999) interrogate baroque painting in the self-consciously political perspectives defined by our own both intensely and inevitably interested and self-referential motives for looking at it. Leonard Barkan's *Unearthing the Past* (1999) combines the methods of Foucault and Warburg art history to show how, in digging up and digesting the ruined artistic legacy of classical antiquity, early modern aestheticians and archaeologists wound up constructing the past to which they imagined they gave "rebirth." Harry Berger's *Fictions of the Pose* (2000) draws on everything from Renaissance conduct books and the Lacanian theory of the Gaze to the political and ecclesiastical history of the United Provinces of the Netherlands and the evolving conventions and studio practices of early modern portraiture to explore how Rembrandt managed to turn the self-portrait into a remarkably prescient instrument of radical ideological as well as artistic critique. Finally, Jonathan Sawday's *The Body Emblazoned* (1995) analyzes the intersections of art, letters, and science typified by their shared interest in the anatomical dissection of the human body to explain the properly modern transformation of Vitruvius's noble cosmological Man into Descartes' demoralized machine. What all of these commentators have in common is the acuity with which they bring the posture of critical suspicion demanded of interpreters of early modern texts to bear on the visual objects that were once the exclusive province of art historical idolatry.

If students of literature have learnt anything in the wake of the theoretical revolutions of the 1960s through the 1980s, it is that texts can never be taken at what the hagiographical norms of pre-structuralist literary interpretation piously present as face value. In "La mort de l'auteur" and "De l'œuvre au texte," a crucial pair of essays that have joined Wimsatt and Beardsley's chapter on the "intentional fallacy" as the obligatory starting point for any course in advanced literary analysis, Roland Barthes puts it this way. What we used unhesitatingly to call "works" of literature are not autonomous inhabitants of a fundamentally neutral cultural space whose (in Stanley Fish's felicitous phrase) "self-announcing" character is readily available to any disinterested and moderately well-informed passer-by; they are rather "methodological fields" whose properties reflect and even demand the questions, concerns, and technologies that supervene the moment we begin to read them.[18] This is partly so on ontological grounds. As in different ways Derrida, Deleuze, and de Man all remind us, the very condition of possibility of the text *as* text, what precisely makes a *text* of otherwise at least notionally self-explanatory speech, is the absence that makes for writing, and the logic of difference writing sets in train. Texts are never what they seem, if only as a reflex of the grammatological and rhetorical displacements that are simultaneously the scene, the instrument, and the repository of the act of writing. (The fact that writing is all three of these things, at once and undecidably, is itself a case in point.) But the conversion of "work" to differential methodological artifact also expresses the work's *historical* dependence—the master theme of Foucault and of Frankfurt Critical Theory, and thus of the "new" historical models they inspire. What a text betokens without being able to embrace it is not just the aporetic nature of its scriptorial medium; it is the system of often conflicting social, psychosexual, and ideological interests that shape the cultural emergencies of which it is the deposit. Shakespeare's *Hamlet*, the Cartesian cogito, or Calderón's *La vida es sueño* are not explicitly *about* the advent of the collective historical personage we have come to call the "modern bourgeois subject"; nor indeed *could* they have been about it, since it is only later, in the light of historical consequences of which subsequent acts of historical interpretation are themselves the telltale product, that the relevant concepts ("modernity," "bourgeoisie," "the subject") come to hand. Nevertheless, the occult social and ideological forces whose beleaguered protagonist turns out to have been the "modern subject" may legitimately and productively be said to mediate the literary and intellectual processes of which Shakespeare's, Descartes', and Calderón's writings serve as the index.

This accounts for the originality of studies like those noted above. Necessarily preoccupied with the far greater effects of presence that visual art deploys, both in its figurative aspect (whatever else a Venus by Botticelli may mean or do, there is the incontestable fact of the Venus herself) and in what Berger terms its "textural" dimension (there is also the fact of *paint,* of its mode of application, of the brush and hand whose traces it bears),[19] art historians were far slower than their literary counterparts to acknowledge and respond to the mediated nature of the media they study. (The same can be said of professional philosophy, especially in the analytic tradition of the Anglo-American scene, where a preoccupation with testing concepts and with adjudicating rival forms of argument have cast a comparably idolatrous spell.) Some sort of outside intervention was therefore required to wake art history from the formalist slumber that the visual rather than (as in literature) directly differential nature of the medium encouraged.

The fact remains that, prodded by the contrarian, deliberately deconstructive efforts of Bryson or Bal, powerful interventions have increasingly come from art historians as well. For a start, of course, there is Holly's revisionist account of the Panofskian foundations of art history itself, seconded not only by Donald Preziosi's *Rethinking Art History: Meditations on a Coy Science* (1989), exposing the discipline's largely unspoken ideological presumptions in order to introduce the necessarily iconomachic perspectives of genuinely historical analysis, but also by more recent contributions like Christopher Wood's introduction to his *Vienna School Reader: Politics and Art Historical Method in the 1930s* (2000), offering a more sympathetic (and accordingly less judgmental) account than Holly's or Preziosi's of the political bearing of the humanistic practice of German-language art history in the tradition of Riegl and Wölfflin in the face of rising Nazi barbarism. But we also have Svetlana Alpers's *The Art of Describing* (1981) and *Rembrandt's Enterprise* (1988); Michael Baxandall's *Painting and Experience in Fifteenth-Century Italy* (revised ed., 1988); Celeste Brusati's *Artifice and Illusion* (1995); Francis Haskell's *Past and Present in Art and Taste* (1987) and *History and Its Images* (1993); Martin Kemp's *The Science of Art* (1990); Barbara Stafford's *Body Criticism* (1991); or Bryan Wolf's *Vermeer and the Invention of Seeing* (2001)—putting the history of early modern art in dialogue with its material bases in the technologies of early modern optical science and anatomy, in the socioeconomic systems of patronage and commissions that enabled artists to work by paying their keep, in the iconophobic yet increasingly graphic conceptions of early modern philosophy, and in the shift from the workshop practices of the generations of Titian and Rubens to the marketplace of Rembrandt and the commercial art dealers who increasingly control the circulation of works of art. Or there is the work of David Summers, *Michelangelo and the Language of Art* (1981) and *The Judgment of Sense* (1987); David Carrier, *Poussin's Paintings: A Study in Art Historical Methodology* (1993); or James Elkins's *What Painting Is: How to Think about Oil Painting, Using the Language of Alchemy* (1999)—all of which urge, in different and, as in Elkins's case in particular, at times eccentric ways, that early modern painting be granted a philo-sophical seriousness that the post-Romantic picture of the painter as *idiot savant* makes difficult.

Finally, as a kind of emblem or epitome of the change in standpoint, there is the deep and far-reaching feminist revaluation of the art historical canon. Griselda Pollock's *Vision and Difference: Femininity, Feminism, and the Histories of Art* (1988); Mary Garrard's *Artemesia Gentileschi* (1988); or the revolutionary collection of essays Garrard co-edited with Norma Broude, *Feminism and Art History: Questioning the Litany* (1982) all come to mind here. But so too do more recent studies—Rona Goffen's *Titian's Women* (1997), for instance, offering a finely nuanced defense of Titian's por-trayal of women against reflex feminist condemnation, or Mary Campbell's *Wonder & Science* (1999), where the rapacious visual practices feminists discover in art are brought into conversation with the unavowed yet powerful erotics of early modern science. By emphasizing the essential unity behind apparent differences in medium and form, and especially how, whatever the medium, women so often emerge as pas-sive objects of visual analysis and consumption, feminist analysis of the image of women set forth in painting highlights the *systemic* character of early modern picto-rial practices. Indeed, the feminist critique reveals just the kind of generalized visual "discourse" that Foucauldian theory posits as the correlate of the hegemonic *episteme* by which early modern culture constitutes a single self-organized and self-reproduc-ing whole. In the process, oppositional accounts of how women are portrayed in early modern painting bring the régime's characteristic *violence* into sharper focus—a vio-lence highlighted by the links between painterly portrayals of the female body and the Baconian-cum-Cartesian rhetoric of "mastery" and "possession" informing the scientific investigation of nature. Feminists have thus unearthed a culture of ocular objectivity that, in defining early modern pictorial practices in the broadest sense, one encompassing literature and philosophy as well as visual or plastic art, at once fed on and propagated what Bal calls a pervasive "semiotics of rape."[20]

To be sure, the complex enterprise sketched here is subject to noteworthy excesses and persistent tensions. In particular, we note a tendency to *patronize* the past, alleg-ing blind spots that are often of our own making. As hinted earlier, it takes a certain judgmental precipitancy to overlook how Marlowe's *Jew of Malta* already fingers the anti-Semitism shaping Shakespeare's *Merchant of Venice*. Similarly, there is a ten-dency to hypostatize, a bad habit contracted from the Continental philosophers on whom so many of us depend. Thus, despite the warnings we might have gleaned from a more scrupulous reading of Wittgenstein on the fallacies attending the careless use of definite articles, there is lots of talk about pseudo-entities like "*the* modern subject" (as though there were only one) or "subjectivity *as such*" (as though *as-suchness* were a door to some really existing conceptual ground rather than an unconscious throw-back to the Scholastic thesis of essential forms). There is also the tendency to simplify by taking special cases for general rules. Bal falls into this trap when she asserts not simply that *some* of the dozens of poems and images devoted to the story of the rape of Lucretia participate in the crime they rehearse or reproduce, but that *all* of them do.[21] This, in turn, is related to the metonymical procedure Harry Berger calls "snip-petotomy." To cite Berger's own example, in Francis Barker's *The Tremulous Private Body: Essays in Subjection* (1984), making a characteristically Foucauldian case for interpreting the advent of "*the* modern subject" as the disciplinary social construc-tion of the privatized individual, an isolated bit of a text (Samuel Pepys's report of destroying his copy of the pornographic *L'Ecole des filles*) is not only overinterpreted (it is far from clear that shame-faced repression of his pleasure in the book made Pepys destroy it), but is also made to stand, first for the entire text (Pepys's mammoth diary as a whole) of which it is a tiny part, and then for the entire culture of which the diary is the merest slice.[22] Or to take another example, the more outstanding for the vivid refutation it receives at Derrida's hands, there is Foucault's snippetotomous overreading of the dismissal of the possibility of madness in Descartes' first medita-tion: a brief passage (about half of a short paragraph) on the grounds of whose very brevity Foucault lays the entire basis for the history of modern Reason.[23]

What all of this comes down to is the reductionism whose form is given in the Panofskian alternative with which this essay began, the monument/document pair I used to characterize the inescapable ambivalence of the posture involved in reading historical texts. Consider an instructive passage from Foucault's *Archéologie du savoir* in which he cites Panofsky's terms as a key to his own method. Foucault insists in the passage that, appearances notwithstanding, the historical "archaeology" of epis-temological categories is not an "allegorical" procedure seeking "an 'other discourse'" beneath or behind the "proper volume" of the historical discourses that form its monuments.[24] It is nevertheless typical of Foucault's method (as in fact—Panofsky's point—of method in general) that the characteristic effect of his analysis is the exact opposite of the one he claims. Insofar, moreover, as the object of analysis is precisely constraining "discourses" rather than the actual works on which they impose their prior conditions, how could it be otherwise? Nor do I cite Foucault's dilemma in order to refute him. The latent systems of constraining discursive conditions of possibility that he brings to light did in fact exist and did in fact operate very much as he reports. The problem, then, lies less in the underlying hypothesis than in the habit of Scholas-tic hypostatizing noted a moment ago—in the tendency to see a given "discourse" as existing apart from the texts, images, or practices it conditions and, as a result, to see it as *determining* rather than conditioning the instances that make its work visible.

Put another way, in order to bring a given "discourse" to light, Foucault is obliged to treat it as a monument of which everything else—that is to say, of which everything *in particular*—is merely a document. Yet though something along these lines may be a necessary point of departure, this is not, in the end, how even "discourses" work, if only because "discourses," like the grammars on which Foucault models them, are an abstraction from the practices they govern—practices, moreover, that, in carrying the enabling "discourses" along them, modify them as they go.

All of which is expressed in the very form of the objects we are trying to account for. We return here to another distinction noted earlier, one both Panofsky and the Ricœur of "Qu'est-ce qu'un texte?" implicitly worry at: the distinction between facts and artifacts, between things that in some sense naturally or mechanically occur and those that have to be made. A first point is that, unlike facts, artifacts are *intended*. As Kant would put it, both their form and their existence betoken a conscious interest and a deliberate purpose, however darkly overdetermined these may be. But this, in turn, means that to grasp them demands not merely explaining, but *comprehending* them—understanding not only how they came to be, but what they are *for* and how that in turn engages them in a life-world no less real for being a reflex of the purposes and presumptions that, in invoking it, also construct it.

This points to what seems to me to be perhaps the great achievement of interdisciplinary research in the early modern era. If texts enable us to understand how painters *thought,* and thus the ideal content or meaning of the images they produced, images help us see what the poets *saw*—the world as they imagined it, the world in which they wrote and thought as they themselves understood it. This grants modes of contact more intimate, more prehensile, and more comprehensive than any one discipline could afford. Yet it does so only so long as we remain *patient* with the past, allowing it to unfold as it were of itself in the light our interest and our questions shed.

To be sure, as Bal in particular insists with exemplary heat, we only see the past as *we* see it, driven by motives, anxieties, certainties of our own. This means that our readings are as artifactual as the artifacts with which they engage. However, if we learn nothing else about the past, at least we learn this: that we do not, in fact, share its understandings, and therefore that a painting of Lucretia, say, is not necessarily what seems so blindingly obvious to us. As the art historian Michael Baxandall urges in a book whose theme is just the Gadamerian problem of those "patterns of intention" that we at once recognize *in* and import *to* images as a reflex of whatever directs our attention to them in the first place, to remain true either to our objects or to ourselves demands a certain kind of historical *tact*.[25] Baxandall opens his book by discussing the classical tradition of *ekphrasis* and its revival not only in, but as the very basis of, the Renaissance literature of images. The lesson he draws is nonetheless addressed to *us*. However clearly and self-evidently images may seem to appear before our eyes and thus to justify what we say about them, it is not, in fact, about *images* that we talk, but rather about images "under description," that is, as prefigured in our field of vision by the particular language that we speak and the questions and concerns that language is capable of articulating. But this means, not that the past is irrecoverably concealed from us, but only that the first work of criticism we perform must be directed at ourselves.

NOTES

1. I cite David Damrosch's presidential address at the 2003 meeting of the ACLA hosted by California State University at San Marcos.

2. See Erwin Panofsky, "The History of Art as a Humanistic Discipline," in *Meaning in the Visual Arts* (Chicago: University of Chicago Press, 1955; Phoenix paper ed.), 1–25.

3. See Joseph Margolis, *Interpretation Radical but Not Unruly: The New Puzzle of the Arts and History* (Berkeley: University of California Press, 1995), 33–34.

4. Paul Ricœur, "Qu'est-ce qu'un texte? Expliquer et comprendre," in *Hermeneutik und Dialektik: Aufsätze (Hans Georg Gadamer zum 70. Geburtstag)*, ed. Rüdiger Bubner (Tübingen: Mohr [Siebeck], 1970), 2:181–200.

5. Since he is less likely to be familiar to most readers, here is a reference for the last author in this list: see Pascal Quignard, *Rhétorique spéculative* (Paris: Calmann-Lévy, 1995).

6. Plato, *Phaedrus* 275; trans. Walter Hamilton in *Phaedrus and Letters VII and VIII* (London: Penguin, 1973), 97.

7. Edward Gibbon, *The Decline and Fall of the Roman Empire*, 2nd ed., ed. Mortimer J. Adler et al. (Chicago: Encyclopaedia Britannica, Inc., 1990), 1:310–13.

8. Gibbon, *Decline and Fall*, 1:296. For a beautifully circumstantial account of the critical historicism shaping early modern philology as a whole, see Anthony Grafton, *Commerce with the Classics: Ancient Books and Renaissance Readers* (Ann Arbor: University of Michigan Press, 1997).

9. See, e.g., Gibbon's "character" of Constantine, *Decline and Fall*, 1:255–58.

10. According to Gibbon's *Memoirs*, the *Decline and Fall* was first conceived "[o]n the fifteenth of October 1764, as I sat musing amidst the ruins of the Capitol, while the bare footed friars were singing Vespers in the Temple of Jupiter" (see *Decline and Fall*, 1:v). It also ends there, at least in remembrance, when, writing the last words, in Lausanne, on 27 June 1787, Gibbon recalls where and when the idea for the book first came to him. See *Decline and Fall*, 2:598.

11. Plato, *Phaedrus* 237; trans., 34.

12. Benedict Anderson, *Imagined Communities: Reflections on the Origin and Spread of Nationalism* (London: Verso, 1983).

13. For a wonderful recent study of the Republic of Letters, the more valuable for approaching it as lived by its members from within, see Peter N. Miller, *Peiresc's Europe: Learning and Virtue in the Seventeenth Century* (New Haven, Conn.: Yale University Press, 2000).

14. See Harry Berger Jr., *Fictions of the Pose: Rembrandt against the Italian Renaissance* (Stanford, Calif.: Stanford University Press, 2000), 456–61.

15. See Mary B. Campbell, *Wonder & Science: Imagining Worlds in Early Modern Europe* (Ithaca, N.Y.: Cornell University Press, 1999), esp. chaps. 4, 5, and 6.

16. Erwin Panofsky, *Hercules am Scheidewege und andere antike Bildstoffe in der neueren Kunst* (Leipzig: B. G. Teubner, 1930; rpt. Berlin: Gebr. Mann Verlag, 1997), vii-viii. I cite Miller's translation, slightly modified, in *Peiresc's Europe*, 15.

17. See Walter Benjamin, *Ursprung des deutschen Trauerspiels* (1928); I cite the English version, *The Origin of German Tragic Drama*, trans. John Osborne (London: Verso, 1977), 149–50.

18. See Roland Barthes, "La mort de l'auteur," in *Le bruissement de la langue* (Paris: Seuil, 1984), 71–80, and "De l'œuvre au texte," ibid., 81–85; and Stanley E. Fish, *Is There a Text in This Class? The Authority of Interpretive Communities* (Cambridge, Mass.: Harvard University Press, 1980).

19. See Berger, *Fictions of the Pose*, 53–58.

20. Mieke Bal, *Reading Rembrandt: Beyond the Word-Image Opposition* (Cambridge, Mass.: Cambridge University Press, 1991), 60.

21. See Bal, *Reading Rembrandt*, chap. 2.

22. See Francis Barker, *The Tremulous Private Body: Essays on Subjection* (London: Methuen, 1984), 50–60. For his critique of Barker's reading, see Harry Berger Jr., "The Pepys Show: Ghost-Writing and Documentary Desire in *The Diary*," *English Literary History* 65 (1998): 557–91; for "snippetotomy," ibid., 563.

23. See Michel Foucault, *Histoire de la folie à l'âge classique* (1961; 2nd ed., Paris: Gallimard, 1972), chap. 2, "le grand renfermement." For his critique of Foucault, see Jacques Derrida, "Cogito et histoire de la folie," in *L'écriture et la différence* (Paris: Seuil, 1967; Points paper ed.), 51–97.

24. Michel Foucault, *L'archéologie du savoir* (Paris: Gallimard, 1969), 182.

25. Michael Baxandall, *Patterns of Intention: On the Historical Explanation of Pictures* (New Haven, Conn.: Yale University Press, 1985). See esp. the intro., "Language and Explanation," and chap. 4, "Truth and Other Cultures: Piero Della Francesca's *Baptism of Christ*," where the kind of "tact" argued for in the introduction is brought to bear on a particularly puzzling Renaissance painting.

CHAPTER TWELVE

Beyond Comparison Shopping

This Is Not Your Father's Comp. Lit.

FEDWA MALTI-DOUGLAS

It is only as I penned the subtitle to my contribution that I realized that I had been educated while an undergraduate at Cornell University and then as a graduate student, first at the University of Pennsylvania and then at UCLA, only by male professors. So when I note that this is not my father's Comp. Lit., the phrase has multiple meanings for me. As a graduate student, I was trained both in America and in France. French criticism in the 1970s was a great liberating movement for me, pulling me beyond my American educational experience toward names I had never heard before. And that is perhaps why I am constantly searching for great beyonds—beyonds that will permit the application of different theoretical models (be they semiotically-inspired, gender-inspired, sexuality-inspired, and so on) beyond any disciplinary confines. Two beyonds strike me as particularly significant in the context of a self-examination by comparatists at the dawning of a new century: beyond the verbal word into a visual universe; and the application of critical theory beyond what we normally define as literature into a wider variety of texts, understood in the largest possible context, and encompassing the rich areas of law, medicine, and science.

Only upon arriving at my first tenure track job at the University of Virginia in 1977 did I learn that not only had the university very recently become co-ed but that we female professors were a new oddity. It was in that context that I began my involvement as a faculty member in programs of comparative literature. As I watched my own career and, more importantly, the careers of my graduate students develop, I began to hear the suave and cosmopolitan voice of Ricardo Montalban telling me not only that this was not my father's Oldsmobile but that this was not my father's Comp. Lit.

Hearing a voice and acting on what that voice is transmitting are two different things. As director of the Program in Comparative Literature at the University of Texas, a program that only awarded Ph.D.s, I watched the interests of graduate stu-

dents evolve. My own pursuits were morphing at the same time. I found myself drawn
to different intellectual worlds far beyond those I had inhabited thus far. I had by
this time assimilated feminism fully into my own research, and gender became a lens
through which I viewed every word I consumed.

But the lures of the beyonds were only beginning. The first siren's call came from
the world of the visual, the world of film, political cartoons, and comic strips. Having
a partner who is a cultural historian meant that when our intellectual interests col-
lided, there was a synergy that benefited each of us. Our research on cinema was exciting, but I personally was drawn much more to the universe of comic strips. When we
embarked on our collaboration in this area, it was French criticism that sustained us.
The work of giants like Pierre Fresnault-Deruelle, Gérard Genette, Roland Barthes,
and many others convinced us that the study of verbal production, those narratives
that had provided our nourishment for many years, could be made even better if we
added the visual component to the verbal one. It is as if, after realizing that we had
supped only on American food, we had suddenly discovered the riches of French
cuisine.

My answering the call of the siren surprised many of my more closed-minded colleagues. I was called the enfant terrible of the profession for delving into the analytical
world of comics. This new wilderness that my coauthor, Allen Douglas, and I had
just entered was full of thorns and discouraging spirits. But decades later, Americans
discovered what the French already knew: the pleasures of the comics medium. It was
partly, of course, that Art Spiegelman had produced his Pulitzer Prize–winning *Maus*
(1986–1991). But American artists had long preceded Spiegelman. To name but one,
Will Eisner, a giant of the genre, has many graphic novels to his name that portray
life in Bronx tenements filled with Italian and Jewish immigrants (e.g., *A Life Force*,
1983). Most recently, he has taken to transforming works of literature like *Moby Dick*
into comic albums.

France has long been a most congenial atmosphere for comic-strip artists, both
those who are French-born and those who adopt the Gallic country as their home.
The annual festival at Angoulême draws fans and artists from around the globe. One
of the most famous names is that of Jacques Tardi, who has illustrated Céline's *Voyage
au bout de la nuit* (1992), among others. With his inserted illustrations, Tardi creates
an altogether different Céline *Voyage*, one that forces its readers to ponder not only
the words but the illustrations as well, creating an unusual type of intertextuality.
Tardi has long transcended his importance as a comic-strip artist, designing book
covers for established French publishers like Gallimard. Talking to Tardi makes one
aware that long before Americans had heard of *Maus*, Spiegelman had been working with Tardi and other artists on the journal *Raw*. Italians can pride themselves

on Crépax, whose frames are a tour de force. In Spain, Max is acknowledged as the master of the medium. The comics published by the Slovenian group Stripburger are often nothing short of enthralling. And this is not to speak of the enormous Japanese production of *manga*. Then there are Mexico, India, and numerous other countries around the globe.

I am convinced that part of the reason that the siren's call went unheeded for so long among American intelligentsia derives from our own cultural insecurity. We need the assurance that our Nathaniel Hawthorne can match Gustave Flaubert, or that our Ernest Hemingway can beat Albert Camus. Comics and graphic novels were for much too long viewed as a production for marginal readers, for the enfants terribles of their field, if you wish.

Can any of us imagine the likelihood of having a book like *Tintin est-il de droite ou de gauche?* [Is Tintin on the Right or the Left?] (2002) produced on this side of the Atlantic? This delightful volume consists of commentaries by members of the French National Assembly (the equivalent of our Congress) on the intrepid reporter and famous comic book character created by Hergé. The participants acknowledged one another as "Tintinologues" (Tintinologists), each arguing that the famous series of albums belonged to his or her political family. Can any of us conceive of members of the U.S. Congress undertaking such a project, say, with Mickey Mouse, who has just celebrated his seventy-fifth birthday? If only!

Fortunately there have been courageous, generous, and inspiring spirits like John Lent, who has tirelessly spent his career on comics, most recently founding and editing *The International Journal of Comic Art*. Every issue is an eye opener, much like the older and equally interesting *Comics Journal*, whose contents complement the more scholarly output of John Lent. Obviously, Lent heeded that first siren's call and courageously served as a model for all of us.

But aside from that, let us be fair and admit that we had grown accustomed to taking our intellectual cues from the Frankfurt School and from Continental figures like Michel Foucault, Jacques Derrida, Julia Kristeva, Tzvetan Todorov, and many others. Perhaps part of it is still our viewing ourselves as a cultural offshoot of Mother Britain and her cousins across the channel. Although it would be wrong to ignore the fact that American queer theory, with the ground-breaking research of Judith Butler, to name but one, has perhaps set the standard in that area.

These critical movements are only beginning to affect the study of comics. The International Comics and Animation Festival (ICAF), in conjunction with the Small Press Expo, is a haven for those of us who derive our intellectual sustenance from comics. And when the ICAF meets with the Small Press Expo, the interweaving of critics, artists, and publishers creates nothing short of a heaven populated by comics enthusiasts. No one speaks anything but comics. The energy that emanates from those meetings can be utterly intoxicating.

It is there that one discovers that comics are not only a man's world. The male superheroes have their counterparts in female superheroes. Dick Tracy was matched by Ms. Tree, a female detective (Mystery, get it?).

In today's rough and tumble world, where AIDS can be tackled by Judd Winick in a graphic novel (*Pedro and Me,* 2000), Phoebe Glockner is not ashamed to pen comics that address child abuse (*A Child's Life and Other Stories,* 1998). If Willem in his *Anal Symphonies* (1996) can show his viewer X-rated materials with erect penises, the Canadian Julie Doucet is willing to match him without so much as a flinch (*Lève ta jambe, mon poisson est mort,* 1993).

In fact, the graphic novel, a longer and more complicated form that permits greater character development and plot twists, has been a liberating medium, I would argue, for female comic-strip artists. They do not shy away from dealing with critical and taboo subjects like mental illness, as Madison Clell does in her moving graphic novel, *Cuckoo: One Woman's True Stories of Living with Multiple Personality Disorder* (2002). More adventurous and witty comics and graphic novels have targeted the law (e.g., those of Batton Lash) and the world of disability (e.g., David B., *L'ascension du haut mal,* 1996).

Comics production is a global phenomenon and provides a rich area for the comparatist. Romance? Violence? Religion? Fantasy? Politics? It's all there for those unafraid to probe the great beyond, the beyond that is not part of our father's comparative literature. I would even argue that there is no one in a better position than comparatists like ourselves, equipped with the necessary linguistic gear, to tackle the heights of stripology. This universe holds many treasures that have only begun to be mined by cultural critics.

The analysis of works that are purely graphic in nature differs from more ambitious projects that could explore multileveled assemblage of creations. Let us take one example. One can easily create comparative topics that span the purely verbal and the combined verbal-visual. How about a study of the graphic novel in English by Peter Kuper (2003) that tackles Kafka's *Metamorphosis,* written originally in German? Obviously a critic would need to be at home not only in the German language but also in the critical languages that would permit the analysis of both artistic creations. What changes were made in the recasting of the book from a purely verbal product to one utilizing both the verbal and visual? The juxtaposition of the graphic novel with the original German (and English translation) creates a textual cross-fertilization whose insights would undoubtedly redefine both the high literature that is Kafka and its up-to-now illegitimate cousin, the more popular graphic novel.

If one examines the history of literature, even high literature, alongside the history of art, it will swiftly become apparent that there are numerous literary texts that have been translated into visual forms. Some of these have, in their latest incarnations, become both visual and verbal at once—that is, comic strips. The possibilities for the comparison of the products of visual and verbal languages are almost infinite.

But this is only the first beyond. There is another insistent siren whose call is much more challenging than that of her earlier colleague. This is the siren of law, medicine, and science.

I am proud to bear the title of the enfant terrible of any profession—if by enfant terrible, we mean what the first academic meant when he called me that. That I was going beyond what the field could tolerate. I could not at that time ignore that siren's song, just as I am now unable to close my ears to the siren luring me to the areas of law, medicine, and science.

Law and literature are by no means strangers to one another. The prolific federal judge for the Seventh Circuit, Richard Posner, has even penned a book entitled *Law and Literature* (1988). But for anyone at home in theory, Posner's volume is at best a frustrating read. Much more provocative is the analysis by Peter Brooks of guilt in law and literature, *Troubling Confessions* (2000).

Yet there is something in the law that remains a mystery. As someone who teaches seminars in a law school, I know the importance of that field for all of us. At the same time, law is an area ripe for comparatists. If one reads transcripts of trials as literary narratives, the results can be eye-opening. Then add to that the live videos of actual court cases (I am not talking here about *Judge Judy, The People's Court,* and other such television shows), and I would challenge anyone to resist these accounts. When I teach the transcripts from the Lorena Bobbitt case, for example, I add the video of the trial. It is no different from analyzing a cinematic production, except that this is not fiction but a process in which an individual's life is in question. Lorena is in the audience, dressed primly in a dark blue suit. When she steps into the witness box, she has shed her jacket—provocative hints of disrobing—and appears in a white shirt like an angel who has just descended from heaven.

The quip by Otto von Bismarck is oft repeated: that there are two things that you do not want to see being made: law and sausages. But how many ever take the time to read a legal statute all the way through from beginning to end? Even law students rarely undertake this exercise. Their education is based chiefly on summaries of statutes and judgments. The experience for anyone with literary-critical, not to speak of comparatist, background is extraordinary. Even a legal document that was mockingly compared to high literature, *The Starr Report* (1998), was rarely read through, I discovered, even by those who chose to write about it. Legal texts are also frequently political texts, and they are among the most revealing objects in our culture. To carefully examine the Americans with Disabilities Act is nothing short of eye-opening, as we watch our own social preoccupations and phantasms, from the cultural to the sexual, mirrored in a legal document.

What I am suggesting is miles away from the approach of Posner or others who teach law and literature. They are mostly concerned with legal issues in high literature. I am looking at the underbelly of the law to see what it can tell us about ourselves.

I can already hear some voices raised in objection. How is this comparative literature? My response? This is an area where comparatists, with their rich cultural and literary background, can make a difference and set a new agenda. It is the borrowing of theoretical methodologies from one discipline and transporting them for application to another, completely different area. If there is one thing that Michel Foucault taught us, it is that our mental structures are the product of numerous layers of our culture and society. And to understand ourselves, it behooves us not to ignore any of these layers.

To view a legal statute with the eyes of a comparatist can be a unique experience. The subtexts of statutes and legal decisions force us to examine a critical element of those mental structures. Even some finely crafted closing arguments with their rich intertextual universe can provide insights for the most jaded critic.

The law, of course, is more than a verbal product in our society. It is also an institution and an inspiration for fiction. Read a novel like John Grisham's *Pelican Brief* (1992) and then view the film by the same name (1993). The cinematic alterations will astound you. Denzel Washington, a magnificent actor and an African-American, plays the role of the reporter. In the novel, this role is left racially undefined, so the romantic ending with the law student can gratify a reader. In the film, that romantic element is abandoned, as Julia Roberts at the end of the adventure sits on a beach sipping a drink by herself. Gender, racial, legal, and political issues take on multiple lives as they cross the novelistic universe to enter the cinematic, all under the umbrella of the law.

If the law can be a subject of study for comparatists, why not medicine and science? (I am aware of the journal *Medicine and Literature*, but that is another venture altogether.) The challenges here can be very fruitful. A study like that of Kathryn Montgomery Hunter (*Doctors' Stories: The Narrative Structure of Medical Knowledge*, 1991) in which she analyzes case studies, among other genres, can teach a great deal to those of us who examine medical fiction or narratives penned by physicians. Medical practice, too, has its mysteries and topoi, and these are revealing of professional and cultural values as well. The short medical tales by Richard Selzer, Oliver Sacks, and

Irvin Yalom, to name but three, can certainly be placed alongside the medical short stories of Egyptian physician-writers like Nawal El Saadawi and Yusuf Idris.

Perhaps what makes the world of medicine and science potentially richest for comparatists is that physicians, biologists, and other scientists are presently grappling with problems that previously were thought to be the purview of traditional humanities disciplines. What is the meaning of life? Of death? What makes a human *human*? What is the meaning of consciousness? Of intelligence? Then, of course, there are the ethical questions that flow from our emerging mastery over the building blocks of life. Some questions link the medical with the legal. In the newly patented chimeras (yes, that is what they are called), how much human DNA does it take to create a legal person? This issue, for example, has been explored by Yvonne Cripps in her study on genetic modification (2004). It's a Brave New World out there (wordplay intended).

Among the more provocative narratives that can enrich our comparative world are the memoirs emanating from the world of science and medicine, each arguing for progress in the areas of social changes, medical advances, scientific breakthroughs, be it through stem-cell research or other issues: those of the disabled, of the transsexuals, of the ill, and so on. If we close our eyes to the enormous American production in these areas, we may still be able to see that the French, to take but one example, have also created a significant corpus on disability, transsexuality, illness, and so on. Imagine, for a moment, a disease that does not discriminate on any basis, breast cancer, and you will come to the realization that the comparative field widens enormously to include other countries and other languages.

As one crosses linguistic borders, this area of the science of the body can be particularly gratifying. When the legendary American Helen Keller met the Arab world's leading modernizer, Taha Husayn, they spoke a corporal language that was absolutely their own. He was blind, whereas she has become the American icon for the physically challenged. Their meeting was immortalized in a photograph that tells its own story through the body language of the participants.

Cross from America to Mexico, and how can you forget the powerful paintings of Frida Kahlo, imbued not only with her political ideas but with her medical problems as well? Then cross the Atlantic, where you will find a life of Frida redefined in Italian by Marco Corona (1998) through the comic strip medium. And this is not to speak of the film *Frida* (2002), yet another comparatist's dream.

Art can force medicine to intersect with the body, as in Kahlo's painting *The Broken Column* (1944), reminding us that the visual, with which we began through the world of comics, should be constantly present on our critical radar. (In fact, many of Kahlo's paintings pit the corporal against the medical in a very in-your-face manner.) If Tracy Chevalier's novel, *Girl with a Pearl Earring* (2001), brings a famous seventeenth-century painting by Vermeer to life, it also intertextually weaves the universe of art into that of words and from there into film (2004).

For me comparative literature must be a world without limits, assuming that one can navigate several languages. It is almost a domain of fantasy, in which high art can be analyzed alongside the cinema, which can be analyzed alongside the comic strip, which can be analyzed alongside a verbal world. It is like a wonderful kaleidoscope that allows comparatists a multifaceted view into the world that we intellectually inhabit. Certainly, many a nay-sayer will not be quite ready yet to take the plunge into these rapids, carrying on his or her shoulder the aging body of the old comparative literature. But so be it. It is precisely *because* it is not our father's Comp. Lit. that we can infuse fresh life into the field.

PART II

RESPONSES

CHAPTER THIRTEEN

World Music, World Literature

A Geopolitical View

KATIE TRUMPENER

Voices of the Peoples

Sketching the early ancestry of comparative literature, Haun Saussy's chapter briefly invokes the work of Johann Gottfried Herder to press instead for the primacy of Herder's protégé Goethe and of Madame de Staël as originators, respectively, of newly cosmopolitan notions of *Weltliteratur* and of comparative cultural analysis. What Herder represents is something different: a comparative paradigm and an investigative spirit that belong to the slightly earlier moment of the Enlightenment and late-eighteenth-century sentimental enthusiasm (with all that its imaginative sympathies imply politically). Herder's work of the 1770s thus encompasses not only his influential essays on Ossian, Shakespeare, and Hebrew poetry but his comparative ethnographic collection, *Stimmen der Völker in Liedern* [*Voices of the Peoples in Songs*] (1778–79). At a moment when most European ballad-collecting is implicitly or explicitly nationalist, Herder collects and juxtaposes songs and oral materials from all over Europe, from Greece to Greenland, with special attention to often-overlooked areas like the Baltic.

In "Conjectures on World Literature," Franco Moretti provocatively measures comparative literature's longstanding rhetoric of global reach against its actual modesty as an "intellectual enterprise, fundamentally limited to Western Europe, and mostly revolving around the river Rhine (German philologists working on French literature). Not much more."[1] Staël and Goethe presumably stand at the beginning of this Rhine-centered discipline. Yet if we see the discipline as stemming no less from Herder's pioneering work, then we might understand comparative analysis as rooted equally in the historical relationship between Western, Eastern, and Central European powers; as including the Danube, the Baltic, and the Black Sea in its disciplinary geography; and as foregrounding, from its origins, the problems of empire, political domination, and forced bilingualism that geography raises.

Herder's *Stimmen* offers an implicit prototype for cross-cultural generic analysis. But Herder also works to fathom the universality of literary expression (and indeed, the nature of language itself) by understanding something of the sociohistorical (and especially, in the case of the subjected Baltic peoples, the geopolitical) circumstances of their creation. In translating an Estonian "Lament over the Tyranny of Serfdom," Herder thus declines to abbreviate it, although that would render it more beautiful to his audience. What must come through is the song's function as "true sigh," originating not "in the poetic" per se, but rather in "the felt situation of a suffering [*achzenden*] people."[2] His transcription and translation of Lithuanian songs, on the other hand, should help erode German prejudices against an "unused, despised" Lithuanian language, believed incapable of "delicacy."[3] In fact, as Herder's mother was wont to say, "the Lithuanian language is itself half poetry"—even if for her, its sound is still that of a little table bell, in contrast to the "big churchbell" of the German language.[4] Even under German or Russian political domination, Herder insists, "minor" languages remain fully capable of producing literature. Consistently self-conscious about problems of translation, Herder's work remains equally attentive to the geopolitical power differential between cultures and languages, including what Emily Apter (chapter 3) aptly dubs "linguistic class struggle."[5]

Madame de Staël followed lines of French and Scottish Enlightenment thought developed by Montesquieu and Adam Ferguson in her attempt to postulate certain economic, agricultural, and sociohistorical preconditions for the development of particular literary forms. Herder, in contrast, saw literature as capable of emerging and thriving everywhere, even—or especially—under socially adverse conditions, and as formulated in part to speak to those conditions. If Herder is included as a crucial figure in the founding pantheon of comparative literature, this may help us to see the discipline as interested, from its beginnings, *not only* in world literature (à la Goethe) as an ambitious, overarching concept that may not find easy instantiation or (à la Staël) as made up of the specific "diplomatic" relations and genetic differences between different key literatures, but also as a model that thinks simultaneously about literary similarities and the political force field within which literature takes place.

In his attention to the social and political function of music and in his interest in the realm of musical *practice,* Herder could also be seen as a founding figure of ethnomusicology. Our disciplinary history, indeed, is not only linked to other forms of philology, but it parallels that of other disciplines emphasizing cultural comparison.

Herder's work insists that the "practical" work of collection, montage, and anthologization constitutes an important form of cultural intervention. Over the last decade, especially, it has been practical musicological work, even more than practical literary work, that has modeled, developed, and mainstreamed new paradigms of cross-cultural influence, as a proliferation of intriguing concerts and recordings have reshaped our collective sense of musical tradition.

What made the 1990s such an exciting era for ethnomusicological rediscovery? Saussy underscores the ways technological changes have catalyzed new scholarly idioms. In the musical realm, too, the advent of the CD, with its accompanying (and sometimes lengthy) CD booklet, has made it newly possible to use musical recordings to launch and document sustained arguments about musical history. But other kinds of historical developments were equally catalytic: the controversies over the Columbus cinquecentennial, for instance, spurred important efforts to document the musical encounter between continents: "Les Chemins du Baroque," for example, ambitiously traced the reach of baroque music (through Jesuit missions) into the major historical centers of New World colonization, where it shaped new forms of musical culture.[6] To be sure, this series still emphasizes the shaping force of European models more than its intermingling with or reactions to indigenous forms of music. Other recordings, however, brought together an even wider range of materials to suggest mutual, multidirectional influence—for instance, reconstructing the way popular Spanish musical idioms like the *vicancicos* (in Spain already linked to regionally marked language and already showing musical influences from North and sub-Saharan Africa), once transplanted into New Spain, began absorbing both indigenous languages and pidgins (Quecha, Nahuatl, Afro-Spanish) and Native and black African rhythms.[7]

In Eastern Europe, too, the collapse of Communist rule catalyzed sustained political stock-taking and soul-searching—and various forms of revisionist (musical) historiography. The dissolution of the Soviet imperium and the redrawing of borders made older cultural and geopolitical formations newly visible. Although long under Russian, then Soviet political control, areas of Central Asia also had an ancient and far longer history as part of the Silk Road—an axis of trade and cross-cultural influence that seemed newly fascinating after 1989 as an alternative model to the empire or the nation state.[8] In post-1989 Eastern Europe, similarly, intellectuals became increasingly engaged by the situation of minority and ethnic communities. On one level, their interest expressed political solidarity in the face of renewed popular scapegoating; on another, it reflected the belief that such communities (having weathered successive regimes bent on their assimilation or destruction) offered important paradigms for how to maintain collective identity in the face of political upheavals.

Already during the late 1980s, intellectuals had become alarmed by the political situation in Rumania, where the Ceauşescus' campaign for rural consolidation involved plans to raze centuries-old ethnic villages (especially those inhabited by long-standing Hungarian and German minorities), to close Hungarian-language schools, and to ban the use of the Hungarian language. Musicians in Hungary showed their solidarity for the Hungarian-Rumanian communities by making repeated (sometimes surreptitious) visits to Rumania and by trying to learn, record, preserve, and disseminate some of the traditional musical repertoire still being played in the threatened villages. In 1989–90, during the tumultuous months of political transition in Rumania, several Hungarian groups released albums documenting this music (and one organized a benefit concert in Hungary for the victims of the Timişoara massacre).[9] So too, in the post-1989 era of neo-nationalism, these groups continued to research and record the music of ethnic groups in other parts of Eastern Europe. Such work implied *not* a politically reactionary yearning for the return of Greater Hungary so much as an insistence on the cultural contribution of ethnic minorities and on a multinational *regional* identity that transcended national boundaries and ethnic identifications. In Transylvania, as one 1993 recording documented, a now-almost-lost Jewish musical tradition developed partly out of Hebrew, Russian, Lithuanian, and Ukrainian sources; even after most of the community died in the Holocaust, this music was partly preserved by Vlach Gypsy musicians.[10]

Other projects, meanwhile, persuasively recontextualized the Eastern European modernist avant-garde in relationship to ethnic or regional folk music. The Pokroveky Ensemble intriguingly re-embedded Igor Stravinsky's 1923 *Les Noces* within the tradition of popular Russian wedding music; while Muzsikás worked to rethink the relationship of folk musical improvisation, Béla Bartók's work as an ethnomusicological collector, and his attempts to develop an indigenous avant-garde.[11] Such work was still implicitly informed by the Marxist tradition of exploring music's role in negotiating group identity and dynamics, yet it was newly freed from political pressures to frame and evaluate either "high" or popular traditions within a preset aesthetic-political schema. Indeed, the recovery of such cross-connections involved not only the full post-Stalinist rehabilitation of a high modernist tradition once anathematized as decadent (and of "émigré" music as an integral part of national musical tradition), but the reclamation of folk music itself from its Stalinist appropriations as well.[12]

In the West, the musical and literary reevaluations of the last decade result in part from the much-discussed opening of the canon and a newly keen interest in the interplay between popular and "high" aesthetic traditions.[13] In Anglo-American literary studies, to be sure, the cultural turn of the 1990s often implicitly involved presentism as well as historicism; moreover, the academy's renewed attention to the internal cultural pluralism of the Americas occurred in part at the expense of the premodern and of other parts of the world. In the realm of music, conversely, the brief but intense popular interest both in early music and in "World Music" involved an alternating exoticization and domestication of the unfamiliar (with mainstream audiences particularly interested in new and old crossings between American pop-rock idioms and "exotic" forms of folk music, and in present-day "remixings" of tribal song or meditational chant with Western techno-beats). Yet for ordinary listeners, nonetheless, the end effect has been an enormous expansion in listening range and cross-cultural curiosity (comparable only, perhaps, to the way the new food culture of the last decade or two has broadened many North American and European palates beyond recognition).

In some ways, the widening of musical taste may be easier to effect than an analogous broadening of reading habits. The linguistic barriers seem less formidable in the musical than in the literary realm—not only for potential listeners (who can find pleasure and perhaps some kinds of cultural knowledge in song even without understanding the words) but also for the musicians and musicologists who (assuming roughly comparable notation systems, good sight-reading abilities, and/or good ears) may be better able to work their way into new kinds of repertoire *without* extended linguistic and cultural retraining. Moreover, even the brief exposure represented by a single concert experience or a single recording may have a dramatic impact and lasting effects, *if* cross-cultural contact, influence, and comparison can be rendered audible, palpable—in the way the drone used in a traditional shepherd's song, for instance, resonates with the abstracted bass-line in a Bartók string quartet. The listener, arguably, will grasp such continuities of rhythm or pitch almost somatically—certainly at a more visceral, less cerebral level than the intellectual processing of comparable "literary" evidence of influence or contiguity filtered through one or more layers of translation. Musicians and musicologists, to put it another way, may have an easier time isolating particular points of overlap and contrast, and helping auditors hear them.

Together, musicians and ethnomusicologists have changed and expanded the West's musical maps. Has comparative literature managed to alter the West's internal literary maps as profoundly? The last decade has certainly seen some ambitious literary projects, which have worked to give (academic) readers and students new texts and models for comparative analysis. Werner Sollors and Marc Shell's huge project on American Literature not written in English has recovered, anthologized, and theorized a vast multilingual body of American literature—and in the process, perhaps begun to change even popular perceptions about the history and future of literary life as well as the inevitability of linguistic hierarchies—in the United States. David Damrosch and others have worked not only to theorize a new pedagogy of world literature but also to compile a new range of teaching anthologies. And Franco Moretti's ongoing investigations into the politics of circulation and reception have taken the quasi-Brechtian form of "media experiments" in their own right, their own form interrogating issues of genre and venue.[14] What such work shares is both an interest in the realm of critical *practice* and a reliance (still unusual among North American humanists) on a research team to diversify its linguistic and conceptual base.

As Damrosch has recently argued, current comparative training in graduate programs does little either to model such collaborative work or to prepare students to undertake it.[15] Yet as we can see from the comparable collaborations feeding the new ethnomusicological practice—field ethnography meeting archival research, performers from different traditions learning to play together—such collective efforts can function not only to recreate past moments and modes of influence but also to develop new modes of performance, new modalities of scholarship. Could world literature, as a critical and cosmopolitan paradigm, someday achieve the same cross-over success (and generate as much local interest and wide-ranging curiosity) as world music? Only if we can find new ways of talking to and working with each other.

History and Area

Ten years from now, and ten years after that, the current ACLA report will still make interesting reading, at least as documents of their moment. Saussy's chapter is particularly ingenious at describing the global economic underpinnings of the current intellectual dispensation as well as the way it presupposes a particular media system. Yet it has comparatively little to say about other forms of political and historical transformation that have shaped the last decade. Djelal Kadir's essay, conversely, reflects deep political anxieties about just what (and potentially how little) our attempts at cosmopolitanism (at the microscopic level of the world literature syllabus and disciplinary debates about methodology) mean in light of the global realignment of political forces. As Kadir rightly points out, our hopes and aspirations about our own institutional practice are at once too utopian and already anachronistic, given the grimness of the current political situation. For what they presuppose is that the American academy will continue to function (as it indeed has, for the last decade and more) as an unusually international intellectual meeting-ground, far more cosmopolitan than its host society, yet as such embodying an important American self-perception as a nation of immigrants, and therefore able to draw on the cultural diversity, intellectual energies, and talent pool of the world. Historically, American universities served repeatedly as places of refuge for émigré scholars—and were greatly enriched, in turn, by the new methodologies and forms of knowledge these scholars brought with them. As late as 1999, when a group of University of Chicago colleagues were working to establish the Scholars at Risk Network, it was still possible for us to envision American universities as welcoming safe havens for scholars under threat throughout the world.[16]

Yet as both the globalization discourse of the last decade and the political events of the last two years have reminded us, the internationalism of our academic life is a direct consequence of our economic, cultural, and political hegemony, our position at the center of a de facto empire. Especially at present, the United States appears to the world community not as cosmopolitan, but as self-righteous, belligerent, and megalomaniacal. Within the United States, moreover, the current "security" climate—including the drastic curtailment of the previous freedoms of speech, movement, reading, and research enjoyed by foreign visitors and resident nationals—are already eroding our universities' abilities to function as genuinely international and poly-cultural institutions, as places of true cosmopolitan exchange.

At the time of the last ACLA report, intellectuals around the world were still reeling from a previous moment of political cataclysm and geopolitical realignment. To an extent clear only in retrospect, the Cold War's apparently permanent and unbridgeable divides also caused, over its decades, a kind of conceptual "stuckness" among intellectuals, East and West. Although the events of 1989 proved this an illusion, the Cold War era itself was experienced as a kind of "end of history" (first in the early postwar period because atomic war seemed imminent, then because the political order and the political geography of Europe seemed immutable). And in retrospect, it seems astonishing how completely Eastern Europe vanished from the West's postwar intellectual and cultural radar, once Cold War conditions rendered the region relatively inaccessible and inhospitable to Western scholars.

So how has the radically changed situation of the last decade reshaped our cognitive patterns and maps? At least so far, fifteen years from the 1989 breakdown of a bifurcated Europe, the ensuing political, economic, and demographic transformation of Europes East and West, and their concurrent partial reconsolidation under the sign of the European Union, have had remarkably little effect on the North American study of European literatures and cultures. (So too the long-anticipated or long-feared devolutionary "breakup of Britain" now in progress has had virtually no impact on the American study and teaching of "English" literature.)[17] Only the demographics of our graduate programs changed markedly in the 1990s, as record numbers of Eastern European students have begun studying at our universities.[18] In contrast—and this is a mark of our inherent institutional and disciplinary conservatism—only a tiny number of Eastern European humanists were recruited to move to North American universities. There may be ongoing excitement about a few Eastern European thinkers, dead (Mikhail Bakhtin) and alive (Slavoj Žižek), but there is no large-scale infusion of Central and Eastern European faculty, methods, and literary sensibilities into the North American academy—at least nothing comparable to the period from the 1930s to the 1950s, when our universities were intellectually reinvigorated by the arrival of émigrés fleeing fascism or communism.

In the early decades of the twentieth century, Central and Eastern Europe saw the rise of the discipline of comparative ethnomusicology; the crucial work done not only by Béla Bartók and Zoltán Kodály in Hungary but also by John Meier in Germany and Constantin Brailoiu in Rumania reacts both to those regions' marked cultural and linguistic variegation and to their political instability.[19] Already in the nineteenth century (as Caryl Emerson's essay here and Saussy's description of the Cluj-based comparatist Hugo Meltzl de Lomnitz both suggest), Eastern and Central European intellectuals were equally crucial for the emergence of our parallel discipline. Since the 1930s, a disproportionate share of North America's most distinguished theorists and practitioners of comparative literature have come from these parts of Europe.[20] Yet because of the implicit geopolitics of the field (and of European notions of where high culture really takes place), these scholars had largely made themselves over into polymathic experts on Western Europe. If very occasionally they referred back to Central or Eastern European materials, they tended to do so with a gesture of slight apology for the necessary obscurity of such references.

Today, as that region's people and governments struggle with ongoing economic, political, and social reconstruction, questions of regional identity and cultural legacy continue to be pressing—with potential ramifications for our models of comparative analysis. To what extent does Central or Eastern Europe remain a useful rubric for understanding the past and present of this region? Does "Central Europe" signal primarily Habsburg nostalgia? Or the unending European wish to be perceived as "more Western," and thus part of the "civilized" world? Or does the concept of "Central Europe" describe a transnational, translinguistic parity of experience that goes as deep as the claims of cultural or linguistic nationalism (given the parallel experiences of neighboring cultures and literatures in this region of Europe, first under Habsburg and/or Russian reign and then as similarly constituted states within the Soviet-controlled Warsaw Pact)?

In Western Europe, the rise of the nation-state entailed the attempted subsumption of regional identity. In Central and Eastern Europe, where the nation-state was late to develop, majority and minority cultures coexisted in many areas—and at certain moments, at least, managed an unusual degree of cultural synthesis. What are the consequences of such zones or periods of overlap for the literary historiography of Europe, so dominated, at least since the nineteenth century, by nationalist and national-language models of literary production? What kind of model might Central and Eastern Europe (if understood as cultural crossroads and linguistic melting pots) offer European culture as a whole?

Our own Central and Eastern European students are potentially capable of generating new paradigms and questions for comparative study based on *their* part of the world, their own cultural backgrounds, and even their own political experiences in two markedly different world orders. Certainly they are uniquely positioned, linguistically, culturally, and experientially, to undertake new kinds of comparative projects that take as their starting point empirical areas of contact and cultural overlap (whether historically or in the present). What if these and other young comparatists, indeed, were encouraged to undertake comparative projects whose linguistic and cultural coordinates actually made "empirical" and regional "sense"?

Indeed, insofar as our comparative literature programs tend to include many international students from a wide range of backgrounds, they perennially represent a huge pool of potential *new* knowledges and new cross-connections. Yet our curriculum tends to run in preestablished grooves. It is still, to be sure, more varied than that of the individual language fields. But how often do faculty try to redesign courses and requirements around the students who are actually there, rather than just assuming that they, too, will want mainly to absorb the Western European and world canon, the canon of methodologies and existing problems?

For foreign graduate students who eventually return to their countries of origin after receiving the Ph.D., the attempt to re-root the materials of their American graduate education in their home university system often produces unexpected and illuminating results.[21] Typically, though, even comparative literature programs tend to lose touch with their foreign graduates if they "vanish" from American academia. During the students' stay in the United States, their programs probably did not do enough to build on and learn from them—and now that they have departed again, their programs and professors may not even grasp what they have gone back to. Comparative literature as a discipline—and the knowledge economy of the American universities more generally—can ill afford this cultural myopia. A more truly global discipline would *care* more about where its students and its paradigms went. And it would prepare students for possible return—and for the most productive possible return—if its curriculum and dissertation advising explicitly called on students to try to use all corners of their background and experience, and to begin the process of synthesis, methodological comparison, cross-reading, and cross-referencing already in graduate school.

Comparative literature needs to give renewed thought to its own mandates, not least in light of the post–Cold War partial defunding (and now, the threatened U.S. government oversight and censorship) of area studies. In fact, some humanists affiliated with area studies programs feel the collapse of that disciplinary paradigm has been approaching for a long time, both for intellectual reasons and for reasons of internal dynamics. In practice, many "experts" housed in area studies programs really only worked on one culture, without particular interest in the others; geopolitical tensions between the various countries were often replicated in department struggles over curriculum, and so on. Given area studies' current crises of funding *and* morale, it seems paradoxical that Gayatri Spivak's recent *Death of a Discipline* diagnoses comparative literature as the discipline near death and argues for a cross-pollination with area studies as the best path to its revitalization.[22] Perhaps, instead, it is an infusion of comparative literature that could reinvigorate area studies, helping to reinvent it or helping it realize in practice what it always might have been.

As Emily Apter rightly reminds us, there is a continual danger that postcolonial studies risk perpetuating colonial cultural and linguistic frameworks—and the same is true for area studies as well. A newly humanistically inflected area studies would need, as its starting point, a historically differentiated sense of cultural and linguistic geography, the ways in which imperial-bureaucratic coordination of regions worked from or against older geopolitical, linguistic, cultural, even geological divides. Comparative literature would also need a clearer consensus that sociohistorical approaches to literature really *were* as valuable as the theoretically saturated, text-immanent ones that were Comp. Lit.'s hallmark in the institutionally prestigious "glory days" of the 1970s and 80s.[23] Some kind of clarifying internal debate would also be needed about the subordinated institutional place of the humanities in the earlier, now ailing or defunct, social-science-oriented model of area studies; and for this, there might have to be frank discussion about the increasing social-science bias of many universities, given trends in research funding and perhaps given humanists' own internal doubts and debates.

Comparatists could and should play a crucial role in forging new, more genuinely comparative and innovative models of cultural studies. Yet they won't be able to do so until deans and other administrators begin thinking quite differently about appointments in their field. As most national literature departments continue to face shrinking enrollments, their hiring schemas are becoming increasingly traditional, conservative, and rigid.[24] At this point, it would take a real paradigm shift to give the person able to teach Polish as well as Russian the chance to occupy a job that encouraged, supported, and rewarded the Polish as much as the Russian expertise, or so that a tenuring department saw work on Latvian or Bulgarian as well as German literature, not as time lost to a nationalist hobby, but as forms of specialized knowledge that expanded the cultural and intellectual range of the humanities and the university as a whole.

The particular intellectual range of our own post-1989 students, in other words, points to a new agenda for comparative literature—one that meshes with growing administrative interest, across the country, in revitalizing international studies, study abroad programs, and intensive language learning. As Mary Louise Pratt has argued more generally for the culturally based study of languages, *our* methods and interests could potentially transform a wide and important segment of humanities teaching—and indirectly, at least, the way future American political leaders, diplomats, and policymakers understand the world outside our own borders.[25]

World Literatures in the New World Order?

Saussy's chapter in this volume reflects skepticism not only about the possibilities or fruitfulness of actual comparison, but especially about the pedagogical realizability of world literature: if all or most texts are necessarily read in translation, he seems to suggest, the result will be a thematically driven, aesthetically and culturally flattened view of global texts. Responding publicly to the draft essays of the Saussy report, Gayatri Spivak has pointedly criticized world literature teachers who venture beyond their own fields of expertise and linguistic competence. For when they teach "foundational" texts like the *Mahābhārata,* she argued, they will likely be oblivious not only to these works' linguistic texture and historical meaning but to the ongoing controversies they engender in their own cultures of origin, whether among local feminist critics or among intellectuals critical of the way current fundamentalisms use these texts to legitimate themselves. When a liberal Western professoriat attempts inclusiveness, Spivak suggested, it risks enshrining a conservative sense of other texts and cultures.[26]

One of Kadir's narrative personae is even more pessimistic, suggesting that comparative literature's "move from the historical density of the literatures of the world to the abstracted construct of World Literature" will, within a few years, have driven the discipline to the brink of extinction. As a still-novice teacher of world literatures, I remain much more sanguine—indeed, convinced that the 2014 ACLA report will find both world literature and comparative literature not only alive and well, but changed for the better by their interdependence.

Over the last three years, enrollment in Yale's world literatures course has more than quadrupled—partly in response, presumably, to September 11th and the current war in Iraq.[27] Our syllabus itself, to be sure, is not overtly topical. In 2003–4, texts included *Gilgamesh;* several-hundred-page chunks of *The Mahābhārata, The Ara-bian Nights,* and *Tale of Genji;* various versions of *Sundjata; The Odyssey, Hrafnkel's Saga, The Breton Lais,* and *Midnight's Children.*[28] We spent a lot of class time talking about formal questions of genre, temporality, narration, narrative consciousness, and perspective. But these texts also, quite insistently, raised questions of foundational violence and the ethics of conflict, of the logics of feud, massacre, terror, and genocide as well as the quasi-theological role of literature in mediating ideological shifts and moments of historical crisis, enacting conversion and convergence.

This year the course will also include Peter Dale Scott's tour de force, his long poem, *Coming to Jakarta: A Meditation on Terror,* as an instance of contemporary, self-consciously "global" writing.[29] A Canadian scholar/poet now teaching at Berke-ley, Scott is a former diplomat with a long history (from the Vietnam War era onward) of activism as a "concerned Asia scholar." An attempt to understand his own moral and aesthetic autobiography in relationship to global political upheavals, his poem meditates explicitly on issues of reciprocal cultural knowledge, political neutrality, the limits of self-knowledge and of global empathy, and the way cosmopolitanism often proves a function of class or caste. All this in an elusive poetry indebted to the *Mahābhārata,* to Ezra Pound, to a range of East Asian (and hybrid West Coast) verse forms, and to a vast array of political and historical scholarship (much of it annotated in the marginal glosses accompanying the poem).

Such works can potentially give world literature students an important intellec-tual and philosophical toolset to begin tackling the varied literary materials of the world. For the most part, however, the course will continue to emphasize non-West-ern texts that have been widely influential within their extended cultural contexts (with special focus on "early" texts students are less likely to tackle on their own).[30] By David Damrosch's standards, most of these texts are "hypercanonical" (above, chapter 2). But hypercanonical to whom? Until our colleagues in other Western lit-erature departments have actually read or reread *Sundjata, The Tale of Genji,* or the Haddawy edition of *The Arabian Nights* and adjusted accordingly their pedagogical and professional narratives about epic as a genre, the cultural function of storytelling, or the rise of the (Western) novel, world literature courses like ours remain a neces-sary intervention into local campus intellectual culture. And such courses also point students toward the more specialized courses offered by the non-Western literature departments, in search of more information about the literary cultures that produced *Gilgamesh* and *Genji.* (We have sometimes joined them there, auditing our colleagues' courses in an attempt to increase the sense of context we can bring to our own future teaching.) Even after the "theory years," comparative literature retains some power to set aesthetic and intellectual agendas for the humanities as a whole. World literature courses can potentially tilt the balance of power in the humanities from its old, implicitly Western orientation simply by broadening students' sense of what is interesting and important to study.

In the current political climate, moreover, the very complexity of the texts we are reading seems important. Potentially, at least, they can arm students—and teachers—against now-pervasive, often astonishingly facile generalizations about other cultural and religious traditions. What world literature courses impart is not only a bigger but a more inflected and more complex sense of the world, as of its literary manifestations.[31]

Some of what they learn also has very local ramifications. Our first week now includes a question-and-answer session with *Gilgamesh* translator Benjamin Foster (Professor of Near Eastern Literatures and Civilizations and curator of Yale's Babylonian Collection). Last year Foster brought some cuneiform tablets with him for students to see; his parenthetical comments about the physical fragility of the cuneiform record and the literary-historical consequences of archaeological looting quietly underscored the cultural costs of the ongoing Iraqi war.[32] Indeed, students who have grasped something of the textual history of *Gilgamesh* and the *Arabian Nights*, or pondered these narratives' evocative accounts of urban culture will have a more complex, considered, indeed, more educated reaction to the news of the bombing of Baghdad or the burning of the National Library of Iraq than students to whom Iraq remains just a place name on a map.

With intelligent and motivated students, at least, such implications scarcely need articulation. They are simply there in the fabric, in the implicit worldview of the course. Meanwhile, course texts and ways of reading can also stimulate students to think about key methodological questions: in our final class last year, my students eagerly debated the usefulness of genre as an organizational principle, whether close reading remained possible in translation (with one student advocating comparative reading of varying translations as a way of exploring semantic fields and horizons of reception), and even whether the close reading paradigms developed in North America (and before that, out of the Western religious hermeneutic traditions) were necessarily appropriate for reading texts from radically different cultural traditions.

As most world literature teachers would readily acknowledge, our own limitations of training make us largely unable to model such culturally alternative modes of reading, however much we might theorize their existence or try to reconstruct them in and from the texts under discussion. In some respects, world literature remains a daunting, perhaps impossible project. But so, of course, is comparative literature itself a utopian ideal to which we can only apprentice ourselves over the long term. This apprenticeship will be largely auto-didactic: ambitious reading in various directions, more language study, conversations and exchanges with a widening array of colleagues. Those of us teaching world literatures are trying to actualize Herder's expansive vision, informed by a sense of the implicit parity between literatures. We are, of course, not fully adequate to the task. But if not us, who? And if not now, when?

NOTES

1. Franco Moretti, "Conjectures on World Literature," *New Left Review* 1 (January-February 2000): 57–67, p. 54.
2. Johann Gottfried Herder, *Stimmen der Völker in Liedern. Volkslieder. Zwei Teile* (Stuttgart: Philipp Reclam, 1975), 244–45. Translations mine.
3. Ibid., 240.
4. Ibid., 239.
5. See for instance, Herder, *Stimmen*, 184.
6. See, for instance, Les Chemins du Baroque, *De L'Altiplano à l'Amazonie. Lima—La Plata. Missions Jésuites* (K617, 1992); *Messe de l'Assomption de la Vierge* (K617, 1992), and *Le chant de la Jérusalem des terres froides. Les Chemins du Baroque en Nouvelle France* (K617, 1995). The initial recordings emerged from a series of 1992 concerts in venues ranging from France, Spain, and Portugal to Mexico, each involving collaboration between European musicologists and local musicians.
7. The Boston Camerata, *Nueva España. Close Encounters in the New World, 1590–1690* (Erato, 1992); see also Hespèrion XXI, *Villancicos y Danzas Criollas de la Iberia Antigua al Nuevo Mundo 1550–1750* (Alia Vox, 2003). Related work has begun to be done in and for Europe as well. Capella Romana's current concert program, "Music for the Fall of Constantinople," for instance, explores the musical contours of Constantinople's decline and fall as the center of Christian Byzantium. As the threatened imperial family tried to shore up Western support through intermarriage with Western European dynasties, Western composers like Guillaume Dufay composed works to celebrate these nuptials, to celebrate the 1426 rededication of a Latin-rite church in Constantinople, and eventually also to lament for fallen Constantinople. The program's own juxtaposition of Byzantine liturgical chant and Western European polyphony, meanwhile, suggests intriguing points of contact and cross-over.
8. Already during the Glasnost era, Libuse Moníková's 1987 novel *The Façade*, trans. John E. Woods (New York: Alfred A. Knopf, 1991), detaches her group of Czech historical restoration experts from their usual work in Bohemia (repairing the crumbling façades of a nationalist heritage) to send them on a picaresque journey across Central Asia so that they can meditate on the past, future, and limits of the Soviet imperium.
9. Muzsikás, *Blues for Transylvania* (Rykodisc, 1990) and Örkös Ensemble, *Transylvanian Portraits. Hungarian Village Music from Transylvania* (Koch, 1993). Experimental cultural criticism like Claudio Magris' 1986 *The Danube*, trans. Patrick Creagh (New York: Farrar, Strauss, Giroux, 1989) and Peter Esterhazy's 1991 *The Glance of Countess Hahn-Hahn (down the Dan-*

ube), trans. Richard Aczel (Evanston, Ill.: Northwestern University Press, 1994) work similarly to establish regionalist frameworks for cross-cultural influence and comparison.

10. See Judit Frigyesi, "The Historical Value of the Record," CD booklet accompanying Muzsikás, *Máramaros. The Lost Jewish Music of Transylvania* (Rykodisc, 1993), 10–18.

11. Pokrovsky Ensemble, *Stravinsky "Les Noces" and Russian Village Wedding Songs* (Elektra, 1994); Muzsikás, *The Bartók Album* (Rykodisc, 1999), as well as their recent joint tour with the Takács Quartet.

12. For a literary meditation on this problem, see Milan Kundera's 1967 novel *Žert* (*The Joke* [New York: Harper, 1992]), as well as my "Imperial Marches and Mouse Singers: Nationalist Mythology," in *Text and Nation: Debates on Cultures in Conflict,* ed. Laura Garcia-Moreno and Peter C. Pfeiffer, 67–90 (Columbia, S.C.: Camden House, 1996).

13. In some respects, canon-breaking republication projects like Virago World Classics (ongoing since 1978 and designed to showcase a broader range of British and English-language female modernist novelists) or University of Illinois' Radical [American] Novel Reconsidered of the 1990s, have been matched by comparable musical efforts—Hyperion's extensive *English Orpheus* recording series, for instance, which attempts to reestablish a fuller range of British composition between 1600 and 1800. Important publishing and musical initiatives have also tried to stake out newly coherent territory, whether in giving literary-historical contours to a resuscitated post-Communist "Central Europe" (see, for instance, the translation series of "Central European Classics" edited by Timothy Garton Ash and published by Central European University Press), in rethinking the varied traditions of Latin America (in Oxford University Press's ambitious Library of Latin America) or in regathering and reassessing the German and other European composers forced into emigration, persecuted, or killed during the Third Reich (London Records' series on "Entartete Musik: Music Suppressed by the Third Reich").

14. On the Brechtian precedent, see Dieter Wöhrle, *Bertolt Brechts medienästhetische Versuche* (Cologne: Prometh Verlag, 1990). Moretti's recent essays—including the manifesto-like "Conjectures" and "Markets of the Mind," *New Left Review* 5 (September/October 2000), 111–15, on current expansive yet generic global film distribution circuits—have been published in *New Left Review,* as if comparative literature (still) mattered to a broader audience of intellectuals—and forcing at least one group of academics to keep up with nonspecialist periodicals if they want to follow the debates in their own field. Moretti's *Atlas of the European Novel 1800–1900* (London: Verso, 1998) experimented with the crossing of literary history, publishing history, statistical analysis, and cartography, attempting quite literally to draw both bigger and denser maps. And Moretti's mammoth five-volume critical anthology, *Il Romanzo* (Turin: G. Einaudi, 2001–2003; planned partial translation in English and other languages), attempts to develop a new, truly global account of a single literary genre—the novel—across time and from the vantage-point of many different national literatures. As Moretti makes clear in "Conjectures on World Literature," he currently advocates a new kind of literary macro-history based on "distant" rather than close reading and derived in part from a synthesis of different kinds of national accounts. Moretti's own editorial model for *Il Romanzo* may draw partly on ambitious collaborative efforts of the preceding decade to rethink nationalist literary culture and cultural history; see, for instance, *A New History of French Literature,* ed. Denis Hollier (Cambridge, Mass.: Harvard University Press, 1989); and *Les Lieux de mémoire,* ed. Pierre Nora (Paris: Gallimard, 1986), three-volume English selections published as *Realms of Memory: Rethinking the*

French Past, ed. Laurence D. Kritzman, trans. Arthur Goldhammer (New York: Columbia University Press, 1996–98).

15. Damrosch, "World Literature, National Contexts," Special Centennial Issue on World Literature, edited by Richard Maxwell, Joshua Scodel, and Katie Trumpener, *Modern Philology* 100: 4 (May 2003): 512–31, p. 516.

16. Now headquartered at New York University, the Scholars at Risk network (www.scholarsatrisk.nyu.edu) encompasses more than 70 universities in the United States and abroad.

17. The phrase comes from Tom Nairn, *The Breakup of Britain: Crisis and Neo-Nationalism* (London: New Left Books, 1977).

18. For somewhat different political reasons, the last decade has also seen record numbers of Chinese students enrolling in American graduate programs. A few months before the opening of the Berlin Wall—and the de facto toppling of communist governments throughout Eastern Europe—pro-democracy students were massacred in Beijing's Tian'anmen Square by order of Chinese officials. In the German Democratic Republic, horror of the Chinese precedent may have encouraged protestors to join in mass marches that summer and fall, while leaving many East German officials determined to avoid similar bloodshed. In China itself, the post-massacre crackdown on dissidents led many intellectuals to flee or emigrate to the United States—where their presence, in various university and extra-institutional contexts, renewed discussions about the function of civil society. China's economic liberalization and social transformation over the past decade, meanwhile, has led to intensified American business and governmental interest in Chinese markets—and to great increases in the numbers of Chinese students in American graduate programs (including comparative literature).

19. See, for instance, Béla Bartók, *Essays,* ed. Benjamin Suchoff (London: Faber and Faber, 1976); Zoltán Kodály, *Folk Music of Hungary* (New York: Praeger, 1971); John Meier, *Kunstlieder im Volksmunde. Materialien und Untersuchungen* (1905; rpt. Hildesheim: Olms, 1976); Constantin Brailoiu, *Problems of Ethnomusicology,* ed. and trans. A. L. Lloyd (Cambridge, UK: Cambridge University Press, 1984), as well as my "Béla Bartók and the Rise of Comparative Ethnomusicology: Nationalism, Race Purity, and the Legacy of the Austro-Hungarian Empire," in *Music and the Racial Imagination,* ed. Ronald Radano and Philip V. Bohlman (Chicago: University of Chicago Press, 2000), 403–34.

20. See Lionel Gossman and Mihai I. Spariosu, eds., *Building a Profession: Autobiographical Perspectives on the Beginnings of Comparative Literature in the United States* (Albany: State University of New York Press, 1994).

21. One need only look, for instance, at the various intellectually ambitious, private "start-up" universities in Turkey, staffed almost exclusively by Turkish academics with recent American Ph.D.s (and who continue to publish with American university presses), to understand what a powerful revitalizing force American graduate education can be—or at least has been—for other academies.

22. Gayatri Chakravorty Spivak, *Death of a Discipline* (New York: Columbia University Press, 2003).

23. One place to start debate might be a collective rereading of Auerbach's fascinating 1958 *Literary Language and its Public in Late Latin Antiquity and in the Middle Ages,* trans. Ralph Manheim, foreword by Jan M. Ziolkowski (Princeton, N.J.: Princeton University Press, 1993), a revelatory counterpart to *Mimesis* in its account of the way cultural processes work themselves

out in literary form and in language, as in its attention to the ongoing struggle between vernaculars, emerging out of locally based linguistic worlds and a "globalizing" imperial Latin.

24. Yet as some chairs have begun to argue, the dreaded administrative amalgamation of once-separate national and comparative literature departments can potentially lead to more interesting hiring. William Moebius, "Comparative Literature: The Lion or the Gnat?" New Institutional Forms of Comparison panel, MLA convention, Philadelphia, December 29, 2004.

25. Mary Louise Pratt, "Building a New Public Idea about Language," *Profession* 2003, 100–119.

26. Gayatri Spivak, "A New Comparative Literature," New Institutional Forms of Comparison panel, MLA convention, Philadelphia, December 29, 2004.

27. The course was founded in the late 1990s by Vilashini Cooppan; her "World Literature and Global Theory: Comparative Literature for the New Millennium," *Symploké* 9 (2001): 15–43, touches on its developmental history and initial purview. Students in Yale's literature major are required to take either this course or a parallel lecture course on world cinema. Many of our students, however, are concentrators in other majors (including economics and the sciences) or freshmen taking the course either as part of a more general distribution requirement or as an elective.

28. The course's sustained attention to the interrelationship of text and performance was anchored not only in primary readings but in works in other media: in Dani Konyaté's feature film, *Keita! The Heritage of the Griot* (Burkina Faso, 1994), documenting *Sundiata*'s continuing recitation, transmission, and relevance in present-day West Africa; in Derek Walcott's 1992 Nobel Prize address "The Antilles: Fragments of Epic Memory," evoking popular *Ramayana*-inspired performances throughout the Indian diaspora, including by lay actors in Trinidad; and in culmination (through a happy coincidence of campus programming), a live, gamelan-accompanied, traditional Javanese shadow-puppet performance of *Mahābhārata*-inspired materials.

29. Peter Dale Scott, *Coming to Jakarta: A Meditation on Terror* (Toronto: McClelland and Stewart, 1988).

30. I write, I should add, as a converted skeptic. Teaching at the University of Chicago a decade ago, I joined other literature colleagues in resisting a decanal initiative to institute a world literature course (implicitly intended to involve more non-Western literature faculty in introductory Humanities Core literature teaching, rather than in area-based Civ. courses). Our faculty group instead developed a multiterm core course, "Reading Cultures," which described the cultural preconditions for Western encounters with the non-West, using rubrics like collecting, traveling, urbanism, and the rise of capitalism as a world system to explore the historical and methodological underpinnings of the humanities. Yet because the course was fairly high-concept, I found it somewhat hard to teach in ways that left texts and issues sufficiently open-ended to spark good discussion. Despite their initial input into the course, moreover, faculty in non-Western literature departments were rarely released from their own departmental or area based courses to teach Reading Cultures. As a long-term result, the course has featured ever-fewer non-Western texts. The Yale course has moved in the opposite direction.

31. To read *Midnight's Children* after *The Mahābhārata* and *The Arabian Nights,* for instance, is to understand something crucial about the novel's narrative genealogies, its programmatic attempt to develop a hybrid fusion of narrative traditions, one of its many strategies to defy sectarianism and partition. Unlike most other courses in which Rushdie is taught (from the seminar on Joyce and Rushdie to the survey of South Asian fiction in English), our particu-

lar context of reading provides a way of placing the postcolonial that does not subsume it back into the rubric of "English" tradition, however broadly defined.

32. Housed in Yale's main library, the Babylonian Collection is North America's largest collection of cuneiform tablets and texts; in spring 2003, Yale librarians responded to events in Iraq with a small exhibit outlining (and mourning) the kinds of cultural records destroyed or lost during the American invasion.

CHAPTER FOURTEEN

Answering for Central and Eastern Europe

CARYL EMERSON

For all our attentiveness to globalization, new media, and re-grafting the disciplines, most of us in the senior ranks of comparative literature, when faced with summings-up of the field, still surreptitiously check out first the fate of our own core languages, cultures, favorite books, and names. Thus did I approach the draft of the ten-year report. What does it have to say about Russia, and even more about the newly liberated Slavic (and non-Slavic) peoples of Central and Eastern Europe?

From the perspective of one sunk deep in this material (an admittedly unreliable position), it would seem to be the perfect test case. All those small peoples who name their streets and public squares, not after generals (for their military victories are few), but after poets. A patchwork of small nations that had long nurtured the literary word as a glorious substitute for political identity or autonomy. Their literatures had been rewarded in the institutionalized sense too. As if following some rule of inversion that the briefer the tradition, the more intensely it was valued, the first university Chair of Russian Literature was established in Russia in 1835, while the *founder* of the tradition, Alexander Pushkin, was still alive (decades before native literature chairs were established in premier universities in England and the United States).[1]

What is more, the region is intuitively "comparative." In Eastern Europe, one town would commonly speak several native languages, belong to two or three empires in the course of a single generation, and assume most of its residents to be hybrids who carried the dividing-lines of nationality within themselves. (As the famous story goes, Franz Kafka and Jaroslav Hašek drank at the same Prague pub, Kafka his coffee upstairs and Hašek his beer downstairs, one writing in German, the other in Czech, both knowing both languages and greeting one another on the stairs.) Exile, displacement, multilanguagedness, heteroglossia, outsideness to oneself and thus a taste for irony, the constant crossing of borders, and the absence of a tranquil, organic, homogenized center that belongs to you alone: all these Bakhtinian virtues and prerequisites for genuine dialogue have long been endemic to Central Europe.

Twenty years ago, this region was still frozen into the fake homogeneity of the Warsaw Pact. In 1984, far before anyone suspected the end, Milan Kundera wrote a bitter essay on the tragedy of Central Europe, a region distinguished, he said, by the "greatest variety within the smallest space," swallowed and flattened by Soviet Russia, whose ideal was "the smallest variety in the greatest space."[2] After the collapse of the Soviet system and the liberations of 1989, some of the consequences of this flattening for comparative literature studies became clear. It was discovered, for example, that Moscow's policy toward her colonies both east and west had been to translate as much as possible from their "native writers" into imperial Russian—but not to sponsor collateral translations among the satellite states themselves—say, Bulgarian into Kazakh, Latvian into Hungarian, Polish into Slovak. (The important exception here was East Germany, another nation with an imperial language, which actively commissioned translations from "minor" peoples.) When Michael Henry Heim, our most accomplished humanist of Eastern European cultures and veteran translator from all the languages of the region, decided in the spring of 1999 to convene a conference and create a Web site for professional translators of the newly independent post-Communist nations, he was astonished to find that they knew very little of one another's work.[3] Literatures of the area had been treated like the politics of the area—or rather, like the logic of a conspiratorial Communist party cell. Satellite nations were the spokes of a wheel, which met and were masterminded at the central hub of Moscow but were not structurally encouraged to communicate among themselves.

By the 1990s, the famous dissidents of the area (Václav Havel, Adam Michnik, György Konrád) had triumphed. It seemed to be a new model for governance—the playwright-president, the literate public intellectual who practiced anti-politics—and as such, the envy of enlightened progressives both East and West. But by 2002 this situation had shifted. Political sensitivities that had become important, even definitive, for comparative literary studies and were encoded in our cultural theory, postcolonialism, post-poststructuralism, and critique of corporate capitalism and American militant imperialism, were not receiving the support from these post-dissidents that we had expected.[4] Havel endorsed the American-led invasion of Iraq; Michnik agreed to work alongside neoconservatives in the Bush administration to fight terrorism and rebuild the Middle East. Where was Kundera's Central European disgust at big nations, with his argument that big armies always had History, and therefore immoral intent, at their side? It turned out that these newly visible Central European languages and literatures were no more pliable or reliably in the mainstream of Western academic protest than they had been when they were trapped inside the repressive Soviet camp. These thinkers and political figures owed nothing to our theories, and did not feel beholden.

In post-imperial Russia herself, of course, political fragmentation and the end of censorship have created rich new institutional possibilities for comparative literary studies. After the thrill of moving all our faddish philosophers and vocabularies into their lexicon—that translation is now almost complete, with glossy textbooks on postmodernism (and on its demise) circulating since the late 1990s—high-profile wars are being fought in the journals over the future shape of literary study in Russia and how open it should be to non-Russian comparative or interdisciplinary rubrics.[5] The Russian problem, to be sure, is different from the Central European one. At stake in freshly post-Communist Russia was not the legitimacy of the national language itself or the opportunity to advertise one's own literary history, traditions, and cultural heroes (after all, the whole world knows Dostoevsky and Tolstoy). Russian professionals sought the right to discuss these and other phenomena through the formerly taboo lenses of Foucault, Derrida, Blanchot, Baudrillard, Walter Benjamin, Paul de Man—in a word, the right to practice in Russian journals what has long been the familiar binding gesture in English and comparative literature departments in the Western academy: a juxtaposition (and thereby a comparison) of disparate national works through some "transnational," transcendent theory. Ever since the abolition of state censorship in August 1991, legal rights to do so have been in place; the current debate is more over the appropriateness, and even the decency, of such a reorientation. For now that those European philosophers are household words there too, Russian culture risks losing the exceptional status she enjoyed for two hundred years as the creator of "obligation literature," literature that stood up to the state and put poets in the front lines of the struggle for humanity. Traditionally, great Russian literature has been, not entertainment but liberation, salvation. The discovery that the free word is neither dangerous, sacred, nor unifying, but rather, banal and noisy, one more competitor for attention in the marketplace, was a disillusionment to many critics of the older generation. Sensing this loss of status in the literary world, and lamenting the empty, nihilistic relativism of many Western theories threatening to take its place, the Russian backlash has been fierce. This curious battle, between the "normalizers" (those who insist that literature has the right to be ordinary, trivial, pleasurable) and the "exceptionalizers" (all Russian literature worthy of the name demands that its readers change their lives), is worth watching as Russia seeks a post-Communist identity.

Unsurprisingly, the "Russian exceptionalist" position has routinely been resisted and ridiculed by Central Europeans. The Czech Milan Kundera and the Pole Tadeusz Konwicki—both confirmed Russophobes—were especially eloquent on this score in the 1980s. What is Russia's suffering to us? Why should we, the Westerners of Central Europe, bow down before (and buy into) that bully nation's cult of sacrifice? In his 1984 essay "The Tragedy of Central Europe," Kundera cited an exchange between Kazimierz Brandys and Anna Akhmatova, where the great Russian poet austerely dismissed the Polish writer's complaints because he hadn't done time in prison. This is simply pretentious and inflated self-pity, Central Europeans agree among themselves: these Russians "sacrificed" their way to the largest land empire in the history of the world, and we are expected to respect them for it. Here is "Comparative Literature" (or rather, competitive suffering) at its most raw.

Such, then, has been my sense of the polemical currents of comparative literary studies in those post-Communist cultures that I watch from a distance and teach, usually in translation, in our classrooms. From that perspective, two things leapt out at me from the ACLA report. First is how small a role that whole part of the world played in the initial conceptualization of the European comparative literature project. In his 1877 article on the "present tasks" of the field, Hugo Meltzl de Lomnitz—a Central European name if ever there was one—"prescribes ten languages as the basis for literary study." Icelandic and Dutch are among them—but not a single Slavic language. And this was all the more peculiar, given the "Habsburg cut" of the list; the Austro-Hungarian empire, after all, contained sizeable Czech-, Slovak-, Slovenian-, and Croatian-speaking populations. Was it all really so invisible and inaudible?

    When the first draft of the report was aired at an ACLA panel at the MLA in San Diego in December 2003, David Damrosch reminded the audience, in response to this comment of mine, that Meltzl de Lomnitz had not included Russian in his list of appropriate languages because, in his view, the censorship policy of the Russian imperial government so undermined the integrity of the Russian literary word that study of it would be tantamount to collaboration with tyranny. What a mournful example of politics swallowing up creativity, I thought. Because evidence suggests the opposite: that free, secure, prosperous cultures produce an ocean of trivial, commercial, and hedonistic works; whereas tragic, besieged, and unfree cultures produce literature of high ethical stature. (Whether or not it can be published in its era is another and quite separate matter.) And I began to remember all the bad-dream anecdotes that people who teach about this part of the world would like to forget: that as late as the nineteenth century, for example, linguists considered Slavic languages to be all dialects of one basic tongue (Russian), although with different alphabet conventions; or that the Habsburg Empire, unable to agree on an official language for administrating northern Croatia because the Hungarians, the Austrians, and the Italians were each pressing their own imperial claim, resolved finally to run the government in *Latin* (it would appear that in Zagreb, the Croatian language was not a serious candidate). And this fantastically rich laboratory of Slavic languages did not figure in to the founding slate of basic literatures out of which our field emerged. My feeling of injury would surely be familiar to Africanists, Islamists, Japanologists, and other specialists in ancient world cultures that were considered, until very recently, off the map by tiny self-centered Western Europe. I felt a pang of sympathy for those disciplines, and for the noisy energy they have had to mobilize to ensure "their slow ascent.

The second impression leaping out of the report was the prominent role played in the elaboration of "comparative ways of thought" by Russian and Central European literary *theory*. What had broken the visibility barrier was not the languages themselves and (except for the eminently translatable Great Russian Novel) not their classic literary texts, but an arsenal of devices, methods, and rationales (such as "literariness") for linking all literary products at some higher level, independent of particulars but made common, and thus comparable, by a set of universal constants. Alexander Veselovskij in the nineteenth century (just now being translated) and Viktor Zhirmunskij in the twentieth are acknowledged leaders in this effort, as are, of course, the Russian Formalists and Prague Structuralists. The latter two groups are famous for having worked out, in the 1920s and 30s, many of the ideas reinvented in Paris in the 1970s and 80s. Why this was so is a fascinating cultural question. In a series of probing essays over the past decade, Galin Tihanov (Bulgarian by birth, British by higher education) has made explicit some of the reasons: the peripatetic, trilingual qualifications of these intellectuals, exiled (or self-exiled) in both East and West, born of nations that adored the literary word but finding themselves always between several cultures and unable to lose themselves in any one of them.[6] And thus the fertile meta-capacities of the Central European mind: cosmopolitan, restless, homeless, a natural translator and hub.

Can we say that comparativist anxieties for this part of the world are the same as the ones Haun Saussy lays out in the ACLA report for European and American academic departments? Yes and no. As regards the changing status of translation (its lessening importance as the medium moves from verbal to visual, as close readings go out of fashion, and as ever more global communication defaults to English), we should admit up front that this remains largely a problem of the United States. Thus, we will be the beneficiaries. For Americans are the ones most routinely embarrassed by inadequate, delayed, and artificial learning of others' languages, whereas Central and Eastern Europeans (like their confrères the Finns, the Danes, and the Dutch) go on growing up with three or four. Will their post-Communist comparative literature departments also feel the pressure of domestic equivalents to our "relevance wars," our cultural studies and post-cultural studies? Doubtless yes, although exact equivalents there will not be. (Russian "culturology," for example, is as nonpolitical and philosophically speculative as cultural studies has been traditionally partisan and activist.) Gender issues will continue to be dealt with differently, due to cultural differences as basic as Turkish influence on the South Slavs and an overall looser, less norm-driven attitude toward "private life" lived eccentrically in public forums—sexuality, aging, disability, ugliness, a messy lawn, or an impossible in-law are all normal and do not need to be hidden. Eastern Europeans, too, suffer from cyber-flattening and a Googlization of the world—and to the extent that e-mail and online are the only things that work in areas too remote or too poor to have an infrastructure, a library, or a paved road, residents in those parts are more dependent on its resources than we. (There was a period soon after the Communist collapses when comparative literature and Slavic departments received a rush of applications from gifted young people in towns so remote—or, under their old regimes, closed and classified—that they weren't on any map.)

But one phrase in the report, near its increasingly politicized conclusion, brought me up short: "Most of the good things in life are inefficiencies." Talk to any post-Communist East European, and they will confirm: the worst aspect of America's becoming the standard to which so much is now reduced is that we move fast and insist on finishing what we begin. But art should slow us down. It should take up our time and make us think. Thus the cooption of art by the marketplace, and by the corporate values of speed, power, consumerism, instant gratification, and instant depletion leading to more consumption, is an obscenity and a disaster. To adjust art to the history-less pace and corporate values of commercial life in hopes of making it "relevant" is to eviscerate it.

No one in those countries seriously wishes for the return of the fake and fatal markets of Communism, of course. Nor do they believe that art should turn back the clock. But it must provide some alternative to what we are otherwise forced to live by. All art, just like every genuine act of comparison, is time-intensive; it does not come ready-made, because it represents an approximation, an imperfect translation, a striving. Corporate or mass culture does not encourage striving—that is, the search for elusive things. Here, in the more "inefficient realms" of the imagination, Central and Eastern Europeans (for all their contributions to the avant-garde) have routinely stood up to Western models of successful art. Anaesthetizing commercialism quickly palls. Politicized, confrontational art brought them to the edge of the abyss. More enduring are the contemplative, affectionate, and humorous modes of artistic communication.

It is no accident that a Russian-born philosopher of culture now teaching at Emory University, Mikhail Epstein, has been the most eloquent champion of a comprehensive reassessment of "identity politics" as an institutional organizing principle in language-and-culture departments of the liberal-bourgeois university. In several essays during the late 1990s, Epstein introduced the idea of "transculture." He invites us not only to abandon, at long last, the old "acceptable" political binary (East versus West) but also to stop hungering after those big convergence schemes, hybridization or globalization. The very idea of majority and minority should be rethought, he advises. In the West, we must let go of our established sense of the legitimate "minorities"—black, female, Hispanic, bisexual, et cetera—just as we've been forced to let go of the political binary. And we should start thinking instead in terms of "variously delineated majorities": people grouped according to their experiences of illness, inspiration, love, creativity, suffering, loss, and other states that transcend identity. For more unites us than divides us, he insists. One must simply commit to finding co-experience as interesting as confrontation and struggle, and commit to defining the proper transcendent categories.[7] If the traditional (and now outdated) humanities were a product of the Renaissance, the "dehumanities" (psychoanalysis, Marxism, semiotics, structuralism, poststructuralism) a product of the twentieth century, then now, with so much sober wisdom born of all the collapses of system, we are ripe for the "transhumanities."[8]

What in the world are the transhumanities? In a recent (2004) speculation entitled "The Unasked Question: What Would Bakhtin Say?" Epstein remarks that the "post-it mode of innovation in the humanities" (postmodernism, poststructuralism, postcolonialism, etc.) is positively self-defeating, dependent on what came before.[9] He also believes—along with most Russian culturologists and many Central European theorists—that in any act of enabling, power is hugely overrated as both a parameter and an operator. Its application usually does more harm than good. In its stead, Epstein recommends a new field: "potentiality." I suspect that what Epstein calls "potentiology" will be part of the core of comparative literature departments of the future.

But what does he mean by "potentiology"? The force behind Epstein's forward-looking, whimsical body of writings rests on a pedagogical and physiological banality—but a profound one. By the time we, the professoriat, are experienced and tenured teachers, we are getting old. Looking back—especially in the humanistic disciplines, which are not progressive sciences and thus do not have a "cutting-edge" of discovery—not only feels right, but feels wise. The past is reliable, documentable, and (most important to our generation) cries out for justice. Study it so that it can be explained, so that its raw or unresolved issues can be addressed. Otherwise, history will repeat itself. But it is by no means clear that historical particulars do, in fact, repeat. And meanwhile, every year our students are younger and younger. To them, the real events of our lives are history or hearsay. They have to be *made* real. Psychologically and physiologically, it is natural for people one-third our age to be more interested in future potentials than in past errors. Yet it's the rare older person (Epstein is one) who provides moral categories and creative tools to think about futures in a buoyant way, that is, free from the mark of our errors, cyber-savvy (in "The Unasked Question" he speaks of "interlations" rather than translations, textoids rather than texts), yet without a hint of commercial cant and with none of the manic utopian intonation that marked the great communist experiment.

Again, Central and Eastern Europeans provide a good pool for this sort of thinking. They have been through every abomination. An ideology or an -ism that takes itself seriously is simply ludicrous. They (and we can now include the imperial Russians) have accustomed themselves to loss. They've had a good look at our Western victories as well as at our patterns of protest and are indifferently impressed. This state of affairs encourages an outside-ness to all things rather than a consuming of them, and is sympathetic to a robust "potentiology." We could begin learning from them.

NOTES

1. See Galin Tihanov, "Why Did Modern Literary Theory Originate in Central and Eastern Europe? (And Why Is It Now Dead?)," in *Common Knowledge* 10(1) (Winter 2004): 61–81, esp. 77.

2. Milan Kundera, "The Tragedy of Central Europe," *New York Review of Books*, 26 April 1984, 33–38.

3. The conference took place, but funds were insufficient to set up and maintain the Web site. Heim still hopes to do so, thereby providing a forum where literary specialists in one country can decide, via domestic reviews, the best works being produced, which they can then propose for translation to fellow members in other language communities.

4. Jeffrey C. Isaac, "Rethinking the Legacy of Central European Dissidence," in *Common Knowledge* 10(1) (Winter 2004): 119–29.

5. Most visibly between the glossy, postmodernist, Western-oriented *Novoe literaturnoe obozrenie* [New Literary Review], funded handsomely by New Russian private subsidies, and the methodologically more conservative *Voprosy literatury* [Questions of Literature], still in its modest Soviet-era format. See the acerbic response to a special "state of the field" issue of *NLO*, "After the History of Literature" (No. 59: 2003), with such cutting-edge rubrics as "After Systems," "After the Nation," "After Literature," "After the Discipline," "After Binariness," "After Canonization," mounted by Igor Shaitanov, editor of *Voprosy Literatury*, in his "Delo No. 59: NLO protiv osnov literaturoveniia" [Case #59: NLO against the Foundations of Literary Study"], in *Voprosy literatury* (September-October 2003): 135–51.

6. See Tihanov, "Why Did Modern Literary Theory Originate in Central and Eastern Europe?" and also his recent comparative-historical projects, such as "When Eurasianism met For-

malism: An Episode from the History of Russian Intellectual Life in the 1920s," in *Die Welt der Slaven* 48:2 (2003): 359–82. Eastern European thinkers were especially well equipped to gather up, analyze, and reintegrate the shards of the monolithically ambitious German "mandarin culture" and investigations into *Bildung* that lay in ruins after the First World War. For a superb example of comparative philology on this terrain, watch for Vladimir Nikiforov, *The Individual in Husserl, Rickert and Bakhtin: The Genesis of a First Philosophy for a World in Ruins*, forthcoming from Mellen Publishers.

7. Mikhail Epstein, "Transculture and Society," in Ellen E. Berry and Mikhail N. Epstein, *Transcultural Experiments: Russian and American Models of Creative Communication* (New York: St. Martin's Press, 1999): 102–12, esp. 105.

8. Mikhail Epstein, "The Rehumanization of the Humanities," in *Transcultural Experiments*, 113–19.

9. Mikhail Epstein, "The Unasked Question: What Would Bakhtin Say?" in *Common Knowledge* 10(1) (2004): 42–60, esp. 44.

CHAPTER FIFTEEN

Not Works but Networks

Colonial Worlds in Comparative Literature

ROLAND GREENE

"A discipline defined by the search for its proper objects": this characterization by Haun Saussy, offered in his thoughtful account of the state of comparative literature at the present time, reflects the discipline as most of us know it, even if some comparatists wish it were otherwise. Saussy persuasively sketches a comparative literature, the history of which "is not one of steadily deepening understanding of a single object of study, but rather a history of attempts to locate that object of study. Receptive to changing definitions of 'literature' to a degree unmatched by any other literary field, . . . comparative literature has a discontinuous history in which it is not always the protagonist." This is the condition of our field, and we should accept it as a virtue, even a privilege. In fact, many disciplines have not always been their own protagonists. Biology has depended on chemistry and physics to catalyze the development of biochemistry and molecular biology, respectively, while the Cold War motivated the emergence of programs in materials science that renovated the discipline of engineering but also affected solid state physics. Several of the social sciences have undergone a turn toward quantitative methods in which those disciplines have been not so much agent as scene.

If comparative literature is the workshop of literary studies, as I wrote ten years ago in response to the Bernheimer report, then we must accept that a good part of our mission is to interpose our particular knowledges against problems that come to us from outside our discipline, thinking comparatively on behalf of literary studies as well as other disciplines altogether.[1] If it locates comparative literature in an oblique relation to the other domains of literary studies, many of which are not nearly so responsive to prevailing intellectual currents in the larger academy, this challenge acknowledges the reality that our discipline has a great deal in common with those areas of scholarship that resemble crossroads more than bounded fields, such as anthropology, geography, and engineering. In the following pages, I intend to consider where the Saussy report belongs in the conversation about the discipline that has been carried on intermittently for the past fifty years, and what the present moment holds for those of us whose scholarship embraces the early modern literatures of Western Europe and the Americas, especially the colonial circuits that connect them and their postcolonial outcomes.

Ten years after the Bernheimer report, that document seems as much a period piece as the reports that preceded it by Harry Levin and Thomas M. Greene, respectively. Each of these assessments of the state of the discipline is the product of uncertainties and anxieties peculiar to its decade. In the case of the late Charles Bernheimer and his committee, these feelings concerned the relation of literature as an object of study to the field of comparative literature and included questions as to whether comparative literature should confirm, resist, or undo its original premises. Those founding principles were staunchly Eurocentric in cultural orientation, both historical and theoretical in method, and literary in object. If there was a pressure bearing on the Bernheimer report from the humanities at large, it came from the seeming momentum of cultural studies as a renovating force. The state of affairs around the Saussy report is different in that there is no such catalyst at hand—or at least nothing not already addressed by Bernheimer and the several compelling essays that his report provoked, such as postcolonial studies or a reinvented philology—so Haun Saussy and the rest of us are obliged to ponder what might be considered the perennial questions of the discipline's self-definition. The various approaches to this occasion are instructive for anyone who cares about comparative literature.

Like the decennial reports written by Bernheimer and Saussy, the addenda and replies to them of the 1990s and the present show some common tendencies. There is the essay composed in the tone of *ubi sunt,* lamenting the fact that priorities that were once thought inseparable from comparative literature have lost their inevitability. There is the dutiful catalogue of recent scholarship of one sort or another, manifesting how busy the field has been but avoiding the central question of whether all this activity is to any purpose. There is the programmatic piece asserting that comparative literature is really about one thing or another—exile, globalization, translation, world literature—and bringing it up to date under the auspices of such labels. One of the most durable gestures in all of this writing about the discipline is the assertion that some large idea will come to validate the institutional arrangements that are already in place and will become an engine of expansion. When cultural studies was believed in some quarters to be such an idea and engine, a few departments even went so far as to rename themselves with "cultural studies" in their titles. A half decade ago, globalization was such an idea: several prominent departments and journals sponsored conferences and special issues on comparative literature and globalization that were probably as much about making the concept work for literary studies as anything else.[2] Meanwhile, some departments and programs have cultivated highly visible emphases in film and other sidelines as a way of staying viable—a bargain that will have implications for whether comparative literature, as a coherent discipline rather than a set of departments, will yet exist in another generation. To me the most striking thing about all of these activities is the emptiness at their heart. It is as though we refuse to see what endures about the discipline in spite of all the changes of emphasis and fashion.

Against the drift of much of this activity, it seems worth insisting that as an intellectual formation, comparative literature is not much different now from what it was ten, twenty, or thirty years ago. Notwithstanding the conversation about crisis in the discipline that has become a continual feature of its self-definition—driving out more reasoned accounts of what the field is and should be—comparative literature remains the one area in literary studies that has no object in the sense of a corpus, a set of languages, or a normative method. Nor is comparative literature "about" literature itself, if that means it treats that category as a single entity. Instead, the discipline concerns itself with the exchanges out of which literatures are made: the economies of knowledge, social relations, power, and especially art that make literatures possible. Not literature but literatures; not works but networks. Naturally, if one undertakes to address literatures comparatively—that is, with the negotiations that construct them in the foreground, emphasizing their constructedness—one must posit something of each literature in itself as well as of literature in general. One must interpret particular novels, employ received concepts, narrate literary histories. But those acts are merely the means that direct us to the end of comparative literature, which is to issue fresh accounts of literatures under negotiation.

The available modes of evoking such negotiations change from time to time: now they might be called history of ideas, later literary theory, still later cultural or postcolonial studies—and later again, perhaps history of ideas or formalism again. All of these approaches seem especially revelatory for as long as they give us fresh entry into literatures under negotiation; by the same lights, most of them lose explanatory power over time because they come to be about literature as already negotiated—about works in themselves, settled terminologies, and predictable results. Means come to be mistaken for ends, national literatures become reified again, and the work overwrites the network that gives it power. These adjustments away from the outlook of comparative literature are not only inevitable but necessary, since the comparative approach depends on—is partly built from—the discoveries of those scholars for whom authors, works, and national literatures are of primary importance. Moreover, the comparatist may sometimes act, not as comparatist, but instead in his or her capacity as scholar of a national literature, working locally or ad hoc rather than relationally. How could it be otherwise? But the drive of the comparatist is to remain committed, not to theory or the visual arts or textual studies as a matter of program, not even to French and Spanish and German literatures themselves, but to recovering that dynamic event of negotiation: how literatures and all their elements come into being out of a process of exchange.

The centerpiece of Saussy's document is an extended consideration of what might be the *tertium comparationis* of comparative literature, the ground or trunk that makes distinct objects comparable. It is always hard to see negotiation or exchange as such a term because such networks seem to exist more in process than in substance and are always at risk of dissolving into the stations they connect with one another. Moreover, despite the corrective efforts of many observers from Foucault and Barthes to Bernard Cerquiglini, Franco Moretti, and Rey Chow, certain totems of literary studies—authors, works, languages, genres, periods—exercise a pull that sometimes counters the comparative import of a critical project, making it seem to be about, for instance, the works rather than the networks. Saussy's promising approach is to suggest, not for the first time, that "literariness" might be an example of the kind of object to which the discipline aspires. Such an agenda will work to the extent that it resists allowing "literariness" and its equivalents to become merely properties of the works in question, and instead forces into view those properties under construction across works, languages, and cultures.

Where Saussy remarks that "some paradoxes [would] follow from the elevation of literariness (or literary language) to the status of characteristic object of study for comparative literature," and goes on to observe that "many activities normally carried out in the field do not find themselves reflected in it," something, in my view, is being missed. Literariness in the sense of an object of study counts as comparative because it is a good example of a property that can be considered only according to a comparative method; studies of the literary that confine themselves to a single language or national literature, while they undoubtedly exist, work against the grain of a question that must be engaged multilingually and cross-culturally. It is not the actual question "what is literary?" that is important here, but the kind of question; and many topics, problems, and practices normal to the field can be addressed in terms of that kind of question. Indeed, all the typical activities of comparative literature can be embodied in such questions, whether or not they concern literariness itself; and that is what makes literariness "a virtual model" for the project of comparative literature. At the same time, such questions entail the exclusion of certain activities only to the degree that they do not satisfy the criterion of showing exchange or negotiation in process. One thinks of Harry Levin's famous course at Harvard called "Proust, Joyce, Mann."

There are ways of teaching a course with that title as properly comparative—for instance, revealing an economy of ideas and techniques among these figures, their moments, and settings—and there are ways in which such a course, despite its attention to novelists of different languages and societies, might not be comparative at all. Does the title of the course name three novelists, or a new explanatory model for modern fiction? Is the course about novels or something larger in which the novels are inlaid?

Saussy's "literariness" is one of several current ways of invoking a negotiational model of the discipline. Recently I have been interested in two alternative formulations, namely, Franco Moretti's and David Damrosch's differing and perhaps incompatible accounts of world literature as a suitable *tertium*—that is, as the object we consider when we read two or more works together. With a bracing disregard for the usual pieties of literary studies, Moretti argues that a serious attention to the novel, not as a genre in the conventional sense, but as a global system of literary production, will entail a mode of reading that emphasizes widely distributed patterns over particular objects, broad-gauge observation instead of interpretation.[3] Unlike many of those who speculate on the discipline, Moretti treats critical practice as answerable to a politics and a worldview ("the way we imagine comparative literature is a mirror of how we see the world").[4] Convinced that the literary regime, from the creation of literary works through the scholarship about them, is organized to maintain the centrality of European and American writing, he asks comparatists to confront this fact by working differently, notably by subtracting close reading from their procedures. The evident impracticality of this demand evidences both the power of the regime that Moretti seeks to neutralize and, what concerns him less, the fact that in practice today, comparative literature is more often a set of conventions and activities than a fully integrated discipline.

Damrosch's angle of approach is more subtle: he insists that world literature is a sort of template that might be applied to any literary event that has crossed the national and linguistic borders within which it was created. We witness such an event in its local context, and we may witness it again as an instance of world literature, and these two modes of reading inform one another, allowing (say) a particular work of Dante or Kafka to live in two elements at once. Scarcely arguing against conventions such as close reading, Damrosch seems to envision a critical outlook that might produce multiple, complementary, but not entirely compatible close readings—say, of the work in its local setting and then again as a specimen of world literature.[5] Damrosch's fundamental insight is perhaps that from the array of literary works that makes the various national literatures, we can and do fashion an alternative canon—world literature—according to which the same works seem different, speak to different concerns in different voices, and weigh differently against one another. As I see it, both Moretti and Damrosch are invested in models of literary studies that emphasize the negotiations that establish literariness over the seeming autonomy and self-sufficiency of the works that result from that process. With Saussy they see literariness as a hieroglyphic rather than a hieratic event, something to be recovered, deciphered, and transposed in its distributed power.[6] At the same time, they recognize the negotiated character of literariness in stark contrast to each other, Damrosch proposing that we acknowledge literary networks by adding a dimension to our interpretive procedure, Moretti suggesting we do the same by subtraction.

To measure how much the climate of disciplinary conversation has changed since the Bernheimer report, one might revisit two prominent investigations that predate it by only a few years, namely Claudio Guillén's and Susan Bassnett's book-length overviews of 1985 and 1993, respectively.[7] Guillén argues for the supranational dimension of comparative literature and is impatient with the national literatures in their depth and complexity; he would rather examine structures that exist across nations, languages, and history, which sounds incontrovertible until we see that his practice is captive to received concepts, conventional literary history, and luminous examples. Meanwhile Bassnett, in a polemical volume of about the same moment as the Bernheimer report, insists on an understanding of literary studies as involving principally the forces that make works legible rather than the formal properties of the works themselves—aligning herself as far as that goes with Bernheimer, Moretti, and Damrosch. The climax of her argument, however, is the claim that comparative literature is not only intellectually but also ideologically incapable of such a project because of its positivist legacy and other factors, and her designation of postcolonial studies and translation studies as two fields that in 1993 are undertaking more or less what comparative literature ought to be doing.[8] While Guillén describes an exaggeratedly continuous and rather platitudinous conception of the field, Bassnett omits the fact that at many junctures in its history, comparative scholarship has considered exactly the types of questions she endorses: what is read and by whom, how literature is received across cultures, what translation makes both evident and obscure. Just as (contra Guillén) these questions are not necessarily in play in what we call comparative literature, so (contra Bassnett) they are not programmatically off the agenda there either, and certainly not for ideological motives that would render translation studies insightful where comparative literature is blind. Rather, certain critical stances are fresh enough in their moment (as translation studies was in 1993) to make the old questions sound contemporary again. The recent history of the field tells of a migrating franchise—from high theory to cultural studies to postcolonial studies—that has kept inviting us to look beyond works to networks, always in a renewed idiom.

The inclusive and exclusive views of the discipline by Guillén and Bassnett, respectively, are to me both symptomatic of their era, in which the history of the discipline is often misunderstood by partisans as either too little or too much differentiated. We ought to be considering instead how the most compelling scholarship, from Curtius to Barthes to Said, evinces a common and evolving set of preoccupations, and how future work should move those concerns forward in aesthetic, political, and other directions. The Bernheimer report represents a hinge between a great deal of disciplinary analysis up to Guillén and Bassnett on the one hand, and the group of striking arguments by Damrosch, Moretti, Gayatri Spivak, and others that have appeared since 1995.[9] I credit the report, and especially Charlie Bernheimer himself, with making this case in a way that balances a respectful and open-eyed account of the field's past with an equally realistic and nuanced view of its future.

The Bernheimer report contained one sentence that became a particular point of contention, but it should be quoted only in the context of the statements that follow it:

> Literary phenomena are no longer the exclusive focus of our discipline. Rather, literary texts are now being approached as one discursive practice among many others in a complex, shifting, and often contradictory field of cultural production. This field challenges the very notion of interdisciplinarity, to the extent that the disciplines were historically constructed to parcel up the field of knowledge into manageable territories of professional expertise. Comparatists, known for their propensity to cross over between disciplines, now have expanded opportunities to theorize the nature of the boundaries to be crossed and to participate in their remapping.[10]

In 1995, the first sentence above was taken to be a synecdoche of the entire report, which was generally seen as acknowledging the rise of cultural studies as a renovative force in comparative literature. Although the report took some care to make the point that the "field of cultural production" in which literature is embedded should only be expanded, and not remapped to push literature aside, some respondents, such as Peter Brooks and Michael Riffaterre, heard a different implication, namely that literature itself, and the high theory that defines it, should not be central to comparative literature. Others, such as Mary Louise Pratt, welcomed the statement as an overdue coming to terms with the realities of the field.[11] Still, nothing in the report did as much to provoke a sense that as a threshold in the life of the discipline was being crossed, some comparatists would find themselves in an unfamiliar position—on the outside.

Ten years later, it seems to me that the report's argument on this point has been borne out, but not because cultural studies has come to revive comparative literature. If anything, the shortcomings of cultural studies, especially its weak hold on history, linguistic specificity, and cultural difference, are more evident than they were ten years ago. We might say that what was heard in 1994 as an endorsement of cultural studies was really an open-ended account of where the field belonged, and that several kinds of scholarship, including colonial and postcolonial studies, would fit that description without any of them being its necessary fulfillment. The central observation was that "phenomena" considered as such had given way to "fields" of production—a view of comparative literature that looks backward as well as forward, demarcating the boundary between this discipline and other varieties of literary studies with a clarity that was (and is) certain to make some people uncomfortable. For those who felt themselves on the outside of the perimeter drawn by this observation, there was perhaps a sense that something vital to literary studies was being written off by fiat; to others, it might have seemed that comparative literature was bringing itself into the present. But it went unrecognized on all sides that this was a description of comparative literature with a strong basis in the history of the discipline. Bernheimer and his committee were making the claim that literary works in the phenomenal sense—poems, plays, novels as such, to be experienced as literary objects, read in and for themselves—are not central to comparative literature, that the discipline exists to treat literature in the expanded sense of genres, canons, and economies—in short, fields. This distinction embodies the terms of an argument that has played out among comparatists in every phase of the discipline, and that every comparatist has probably had with himself. Of course comparative literature concerns itself with literature; to insist on that is to say everything and nothing. But literature is a metonymy for many things, and one's understanding of the discipline depends on which dimensions of literature one invokes metonymically—those that foreground what is intrinsic to the category and particular to its works, or those that emphasize what is brought about by proximity, contingency, and exchange. If there are now opposed parties within the field—say, those who see the field in a dynamic conversation with the present, and those who take a more conservative view that something essential has been lost—then they might be represented by these two ways of thinking about what comparative literature can be.

In a provocative essay that speaks to this moment in the discipline, Rey Chow has argued from a different angle—a geopolitical one—that two paradigms for comparative literature are now available. The older of the two, which represents the established tradition of comparative literature, might be called "Europe and Its Others":

> In this formulation, the rationale for comparing hinges on the conjunction *and;* the *and* . . . signals a form of supplementation that authorizes the first term, Europe, as the grid of reference, to which may be added others in a subsequent and subordinate fashion.

An outcome of this kind of comparison is an often asymmetrical distribution of cultural capital and intellectual labor, so that cultures of Europe (the grid), such as French and German, tend to be studied with meticulousness while cultures on the margins of Europe, such as those in Latin America, Africa, or Asia, even when they are differentiated by unique, mutually unintelligible linguistic traditions, may simply be considered examples of the same geographical areas (and hence not warranting comparative study). ... The *and* thus instigates not only comparison but also a politics of comparison: on the one side, the infinite opening of histories, cultures, and languages in their internal vicissitudes in such a manner as to enable their studies to become ever more nuanced and refined; on the other side, a crude lumping together of other histories, cultures, and languages with scant regard to exactly the same kinds of details and internal dynamics of thought that, theoretically speaking, should be part of the study of any tradition. These other histories, cultures, and languages remain by default undifferentiated—and thus never genuinely on a par with Europe—within an ostensibly comparative framework.

The other model, to which Chow attaches the label "Post-European Culture and the West," is adumbrated in the recent work of several scholars from particular national literatures, only some of whom identify themselves as comparatists, and involves a different sense of comparison—one that, I believe, gives substance to a field- or exchange-oriented account of what we do:

No longer simply a spontaneous act occasioned by, say, the taxonomic arrangement of multiple linguistic spheres, comparison is understood by these critics as a type of discursive situation, involuntarily brought into play by and inextricable from the conditions of modern world politics—a discursive situation that in the end does not quite conform to classical comparative aspirations. Unlike the old-fashioned comparative literature based on Europe, none of the studies in question vociferously declares its own agenda as international or cosmopolitan; to the contrary, each is firmly located within a specific cultural framework. Yet, in their very cultural specificities, these studies nonetheless come across as transcultural, with implications that resonate well beyond their individual locations.[12]

To Chow's acute observation I add the following: what I am calling (after Bernheimer) the phenomenal approach to comparison is tacitly encouraged by the paradigm she calls "Europe and Its Others," in that an asymmetrical program of comparison tends to protect the conditions for seeing certain literary materials with a great deal of cultural capital—the *Trauerspiel,* French realist novels, or modernist long poems—as phenomena whose qualities override any negotiation within a literary and social economy. It is not that an approach limited to Europe cannot discern such negotiation and exchange: Walter Benjamin's work on the German baroque drama, not to mention a reasonable body of comparative scholarship on the novel and on modernist poetry, demonstrates that it is possible to work in local as well as transcultural terms within a European orbit. At the same time, as a disciplinary model, "Europe and Its Others" tends to represent a methodological bias writ large; the same assumptions that authorize European productions as "the grid of reference" can make those productions seem constructing rather than constructed. The cosmopolitanism of traditional comparative literature might thus be cast, in caricature, as a serviceable cloak for those critics who prefer works to networks, phenomena to economies—a cloak the most searching comparatists have always refused.

The attraction of Chow's alternative model, as I understand it, is that in accord with its very different politics of comparison, this model assumes that to speak of literatures is to document and theorize the transactions out of which works, genres, and periods arise. Even where only European materials are involved, it ought to be possible to eschew grids of reference and closed taxonomies and to understand comparison as inherently problematic—a politics writ small. Exact correspondences aside, my argument about what is fundamentally at stake in comparative literature—which I take to overlap in local and approximate but important ways with Saussy's and Bernheimer's statements, with Damrosch, Moretti, and Spivak in broad outline, and with the classic canon of disciplinary practice from Auerbach and Curtius forward—converses vividly with Chow's argument. All of these accounts accept the seemingly trivial but propitious episode of Saussy's conclusion to his report's first part, in which he insists on what he calls "the politics of the adverb," namely, that comparative literature is about how we read: with what awarenesses; what politics; what provisions against the tyranny of the work, the period, the genre—in other words, against all that is disciplinary rather than paradisciplinary (as I put it ten years ago) or metadisciplinary (as Saussy has it today).

It remains for me to conclude with a few remarks about colonial and postcolonial studies in comparative literature. The continual challenge of this kind of scholarship is to maintain a focus on *how* rather than *what* we are reading, or in Chow's terms to construct a politics of comparison that does not borrow the inequalities and disproportions of the colonial world itself. Of course, if any branch of comparative literature should be prepared to keep networks and exchanges in sight, it ought to be colonial studies. The most invigorating scholarship in this area situates particular works in their social and aesthetic contexts, treats authors as in some measure the products of colonial processes, examines works from the metropolis and its colonies alike in local and cross-cultural perspective, and allows for all of the terminals on the colonial circuit to participate in defining the terms of the literary project at hand.

And yet we are scarcely able to say that because we have accounted for the networks that give meaning and power to colonial works, we have overcome the challenge of reading comparatively. For me a compelling dimension of that challenge has been to ask continually: what is a network, a circuit? Old and new, the arguments that have influenced me most profoundly in the past several years have been the ones that did the most to unsettle my sense of how to define and apply the idea of a colonial context—that expanded, redefined, and renamed the contexts with which I was already familiar.[13] The device "not works but networks" avails only as long as we keep our networks open in both historical observation and theory, "unworking" them from time to time—and this project may be especially vexing in the colonial and postcolonial terrain, where the patterns of travel and exchange established by earlier scholarship can come to seem as inevitable as periods, styles, and works do elsewhere.

As colonialists, we are obliged to qualify the distinction in the motto of this essay: while the literary works that concern us may or may not seem to overwrite their contexts as readily as do realist novels or modernist long poems, the networks we construct to explain those works are really, openly, the objects of our attention. In this sense, our local field of colonial and postcolonial studies is a limit-case that shows how inseparable works and networks are, how often works must be reinvigorated within networks even as the networks themselves are reinvented again and again—in the case of colonial networks, by restaging the conversations between past and present. The mid-twentieth-century historians of the baroque Americas, present-day scholars of colonialism from the postcolonial world, scholars of and from the indigenous "fourth world," and, of course, practitioners of other disciplines—geographers, historians, anthropologists—who concern themselves with the cultural traffic of colonialism: all of these can be made to unsettle and "unwork" the networks of colonial and postcolonial studies.[14] With the fresh or forgotten information of these interlocutors, we rebuild a comparative literature from the outside in.

A stark necessity in the colonial and postcolonial field, this imperative is probably less vivid but no less necessary in the rest of comparative literature. And as we reinvent our field, we ourselves enact an exchange, because we give something back to the historians, geographers, and scholars of national literatures—as Wellek, Said, and Spivak have all given back. In the twenty-first century we comparatists can take nothing for given, certainly not our influence. Still, our discipline continues to offer something provocative and even transformative, as the laboratory or workshop of literary studies where interpretive formations, reanimating concepts, and comparison itself make new again the worlds of literature and culture.

NOTES

1. Roland Greene, "Their Generation," in *Comparative Literature in the Age of Multicultural-ism*, ed. Charles Bernheimer (Baltimore: Johns Hopkins University Press, 1995), 143.

2. For example, "Globalization and the Humanities," *Comparative Literature* 53 (2001).

3. Franco Moretti, "Conjectures on World Literature," *New Left Review* 1 (2000): 54–68. He continues the argument in "More Conjectures," *New Left Review* 20 (2003): 73–81.

4. Moretti, "More Conjectures," 81.

5. David Damrosch, *What Is World Literature?* (Princeton, N.J.: Princeton University Press, 2003), 5, 26.

6. Gregory Jusdanis, "World Literature: The Unbearable Lightness of Thinking Globally," *Diaspora* 12 (2003): 103–30, conducts an extended critique of arguments such as Moretti's and especially Damrosch's.

7. Claudio Guillén, *Entre lo uno y lo diverso: Introducción a la literatura comparada* (Barce-lona: Editorial Crítica, 1985), trans. as *The Challenge of Comparative Literature* by Cola Franzen (Cambridge, Mass.: Harvard University Press, 1993); and Susan Bassnett, *Comparative Litera-ture: A Critical Introduction* (Oxford: Blackwell, 1993).

8. Bassnett, *Comparative Literature*, 9–10, 159.

9. Gayatri Chakravorty Spivak, *Death of a Discipline* (New York: Columbia University Press, 2003).

10. "The Bernheimer Report, 1993: Comparative Literature at the Turn of the Century," *Comparative Literature in the Age of Multiculturalism*, ed. Bernheimer, 42–43.

11. Michael Riffaterre, "On the Complementarity of Comparative Literature and Cultural Studies," in *Comparative Literature in the Age of Multiculturalism*, ed. Bernheimer, 70–71; and in the same volume, Peter Brooks, "Must We Apologize?" 103–4, and Mary Louise Pratt, "Com-parative Literature and Global Citizenship," 59–61.

12. Rey Chow, "The Old/New Question of Comparison in Literary Studies: A Post-Euro-pean Perspective," *ELH* 71 (2004): 294–95, 301.

13. For instance, Barbara Fuchs, "Imperium Studies: Theorizing Early Modern Expansion," in *Postcolonial Moves: Medieval through Modern*, ed. Patricia Clare Ingham and Michelle R. Warren (New York: Palgrave Macmillan, 2003), 71–90; and the recent unpublished work by Timothy Reiss on the relations between imperial expansion and Baconian natural philosophy.

14. Examples old and new include Mariano Picón-Salas, *A Cultural History of Spanish America: From Conquest to Independence*, trans. Irving A. Leonard (Berkeley and Los Angeles: University of California Press, 1963); Vicente L. Rafael, *Contracting Colonialism: Translation and Christian Conversion in Tagalog Society under Early Spanish Rule* (Ithaca, N.Y.: Cornell Uni-versity Press, 1988); Gordon Brotherston, *Book of the Fourth World: Reading the Native Ameri-cas through Their Literature* (Cambridge, UK: Cambridge University Press, 1992); and Jorge Cañizares-Esguerra, *How to Write the History of the New World: Histories, Epistemologies, and Identities in the Eighteenth-Century Atlantic World* (Stanford, Calif.: Stanford University Press, 2001).

CHAPTER SIXTEEN

Comparative Literature

Congenitally Contrarian

LINDA HUTCHEON

Congenitally contrarian: neither a medical symptom nor a political affiliation; not even a description of departmental politics, though Haun Saussy has remarked above that "a comparative literature department without confrontations is a collection of inert elements." Although the word *contrarian* has "contrary" built into it, I do not even want to suggest that comparative literature as a discipline should only focus on the contestatory and the oppositional. What I do mean is that I believe comparative literature to be *inherently* contrarian—that is, by its very nature. Saussy deems comparatists fortunate to "inhabit a multipolar profession" in a unipolar, globalized world. But he notes that "the times" make this a "contrarian" model; it is this off-hand remark that I take up here in responding to the ACLA's latest reevaluation of the state of the discipline.

The *Oxford English Dictionary* informs us that to be contrarian is to oppose or reject popular opinion, something comparatists have done quite regularly—regarding everything from the singularity of national cultures to the fixity of what constitutes the "literary." The history of this academic discipline in North America offers plentiful evidence of this side of its contrarian nature. Closely related to this fact of identity is another obvious fact: that every decade or so, comparative literature on this continent has reexamined its own working assumptions in the light of changes in both the profession and the world at large in which it professes (e.g., in 1965, 1975, 1993, and again in 2004). I have not noticed that any of the national language and literature disciplines have undergone this kind of regular self-scrutiny, and so few others can lay claim to comparative literature's resulting institutional and intellectual, self-reflexive self-examination. I would argue that this "meta-disciplinarity" is the real reason why what we call "theory" took such firm root in comparative literature departments. It was not simply because they had faculty and students who could speak the languages needed; it was because the ground was already prepared for what Terry Eagleton calls the "systematic reflection on our guiding assumptions" that constitutes "theory."[1]

It is this habit of self-interrogation that makes the discipline perhaps uniquely responsive to change: comparative literature has always been open to rethinking; it is always aware of the state of the intellectual economy, if you will. I deliberately turn to an economic metaphor here because the dictionary definition of a "contrarian" is one who resists popular opinion, but does so specifically *in stock exchange dealing.* I am well aware that there are very different opinions of this discipline's success in the "marketplace of ideas," so to speak. Saussy's evaluation asserts that, despite comparative literature's *institutional* "wraithlikeness," comparatist *ideas* and *practices* are omnipresent now: "Our conclusions have become other people's assumptions," he claims. And he may be right, given the number of sessions, for example, at the 2004 convention of the Modern Language Association that dealt with globalization and comparativity (of everything from Queer to Early American literature). But this very same focus of scholarly attention can also be found in conferences of many different stripes around the world today. At the other extreme, however, is Gayatri Spivak's lament for the end of comparative literature, for the "death of a discipline."[2] If she is right, then I cannot be alone in noting the obvious irony of its demise at the very moment in history when its disciplinary focus on those mobile networks of ideas, connecting and circulating around the globe, can be most useful.

As George Steiner and others have explored, comparative literature's expansion in North America after World War II was the direct result of "marginalization, . . . [of] partial social and ethnic exclusion."[3] What he meant, of course, is that this became the discipline of the (largely Eastern and Central) European polyglot exile. Therein lay its strength—and increasingly its limitation, in geographic and cultural terms. If, to use Steiner's image, comparatists are forever "jubilant at the intractable diversity of Babel,"[4] that diversity has been a decidedly limited one. As Franco Moretti has reminded us, the discipline's rhetorical reach has decidedly exceeded its geographical grasp.[5] I shall not rehearse here the many arguments, historical and other, mounted against the resolutely European focus of earlier comparative studies. For over a decade now, the discipline has been facing head-on the need to go beyond its roots and to broaden the linguistic and cultural scope of its work to include the rest of the world: the East as well as the West, the South as well as the North.

Yet, if comparative literature really is as "congenitally contrarian" as I hope it is, on the intellectual stock market, it will not abandon Europe completely, despite its current lack of fashionable appeal (and almost political correctness), especially among its younger scholars in North America. In an academic and intellectual environment like the current one, in which we are all grappling with the complex issues surrounding globalization, for many not only has the question of Europe not been answered, but Europe is now out of the question (as well as out of fashion). Yet the revival of ethnic and religious nationalisms after the dissolution of the Soviet Union and the break-up of the former Yugoslavia marked a major geopolitical realignment, and with that came great pain along with some gain. Our current preoccupation with Iraq, in other words, should not make us forget Kosovo. Comparatists have always attended to history and memory.

Why should we not forget Europe? In the ever-expanding economic grouping that is the European Union, there is more than ever a need to find cultural as well as economic commonalities amid manifest national and historical differences between East and West, North and South. To precisely this end, in 1986 the EU adopted an anthem: "Ode to Joy," the finale of the fourth movement of Beethoven's Ninth Symphony (in D minor, Op. 125),[6] but *without* the famous choral text, the composer's shortened adaptation of "An die Freude," a 1785 ode by Friedrich Schiller. The official EU orchestral version was arranged and shortened to two minutes by the conductor Herbert von Karajan.[7] When you think about it, this choice of anthem was intensely German in its music (and its silenced text). The music alone was deemed share-able, supranational, "representative of European genius and therefore capable of uniting the hearts and minds of all Europeans."[8] It is hard not to make a connection here with the parallel aspirations of Goethe's *Weltliteratur,* with its interweaving of literary traditions to combat isolationism and nationalist arrogance. But Steiner's evaluation of the *actual* situation of the union of the historically warring countries of Europe, though written now a decade ago, is still relevant: "The notion of a European concord, except on a commercial, fiscal, or mercantile basis . . . seems to recede from realistic expectations."[9]

Does this choice of a European anthem help the cause of a greater (ideological and cultural) unity in any real or, for that matter, any symbolic way? And is there a lesson to be learned from this choice? Schiller's original long ode had offered a message of utopian unity, through magic ("Zauber"), of what custom had once strongly divided ("Was die Mode streng geteilt"). One might be forgiven for thinking that, despite the obviously limiting feature of the words being in only one of the European languages, this would seem a good start for an anthem meant to provoke as well as symbolize pan-European unity. Beethoven, in his shortened version, had kept this message and its rousing conclusion that all men shall become brothers ("Alle Menschen werden Brüder"). Both versions celebrate friendship, marital love, and, more interestingly, the salvation of the good and the evil together ("Alle Guten, alle Bösen"). On both poem and lyrics, all the world's "brothers" are exhorted to run their race joyfully, just as a hero goes to victory ("Laufet, Brüder, eure Bahn, / Freudig, wie ein Held zum

Siegen"). Presumably then, including the nonracing women, the world's millions are to be embraced ("Seid umschlungen, Millionen"); they are also to bow down ("ihr stürzt nieder") to the Creator ("den Schöpfer").

In shortening the long ode, Beethoven had deleted such things as Schiller's message of courageous endurance for a better world ("Duldet mutig, Millionen! / Duldet für die bess're Welt"), along with the poet's urging that anger and revenge be forgotten and enemies forgiven ("Groll und Rache sei vergessen, / Unserm Todfeind sei verziehn"). In the original version, the entire world would be reconciled ("Ausgesöhnt die ganze Welt!") in the joy of divine forgiveness. But if the composer cut some of the stanzas of the ode, he arguably retained their general ideology, not to say, their sentiment. Even though he lived in a less politically correct age than our own, Beethoven was perhaps wise to cut the poem's line about cannibals drinking gentleness ("Trinken Sanftmut Kannibalen"), as all the reunited others imbibe the golden wine of joy. But he kept the general message of brotherhood and divinely assisted human unity.

The European Union's decision to use only the music of the "Ode to Joy" without any of the actual words of Schiller's utopian message of brotherhood has a number of interesting consequences. Yes, there are obviously other languages than German spoken in the Union, but it is also likely true that many people hearing the music will recall the sense, even if not the precise words, of the lyrics. More importantly, however, as the musicologist Caryl Clark has argued, the decision to omit the words ignores the complicating musicological fact that the instrumental music alone, with its "inner conflicts and irregularities" semiotically signals "disorder not harmony, deviance not complacency, difference not collectivity."[10]

Given this discrepancy, I would like to suggest that the European Union's symbolic, if ironic (and I suspect totally unintended), acceptance of discordant musical multiplicity instead of an articulated message of unity may suggest a model for comparatists to intervene in European (and even global) debates. The reason for my excursion into the ironies of European musical politics is that I believe these very ironies teach us, by analogy, that one kind of unity need not suppress or deny diversity and difference, or even discord. As Elizabeth Deeds Ermarth has argued, in a postmodern world in which individual as well as national identity is "multi-laminated" and complex, difference is both constitutive of identity and something to be constantly negotiated. Difference cannot be denied or reduced to common denominators: that way—the way of modernity, she argues—lies the conflicts over Truth that have brought our world totalitarianism and genocide.[11]

In the considerably less contentious field of comparative literature, certain ambitious embracings of unity-respectful-of-multiplicity-and-difference stand as exemplars, as both solo and collective models for the discipline as a whole. I am thinking of works like Franco Moretti's *Atlas of the European Novel 1800–1900* or John Neubauer and Marcel Cornis-Pope's multiply authored collaborative mega-project, the multi-volume comparative *History of the Literary Cultures of East-Central Europe: Junctures and Disjunctures in the Nineteenth and Twentieth Centuries.*[12]

If comparative literature really is (and I believe it is) a discipline that "teaches us to adjust to multiple frames of reference and attend to relations rather than givens," as Saussy claims, then it is incumbent upon it to bring its insights and skills to the cultural redefining of Europe. That this should not be its only mission should by now go without saying. The literary, cultural, and historical relations among northern and southern, among eastern and western parts of the globe are crucial to its new identity in the twenty-first century. But I would like to think that this discipline's contrarian temperament means that it won't forget its roots, that it won't forget Europe. Congenitally contrarian, it should always be willing to "move the other way"—as in "contrary motion" in music.

I live in a country that shares a contrarian identity with the discipline I study. Like comparative literature, Canada is intensely self-reflective—another way of saying that it has a persistent identity crisis, or at least persistent doubts about how to talk about itself. It too is founded historically upon exile, immigration, and displacement. It too has worries about separation, that is, about its "intactness": Quebec, with its recurrent sovereignty-or-separation aspirations, may be to Canada what cultural studies (or area studies, or ethnic and postcolonial studies) are to comparative literature. Both my country and my discipline are deeply concerned about things they feel are central to their identity that are threatened today: health care policy, on the one hand, linguistic polyglottism, on the other. Both fear engulfment by economically and politically more powerful entities: for Canada, it is the United States; for comparative literature, it is the national literature departments. Each has experienced what Saussy calls "a discontinuous history in which it is not always the protagonist." Like Canadians, comparatists often have difficulty explaining themselves in other than negative terms—as what we are not.

This is not the place to attempt to solve problems of my *national* identity, but perhaps the moment is ripe for looking for more positive terms of self-definition for our discipline, paradoxically flourishing yet feeling beleaguered. Saussy uses the image of comparative literature as a "test bed for reconceiving the ordering of knowledge, inside and outside the humanities"—a strong and attractive image. I would like to suggest another image, more modest but, I think, apt: the humble but infinitely useful device without which few of us would travel these days to any other continent: the electrical converter. Like this compact, enabling device, comparative literature makes energy (in its case, intellectual energy) *usable* in different places and in different contexts. This intellectual energy is contrarian, even counter-disciplinary as well as meta-disciplinary, as Saussy argues. And, if I may continue the electrical metaphor, another way to think about comparative literature's usable but not totally consumable energy—whether alternating or direct—is as *power.*

NOTES

1. Terry Eagleton, *After Theory* (New York: Basic Books, 2003), 2.

2. Gayatri Chakravorty Spivak, *Death of a Discipline* (New York: Columbia University Press, 2003).

3. George Steiner, *"What Is Comparative Literature?" An Inaugural Lecture Delivered Before the University of Oxford* (Oxford: Clarendon Press, 1995), 7.

4. Ibid., 10.

5. Franco Moretti, "Conjectures on World Literature," *New Left Review* 1 (2000): 54.

6. Premiered on May 7, 1824, in Vienna.

7. On January 19, 1972, the Council of Europe had earlier adopted it as its anthem at Strasburg.

8. Caryl Clark, "Forging Identity: Beethoven's 'Ode' as European Anthem," *Critical Inquiry* 23(4) (1997): 789.

9. Steiner, "What Is Comparative Literature?" 18.

10. Clark, "Forging Identity," 806.

11. Elizabeth Deeds Ermarth, "Agency in the Discursive Condition," *History and Theory: Studies in the Philosophy of History* 40 (December 2001): 52–54.

12. Respectively, London: Verso, 1998, and Amsterdam: John Benjamins, 2004, with more volumes forthcoming.

CHAPTER SEVENTEEN

Penser d'un dehors

Notes on the 2004 ACLA Report

ZHANG LONGXI

Flying literally from the other side of the globe to Philadelphia for the MLA meeting, I come from a place far enough away to provide me with a standing point where I can have my reflections relatively uncompromised by the internalized knowledge of someone inside the loop. On that basis I am making a claim to the possibility of thinking from the outside, *penser d'un dehors*. I may claim to have an outsider's perspective which, by virtue of being outside, might perhaps be able to shed some light on matters that lie invisible to the insider's blindness. But no—I do not wish to make such a pretentious claim, because an insider's blindness may just be matched by an outsider's ignorance. What I do claim, however, is not that an outsider can think better, but that he can think differently, not following the protocols widely accepted by insiders, and thus think independently and critically. For me, therefore, *penser d'un dehors* really means to take an unconstrained position where one dares to think freely, *ose penser pour soi-même*, and refuses to follow any particular opinion, any particular theory or critical approach that happens to be popular or influential at the time.

Ironically, however, *penser d'un dehors,* or assuming a culturally other or marginal position, or a perspective on the periphery, is precisely what seems popular or fashionable these days, so my effort at an outsider's independent thinking must also reject that disingenuous otherness of a privileged outsider's position. Therefore, coming from the outside, I do not think of myself as a real outsider, though not exactly as an insider either. In between these positions is where I see myself situated, but in-between-ness is what I believe to be just the position for a student of comparative literature; and it is from such a position that I come to reflect on the new ACLA report.

The story Haun Saussy told of comparative literature winning its battles but losing its identity is very much true to the reality of the academia we experience, and also somewhat alarming. With its multilingual requirement and constant demand to go beyond national boundaries, comparative literature does not easily find a home, nor does it easily feel at home, in any disciplinary space of a single language and literature department. The identity problem, or the crisis of comparative literature, as René Wellek and others have indicated, may have started with its very name and nature.[1] The first term in the name, *comparative,* does not describe its nature, and now the second term, *literature,* seems also losing out and thus damaging its nature. As Saussy observes in the first chapter, just as a theoretical linguist may not know a lot of languages, a literary scholar these days could "make a career in literary studies without making sustained reference to works of literature." Much of the "space of comparison" in literary studies is a sort of borrowed space from other disciplines—"anthropology, history, sociology, political science," among others, with the dangerous consequence of comparative literature risking "giving up what autonomy it has and becoming an area of application for the disciplines that define it." That is of course just the flip side of comparative literature's victory in invading other disciplines with its theories and methodologies, but by moving away from literature as its focus, comparative literature stands to lose its identity as comparative *literary* studies. It is therefore important for comparative literature at the present, as Saussy argues, to reexamine the idea of "literariness" and to reclaim literary studies with new perspectives and the possibility of new insights.

It seems that many literary scholars are now turning to film studies, popular culture, and other subjects, presumably because they believe that they can march into those other fields equipped with critical theories easily applicable to whatever is considered an object of study under the rubric of text or textuality, whereas literature has long been a conquered territory, worked many times over with various critical approaches, not to mention the presumption held by many that literature, particularly premodern and early modern literature, is somehow elitist and politically suspect of being part of a complicity with power, representing conservative values of a repressive tradition, or even alleged to be, as Christopher Braider noted in dismay, "the wicked laboratory of the technologies of cultural fabrication and control embodied in Michel Foucault's favorite icons of the hegemonic modern state" (chapter 11). Abandoning literature for films, multimedia, popular culture, and other forms of contemporary middle-class, urban lifestyle in the West may be legitimized as "radical subject choices," as Susan Bassnett puts it, while comparative literature and traditional literary criticism are "increasingly seen as dinosaurs from a liberal-humanist prehistory."[2]

That is all very well, but is there also the danger of legitimizing one's very own lifestyle, of egocentric narcissism and identity politics, the total neglect or amnesia of history, and fostering and catering to the taste of a fast-food population accustomed to quick assimilation of sound bites and color pixels but unconformable with patient, intensive reading and slow, rigorous thinking? In an age of information with Google delivering a sort of Cubist matrix of massive data for each keyword search, but much flatter and more amorphous data than what is relevant and useful, "close readings and paradoxes of traditional literary criticism," as Saussy remarks above, "must have been symptoms of the information-poor communications networks of the past, when details mattered." "In a rapidly changing age," Aldous Huxley already said as early as 1933, "there is a real danger that being well informed may prove incompatible with being cultivated. To be well informed, one must read quickly a great number of merely instructive books. To be cultivated, one must read slowly and with a linger-ing appreciation the comparatively few books that have been written by men who lived, thought and felt with style."[3] Huxley certainly anticipated the current debate about information and real knowledge, but his remarks are also obviously marked as outdated in maintaining that only a few books written by men are worth read-ing. Most likely, Huxley now counts as one of Bassnett's "dinosaurs from a liberal-humanist prehistory," and his call for slow reading and cultivation is hardly heard in today's academia. In any case, literature does seem to fade out, literary studies are being displaced by cultural studies, and comparative literature, or what Bassnett derisively characterized as "the Literature-as-universal-civilizing-force approach," is pronounced dead.[4]

But of course all those obituaries, however dramatic they may sound, turn out to be false, because comparative literature simply ignores all those prophecies and writings on the wall and lives on. One reason some may consider comparative lit-erature dead is that it is still, despite good intentions and genuine efforts on the part of many comparatists in the West, largely restricted within limits of a Eurocentric or West-centered discipline, even when it is trying to go beyond that limitation. But have we really exhausted all possibilities in literary studies? Have the major works of literary traditions *outside* the West become as familiar to comparatists in Europe and North America as the old and new canonized writers in the West? Even post-colonial studies, which emerge as a political as well as intellectual reaction against European colonialism, are not really beyond Eurocentrism, because critical attention is still concentrated on the relationship between European powers and their former colonies, now grouped together on the basis of linguistic as well as political ties. As Emily Apter comments, "Even newer forms of postcolonial comparativism have in-advertently perpetuated neo-colonial geopolitics in carrying over the imperial carve-up of linguistic fields" (chapter 3). In that context, her discussion of Alain Badiou's *comparatisme quand même* offers an intriguing alternative. Without relinquishing commitments to postcolonial literature, such a comparativism calls for an expansion of vision and horizon beyond the usual and obvious bonds and relationships, and that is precisely what I believe to be necessary for comparative literature to grow and develop further.

For a strong advocacy of one such expansion, that of East-West studies, we may look to another eminent comparatist, Claudio Guillén, who does not work with Chinese or other Asian languages. For Guillén, the space of comparison is located, not in national or even international, but in supranational considerations. Supranationality dissociates comparative literature from nations and their interrelations and thus also from those nagging questions of inequality between influence and indebtedness, center and periphery, the West and the rest, and so forth. Going beyond historical contacts, cultural homogeneity, and linguistic affinities, questions of literary theory become important in providing the basis for wide-ranging comparisons; and in that context East-West studies become the most promising area that "permits the dialogue between unity and diversity that stimulates comparativism to focus on the open confrontation of criticism/history with theory; or, if you prefer, of our knowledge of poetry—supranational poetry—with poetics."[5]

With René Etiemble, Guillén argues for the expansion of comparative literature beyond what he calls "European or Eurocentric chauvinism," while ambitiously advocating acquiring knowledge in the world's various languages and literatures. In a way anticipating Alain Badiou's argument for comparison of radically different works, Guillén considers comparative study of historically unrelated works "the most promising tendency in comparative literature."[6] That of course does not mean simply to put disparate texts together without any grounds for comparison. Guillén justifies comparison on the basis of theoretical affinities rather than the positivistic *rapports de fait* or historical contacts, and therefore he sees East-West studies as "offering especially valuable and promising opportunities" for comparative literature today.[7] East-West studies will give comparative literature not just a new lease on life, but a new perspective from which the limited vision of local and parochial concerns will be exposed, and possibilities of doing comparative work in new ways and asking new questions will open up as challenges as well as potential insights. If comparative literature is really ready to go beyond traditional Eurocentric concerns, even the limitation of postcolonial concerns, then East-West studies and world literature studies may hold out the hope of further development.

Again, as I already mentioned above, to engage in wide-ranging comparisons of historically unrelated works must not be a mere juxtaposition of disparate texts, and when comparability is not justified by historical relations, it must be located in theoretical affinities. That, I believe, is what Guillén means by the dialogue or confrontation of criticism/history with theory, or poetry with poetics. Precisely because they deal with literatures that are not closely related except in recent modern history, East-West studies offer a whole new ground for theoretically justifiable comparisons. But here we must pause to consider a serious question: Is the vast field of non-Western literature just a new virgin soil yet to be ploughed and conquered by applying the same critical theories that have become so predominant in American universities? When theories travel, how do they accommodate the changing cultural and political environment? What are the transformations and distortions involved in translating ideas and theories across linguistic, cultural, and political boundaries? How is a theoretical idea "to some extent transformed by its new uses, its new position in a new time and place"?[8] Edward Said asked that question in his essay "Traveling Theory," but from where I come from, a wholesale and mechanical application of Western theory, including Said's own, has to some extent created problems of a simplistic antagonism between the West and the East, a kind of surging nationalistic mentality and "anti-Westernism" that Said himself found regrettable and described himself as "trying hardest . . . to overcome."[9]

For comparative literature to really go beyond the European and Western horizon, then, a high degree of sensibility to, and an intimate knowledge of, the different local cultures, literary traditions, and historical and sociopolitical conditions are prerequisite for adequate understanding and successful comparison. Simple application of Western theories to non-Western materials is an anathema, and comparative work must start from ground up, beginning with the basic materials, basic issues, and basic human experiences that exist in any literature and culture, such as language, expression, meaning, understanding, interpretation, and so on. Only by looking at how theoretical questions arise from such basic materials, issues, and experiences in different cultural and literary formulations on an equal footing can we hope to avoid a simplistic application of Western theory to the non-West and thus avoid ironically repeating, on the theoretical level, the colonization of the East by the West.

In this sense, I fully agree with Haun Saussy's emphasis on the "linguistics of literariness" and his reluctance to depend on translation, because this puts literature back at the center of our attention and reminds us of the importance of understanding literature in its specific linguistic formulations. I also agree with him that although comparatists usually do well in proposing equivalences, "their rejection by specialists is a further and instructive moment in literary-theoretical interaction." The rejection or suspicion of the comparatist's work by specialists is all too familiar, but such rejection may have as much to do with the narrow-mindedness and limited vision of the specialists as with the rigor of their discipline and their in-depth knowledge of the subject under discussion. Our response should be that the comparatist must also be a specialist, but a specialist with broader interests, knowledge, and vision.

A comparatist is someone who knows too much of other literatures and cultures to be satisfied with just his or her own, who has seen the great ocean and can no longer be content with just the river in the village from which he gets his drinking water. The ability to speak other people's languages and to read more widely than one literature is the defining character of a comparatist, but that does not necessarily pit comparative work against translation and thematics. When Saussy equates thematics with enumeration and says that "with a horizon of universality, one has never finished enumerating," I feel that thematics gets short-changed. To be sure, "it is never enough simply to discover the same themes appearing in different places," but thematics worth its name is never a simple juxtaposition or enumeration; it can be a careful way to negotiate the balance between specificity and relation and to engage in just the kind of comparative work Saussy calls for, which creates relations among different texts and establishes a new perspective to read them beyond the specialist's limited horizon. When you engage in imaginative readings and can discern the thematic patterns arising from the encounter of different texts and textual traditions, then you have something to show the specialist that is unavailable from the perspective of each of the textual traditions in isolation. That is, I think, a good enough justification of our discipline, which is more than one specialization.

Whether translation is only good for the transmission of subject matter is more debatable, as is the question whether whatever is not readily translatable is the thing worth knowing in a literary text, but I agree with Saussy that a high level of linguistic complexity and sophistication may become a barrier for the greatest poets in a particular literary tradition to be adequately translated and to circulate in the world of world literature for international appreciation. For example, of all the great Tang poets in classical Chinese literature, the best known, first in Japan and then elsewhere, is Bai Juyi (772–846), but not Du Fu (712–770), the most revered poet in the native Chinese tradition. Such a discrepancy definitely has something to do with the level of difficulty in understanding the works of these two poets. Compared with the far greater Du Fu, Bai Juyi is much more readily readable and translatable. But instead of acknowledging the failure of translation and leaving the matter to the hands of specialists, I would argue that a job is cut out for the comparatist to investigate the "linguistics of literariness" in the works of these poets and to give the best explanation of the discrepancy in their reception in and outside the native tradition.

Comparative literature may be singularly self-conscious among humanities fields, a discipline that seems always in some sort of a crisis, but I do not share the pessimism that haunts its self-questioning of identity, nor do I believe that much of the anxiety about its impossibility or demise is genuine. The best proof of the validity of our discipline is actually doing the comparative work and doing it well. It is in the work we do that we will be able not only to prove the worth of comparative literature, but to create possibilities for its further growth in the future.

NOTES

1. See René Wellek, "The Crisis of Comparative Literature" (1958), in *Concepts of Criticism*, ed. Stephen G. Nichols (New Haven, Conn.: Yale University Press, 1963), 282–95.

2. Susan Bassnett, *Comparative Literature: A Critical Introduction* (Oxford: Blackwell, 1993), 5.

3. Aldous Huxley, *Texts and Pretexts: An Anthology with Commentaries* (New York: Harper and Brothers, 1933), intro., p. 3.

4. Bassnett, *Comparative Literature*, 47. See also Gayatri Chakravorty Spivak, *Death of a Discipline* (New York: Columbia University Press, 2003).

5. Claudio Guillén, *The Challenge of Comparative Literature*, trans. Cola Franzen (Cambridge, Mass.: Harvard University Press, 1993), 70–71.

6. Ibid., 86, 87.

7. Ibid., 70.

8. Edward Said, "Traveling Theory," in *The World, the Text, and the Critic* (Cambridge, Mass.: Harvard University Press, 1983), 227.

9. Edward Said, "East Isn't East: The Impending End of the Age of Orientalism," *Times Literary Supplement*, 3 February 1995, 3. I have discussed related issues in "Postmodernism and the Return of the Native," in Zhang Longxi, *Mighty Opposites: From Dichotomies to Differences in the Comparative Study of China* (Stanford, Calif.: Stanford University Press, 1998), 184–212; and also in a book in Chinese, *Zouchu wenhua de fengbi quan* 走出文化的封閉圈 [*Out of the Cultural Ghetto*] (Hong Kong: Commercial Press, 2000; 2nd and exp. ed., Beijing: Joint Publishers, 2004). See also Haun Saussy, "Postmodernism in China," in *Great Walls of Discourse and Other Adventures in Cultural China* (Cambridge, Mass.: Harvard University Asia Center, 2001), 118–45.

CHAPTER EIGHTEEN

Comparative Literature, at Last

JONATHAN CULLER

Like the linguistic sign, disciplines and departments have a differential identity: as Ferdinand de Saussure put it, "Their most precise characteristic is to be what the others are not."[1]

Once upon a time, comparative literature focused on the study of sources and influence, bringing together works where there seemed to be a direct link of transmission that subtended and served to justify comparison. But then comparative literature liberated itself from the study of sources and influence and acceded to a broader regime of intertextual studies—broader but less well-defined, except differentially. In its recent history in the American academy, comparative literature has been differentiated from other modes of literary study because it did not take it for granted, as did the departments of English, French, Spanish, Italian, Chinese, that a national literature in its historical evolution was the natural and appropriate unit of literary study. Since comparative literature could not avoid the question, as the national literature departments could, of what sorts of units were most pertinent—genres? periods? themes?— it also became the site of literary theory, while national literature departments frequently resisted, or at least remained indifferent to, the sorts of theory that did not emanate from their own cultural spheres. Comparative literature was thus distinguished by its interest in addressing theoretical issues as well as knowledgeably importing and exploring "foreign" theoretical discourses. It was where those questions about the nature and methods of literary study begged in other literature departments were taken up, argued about, even made the focus of teaching and research.

If neither of these features suffices any longer to distinguish comparative literature, it is because so many people in other departments have jumped on these bandwagons or gradually come around to the views of comparatists. Even the study of American literature, once committed to exceptionalism and totalization (Americanists had to have a theory about the nature and distinctiveness of American literature), is now in the process of reconfiguring itself as comparative American literatures. The question of comparative literature has become everybody's question or, in Haun Saussy's formulation, comparatists have been "universal donors."

Whatever the reasons for the spread of these formerly distinctive features, comparative literature has triumphed, and one might therefore expect a triumphal tone to the 2004 report on the state of comparative literature.[2] But of course the triumph of what once distinguished the field leads to a lack of distinctiveness and thus a crisis of identity, and the tone of Saussy's magisterial review of the history of the discipline is scarcely a triumphant one. For good reason: departments or programs of comparative literature have not reaped the benefits of this success. (Saussy fantasizes that people in national literature departments should have to pay a small tax to comparative literature each time they cite De Man, Said, Spivak, Auerbach, and so on, which would do wonders for the field.) Programs in comparative literature are still small or struggling, and we have to tell the very smart and interesting graduate students that we admit: "Welcome to comparative literature, where we do not believe that the national literature is the logical basis of literary study, but be warned that while doing Comp. Lit. you also need to act as if you were in a national literature department so as to make yourself competitive for a job in one." Though comparative literature has triumphed, and many others are comparatists now, the jobs are still in the national language and literature departments.

Taking an intellectual rather than an institutional view, one should be pleased at this triumph. And it is worth noting that the triumph of comparative literature is similar to other triumphs that do not give cause for celebration. Theory has triumphed in that it is everywhere these days—one needs only to be involved in a search to see how far job candidates have been influenced by theory, in the questions they are posing, in the references that are expected of them, even as people write books and articles declaring the passing of theory. Feminism, too, alleged to be dead, can be said to have triumphed in the academy, in that much of what feminist critics and theorists struggled for has come to be taken for granted. Gail Finney notes in chapter 8 that women students take for granted the equality sought by feminism: "They reject the label 'feminist' but have internalized . . . the goals of the ideology." This is a triumph, like the triumph of theory and the triumph of comparative literature, that one cannot *not* wish to have happened, though one still would rather that such triumphs were not so easy to identify with the death of what is triumphing or that they gave more cause for joy.

There is little joy in this ACLA report, though it is too disparate and dispersed for one to speak of any consistent tone or take. Still, one can identify some contrasts with the previous ACLA report of 1993, "Comparative Literature at the Turn of the

Century," published with sixteen responses or position statements as *Comparative Literature in the Age of Multiculturalism.* That report recommends two courses of action, each of which has a good deal to be said for it. On the one hand, it urges comparative literature to abandon its traditional Eurocentrism and turn global—an injunction entirely justified, both as a reflection of contemporary cultural realities and as a response to the growing understanding that Western cultures have been determined in part by their relations to non-Western others. On the other hand, the 1993 report recommends that comparative literature turn from a concentration on literature to the study of cultural productions or discourses of all sorts. This too is a course for which a good case can be made. Scholars of literature have discovered that their analytical skills can shed light on the structures and the functioning of the wide range of discursive practices that form individuals and cultures; and comparatists' contribution to the study of philosophical, psychoanalytical, political, medical, and other discourses, not to mention film, conduct books, and popular culture, has been so valuable that no one could wish to restrict literature faculties to the study of literature alone. Treating literature as one discourse among others, as the report recommends, seems an effective strategy.

Each of these turns, then, can be amply justified, but the result of both moves together, going global and going cultural, is a discipline of such overwhelming scope that it no longer sounds like an academic field at all: the study of discourses and cultural productions of all sorts throughout the entire world. If one were creating a university from scratch, one could doubtless construct a large department of comparative literature charged with global cultural studies, but then the question of differential identity raises its head: would there be any other departments in the humanities to contrast with comparative literature? Would there be a need for music and art and literature and philosophy departments, or departments to study different areas of the world, or would comparative literature in this new dispensation cover everything in the humanities and much of the social sciences?

As soon as one tries to think about the place of the new global and cultural comparative literature in the university, one wonders whether the 1993 report is less a proposal for the reform of a particular department or discipline than a recommendation for how literary and cultural studies in general should proceed. In fact, isn't this how things ought to be? Shouldn't a report on comparative literature project a future for the humanities? Comparative literature has functioned as a vanguard discipline in the humanities, open not only to various national traditions and their theoretical texts—Marx, Kierkegaard, Hegel, Nietzsche, Saussure, Freud, Durkheim, Wittgenstein—but to experimentation with modes of critical engagement and critical writing, since there was no presumption that understanding a national literary tradition in its historical evolution was the overriding goal. Comparative literature has been the field where critical and theoretical interdisciplinary projects could be freely tried, with results that are exemplary for others and thus affect the direction of literary and cultural studies at large. But this success of comparative literature brings a loss of identity.

The most controversial topic in the Bernheimer report and the associated position papers was the role of literature in a comparative literature that was simultaneously going global and going cultural. In that report and the responses to it, those of us who defended literature, or opined that the study of literature ought to retain a central place in comparative literature, were belittled by Charlie Bernheimer—who in a fashion typical of him, disregarded everyone's comments to write just what he wished. Defenders of literature were treated as old fogies who were inexplicably resisting getting with the program. Close reading of literary texts in the original languages manifestly seemed dispensable to Bernheimer—not a necessary part of the new dispensation.

In my own response to the Bernheimer report, I argued that as national literature departments have increasingly given a role to theory—or, perhaps more accurately, allowed literary and cultural studies to reorganize themselves around questions that have emerged from theoretical debates rather than the conventional literary-historical periods—and as these departments have increasingly brought a wider range of cultural productions into their purview—not just film and popular culture but discourses of sexuality, the construction of the body, and the formation of national and cultural identities, for instance—they became in effect departments of national cultural studies: English and American Studies, French Studies, German Studies, Hispanic Studies. The turn to culture makes sense for national literature departments: the division of literature by national or linguistic boundaries was always rather dubious, but such divisions as these are a very reasonable way of organizing the study of culture. Perhaps, as German literature departments turn to German cultural studies, French literature departments to French studies, the national names will finally represent fields that are more intellectually coherent. And as the national literature departments turn to culture, they will leave comparative literature with a distinctive role. If, having in large measure made possible the expansion of literary studies into cultural studies, comparative literature does not insist on claiming that field for its own, it might find itself with a new identity, as the site of literary study in its broadest dimensions—the study of literature as a transnational phenomenon. The devolution of other fields would have left it with a distinctive and valuable identity at last.[3] As the site of the study of literature in general, comparative literature would provide a home for poetics.

This does not mean that members of comparative literature departments should be discouraged from studying literature in relation to other cultural practices, or even pursuing projects to which literature is only marginally related—far from it. As always, comparatists will participate in the most interesting methodological and theoretical developments in the humanities, wherever these take them. Since literature is not a natural kind but a historical construct, the study of literature in relation to other discourses is not only inevitable but necessary. But as opposed to the other departments of the humanities, comparative literature would have as its central responsibility the study of literature, which could be approached in the most diverse ways.

My argument that comparative literature should accept the differential possibility that the evolution of literary and cultural studies has created, as the site for the study of literature as a transnational phenomenon, did not gain many adherents; and the question of what comparative literature should be has remained as much in dispute as ever, except insofar as we agree that it is the nature of comparative literature to be the site at which the most diverse options of the humanities contend—not just a discipline in crisis, but by its very nature a site of crisis. It is striking, though, that since 1994 the sense of literature as under siege has somewhat abated. While the question of the role of literature in comparative literature was central to the 1993 report, in the 2004 report the place of literature no longer seems such a contentious issue. This might, of course, be because the proponents of cultural studies have won and so no longer need raise the issue, but then you would expect the partisans of literary study to be complaining that literature has been forced out of comparative literature, and that seems not to have happened. Haun Saussy, speaking of comparative literature as "comparisons with literature," presumes the centrality of literature, in the sense that comparative literature involves reading texts of diverse sorts but "reading literarily."

One could say that while the legitimacy of comparative literature projects that do not involve literature has become established, the centrality of literature is not in question as it formerly was—if only by a swing back of the pendulum. This conclusion drawn from the 2004 report seems to me confirmed by observation: there is manifestly an increasing interest in aesthetics, which for a while was a dirty word. In running a very broad search for faculty in comparative literature, which attracted applications from many candidates working in postcolonial studies, I was struck by the extent to which even dissertations that focus on social and political issues and would not need to address literature at all seem to include several chapters on Anglophone novelists—demonstrating that there has come into being a new hypercanon of Anglophone writers: Rushdie, Achebe, Walcott, and Coetzee, among others.[4] The role of literature in comparative literature seems very robust these days, even if literary works are frequently read symptomatically.

In fact, if there is an issue that emerges from the disparate essays that make up the 2004 report, it is not whether literary or cultural studies should predominate but how comparative literature should deal with "world literature." I emphasize that term, for the question is not whether we should study all the literatures of the world, but about the stakes in the construction by comparative literature departments of "world literature," as displayed most concretely in world literature courses.

This returns us to the problem of comparability, to which the fate of comparative literature seems inexorably tied—testimony to the power of a name. As comparative literature liberated itself from a comparability based on attested relations of contact, thus on sources and influence, and acceded to a broader regime of intertextual studies where in principle anything could be compared with anything else, we began to hear talk of a "crisis of comparative literature," no doubt because of the difficulty of explaining the nature of the new comparability that served to structure and, in principle, to justify comparative literature as a discipline. This problem of the nature of comparability is certainly rendered more acute by the shift of comparative literature from a Eurocentric to a global discipline, though in some respects this has been concealed from us. There has been a phase, one might say, where the problem of comparability might apparently be set aside because a good deal of new work has focused on cross-cultural contacts and hybridity within postcolonial societies and within the literatures of colonizing powers. A lot of exciting work has in effect been a sophisticated modernized version of the study of sources and influences: insofar as comparative study addresses the diverse literary and cultural influences at work in Derek Walcott's *Omeros*, or Salman Rushdie's *The Satanic Verses*, or Ousmane Sembène's *Les Bouts de bois de Dieu*, or Rodolpho Gonzalez's *I Am Joaquin (Yo soy Joaquin)*, comparison is based on direct cultural contacts and traceable influences. But in principle, the problem of comparability remains unsolved and more acute than ever. What, in this newly globalized space, justifies bringing texts together?

World literature courses that bring together the great books from around the world seem to base comparability on a notion of excellence that resonates, for me at least, with Bill Readings's brilliant analysis of the "University of Excellence" in *The University in Ruins*. Kant gave us the model of the modern university organized by a single regulatory ideal, the principle of Reason. Humboldt and the German Idealists replaced the notion of Reason with that of Culture, centering the university on the dual task of research and teaching, the production and inculcation of national self-knowledge. But now the model of the University of Culture, the university whose task was to produce cultured individuals, citizens imbued with a national culture, has in the West given way. Today, Readings writes, "no one of us can seriously imagine himself or herself as the hero of the story of the University, as the instantiation of the cultured individual that the entire great machine labors day and night to produce. . . . The grand narrative of the university centered on the production of a liberal, reasoning subject, is no longer readily available to us."[5]

Similarly, while once we might have imagined the study of comparative literature as leading to the production of the immensely cultured individual—a Curtius or an Auerbach—who had mastered the literatures of Europe, now the subject is so large and so diversely specialized that no such exemplar can exist. The best we can imagine are accomplished comparatists with very different interests and ranges of knowledge, who would all be excellent in their own ways. Thus, the University of Culture gives way to the "University of Excellence."

The crucial thing about excellence, Readings points out, is that it has no content (there need be no agreement about what is excellent).[6] In that sense, it is like the cash nexus. It has no content and thus serves to introduce comparability and bureaucratic control. As Readings explains, "its very lack of reference allows excellence to function as a principle of translatability between radically different idioms."[7] The idea of excellence enables us to make comparable entities that have little in common as to structure or function, input or output. But that is only half of its bureaucratic usefulness. It also makes it possible to avoid substantive arguments about what teachers, students, and administrators should actually be doing. Everyone's task is to strive for excellence, however that might be defined. I am interested in the relationship between the comparability of comparative literature and the comparability instituted by excellence, which, to sum up, has the following characteristics: (1) it purports to have content but actually does not; (2) it grants groups considerable freedom (it doesn't matter what you do, so long as you do it excellently), which is crucial to bureaucratic efficiency; but (3) ultimately it is a mechanism for the reduction or exclusion of activities that do not succeed by this measure. How does the comparability of comparative literature compare with this?

The intertextual nature of meaning—the fact that meaning lies in the differences between one text or one discourse and another—makes literary study essentially, fundamentally comparative, but it also produces a situation in which comparability depends on a cultural system, a general field that underwrites comparison. The meaning of a text depends on its relations to others within a cultural space, such as that of Western European culture, which is in part why comparative literature has been so much inclined to remain Western and European in its focus. The more sophisticated one's understanding of discourse, the harder it is to compare Western and non-Western texts, for each depends for its meaning and identity on its place within a discursive system—disparate systems that seem to make the putative comparability of texts either illusory or, at the very least, misleading. What has made possible much recent work in comparative literature has been the identification, largely by postcolonial theory, of a general postcolonial context within which comparabilities can be generated.

What sort of comparability, then, could guide the transformation of comparative literature from a Eurocentric discipline to a more global one? There is a difficult problem here. On the one hand, as Natalie Melas argues, comparison such as justifies a discipline consolidates a standard or norm that then functions to give value to works that match up to it and to exclude those that do not, so that comparison—the principle of comparability—rather than opening new possibilities for cultural value, more often than not restricts and totalizes it.[8] But on the other hand, as we try to avoid this imposition of particular norms, we may risk falling into the alternative practice, which Readings's account of excellence describes, where the standard is kept nonreferential—vacuous—so that it is not imposing particular requirements, but where in the end, it provides a *bureaucratic* rather than an intellectual mechanism for regulation and control. And indeed, the danger of world literature is that it will select what is regarded as excellent without regard for the particular standards and ideological factors that might have come into play in the processes of selection.[9]

The problem of comparison is that it is likely to generate a standard, or ideal type, of which the texts compared come to function as variants. Comparatists today are eager to avoid this implicit result of measuring one culture's texts by some standard extrinsic to that culture. Yet the more we try to deploy a comparability that has no implicit content, the more we risk falling into a situation like that of the University of Excellence, where an apparent lack of concern for content—your department can do what it likes provided it does it excellently—is in the end only the alibi for a control based on bureaucratic rather than academic and intellectual principles.

The virtue of a comparability based on specific intellectual norms or models—generic, thematic, historical—is that they are subject to investigation and argument in ways that the vacuous bureaucratic norms are not. One solution, then, is to attempt to spell out the assumptions and norms that seem to underwrite one's comparisons, so that they do not become implicit terms. A model here might be Erich Auerbach's conception of the *Ansatzpunkt:* a specific point of departure, conceived not as an external position of mastery but as a "handle" or partial vantage point that enables the critic to bring together a variety of cultural objects. "The characteristic of a good point of departure," writes Auerbach in his essay "Philology and *Weltliteratur,*" "is its concreteness and its precision on the one hand, and on the other, its potential for centrifugal radiation."[10] This might be a theme, a metaphor, a detail, a structural problem, or a well-defined cultural function. I can imagine basing cross-cultural comparison on linking principles whose very arbitrariness or contingency will prevent them from giving rise to a standard or ideal type, such as comparing works by authors whose last name begins with B, or works whose numerical place in a bibliography is divisible by thirteen. I confess, though, that this is scarcely the sort of thing Auerbach had in mind and not a general or principled solution to the problem of comparability. A further possibility is to attempt to locate the comparative perspective geographically and historically: instead of imagining the comparative perspective as a global overview, one might stress the value, for instance, of comparing European literatures *from* Africa, for their relations to the cultural productions of a particular African moment. Better such points of departure that impose criteria and norms than the fear that comparisons will be odious. The danger, I repeat, is that comparatists' fear that their comparisons will impose implicit norms and standards may give rise to a vacuousness that is as difficult to combat as is the notion of excellence that administrators are using to organize and reorganize the American university.

The 2004 report, as I say, makes world literature a central problem of comparative literature. The teaching of what Djelal Kadir calls the "abstracted construct of world literature" is ably championed by David Damrosch in "World Literature in a Postcanonical, Hypercanonical Age" (chap. 2) and by Katie Trumpener in her response, entitled "A Geopolitical View" (chap. 13).[11] And the reservations expressed in this report by both Haun Saussy and Emily Apter are pursued most vigorously by Kadir in "Comparative Literature in an Age of Terrorism" (chap. 5). The charge, of course, is that world literature is constructed from the perspective of a hegemonic power, which admits representatives on the terms that it establishes in order to compose and compare, and that this a McDonaldization, in which globalizing America colonizes various cultures, representing them by a bit of local flavor. Kadir cites the "risk of instrumentalizing the literature of the world as objects of neocolonial usurpation and imperial subsumption." However, Katie Trumpener, describing a Yale world literature course to which a lot of thought and a lot of faculty expertise has obviously been devoted, argues that one can avoid "a thematically driven, aesthetically and culturally flattened view of global texts" by focusing in a well-constructed course on, for instance, "questions of foundational violence, of the logic of feud, massacre, terror, and genocide as well as the quasi-theological role of literature in mediating ideological shifts and historical crisis, enacting conversions and convergence." Concentrating on a number of major narratives, one can also focus on questions of genre; temporality; and narrative technique, consciousness, and perspective, and thus prevent such a course from becoming an imperialistic sampling of national thematic flavors.

One can add that world literature is not just a construct of comparative literature departments, important though our role may be in articulating, for a public of students and former students, a world literature. Pascale Casanova's *La république mondiale des lettres*, recently translated as *The World Republic of Letters*, describes a world literary system as a set of discursive practices, a system of power/knowledge, in which literary works from around the world come to engage—with reviews, translation, prizes, cinematic adaptation—a system in which innovation has frequently come from the periphery and recognition emanates from various centers (especially, in her view, Paris).[12] So before we comparatists spend too much time and effort castigating ourselves for imperfectly and imperialistically homogenizing the literatures of the world into world literature, we should recall that such processes already take place in the world of literature and have done so for a long time. If we prefer, we can think of ourselves as engaging critically, as Casanova thinks of herself as doing, with the world system of literature. Undertaking a critique of "world literature" may suit some of us more than constructing it. I should say that I have not been a partisan of world literature, but I do find Katie Trumpener's "Geopolitical View" compelling; and at any rate, I think we should bear in mind her concluding questions. Acknowledging that in some respects world literature remains a daunting, perhaps impossible project, she asks: "But if not us, who? If not now, when?"

Why not now? If America has forfeited any possibility of claiming to survey judiciously the riches of world culture, our horrific role in the world gives us all the more reason to try to see to it that new generations of Americans have some knowledge of the complexity of the products of some foreign cultures. This is a teaching project more than a research project, though research in comparative literature can focus on theoretical questions about possible approaches to world literature, their dangers and virtues. But if it looks as though the field may in the coming years be in part defined by the problem of world literature, comparative literature should also be defined by those features that draw people to the field. And I will guess that this is not "world literature."

The attraction of the field for students and teachers has been tied, I believe, either to a polyglot experience or to an idea of cosmopolitanism. Some people who have lived multilingual, multicultural lives become comparatists because other choices would foreclose possibilities already available to them. American comparatists without a polyglot experience have been driven by a desire to avoid American parochialism, by an interest in other languages and cultures, especially European, both in relation to our own and in relation to the theoretical questions that arise in transnational literary or cultural study.

It is possible to take an interest in the literature of the world as a repertoire of possibilities, forms, themes, discursive practices: comparative literature, I have argued, is the right place, especially today, for the study of literature as a discursive practice, a set of formal possibilities, thus poetics. But it is scarcely possible to take an interest in all the literatures *and* cultures of the world, so comparative projects are likely to remain driven by particular interests, animated on the one hand by singular knowledge, interests, and languages, and on the other by the general theoretical questions that arise when one reflects on one's interest in multiple kinds of texts. In his essay in this report, "Indiscipline" (chap. 6), David Ferris remarks that comparative literature always seeks to incorporate what remains other to it; and it is the combination of that comparative, lateral move, with the *meta* move, that is most distinctive of the discipline and that makes it, as Haun Saussy puts it, the "test bed for reconceiving of the order of knowledge." As such reconceiving occurs, this should count as the triumph of comparative literature, but once again this will not allow comparative literature to feel triumphant. As with theory, so with comparative literature: our triumphs seem destined to be triumphs without triumph.

NOTES

1. *Cours de linguistique générale* (Paris: Payot, 1972), 162.

2. The bylaws of the American Comparative Literature Association mandate that a report be prepared every ten years. The 1993 report, "Comparative Literature at the Turn of the Century," was a collective document (though largely written by Charles Bernheimer) and was published as *Comparative Literature in the Age of Multiculturalism*, ed. Charles Bernheimer (Baltimore: Johns Hopkins University Press, 1995). The 2004 report avoids the appearance of consensus.

3. My comments are published in *Comparative Literature in the Age of Multiculturalism*, 117–21.

4. See David Damrosch, "World Literature in a Postcanonical, Hypercanonical Age," in chapter 2 of this volume.

5. Bill Readings, *The University in Ruins* (Cambridge, Mass.: Harvard University Press, 1996), 9.

6. When Readings was working on this book, I was able to provide him with the example of Cornell's Department of Transportation Services (responsible for campus buses and parking), which had received an award for excellence from its professional organization, whatever that is—apparently for its success in discouraging parking on campus (success in "demand reduction," they called it), by increasing fees for parking permits and progressively eliminating convenient parking spaces. But it is not utterly impossible to imagine that excellence here might have been assigned precisely the opposite content: excellence might consist of making it easier for faculty to park on campus, though I agree that this is not very likely.

7. Ibid., 24.

8. Natalie Melas, "Versions of Incommensurability," *World Literature Today* 69:2 (Spring 1995): 275–80.

9. In his superb book, *In the Context of No Context*, which deserves to be better known as a guide to our condition, George W. S. Trow identifies as a crucial though unrecognized watershed in the history of American modernity: "the moment when a man named Richard Dawson,

the host of a program called *Family Feud*, asked contestants to guess what a poll of a hundred people had guessed would be the height of the average American woman. Guess what they've guessed. Guess what they've guessed the average is" (*In the Context of No Context* [Boston: Little Brown, 1981], 58).

10. Erich Auerbach, "Philology and *Weltliteratur*," *Centennial Review* 13:1 (Winter 1969): 15. I owe this reference to David Chioni Moore's stimulating discussion in "Comparative Literature to *Weltkulturwissenschaft*: Remedying a Failed Transition," a paper for the Twentieth Southern Comparative Literature Association meeting, Raleigh, North Carolina, October 1994.

11. Damrosch, be it noted, is the editor of the leading anthology of world literature (Longmans) and author of a judicious discussion of the problems, *What Is World Literature?* (Princeton, N.J.: Princeton University Press, 2003).

12. Pascale Casanova, *The World Republic of Letters* (Cambridge, Mass.: Harvard University Press, 2004).

CHAPTER NINETEEN

Multum in Parvo; or, Comparison in Lilliput

MARSHALL BROWN

Auch kleine Dinge können uns entzücken,
Auch kleine Dinge können teuer sein   —*Paul Heyse*

Jeder Mensch ist seiner Natur nach auf bestimmte, mitunter sehr, sehr
kleine Dinge gestellt, Dinge, die, trotzdem sie klein sind, für ihn das
Leben oder doch des Lebens Bestes bedeuten.

—*Botho von Rienäcker*

When I sat down belatedly—or, actually, lay down—to read this report, I doubted
I would have anything of weight or moment to contribute. Rightly so. After all, who
am I to pronounce on the future of a discipline? I have spent a career contentedly plowing a smaller vineyard than most of the original authors, extending a few hundred miles
around, say, Strasbourg, and a hundred years more or less (mostly less) around 1800. I
admire much of what goes on in the larger world of the ACLA, occasionally adapt or debate a bit, practice too little of what I hear being preached in this volume and outside it.
Sure, there are singularities of the decade that I would like to notice: the subordination
of time to place and of history to geography (or "cartography," as Emily Apter designates it); the growing centrality of margins; the presentism that several contributors
bewail (though the Yale course Katie Trumpener describes corrects it with manifest
success). These are tendencies much in evidence, not needing me to point them out;
they can be heartily welcomed to the extent that they serve as remedies but are rightly
suspected when they turn counter-hegemonic. We should foster debate and not inflict
our creeds on others, not even on the others whose offices are next door. Who could
argue? No one needs me to praise apple pie, nor do I have any special credentials for
doing so. If I have anything to contribute, it will have to be lighter in weight, more

restricted in scope, more momentary and less momentous. If it's not too foolish to say so, it will have to come (as all our work should come) from the heart.

Genuine feelings, heartfelt, honest, responsive. The new aesthetics is telling us we need more of these kinds of sensitivities. Again, who could disagree, deep down? That is, I might dispute the authenticity of your jargon, but my little promptings, pruned of overweening, how could I suspect them? They won't shout too loud or ruffle too many feathers. If I know and keep my place, my little voice may strengthen its part in the chorus, and that's as much as most of us can hope for. On that score, I'll sing a little tune, answering to the music of this volume.

You may have noticed some mix to my metaphors. I point to the self for validation but to the collectivity for resonance. I can look in my heart and write, but if what comes forth is a sonnet, have I really relied on pure Invention and shunned stepdame Study? Without a doubt, whatever I most deeply feel has been instilled within me. My identity, my voice, is not mine alone. If I am going to say anything rooted, I'll first have to find out and confess who I am. "Denn es muß von Herzen gehn, / Was auf Herzen wirken soll."

I could start, as some have done in the last decade, with my ancestry (mixed, like everyone else's, and only trickling down to me in family lore); my experience; my situation of the decade, the year, or (reading in bed) the moment. That's not the point, you respond. Grander issues are at stake—for some of the contributors, inconceivably, impossibly grand ones. Yes, but . . . Roland Greene remarks shrewdly on the self-inflation predictable in a document like this one. Maybe the state of our discipline tells us about the state of the world (which, much like our field, is pretty awful in some parts and pretty wonderful in others, though good news is always less gripping than tragedy). Maybe the state of our scholarship doesn't finally tell us much about dailiness—such as about our teaching or our institutional settings, which are only sporadically noticed in this volume, chiefly by Haun Saussy, David Damrosch, and Katie Trumpener. But the pressure to say something important is felt enough that every so often I wanted to cry: "Is this real?"[1] But then, my little voice tells me, even reality can take us only so far. For when I start looking for bedrock—*who, at bottom, am I, to be telling you what to think and do?*—I find nothing but quivering jelly. "Shifting ground and sand," Descartes calls the vagaries of experience, and his younger contemporary Andreas Gryphius encapsulates the sentiment in the locally famous line, "Du siehst wohin du siehst, nur Eitelkeit auf Erden." Such war-torn waifs speak to us. Life is compounded of casualness, casualty, casuistry. Contingency is all I come up with, all the way down. Weather. If our studies concern human experience, maybe they can use a dash more humility, a shade less assertiveness than all of us pedagogues are inclined toward.[2]

I'll get to comparative literature after a bit, and to this report. But first please join me in an excursion to Kessin, a remote Prussian village, erstwhile home of the Baroness Effi von Innstetten, née Briest. Remote, perhaps, but easy enough to reach by train from Berlin (with which its name shares a regional, Slavic-derived suffix). The population appears as indigenous and untouched by globalism as that of Highbury, Raveloe, and so many other fictional villages, let alone the would-be aborigines studied by Lévi-Strauss or Bourdieu, Sahlins or Clifford. Like them, though, Kessin is far more planetary than seen at first glance. To be sure, the residents seem little affected by the lesser Prussian aristocracy visiting their beach resort in season, let alone by Bismarck, who sometimes summers unremarked in the vicinity. But no man is an island. This is, after all, Swedish Pomerania, "skandinavisches Vorland" in the eyes of a Brandenburger.[3] Sailors' territory. And before the Norsemen were the Slavs, and before them . . . The local relics are not alien, yet all the more exotic for their primitive wildness: "Das mit den Opfersteinen und mit dem Herthasee das war ja schon wieder viel, viel früher, ganz vor Christum natum; reine Germanen, von denen wir alle abstammen . . ." (280; Fontane's suspension points). We have met the Heathen and they are us. And in the present, there is the haunted-house legend of a Chinaman who seduced a local maiden. The global pervades the local. In despair over his failed marriage, Innstetten dreams of escape. But, as his senior colleague reminds him, there is no getting away from oneself. Running off to Africa, he is told, is kid stuff. And how is this said? "Wollen Sie mit einem roten Fes einem Palaver präsidieren oder mit einem Schwiegersohn von König Mtesa Blutsfreundschaft schließen?" (288). The fact is, you can't get away from Prussia to Africa because Africa is present in the Prussian consciousness: even a Prussian bureaucrat's language encompasses the fez, palaver (a word borrowed from Portuguese explorers' lingo), the foreign-sounding "präsidieren," and the tongue-twisting yet evidently recognizable Mtesa: Innstetten's consciousness and his identity (like mine, like yours) are riven by differences within and without.

Kessin thus reminds us that we don't need to voyage to witness the clash of cultures, even on a global scale. It hits right at home. Every character in Fontane carries her distinct culture in her identity and language, his clash of cultures in his manifold identities and jargons. Identity in Kessin is just as multiple as in Mashpee or Proust's Balbec, or (as Gail Finney points out) in today's feminisms. Hungarian may or may not be sufficiently alien; the ideal is to master all the regional languages of Bengal (Gayatri Spivak knows several, but her father, she once told me, knew more) and a hundred African dialects.[4] But strangeness can lie just around the corner, or on the other side of the bed (or actually, since double beds have never been common in Germany, in the next bed): "Innstetten war immer ein vortrefflicher Mann ['husband'? or the more distant 'man'?], so einer, wie's nicht viele gibt, aber ich konnte nicht recht an ihn heran, er hatte so was Fremdes" (215). We can have a powerful cultural encounter, maybe even more vivid than a transnational one, just down the road. "Du sprichst immer von Nest, und nun finde ich, wenn du nicht übertrieben hast, eine ganz neue Welt hier. Allerlei Exotisches" (45). This reaction comes early in the book; in actuality, the teenage bride underestimates how alien and, for the most part, unwelcome she will be in Kessin, which is not just exotic but ultimately repellent, not just full of "all kinds of exoticism" in general, but of a particular assemblage of quirks, foibles, and vices. "The exotic," when we meet it, turns out to be people, with some soft spots but not enough, and too many edges.

We can suffer Antoine Berman's "test of foreignness," alluded to by Haun Saussy, with our next-door neighbor, or our servant. For they too speak a different language. *Effi Briest* handles dialect with far greater restraint than many realist works (including several of Fontane's other novels), but the effects are no less pervasive and threatening. There is the shrewd servant Roswitha, whom Effi providentially picks up off the street and who remains attached to her in her misery. Roswitha speaks Thuringian Low German; it is marked only in the first encounter, but that is enough to type her outsider's affinity with Effi. "'Ich heiße Roswitha.' 'Ja, das ist selten, das ist ja . . . ' 'Ja, ganz recht, gnädige Frau, das ist ein kattolscher Name. Und das kommt auch noch dazu, daß ich eine Kattolsche bin. Aus'n Eichsfeld. Und das Kattolsche, das macht es einem immer noch schwerer und saurer'" (112; Fontane's suspension points).[5] Only once in this book does the local Low German accent emerge (not full-blown dialect, but even an accent embodies foreignness in language). A minor character named Kruse addresses Roswitha, laughing as (in the continuation) he makes an off-color joke about a hen that doesn't lay: "Un wenn ich ein reines Hemd anziehen will, fehlt ein Knopp. Un so is es nu schon" (175).[6] Here, to be sure, Roswitha passes the test of the foreign. For the language with which she has just approached Kruse bears the mark of their shared northernness: "Ihre Frau will mir bloß noch was erzählen; aber es is gleich aus" (175). The two lower-class characters, whose different accents share the northern "is," meet on the common ground of their distance from metropolitan German. It would be a mistake to regard Fontane's orthography here as phonetic precision, for no German would actually pronounce the "t" conversationally in the consonant cluster "ist gleich." Everyone says "is" in this formula. Rather, through an approximate image of a language, Fontane is intimating an encounter that one would exaggerate in calling cultural yet would derogate by confining to the merely psychological.[7] The meeting ground of the impossibly infinite and the irredeemably particular is the terrain of literature, and no one is more brilliantly economical at it than Fontane at his frequent best.

If cultural encounter falls under the sway of virtually infinitesimal difference, so too, a novel like this shows, does historical action. I mean historical primarily with a small "h" here, to be sure, the intrigue of the *Geschichte*. The catastrophe is precipitated when Innstetten discovers a bundle of love letters to Effi (or what passes as such in the repressive culture of Berlin). Here are the minutely detailed circumstances: The daughter, Annie, whose occasional wildness is certainly not inherited from her stuffed-shirt father ("Das hast du von deiner Mama, die war auch so," says Effi in their tragic final meeting [273]), challenges the good-natured but fat Roswitha to a race upstairs. Annie is overexcited from a number of factors: her mother has remained away in a spa longer than expected; her longing for Effi's return has been stimulated by Effi's exuberant letters and probably by the unusual heat (mentioned only by Effi, but the weather in Berlin is likely to follow that in Ems), by her father's impatience for Effi's return, by the suppressed antagonism of Roswitha and her fellow-servant Johanna (merely hinted here, it breaks into the open later), and by a doggerel poem rehearsed and argued about for the happy occasion (poems often spell trouble in realist novels). Annie stumbles and bruises her chin; the flustered servants can't raise the elderly doctor (who in the end proves to be Effi's one true friend) and, in their bumbling, decide to break open Effi's sewing desk to look for a bandage. Innstetten's return, the bustle to calm Annie, and the doctor's eventual arrival all forestall tidying up; and Innstetten winds up noticing the bundle of letters and, after hours of gradual realization, hesitation, and deliberation, finally reading them. The letters have lain there, unopened and nearly forgotten, for six years; the crisis results from a superabundance of chance factors, yet each factor is in itself so circumstantially motivated and (as I have indicated only in part) so resonant with symbolic meaning—that is, so fully psychologized and/or acculturated—as to seem virtually inevitable.

One realizes in retrospect that Effi and Innstetten were destined for a clash, if not in the form of a sudden debacle ("ein Blitz aus heiterem Himmel" [277], as Effi calls the letter of denunciation she receives while still dallying in Ems, echoing a topos that goes back to Pindar[8]), then in that of the gradual unraveling of the marriage whose lovelessness had encouraged Effi's thoughtless and trivial dalliance in the first place. There is a perfect coalescence of fate and chance, of the universal and the particular, the other who is near enough to matter and the self who is scattered enough to lose control of situations. The whole inventory of Katie Trumpener's thematic study (chap. 13) is here in a nutshell: "questions of foundational violence [of the subtlest, most inescapable variety] and the ethics of conflict, of the logic of feud [as between the portly Johanna and the obese Roswitha], massacre [the traversing of the open territory by so many now vanished civilizations], terror [especially the psychological manipulation of Annie by her father that becomes evident in the final interview, and also the brutal letter from Effi's mother disowning her following her divorce], and genocide [not genocide per se, to be sure, but the kinds of group persecution and demonization—of women and Catholics and Chinamen and subordinates at work and those outside whatever group is looking at them—that have led to genocide], as well as the quasi-theological role of literature [named after a saint and brutalized by her father for a youthful infraction, Roswitha is a Mary Magdalen figure] in mediating ideological shifts and moments of historical crisis [the intolerable mores of Wilhelmine Prussia], enacting conversion and convergence." Around the edges, the novel hints at the seductions of grand tragedy: *King Lear* is mentioned, Gretchen from Goethe's *Faust,* and Wagner's *Flying Dutchman,* along with the ring parable from Gotthold Ephraim Lessing's *Nathan the Wise,* representing quasi-theological conversion and convergence. But the novel skirts these models, as it bypasses all of the actual incidents in Effi's life (betrothal, wedding, childbirth, most of the scene of adultery, death, funeral) apart from the epistolary denunciations by Innstetten and Effi's mother (lovers decades before), whose cruelty is foregrounded by the fact that they alone are actually narrated. It opts instead for a less flamboyant variant of turn-of-the-century realism, one of many novels of its era to which the opening sentence of Ford Madox Ford's *The Good Soldier* might be applied: "This is the saddest story I have ever heard." Bismarck is there in the novel, but the wars that really matter to it are wars of the spirit and not of polities nor, as current idiom has it, cultures.

"Is" instead of "ist." There you have it to a t. It reminds us how the big T, Theory, doesn't have to travel far at all to confront us in all the ways described in this volume. A novel like *Effi Briest* is neither cosmic nor cosmopolitan, but life rarely is. Djelal Kadir correctly alerts us that we are more closely surrounded by regimes of terror than we like to admit, as the increasingly despondent Effi is persecuted by her parents and husband. Still, moment to moment and day to day, we and our students confront muddles more often than mayhem; to that extent, we are less in need of tactics of resistance than of the everyday resources of conduct, comprehension, and communication that a writer like Fontane schools us in. Big Others and big brothers may peer over our shoulders, but most of our others come to us dressed in small letters.[9] We can use comparison, and literature, and comparative literature on every scale of existence.

Consequently, I am less surprised than Caroline Eckhardt (chap. 10) that single-author studies might be classified as comparative literature. When my graduate department turned down my dissertation proposal on the ground that it wasn't international (though it was certainly interdisciplinary by the standards of the day), I pointed to prior dissertations on the shelves concerning single authors and works.

Eventually it went through and became a book on German romanticism, the first stage in work that has been international enough by today's standards, if not by those we might hope for some future decade. The spirit is what matters, not topic, not doctrine.

For the same reason, while I too deplore the loss of the past, I am somewhat less alarmed than Eckhardt appears to be. For like other kinds of otherness, the foreign country that is the past lies all around us, near at hand. If it didn't, there would perhaps be less need to study it, but because it does, there is more than one way to combat presentism. Shakespeare and Lessing and (more obliquely) Pindar, Germanic and Slavic and Scandinavian invasions, the history of everyday life and the prehistory and destiny of the modern German Reich, economic conditions (traders and farming conditions, with—as was typical of Wilhelmine Germany—no industry on the horizon), all are richly encoded in this moderately short, dense novel. There is even a film version (a long, slow one by Rainer Fassbinder), for those willing to sit through it. Cultural longevity works in both directions; if we must sacrifice the enduring past, we can partly compensate with the deep-rooted present. Northrop Frye's *The Secular Scripture*, for instance, can point the way toward sempiternal dimensions of modern plots (this is not to say that age-old is identical with historical, but both are desirable). So can Trumpener's experiment with teaching Peter Dale Scott.

I cheer for Saussy's formulation that "literature has a lot to do with . . . giving disproportionate attention to small things." Not enough of the authors in this volume echo his sentiment, but I am heartened by David Damrosch's call for intensive exploration (cited by David Ferris, chap. 6) and Roland Greene's for "a politics writ small." Christopher Braider belittles snippetology, but the real villain there is reading badly, not reading small. I studied during the acme of the vogue for literary structuralism, whose aim was a comprehensive science of literature. I have never forgotten an English Institute paper by the young Tzvetan Todorov, crusading for a systematic account of literary genres. Paul de Man, in response, asked a very short question: "Those texts that you classify, do you read them first?" If I understand Gayatri Spivak correctly—no easy task—then I agree with numerous authors in this volume that planetarity as a slogan is superior to globalism for its readier recognition of the material underpinnings of ideologies. But difference disseminates into differences, and Kadir's terroristic, reified oppositions are crossed by countless smaller fault lines. Reading the lines, and between the lines, is not just our métier; it is the moral heart of our discipline. To that extent, despite grave tonal differences, I could affiliate with the letter (and perhaps with the spirit) of David Ferris's proposal; it is truer to the delightful inefficiency of literature to call it, not a discipline, with all the punitive overtones we now hear in that word, but an indiscipline.

I think—no, I feel—that the task for the comparatism of the coming decade is to counter misguided globalisms and hegemonic canons with localisms of all sorts. Imperial aspirations were not unknown to structuralism, nor to orthodoxies before and since. Comparisons need rather to highlight contrasts, both between and within. The attention to differences within is associated with the work of Barbara Johnson, who fruitfully pursued a comparatist agenda even when she moved out of a French department and into an English department, where she increasingly studied writings in English by racial others. Most members of ACLA, after all, teach in national literature departments; our day-to-day work is more often focused on the complexities of a single work or linguistic tradition than on international intersections. The work of the negative is the indispensable element I would like to see us share (and here I can in no way affiliate with Ferris's jibes at Hegel), and our particular but not exclusive calling should be the work of the negative between and within languages. I take that to be Emily Apter's and Steven Ungar's shared message as well.[10]

One final topic weighs on my heart. Internal difference to me means irony. Life's little ironies should be central to our perceptions. To be sure, they can be far from inconsequential. The lightning from a clear sky that strikes Effi Briest down reappears in Thomas Mann's *Buddenbrooks* (named after a cameo character in Fontane's novel) as "the little bit of hail" that destroys a crop and ruins a family. Still, it can be redemptive to keep the spirits up. The last few decades have taught us to take lightheartedness seriously, but life as a result has grown awfully downbeat and apocalyptic. Sometimes letting go is a good thing.[11] Not much of Caryl Emerson's admiration for Epstein's whimsy and her recognition of the ludicrousness of self-importance survives in the contributions to this report, nor much of the infectious gusto of Fedwa Malti-Douglas's enthusiasms. It behooves us to be mindful that humor translates worse than anything else. (The English translators of Freud's study of humor had to find substitute jokes.) That is true interculturally and interdialectically. One guy's joke is another man's slur. But the arrow points both ways. If each culture (each group, each individual, each moment) has its way of making meaning, they also all have their ways of deflating meaning, of mimicking their colonizers, their bosses. I was struck recently reading in Stephen Owen's massive anthology of Chinese literature at the prominence of eccentrics and figures of ridicule, just as I had been struck previously, reading Earl Miner's condensed history of Japanese literature, at the potential for complex word play that lurks in a borrowed script and an ingrown, infinitely allusive poetic tradition.[12] Nothing is more satisfying than discovering someone else's sparks of wit. They may not be foundational (in Trumpener's sense), but they may help us cope and may forestall the collective heroizing and scapegoating that we already have too much of. The threats to the planet are real and need to be addressed head on, but in striking a balance for the coming decade, let us be appropriately wary of taking others, or ourselves, more seriously than they take themselves. Comparative literature—reading it, teaching it, studying it, and, heavens (and here speaks the editor in me), writing about it—should be, along with everything else, fun.

NOTES

1. I wish my cry from the heart, at least, were a cry from *my* heart. No such luck. I am quoting Harry E. Shaw quoting Walter Scott quoting the title character of his novel about a historical incident that never happened: *Narrating Reality: Austen, Scott, Eliot* (Ithaca, N.Y.: Cornell University Press, 1999), 1.

2. In his foreword, Ross Chambers says that he owes his recent *Loiterature* (Lincoln: University of Nebraska Press, 1999) to a moment when "summer twilight crept through the valley of the Rhône, swallows swooped over ancient red tiles" and another "in Rushcutters Bay Park in wintry Australian sunlight, watching boats bobbing and hearing the roar of Sydney at a tranquil distance" (xi). And the main text opens: "I've been giving up caffeine for years now, but a caffé latte steams at my elbow. Midsummer" (3). At the start of a hard-working and sometimes explicitly melancholy book, I value the wry recognitions of contingency.

3. Theodor Fontane, *Effi Briest*, ed. Walter Keitel and Helmuth Nürnberger (Frankfurt am Main: Ullstein, 1974), 279. Hereafter, citations of this work will be made parenthetically in the text.

4. I allude to a recent book, a model of twenty-first-century comparatism, Isabel Hofmeyr, *The Portable Bunyan: A Transnational History of The Pilgrim's Progress* (Princeton, N.J.: Princeton University Press, 2004), which studies the diffusion of Bunyan's work through some eighty translations into African languages. Hofmeyr actually knows only one indigenous language (better than most of us!), and studies the many other versions, illuminatingly, through their externals and the English-language elements they contain.

5. "Kattolsch" here replaces "katholisch." No more is needed to characterize Roswitha's language for the book, and indeed none of the dialogue is the least bit obscure linguistically. To be sure, the narrator reports somewhat later: "Roswitha wiegte das Kind und sang in einem thüringischen Platt allerlei Wiegenlieder, die niemand recht verstand, vielleicht sie selber nicht" (118). So much for roots! The novel is rife with generalizations of national and regional characteristics, always contestable and usually contested.

6. Regional forms are "Knopp," "Un," "is," and "nu," for "Knopf," "Und," "ist," "nun."

7. On "image of a language" see Bakhtin, *The Dialogic Imagination: Four Essays,* ed. Michael Holquist, trans. Caryl Emerson and Michael Holquist (Austin: University of Texas Press, 1981), 354–66. The experience of the foreign in one's neighbor's dialect or idiolect, not needing the expense of study abroad or the rigors of learning Swahili, is a fixture of the European realist novel. Obvious as this is, a reminder is perhaps useful here. There is a programmatic example right at the start of George Eliot's first full-length (and most programmatic) novel, *Adam Bede* (chap. 2): "They're cur'ous talkers i' this country, sir; the gentry's hard work to hunderstand 'em. I was brought hup among the gentry, sir, an' got the turn o' their tongue when I was a bye. Why, what do you think the folks here says for 'hev n't you?'—the gentry, you know, says, 'hev

n't you'—well, the people about here says 'hanna yey.' It's what they call the dileck as is spoke hereabout, sir. That's what I've heared Squire Donnithorne say many a time; it's the dileck, says he." If world literature teaches us to approach the Other with as much respect and understanding as we accord the people next door, local literature teaches us to approach the people next door with as much tact and circumspection as any other Other. The two domains are equally necessary, largely but not completely overlapping, and complementary.

8. See John T. Hamilton, "Thunder from a Clear Sky: On Lessing's Redemption of Horace," *Modern Language Quarterly* 62:3 (September 2001): 201–18.

9. See Anthony Cuda, "Who Stood over Eliot's Shoulder?" *Modern Language Quarterly* 66:3 (September 2005): 329–64, decoding the supernatural as figures of the Freudian unconscious.

10. Apter and Ungar point in particular to the so-called Translation Studies community. To my mind, the negatives advocated by Lawrence Venuti, Susan Bassnett, and their group remain too one-sidedly contestatory and too little engaged—a danger they warn against but are not free from. I prefer looking to other translation theorists (and, I hope, to forthcoming work from Apter and Ungar). Compare, for instance, these two programmatic utterances, the first and more categorical from Lawrence Venuti, *The Scandals of Translation: Towards an Ethics of Difference* (London: Routledge, 1998); the second and more responsive from George Steiner, *After Babel: Aspects of Language and Translation* (New York: Oxford University Press, 1998). Venuti: "*Any* agenda of cultural resistance for translation *must* take specifically cultural forms, *must* choose foreign texts and translation methods that deviate from those that are currently canonical or dominant" (85; my emphases). Steiner: "Good translation . . . can be defined as that in which the dialectic of impenetrability and ingress, of intractable alienness and felt 'at-home-ness' remains unresolved but expressive. Out of the tension of resistance and affinity, a tension directly proportional to the proximity of the two languages and historical communities, grows the elucidative strangeness of the great translation" (413).

[Emily Apter's book *The Translation Zone: A New Comparative Literature* (Princeton, N.J.: Princeton University Press, 2006) arrived as this book was in proof. With only a passing note to Venuti (280–81) and none to his activist translation practice, it treats translation as a "problem" (251, in the final phrase of the text) compounded by aporetic negations (246, drawing on Derrida) and interlinguistic interferences. Without pursuing Apter's itinerary all the way to indigestible, sublinguistic digitalizations, I heartily concur in her endorsement of Edouard Glissant's vision of a "world system comprised of multiple linguistic singularities or interlocking small worlds" (245), resonantly reflected in the book's wide-ranging vignettes. Leo Spitzer is Apter's unexpected Nestor. My restricted comparatist economy looks up admiringly to her general economy through the lens of her rich chapter on Spitzer in Istanbul, which eloquently presents philology's "close reading with a world view" as the "micrological counterpart" to planetarity and to Franco Moretti's ideal of distant reading. "The practice of global *translatio* as Spitzer defined it is patterned after untranslatable affective gaps, the nub of intractable semantic difference, episodes of violent cultural transference and countertransference, and unexpected love affairs" (64).]

11. See Ross Posnock, "Letting Go," *Raritan* 23 (2004): 1–19.

12. Stephen Owen, ed. and trans., *An Anthology of Chinese Literature: Beginnings to 1911* (New York: Norton, 1996); Earl Miner, Hiroko Odagiri, and Robert E. Morrell, *The Princeton Companion to Japanese Literature* (Princeton, N.J.: Princeton University Press, 1985), esp. 3–111, "A Brief Literary History."

EMILY APTER, a professor of French and Comparative Literature at New York University, has recently published *Continental Drift: From National Characters to Virtual Subjects* (Chicago, 1999) and *The Translation Zone: A New Comparative Literature* (Princeton, 2005).

CHRISTOPHER BRAIDER is a professor of French and Comparative Literature at the University of Colorado at Boulder. His publications include *Baroque Self-Invention and Historical Truth: Hercules at the Crossroads* (Ashgate, 2004).

MARSHALL BROWN, a professor of English and Comparative Literature at the University of Washington, has edited *MLQ* since 1990. His books include *Preromanticism* (Stanford, 1991) and *The Gothic Text* (Stanford, 2005).

JONATHAN CULLER is Class of 1916 Professor of English and Comparative Literature at Cornell University. His many books include *Structuralist Poetics* (Cornell, 1975), *The Pursuit of Signs* (Cornell, 1990), and *Framing the Sign* (Oklahoma, 1990), as well as the edited collection *Just Being Difficult? Academic Writing in the Public Arena* (Stanford, 2003).

DAVID DAMROSCH, a professor of English and Comparative Literature at Columbia University, is chief editor of the *Longman Anthology of World Literature* (2004) and has also published *We Scholars: Changing the Culture of the University* (Harvard, 1995) and *What Is World Literature?* (Princeton, 2003).

CAROLINE D. ECKHARDT, a professor of English and Comparative Literature at the Pennsylvania State University, has published numerous books and articles on medieval literature, including a three-volume study of *Castleford's Chronicle, or The Boke of Brut* (Oxford, 1996 and forthcoming).

CARYL EMERSON is the A. Watson Armour III University Professor of Slavic Languages and Literatures at Princeton University, where she is also a professor of Comparative Literature. Her books include *The First Hundred Years of Mikhail Bakhtin* (Princeton, 1997) and *The Life of Musorgsky* (Cambridge, 1999).

FERRIS, a professor of English and Comparative Literature at the Univer-
of Colorado at Boulder, is the author of *Theory and the Evasions of History*
hns Hopkins, 1993) and *Silent Urns: Romanticism, Hellenism, Modernity*
(Stanford, 2000). He has also edited the *Cambridge Companion to Walter Benjamin* (2004).

GAIL FINNEY is a professor of German and director of the program in Comparative Literature at the University of California, Davis. Her books include *Women
in Modern Drama: Freud, Feminism, and European Theater at the Turn of the
Century* (Cornell, 1989), *Look Who's Laughing: Gender and Comedy* (Gordon and
Breach, 1994), and *Christa Wolf* (Twayne, 1999).

ROLAND GREENE, a professor of English and Comparative Literature at Stanford
University, is the author of *Post-Petrarchism: Origins and Innovations of the Western Lyric Sequence* (Princeton, 1991) and *Unrequited Conquests: Love and Empire
in the Colonial Americas* (Chicago, 1999).

LINDA HUTCHEON is University Professor of English and Comparative Literature at the University of Toronto. Among her many books are *Irony's Edge: The
Theory and Politics of Irony* (Routledge, 1995), *Theory of Parody: The Teachings
of Twentieth-Century Art Forms* (Illinois, 2000), *Rethinking Literary History: A
Dialogue on Theory* (with Mario J. Valdés; Oxford, 2002), and *Opera: The Art of
Dying* (with Michael Hutcheon; Oxford, 2004). She received the Killam Prize of
the Canada Council of the Arts in 2005.

DJELAL KADIR, the Edwin Erle Sparks Professor of Comparative Literature at
the Pennsylvania State University, is the author and editor of numerous books
including *Questing Fictions: Latin America's Family Romance* (Minnesota, 1986),
*Columbus and the Ends of the Earth: Europe's Prophetic Rhetoric as Conquering
Ideology* (California, 1992), and *The Other Writing: Postcolonial Essays in Latin
America's Writing Culture* (Purdue, 1993).

FRANÇOISE LIONNET, a professor of French and Francophone Studies at UCLA,
is the author of *Autobiographical Voices: Race, Gender, Self-Portraiture* (Cornell,
1989), *Postcolonial Representations: Women, Literature, Identity* (Cornell, 1995),
and *Minor Transnationalism* (with Shu-mei Shih; Duke, 2005).

FEDWA MALTI-DOUGLAS, the Martha C. Kraft Professor of Humanities and an
adjunct professor of law at Indiana University, has published numerous books,
among them *Woman's Body, Woman's Word: Gender and Discourse in Arabo-
Islamic Writing* (Princeton, 1991), *Hisland: Adventures in Ac-Ac-ademe* (SUNY,
1998), *Power, Marginality and the Body in Medieval Islam* (Ashgate, 2001), *Medi-
cines of the Soul: Female Bodies and Sacred Geographies in a Transnational Islam*

(California, 2001), and *Arab Comic Strips: Politics of an Emerging Mass Culture* (with Allen Douglas; Indiana, 1994).

RICHARD RORTY, a professor of Comparative Literature, Emeritus, at Stanford University, is the author of many books including *Philosophy and the Mirror of Nature* (Princeton, 1979), *Consequences of Pragmatism* (Minnesota, 1982), *Contingency, Irony, and Solidarity* (Cambridge, 1989), *Achieving Our Country* (Harvard, 1998), *Philosophy and Social Hope* (Penguin, 2000), and three volumes of *Philosophical Papers* (Cambridge, 1991, 1991, 1998).

HAUN SAUSSY, a professor of Comparative Literature and East Asian Languages and Literatures at Yale University, is the author of *The Problem of a Chinese Aesthetic* (Stanford, 1993) and *Great Walls of Discourse* (Harvard Asia Center, 2000).

KATIE TRUMPENER, a professor of English and Comparative Literature at Yale University, is the author of *Bardic Nationalism: The Romantic Novel and the British Empire* (Princeton, 1997) and *The Divided Screen: The Cinemas of Postwar Germany* (Princeton, 2006).

STEVEN UNGAR, a professor of French and Comparative Literature at the University of Iowa, has published *Roland Barthes: The Professor of Desire* (Nebraska, 1983), *Scandal and Aftereffect: Blanchot and France since 1930* (Minnesota, 1995), and *Popular Front Paris and the Poetics of Culture* (with Dudley Andrew; Harvard, 2005).

ZHANG LONGXI, a professor of Comparative Literature and Translation at the City University of Hong Kong, also directs the Center for Cross-Cultural Studies. Professor Zhang's many publications in English and Chinese include *The Tao and the Logos: Literary Hermeneutics, East and West* (Duke, 1992), *Mighty Opposites: From Dichotomies to Differences in the Comparative Study of China* (Stanford, 1998), and *Zou chu wenhua de fengbi quan* (*Out of the Cultural Ghetto*; Shangwu, 2000).